THE CONQUERING COMMANDER

"A revealing portrait of an innovative warrior"
Kirkus

"A sound and long-overdue biography . . .
detailed and balanced"
Booklist

"FOUR-STAR READING"
Chattanooga News Free Press

"LeMay is captured in full flight in these
anecdote-rich pages."
Publishers Weekly

"AN EXCELLENT STUDY"
Ft. Worth Star-Telegram

IRON EAGLE

The Turbulent Life of
GENERAL CURTIS LeMAY

THOMAS M. COFFEY

AVON
PUBLISHERS OF BARD, CAMELOT, DISCUS AND FLARE BOOKS

Grateful acknowledgment is given for the extract taken from "At a U.S. Bomber Station Somewhere in England," which appears on pages 53–55. Used by permission of The Associated Press.

AVON BOOKS
A division of
The Hearst Corporation
105 Madison Avenue
New York, New York 10016

First Avon Books Printing: April 1988

AVON TRADEMARK REG. U.S. PAT. OFF. AND IN OTHER COUNTRIES, MARCA REGISTRADA, HECHO EN U.S.A.

Printed in the U.S.A.

K-R 10 9 8 7 6 5 4 3 2 1

PART I

CHAPTER ONE

In the autumn of 1965, eight months after his retirement as U.S. Air Force chief of staff, Gen. Curtis E. LeMay published a book, *Mission with LeMay,* which was presented as his autobiography but which was actually written by the popular novelist MacKinlay Kantor.

On page 565, referring to America's already faltering Vietnam War efforts, Kantor wrote in the name of LeMay: "My solution to the problem would be to tell them frankly that they've got to draw in their horns and stop their aggression, or we're going to bomb them back into the Stone Age."

Reviewers of the book immediately pounced on the shocking quotation and LeMay has been saddled with it ever since. Those words, which he never uttered but which he failed to catch in reading the manuscript, have helped make him one of the most controversial military men of our time. That one quotation alone didn't do the job, of course. LeMay himself helped. He was, throughout his career, so blunt, uncompromising, and unpolitical his closest friends called him, with irony, "The Diplomat." And whether right or wrong in the controversies that swirled around him, LeMay allowed them, cumulatively, to do him one big disservice: They have obscured in the public mind the fact that in the minds of most military experts, Gen. Curtis E. LeMay is the greatest air commander the United States has yet produced.

In World War II he was so daring, ingenious, and effective, against first the Germans and then against the Japanese, that his fame and ingenuity as an air commander far exceeded even that of Gen. George Patton as a ground commander. Two years before Patton sent his tanks ahead of him into an almost prostrate Germany, LeMay personally led his Flying Fortresses across fiercely defended German skies in some of the most vicious air battles of all time. He had about him the same aura of unflinching toughness as Patton. He was so tough, in fact, that his men called him "Iron Ass," though not to his face. And he often directed these men from the lead plane in his force, spearheading the attack. Time after time, LeMay led his bombers through storms of German flak and bullets.

He also devised some of the most innovative aerial strategies in World War II—the staggered formation, which increased his bombers' firepower against the enemy; the no-evasive-action bomb run, which increased bombing accuracy (measures that soon became standard in the war against Germany); and the low-level B-29 night attacks, which devastated Japan. After the war, when the Russians threatened new aggression in occupied Germany, LeMay instituted the airlift that prevented the Red Army from taking over Berlin. And he later developed the Strategic Air Command, which even now has an armada of planes in the air every day, ready to retaliate against any possible attack on the United States. Yet in spite of his record as one of the most celebrated heroes of World War II, and as the creator of the SAC air umbrella, which still dominates the nation's defense system, General LeMay is not a popular figure. Among millions of Americans, the mention of him evokes a negative response, the most common being, "Oh yes, he's the guy who wants to bomb everybody back into the Stone Age."

That "Stone Age" quote will always haunt him. Because he has never tried to explain or deny it, people naturally continue to pin it on him and criticize him for it. He has become the symbol of a military strategy that most Americans once accepted but many now question. In an earlier day, men like "Billy" Mitchell and "Hap" Arnold became national heroes by goading the country into developing its air power. But with the 1960s came America's tragic involvement in the Vietnam War and the continuous but fruitless bombardment of the Vietnam countryside. LeMay made none of the major decisions about the use of air power in Vietnam, but he never made that clear, either. In the public mind he became the man who wanted to bomb everything and everybody, the chief exponent of the idea that aerial bombardment was the solution to all problems.

At the same time, the public, disenchanted with the Vietnam War, was swinging toward the belief that bombing solved no problems. A large portion of the American public still holds that belief. But it was not always so. In the days before our entry into World War II, when Adolf Hitler's airplanes were dropping bombs with great success all over Europe and then the Japanese dropped their bombs with spectacular success all over Pearl Harbor, the American people were virtually unanimous in the belief that aerial bombardment was not only an acceptable but an absolutely necessary method of warfare, and that American bombers offered the best hope of restoring freedom to the world.

It was a different America in those days, vastly different from the country as we now know it. Not in every way, to be sure. People worked hard but loved fun. They followed fads, they were obsessed with cars, gossip, popular music, and sports. Though they didn't jog or indulge in extreme diets, they were determined to stay young and attractive. But there were only half as many of us in the country at that time—132 million—and in many ways we were just beginning to wake up to the realities of the world.

We knew about hunger and personal hardship; the Great Depression had taught us that. In fact we hadn't yet gotten through the Great Depression though we seemed to think we had. More than five million men were still unemployed. How many women, we'll never know. They didn't count women very closely then. No one had even thought of women's liberation or the Women's Movement. But not for long would unemployment be a problem. The United Mine Workers went on strike to raise their thirty-five-dollar-per-week wages; the auto and steel workers did likewise, all with some success because the nation's factories were filling up with defense contracts. There would soon be enough work, even for women, though at lower wages.

There was a feeling in the air that the "hard times" were over. Lighthearted tunes like "The Hut Sut Song" and "Six Lessons from Madame LaZonga" were at the top of the Hit Parade. Among the best-sellers were A. J. Cronin's *The Keys to the Kingdom*, Edna Ferber's *Saratoga Trunk*, and J. P. Marquand's *H. M. Pulham Esquire*. Among the movies were *The Philadelphia Story*, *Citizen Kane*, *The Little Foxes*, *One Foot in Heaven*, and the zany Bing Crosby-Bob Hope *Road to Zanzibar*. Harvard students had started the fad of swallowing goldfish. The wealthy fathers of debutantes struggled to outspend each other for their daughters' "coming out" parties. Women faithfully and almost uniformly followed the dictates of fashion. When designers sent hemlines up or down, hemlines all over town went up or down.

When brown-and-white saddle shoes and baggie-maggie sweaters were popular on campuses, they were popular with almost all coeds on all campuses. We were a conformist nation pretending to be free-spirited. We saw things simply. Other countries were warlike; we were peaceful (even though we had been engaged in seven major wars during our 160-year history). Other countries were colonialist and greedy to swallow up their neighbors. We had no territorial designs on any nation. We had a highly advertised "Good Neighbor" policy toward South America and we were granting independence to our Philippine Islands, though we were retaining economic domination of both and warning other nations to keep away from them.

We were sinfully wasteful in the uses of our natural resources. The word *ecology* was used only by biologists, to describe the relationship "between organisms and their environment." No one had yet thought of what we now know as the environmentalist movement. Though the phrase "planned obsolescence" wasn't yet in vogue, the practice was. When you bought a car battery with a two-year guarantee, you had to be ready to buy another battery two years and one day later.

We were an open-hearted, guileless, self-satisfied, churchgoing people, but often naïve, even about ourselves. We thought of ourselves as democratic, charitable, generous, unprejudiced champions of freedom. In many ways we were, yet our speech was full of words like *Jap, Chink, Hun, wop, kike*, and *nigger*. And we had cliché labels for every group to which we didn't belong. Blacks were stupid (but fast afoot), Jews were rich and crooked, the English were humorless, the Irish were drunks, the Scots were tight-fisted, the "Japs" were sneaky (but good gardeners), and the "Huns" were arrogant.

We were aware that we might soon have to go to war against the "Huns" and the "Japs." The signs of it were everywhere. Congress had approved by a one-vote margin the first peacetime draft in our history and the Army, which had limped along with a skeleton force of about three hundred thousand men since World War I, would soon have several million. The Navy was building new battleships, cruisers, destroyers, and even a few aircraft carriers. The Army Air Corps, which had only twenty thousand officers and men in 1938, was now recruiting crews for fifty thousand planes. In addition to the other movies, there were sobering war films like *Sergeant York* and *A Yank in the R.A.F.* And also among the best-sellers were Winston Churchill's *Blood,*

Sweat and Tears, William L. Shirer's *Berlin Diary,* and Jan Valtin's *Out of the Night.* The news from Europe was grim. German planes were still pasting London. German armies were punching deeper into Russia. The Japanese, while still technically at peace, were threatening all of Asia.

It was no secret that war was approaching. And a small though significant isolationist faction, led by men like Charles A. Lindbergh and Senator Gerald P. Nye of North Dakota, campaigned against any American commitment to it. But the majority of Americans realized we were very nearly committed already. And to most people what this meant, at least so far, was an increase in jobs and wages, more money in the pocket. You couldn't find many people complaining about that. The realization we might be sending our sons or ourselves abroad to fight was more abstract than urgent. It didn't translate itself into the deprivation, agony, and death that is the reality of war. We were so confident we couldn't imagine ourselves being threatened seriously by anybody or anything. If we had to go over to Europe and settle their war, we'd soon show them how it was done, just as we had shown them in 1918. America, after all, was the greatest goddamn country in the world. Hadn't we invented everything from the steamboat to the airplane? Didn't we have the world's highest standard of living? As any fool could see, God had "shed His grace" on us. Hitler might do well against corrupt, weak, or Communist countries like France, England, or Russia, but how would he do against our brand-new M-3 tanks, Garand rifles, P-40 fighter planes, and Flying Fortress bombers?

There were better-informed Americans, of course, who were not so comfortable and confident. In late September 1941, Brig. Gen. Arnold Krogstad of the Air Corps visited the Thirty-fourth Bomb Group stationed at Westover Air Base near Holyoke, Massachusetts, and delivered some words of advice to the staff.[1]

You fellows had better get ready for war, he said, because it's coming at us faster than you might think. We'll soon be in it.

Among his listeners was thirty-five-year-old Maj. Curtis LeMay, who only eighteen months earlier had been a lieutenant. Broad-chested and stocky, with a wide jaw, piercing eyes, and a serious face that seemed little disposed to smile, he looked impenetrable and fearsome. But on this day, as he listened to General Krogstad's dire prediction, he was, in fact, more fearful than fearsome. Like everyone else in the Air Corps, he was convinced the United States would eventually get into the war against Hitler. But "soon"! What did the general mean by "soon"?

Krogstad could not be more specific. All he could say was "soon." But he said it in a way that made it sound like tomorrow or next week or next month. And that would be impossible. The country wasn't yet ready. The Air Corps wasn't ready. It took time to build the fields and schools and factories, train the pilots and crews, design the planes and get them through the assembly lines. Sure as hell the Thirty-fourth Bomb Group wasn't ready. LeMay knew that because he was the group's operations officer. It had at its disposal only two untested B-17s and three obsolete twin-engine B-18s.

LeMay felt a sinking sensation in his stomach that didn't go away even hours, days, and weeks after General Krogstad's visit.[2] With the rapid expansion of the Air Corps' organizational structure, the old established groups had been split up to form the nuclei of new groups in the making which, as of now, existed mostly on paper. At this stage, none of them had the men, the planes, or the equipment needed to fight a war. As operations officer, he was responsible for the Thirty-fourth Group's training program, but how could he start any kind of program when he didn't yet have the crews to train or the planes in which to train them? What kind of training would be needed even if he did have the crews and planes? Under the peacetime Air Corps system, every group had its own training program and got only a general directive from higher headquarters. But there would be significant differences between peacetime and wartime training. These young men coming in from cadet flying schools, with shiny faces and shiny new wings, wouldn't get the time to learn operational procedures gradually. How could he manage enough flying hours for the pilots? Where would he find enough practice bombs for the bombardiers? Where would he get the navigators for long-range training flights? Besides not knowing what he ought to do, he lacked the resources to do it even if he had known. For one of the few times in his life, Curtis LeMay felt completely helpless. And his feelings hadn't changed when he got out of bed the morning of December 7, 1941.

It looked like another ordinary Sunday morning in Holyoke, where Major LeMay, with his regally elegant wife, Helen, and their three-year-old daughter, Patricia (whom they called Janie), had lived in a rented house since his assignment to the Thirty-fourth the previous winter.[3] He got up early as was his habit from childhood when, out of necessity, he first became acquainted with work as a way of life. There was a lot of it waiting for him at the base. The new crews were trickling in, a few at a time, and so were the planes. But because it was Sunday, he intended to work only during the morning. He couldn't be blamed for wanting at least a little time with his wife and daughter. Since early spring he had hardly seen them at all. First he had been on detached duty, flying high-priority passengers in a new B-24 Liberator bomber across the North Atlantic to England as part of President Roosevelt's program to help the beleaguered British. Then he had been the navigator on a path-finding flight to South America and across to Africa, seeking an easier air route, especially for shorter-ranged fighter planes, from the United States to Europe. After completing this flight he had returned to duty at Westover. But his efforts to develop training programs now took almost all of his time. His little daughter was usually asleep when he left home in the morning and already asleep again when he got home at night. She'd soon forget what her father looked like if he didn't at least get a chance to pick her up and hug her once in awhile.

True to his resolve, he did knock off work about one o'clock in the afternoon and was on his way home, listening to the New York Giants–Brooklyn Dodgers football game on the car radio, when a studio announcer broke in with the news flash that everyone who heard it will always remember. The Japanese had bombed Pearl Harbor.

LeMay's reaction was strange, yet understandable. He could sympathize with the victims of the bombing, if there were any victims, yet he also felt "some sense of relief" that it had finally happened. At least he knew now where he was going. He was going to war. And he could quit wondering when. He continued on home and broke the news to his wife. Then he returned to the base where more work and a lot of confusion were waiting for him.

In the aftermath of the Pearl Harbor attack and the country's entry into the war, a wave of anti-Japanese hysteria and invasion fear hit the West Coast, particularly California. It was a widely held American notion that all Japanese, including Japanese Americans, were sneaky, and that a lot of them had tiny cameras hidden on their persons, in such unlikely places as their mouths and their belly buttons, with which they took pictures of American military secrets, to be sent to Japan. These being acceptable beliefs at the time, it seemed reasonable to the authorities that all these actual or potential spies on the coast be dispatched to inland concentration camps. No sooner said than begun. The camps were quickly built, in such safe places as the High Sierras and Arizona, and the first of the one hundred twelve thousand West Coast Japanese were herded onto trains, with their children and with the pitifully few belongings they were allowed to take, but without the benefit of due process of law. Almost no voices were raised against this outrage. No one asked why the German and Italian Americans on the coast were not to be put away, though we were also at war with Germany and Italy. Nor did anyone suggest that the Japanese in Hawaii should also be put away. If the California Japanese were dangerous, how much more dangerous were the Hawaiian Japanese, many of whom were thought to have sent up signals, guiding the attack planes over Pearl Harbor. The Hawaiian Japanese presented a problem because there were one hundred sixty thousand of them—almost one-third of the entire population—and even the most jittery of our authorities realized the economy of the islands would collapse without them, whereas the incarceration of the West Coast Japanese would have little effect on the economy there except to create opportunities to buy Japanese-owned property at a fraction of its value.

The anti-Japanese hysteria up and down the coast increased when, on February 23, 1942, a Japanese submarine surfaced a mile offshore, near Santa Barbara, and erratically lobbed sixteen shells in the general direction of an oil refinery.[4] Only minor damage was inflicted but four Japanese in the area were immediately arrested. The *Los Angeles Times* reported: "Two Japs were said to have been riding around the city during the blackout in a station wagon armed with guns. For more than two hours after the raid, brilliant yellow flares burst over darkened Ventura. Authorities said it was clearly an effort to signal the enemy."

Under these bizarre circumstances, it was not surprising that the armed forces also fell prey to the fear of imminent invasion. The Air Force hastened to send every spare unit scurrying westward "as a rabble," in the words of Curtis LeMay. And his Thirty-fourth Bomb Group was part of that "rabble."[5]

Even before the American entry into the war, the pilots of the Thirty-fourth had been patrolling the north Atlantic in search of German submarines. But since their planes had no bombs or depth charges to drop on a U-boat, if one by chance was sighted, nothing was lost by sending the group from the Atlantic to the Pacific. So everyone packed up and headed across country to Pendleton, Oregon. The LeMays put their furniture in storage and Helen LeMay took their little daughter to her parents' home in Lakewood, Ohio, a suburb of Cleveland where her father was active as a corporation lawyer. But if she thought she was settling in for the duration, she almost immediately learned otherwise. When her husband landed at Pendleton, a War Department telegram was waiting for him. He was to return east to Wright Field in Dayton to take part in service tests of the four-engine B-24 Liberator bomber, a plane the United States was already selling to the British even though it wasn't yet completely tested.

The B-24 was still so new at the beginning of 1942 there were only a few Air Corps pilots who had even seen it; fewer still who could fly it. LeMay was one of the latter because he had flown B-24s across the Atlantic to England. The story of how he had learned to fly them offers a fairly typical picture of the helter-skelter way things were done in the hectic days when the country was preparing for war.

One Saturday morning in the spring of 1941, LeMay, at Westover, received a phone call from an Air Corps colonel, C. V. Haynes, who, for some strange reason, was in Montreal. LeMay had known Haynes for several years. In August 1938, Haynes was the lead plane pilot, and LeMay the lead navigator, on a much-publicized pathfinder flight from Washington to Bogotá, Colombia. A simple flight today, but in those days of either primitive or nonexistent navigational aids, an explorative and dangerous mission. It was not by chance that LeMay became the mission's lead navigator. Besides being a highly respected pilot, he had by that time proven himself, on numerous pathfinder flights, to be the most skillful navigator in the Air Corps. On May 12, 1938, for instance, he was the lead navigator for a flight of B-17s that intercepted the Italian liner *Rex* more than seven hundred miles at sea, in an exercise designed to show the U.S. Navy that the Air Corps was also capable of a role in defending American shores.

When Haynes called LeMay in the spring of 1941, he told him to trade his uniform for civilian clothes, get on an airliner, and meet him in Montreal the next morning.[6]

"Where in Montreal?" LeMay asked.

"ATFERO," Haynes said.

"At Farrell?"

"No. I'll spell it. A-T-F-E-R-O."

ATFERO? What did that stand for? Haynes didn't know what the initials meant. Where in Montreal was it? Haynes had apparently been driven to it. He didn't know the address. "You'll have to find it for yourself," he said.

By commercial plane and then (after a snow-forced landing) by taxi, LeMay reached Montreal the next day and eventually did find ATFERO, whereupon he learned that the initials stood for Atlantic Ferry Organization, an agency of the British Ministry of Aircraft Production. Its purpose was to ferry U.S. war planes from Canada to England because it was illegal, under the U.S. Neutrality Act, to ferry planes directly from the United States to Europe. Haynes, and now LeMay, were being assigned to take part in the operation because Gen. Henry H. "Hap" Arnold, the Air Corps commander, realized that a lot of his own planes and men might soon be making the north Atlantic flight as belligerents, and the Air Corps had better find out how it was done. Because the planes to be ferried were B-24s, none of which had even come off the assembly lines as yet, the first item of business for Haynes and LeMay was to go look at one and learn how to fly it.

At Wright Field a few days later they were introduced to the first B-24 out of the factory. A check pilot ushered them aboard with two other Air Corps pilots—J. B. Montgomery and C. J. Cochrane—and after a few words of instruction, invited Colonel Haynes to take the pilot's seat.

With a little more instruction, Haynes managed to start the plane, take it off the ground, fly it around the field, and land it. One more time he took it off and landed it. Then he said, "Okay, LeMay, get in here."

LeMay made one takeoff and landing, Montgomery made one and Cochrane made one, whereupon the check pilot certified all four as qualified B-24 pilots, which meant that LeMay had to his credit fifteen minutes of flying time in a B-24 before he flew one across the Atlantic Ocean to England.

Having survived several transatlantic flights in the spring and summer of 1941, LeMay was considered an expert on the plane by the time the United States entered the war. Hence, his orders to get right back east on the earliest possible plane from Pendleton, Oregon, and report to Wright Field for the belated B-24 service tests. They should have been conducted, of course, before any B-24 was flown across the Atlantic, but the fact that B-24s and other American military planes were flown to England in those days without adequate testing was not a result of carelessness. It was a measure of England's desperate need for aircraft.

Since LeMay had no idea how long he would be at Wright Field—if they considered him a B-24 expert he might have a hard time breaking away—he called Helen and asked her to meet him there, which she did, with little Janie. But neither of the LeMays, or anyone else, had ever fully envisaged the madness of the wartime rush for housing around military institutions. In some places the wives and families of servicemen could find nothing to rent but barns and even chicken coops. LeMay found all the air-base housing taken and all the Dayton hotels full. Fortunately he stumbled upon an old Air Corps friend who had a house on the base and was able to squeeze them in for a few nights, so he spent his days testing B-24s and his evenings looking for a place to put his wife and daughter. Then suddenly, a miracle. He located a couple of furnished rooms for rent in Yellow Springs, about fifteen miles east of the base. But if Helen thought she could settle in there, she soon learned otherwise. In a month, she and her child were again on their way to Cleveland and her husband was again on his way to Pendleton, Oregon, though not for long. Shortly after his arrival in Pendleton this time he was assigned as executive officer to the 306th Bomb Group, which was just in the process of birth. He was on his way to meet this brand-new unit in Wendover, Utah.

Anyone who doesn't shudder at the thought of being stationed in Wendover, Utah, simply hasn't been there. It was an ideal place to prepare young men for the hardships of war. The front wouldn't seem so bad after a tour of duty in Wendover. When Curtis LeMay (Lieutenant Colonel LeMay since January 5, 1942, as a result of the accelerated wartime promotion policy) stood pipe in mouth on the rise northwest of Wendover, looking down on the flat, white Salt Lake Desert that stretched 130 miles east toward Salt Lake City, he thought to himself, "Good place to land and take off." That was about all he could say for it. He wished he could take off immediately.

"There was a rudimentary runway," he later recalled, "but no hangars. No barracks. Everybody was in tents. [And] no adjacent civilian residential areas." There were no more than three hundred residents of Wendover at that time.

Set precisely on the state line between the most sparsely populated part of Utah and the most sparsely populated part of Nevada, it had little to offer its residents except a choice between the Mormon virtues of one state and the ever-hopeful vice of the other. The Nevada gambling places, which included such lavish establishments as a two-pump gas station, a mom-and-pop grocery store, and some dingy bars, had been built as close as possible to the Utah state line so that each could offer a gambler the "last chance" to lose his money. But only the State Line Hotel could offer the ultimate "last chance." Because it straddled the line, a bettor could lose his money in one half of the building but not the other.

When LeMay arrived, the 306th had one officer, Col. Charles Overacker, in command of about five hundred brand-new privates and one corporal, a transferee from the Field Artillery. The first and most urgent need was for at least a few experienced cooks so the men could be adequately fed, a few office clerks so they could be recorded and paid, and a few mechanics to service the four B-17s assigned to the group. Fortunately the Second Air Force was able to spare a few of each, but only a few. All the other new groups were equally desperate for experienced people.

More new men were soon pouring into the 306th from basic training or from the various flying and technical schools. They were dirty and unshaven after long rides on coal-burning trains whose steam engines left cinders in their wake to drift through the open windows of the crowded cars. Now that the country was at war, every obsolete passenger car still equipped with wheels had been pulled from graveyard sidings and returned to service in the desperate scramble to handle the increased traffic. Few of these cars were air-conditioned. Some were so old they featured gaslights.

"A lot of the men didn't even have a change of clothes," LeMay recalled, "because half their baggage would go one way, and the other half another. And they had no money because they hadn't been paid. We'd line them up, pick out the smart-looking fellows, and say, 'Okay, you're a corporal,' or 'You're a sergeant.' Then we'd tell the troop, 'Go over to that tarpaper building. Get yourself a tent, go out to where you see those stakes and put up your tent. That's where you'll live.' "

Among the arriving officers of the new 306th was Maj. (later Gen.) Delmar Wilson, who soon became the group's operations officer. Since his desk was directly across from that of the executive officer, he had an excellent opportunity to observe LeMay's method of thinking.

"He would sit there for two or three hours, smoking his pipe, twirling the forelock of his hair, thinking about something, and never say a word," Wilson has recalled, "then bang! He would come up with an idea, something we should do to train those crews."[7]

LeMay himself felt at this time that he was caught in a mess as unreal as it was terrible. None of the time-honored Army traditions addressed themselves to such a situation. No framework had been set up to solve such problems. "It seemed like this whole enterprise would evaporate, diffuse into space any moment. Or worse than that: descend into a dragged-out, incompetent future." There was a war in progress and he was a soldier. His whole career had supposedly trained him for war. Would he ever see it?

As if his spirits weren't low enough at this time, he received a letter from his younger brother, Leonard, a sophomore at Ohio State who had been drafted shortly after Pearl Harbor and sent to Engineers' Officer Candidate School. He was now a second lieutenant, already in northern Ireland, prepared for the invasion of Europe. "When in hell are you going to get here?" he wrote. "You've been in service a long time. You're supposed to be over here doing something."[8] But here he was in Wendover, Utah. Even trench warfare would be preferable.

While trying to find a way out of this desperate dilemma, he had the additional bad luck to secure a room in the State Line Hotel, so once again he sent for Helen and, once again, long-suffering Army wife that she was, she came with Janie on one of those above-described trains, this time to scenic Wendover. More than that, she stayed for as long as he was there, a whole month, which proved beyond any doubt that she truly loved him.

CHAPTER TWO

LeMay's tenure as executive officer of the 306th was, mercifully, of short duration, but it was a fitting introduction to his next assignment. In June 1942, he took over a group of his own, the 305th, which had already been organized, in a manner of speaking. Within three months, the 305th had seen three commanding officers come and go. Its staff and squadron officers were being moved back and forth from job to job like chess pieces. Its enlisted men got up each morning wondering who would be in charge today.

Since the group, whatever there might be of it, was camped out near Salt Lake City, but was destined to move on, no one yet knew where, the LeMays packed their bags one more time, said farewell to Wendover and its State Line Hotel, and set out across the Great Salt Lake Desert.

When LeMay reached the Salt Lake City Army air base at the end of May 1942, he found the 305th in just about the same condition as the 306th.[1] The day he assumed command, June 4, the group had only four B-17s with which to train the incoming pilots. No navigators or bombardiers had yet been assigned to it. And only two pilots on his staff, besides himself, had ever flown a B-17. One was Group Operations Officer Capt. John H. de Russy. The other, Capt. Joseph Preston, was the group's most notable novelty—a man who had actually seen some combat. Preston had been with the Nineteenth Bomb Group in the Philippines on Pearl Harbor day. During the disastrous Philippine campaign, he flew several missions against the Japanese, and when the Philippines fell, he escaped to Java in his B-17, where he flew a few more missions before being sent back to the States.

The young pilots arriving fresh from cadet training had never seen a B-17. Worse than that, they had never flown multiengine airplanes of any kind. Each had flown about two hundred hours in single-engine planes at flying schools. They had yet to learn even the concept of synchronizing four engines. There had been so many changes of staff personnel in the 305th that no one had gotten around to teaching them. Conditions here were even more chaotic than in the 306th.

For LeMay, however, there was one difference here. Because he was now a commanding officer, the chaos was his direct responsibility, and he'd better do something about it in a hurry or he would soon go the way of the group commanders who had preceded him. There was no doubt in his mind as to what was needed. Training, training, and more training. Five years earlier, when he himself first flew a B-17, he had come under the insistent tutelage of an older officer, Col. Robert S. Olds, who had made it clear to him that flying in the Air Corps was not just a barnstorming adventure, that he must never forget he was preparing himself and his men for war, and that the word for preparation was *training*. But how could he train these fledgling pilots for war when he had only four planes and three "instructors," including himself, who could fly the planes? Eventually there would be more planes but the war, with the country six months into it, wasn't waiting for the 305th Bomb Group to get ready. In two or three months, the group would be called to action and a lot of people in it would be killed needlessly if they weren't trained. There was only one thing to do—train people around the clock. Keep those four planes in the air at all hours. So his first order as commander of the 305th was to institute immediately an unheard-of policy—a twenty-four-hour-a-day, seven-day-a-week training program.

Such a hopeful plan would depend, of course, on the ability of the maintenance crews to keep the planes in flying condition. Here LeMay had two advantages on which he could depend. The first was a man named Ben Fulkrod, a lieutenant who had been a technical sergeant and an assistant line chief on a B-17. LeMay could see immediately that Fulkrod knew everything there was to know about a B-17. And the reason LeMay could see this was his second advantage. He himself knew everything there was to know about the plane. Not content with learning to fly it, he had studied every aspect of it—mechanical, aerodynamic, and military. If there was a mechanical problem a crew chief couldn't solve, LeMay would put on his coveralls, take tools in hand, and show the man how to solve it. Maj. Ralph Cohen, the group armaments officer at that time, later recalled his amazement as he watched this new commander: "I've seen LeMay go out to squadron engineers and tell them what to do with an engine, then show them how to do it. He was a better engineer than any of the engineering officers."

"So we started working," LeMay said in an interview conducted in England a year later.[3] "None of the personnel was ready for combat at all. There were forty-eight [pilots] and four airplanes. . . . To start out with, they had to learn to fly the airplane before we could learn to fly formation. Then we had to go to altitude. But most of the training that we consider essential for operation in this [the European] theater, they never received at all, because there wasn't time."

Though LeMay's ambitious idea dictated that he, de Russy, and Preston spend eight to twelve hours a day (or night) in the air as teachers, the training program made some progress until, after only one week, it was interrupted by the Japanese navy. American intelligence had learned that the bulk of the enemy fleet was speeding across the Pacific toward either Hawaii or Midway Island. If the Japanese were to take Hawaii, the entire West Coast would be vulnerable to attack or invasion. The Army Air Corps decided to meet this new threat with what might be referred to as "a barrage of paper"—several new bomb groups which, for all practical purposes, were organized on paper only.

Since the 305th was one of these groups, LeMay gathered what he called his "raggle-taggle gypsy crowd" and moved them, with their four planes, to Geiger Field near Spokane, Washington. About the time they arrived, Air Corps headquarters decided it would be pointless to send any more skeleton groups. Using the 305th as a nucleus, and leaving LeMay in command, they simply sent crews and planes from other groups, which meant the 305th soon had a full complement. But not of B-17s. Several of the arriving planes were B-24s, which differed radically from the 17s in flight characteristics and in equipment requirements. LeMay now had the job of figuring out how to weld these two kinds of planes (completely incompatible) and one kind of crew (woefully untrained) into a force that could strike some kind of blow against an invading fleet.

He began scrounging frantically for all the items he would need in actual combat—bomb racks (B-17 type and B-24 type), bombs, fuel, ammunition, quarters, food, etc. He worked out a crude, provisional but hopeful plan of operations. And he even conducted a few practice bomb runs—on land because there were no targets to bomb at sea. But fortunately, the Battle of Midway intervened (June 4–6), routing the Japanese fleet and saving LeMay from the hideous possibility that he might have to put his pathetic plan into action.

As soon as the Japanese threat evaporated, so did the 305th Bomb Group's full complement of planes and crews. All the newcomers returned to their original units, leaving LeMay with his "raggle-taggle crowd" and four B-17s. But before they had time to return to Salt Lake City, new orders arrived sending them to Muroc Dry Lake (now Edwards Air Force Base) in the heart of California's Mojave Desert.

When the move to Muroc was completed, on July 4, LeMay resumed his twenty-four-hour, seven-day training program, but not before hearing the moans and gripes of his men about the conditions they found there. Edwards is a huge, busy, well-constructed, exceptionally well-equipped, and air-conditioned facility today. In 1942, it was simply a vast expanse of dry lake bed, attractive to the Air Corps because it offered mile after mile of flat, dry-lake landing surface, so hard it didn't have to be paved. But it was so barren it made Wendover, Utah, look like the Garden of Eden. The only building available to the 305th was a deserted stone house with no windows and half of a roof. This monument to the rigors of the desert became group headquarters. Since there were no barracks, everyone, including LeMay, had to live in tents that became ovens during the 120-degree days and refrigerators during the 40-degree nights. Though he had become a full colonel while at Geiger Field, Spokane, and enjoyed there for two weeks the prerogatives of his new rank, he was sharply reminded now that promotion didn't guarantee comfort. He used the same hand-dug latrines and ate the same canned rations as everyone else. And he listened to his men bitch about the place. But he didn't listen for long. He had what he thought was a sure-fire way to distract them from their miseries. He would work their asses off.

With the few planes he had, he got the crews into the air, one after another. Whenever a plane landed and a crew got out, the next crew got in and took off, with LeMay, de Russy, or Preston remaining aboard to instruct them. They would keep flying a plane, day and night, until something broke, then nurse it back to the base and put Fulkrod's mechanics to work repairing it. But not in hangars. There were no hangars, a fact that forced

LeMay to accept, grudgingly, the first modification of his training regimen. The desert sun was so hot in July the mechanics simply could not work on the planes during the daytime without blistering their hands. Broken-down planes, therefore, had to be repaired at night, which sharply curtailed the schedule of night flights.

LeMay found it so difficult to accept this limitation that it disappointed him to learn his men applauded it. What the hell was wrong with these men? It seemed to him they ought to welcome all the training they were getting because they would soon go into combat, and the better prepared they were, the better chance they had of surviving. But most of them didn't seem to feel that way, and he had a hard time forgiving them for it. He didn't think very highly of this "raggle-taggle crowd" of his. It seemed to him a lot of these mama's boys, farmboys, drugstore cowboys, and college boys just didn't have the guts they'd need in combat. Several of them were openly frightened and obviously unsuited for what they'd be expected to endure. Even some of the gunners, though graduates of gunnery schools, seemed only now beginning to realize that when they fired real bullets at a real enemy, they had to expect the enemy to return the fire. A few of these gunners, after being introduced to the exposed positions they were supposed to occupy in the waist or tail of the B-17, said no thanks, they didn't choose to make themselves so vulnerable. But even after weeding these men out, LeMay had reservations about those he kept. He would flop down on his cot at night thinking, "How could anyone have the gall to bring a rabble like this into battle?"

Underlying his uneasiness was a degree of uncertainty he also harbored about himself.[4] While he had often assumed, abstractly and almost casually, that he would be killed during the war, he was only now staring at it as an immediate, inescapable probability. How would he himself stand up under fire? Maybe he knew more than his men about being a pilot, about navigation and gunnery, but, he asked himself, what did he know about how it feels to be in combat? Would he stand up to it? Would he have the nerve to ask his boys to stand up to it? Especially boys like these who seemed so dismally lacking in what he called "intestinal fortitude"?

While LeMay didn't think much of the men assigned to his group, they didn't think much of him, either. He was a cold, mean son-of-a-bitch if ever they saw one. And he was a different kind of son-of-a-bitch from any others they had encountered during their short time in the Air Corps. In basic training or flight training they had been subjected to officers or sergeants who shouted and cursed at them, stood them at attention and chewed them out unmercifully. This miserable bastard didn't shout at them at all, seldom spoke, and then in a quiet voice which usually uttered only a few terse words. But what those terse words said, in effect, was—You can do it better than that. Do it again until you get it right. And they did it again, and again, and again until they couldn't stand the sight of this uncompromising, unshakeable, indefatigable, demanding man. It wasn't long before one of them came up with a name that seemed to fit him perfectly—''Iron Ass.'' It was a name that stuck, a name that was soon heard throughout the group. Iron Ass LeMay. No one said it within earshot of him. Yet inevitably he heard about it. And a faint smile crossed his face.

Men who couldn't take his relentless pressure were soon on their way elsewhere and new men arrived to replace them. The number of pilots and crews in the group's four squadrons (364th, 365th, 366th, and 422nd) began approaching full strength as July faded into August. New ground units had also been attached: the 679th, 163rd, and 794th Quartermaster; the 57th Signal; the 114th, 517th, and 856th Chemical; the 715th and 423rd Ordnance. And one by one, six or seven more B-17s arrived. The 305th Group was almost beginning to look like a complete outfit, though not a happy one.

LeMay, oppressed by the responsibility of training his men, but also well aware of the morale problem, decided he should give everybody one day off per week if possible. But to turn men loose in the middle of the Mojave Desert would be almost like turning them loose in the Sahara, so he used the group's one transport plane to institute a daily shuttle from Muroc to the Douglas Aircraft Company's field in Santa Monica. The men actually got more like one free day every two weeks because training still took precedence, but at least they could begin to hope for a few days off. Their wives and sweethearts, sharing this hope, began to gather around Santa Monica, waiting for that plane, praying the right man would be on it. Among them, naturally, was the tireless Helen LeMay, who arrived once more with Janie. But once more, almost for naught. Her husband was even harder on himself than on his men. Helen saw him only a few times, a few hours at a time, before she made another long train trek back to her parents' home in Ohio.

LeMay had been hoping for at least two months of intensive work at Muroc, but he didn't get even that much time. On August 23, his ground echelon moved out by train to Fort Dix, New Jersey, for embarkation, presumably to England. He and his crews, now with no support units, were left like orphans at Muroc until he arranged to fly them to Tucson, Arizona, and combine them with another group in training there. But after ten days in Tucson, the orphan crews of the 305th lost even their training planes, which were dispatched to Geiger Field for use by another group in the process of organization there.

The crews were now ready, supposedly, to receive their brand new F-model B-17s with which they were scheduled to fly into battle. Since several of these planes were to come out of factories in Cheyenne, Wyoming, and Tulsa, Oklahoma, LeMay sent some of his crews there to pick them up and fly them east, while he and the rest of the crews traveled east by train to pick up the balance of their thirty-five big bombers at Syracuse, New York. Not surprisingly, under the prevailing wartime conditions, there were no planes ready to be picked up either at Cheyenne or Tulsa. The disappointed crews who went there got on trains and hurried east to Syracuse. But there was actually no need for them to hurry because, as the crews at Syracuse had learned, the planes weren't ready there, either. They needed modifications, especially in the ball turrets.[5]

LeMay, impatient as usual, sent his crews into the factory to help work on the modifications while he, reminded by a sudden October cold spell that he was no longer in the hot California desert, and that his group would soon be flying into a cold, damp English winter, drove a truck out to a quartermaster depot near Syracuse and scrounged all the winter clothing they were willing to give him. Having no authority to requisition such equipment, and lacking even the required Army forms, he simply went in and demanded what he needed.

"By God, we're going overseas!" he cried, pounding dramatically on a desk. "We need underwear. Anything you've got. Let me have it. Overshoes . . ."

Before he was through, he drove away with two truckloads of heavy underwear, boots, galoshes, overcoats, blankets, and sweaters. Not quite as much as the group would need, but, as he eventually learned, more than most groups had when they got to Europe.

As the cold spell in Syracuse continued, LeMay noticed for the first time a personal problem that frightened him enough to send him scurrying to the base hospital. One night he developed such a severe backache he couldn't sleep. At the hospital the next day they put him under a heat lamp, left him there until he felt he was someplace between rare and medium, then sent him back to his quarters.

By the following morning, the pain, as if to avoid the heat, had raised itself to the back of his neck and seemed to be firmly, rigidly ensconced there. Deciding it was just a cold, he worked all morning and went to lunch telling himself he was not about to surrender to a little thing like a pain in the neck.

After ordering a cup of coffee, he raised it to his lips and took a whole mouthful.

A moment later, he looked down to find every drop of it dripping down his shirt front.

He couldn't believe it. What was the matter with him? Didn't he know enough to close his mouth after filling it with coffee?

Doing his best to preserve his dignity in the crowded dining room, he stood up and hurried to the latrine to wipe off his shirt, but by the time he got there he was no longer thinking about his shirt. "When I looked in the mirror," he later recalled, "I knew something was radically wrong with my face and mouth."

A few minutes later, when he arrived back at the hospital, he was fortunate enough to be referred to Dr. Maurice Walsh, a young flight surgeon who, until his enlistment in the Air Corps, had been affiliated with a paralysis clinic.

"You've got Bell's palsy," Walsh said to the worried colonel.[6]

It was not an assuring thing to say to an aircraft pilot. When one thinks of palsy, one envisages shaky hands, hardly conducive to smooth flying.

"What in hell," LeMay demanded, "is Bell's palsy?"

Dr. Walsh gave him a short lecture on the subject which was scary at first, reassuring in the end. Bell's palsy, he explained, was a type of facial paralysis named after the man who first noticed it, Sir Charles Bell, an early-nineteenth-century Scottish anatomist. It was caused by inflammation of certain nerves, usually as a result of exposure to cold. The nerves freeze, then become swollen, cutting off the blood supply. Finally they degenerate, disconnecting some of the facial muscles from the central nervous system.

In LeMay's case, Dr. Walsh believed the palsy had been caused by flying B-17s at high altitudes, where the temperatures were as low as twenty, thirty, or even forty below zero. The B-17 was not as well sealed from the cold as it should be. Only the nerves on the right side of LeMay's face were affected, but that was enough to make one eyelid droop and his mouth sag noticeably to one side, stamping what looked like a perpetual sneer on his face. It made him appear even tougher, more hard-nosed than ever, a circumstance that might make his men fear him more than ever, but wasn't likely to increase either his popularity or his comfort.

If the swelling went down, the flight surgeon said, the nerves would regenerate and his face would return to normal. If not, he'd have trouble with it.

"Give me the ungarbled word," LeMay demanded. "Are you going to do anything about it? Or can you do anything about it? What's the treatment?"

There were a lot of treatments—heat, electric shock, massage, various kinds of physical therapy. But, Dr. Walsh said, "as nearly as we could discern, the cases we didn't treat at all came through just as well as those we treated."

"You've named my treatment," LeMay said. "Good-bye."

As he was rushing out, the doctor had some sensible suggestions for him. "Keep the right side of your face warm. Stay out of drafts. And stand in front of a mirror every day for at least an hour, trying to move your facial muscles."

Since LeMay was firmly committed to flying those cold B-17s, and since he was scheduled to leave soon for England where drafts were prominently featured in nearly every building, and since he couldn't easily fit an hour's worth of mirror-gazing into his already twenty-hour-a-day schedule, he decided to ignore his palsy completely, hoping it would eventually feel slighted and go away, which about 95 percent of it did after a year or so.

As the ball turret modifications were completed, the 305th finally began receiving its new B-17s, bright, shiny, and redolent of that combination—metal, leather, and oil—which creates the distinctive aroma of new airplanes. By mid-October, thirty of their thirty-five had been delivered. Besides being huge by the standards of its day—seventy-four feet long, one-hundred-four-foot wingspan, twenty-four tons fully loaded, forty-eight-hundred horsepower in its four engines—the B-17 was a beautiful machine, with its long, graceful lines and high, distinctive tail. A proud machine. But LeMay didn't give his boys much time to beam over it. He hurried them into the air. They practiced a few high-altitude flights and one day they flew out of Syracuse on a twelve-hour "navigational" flight to Florida, which was no more than an orientation flight for the navigators. They hadn't even joined the group until two weeks before its arrival in Syracuse. None of them had ever navigated a B-17 on a flight of any length, just as none of the bombardiers had ever dropped a real bomb.

In LeMay's estimation, his crews were still so green he cherished every extra day of work before they had to make the long flight from Syracuse to Presque Isle, Maine, to Gander, Newfoundland, and then across the cold, dark north Atlantic to Prestwick, Scotland. The pilots had logged an average of only about one hundred hours in B-17s. The navigators had experienced only the one long flight, the easy cruise down the Atlantic coast to Florida and back. The gunners had fired only a few rounds of ammunition in air-to-air practice. And the bombardiers had never dropped anything but stove-pipe mock bombs, in bright sunshine over the Mojave Desert.

LeMay was still hoping to cram more training into these men when, on October 20, he received a visit from Col. Fred Anderson, an old friend and flying-school classmate who was now on the Air Corps staff in Washington.[7]

"How soon," Anderson asked LeMay, "can you get ready to go to the South Pacific?"

They were in LeMay's makeshift headquarters. He looked up in astonishment at his slender, sandy-haired friend. "What did you say, Fred?"

"You're almost ready to go," Anderson observed. "And they're thinking of sending you. MacArthur needs help down there."

By this time LeMay was pacing the floor, trying to get hold of himself. "Christ, you can't do that, Fred." But as he well knew, it wasn't Fred who would be doing it. Anderson was simply warning him what was going on in Hap Arnold's Washington office. "My ground echelon is already in England. All we've got here is the air echelon. You send us to the Pacific, we won't be worth a damn when we get there, except as replacements."

"I know it doesn't make sense," Anderson admitted, "but

they're yelling their heads off for a heavy bomb group out there. At the moment, you're more ready to go than anyone else.''

LeMay was appalled at the prospect. ''All our baggage is in England,'' he pointed out. ''And all our equipment. You should see the maintenance equipment we sent over there. Our ground crews are there, the people we've been working with. This will be one screwed-up mess if they try to send us to the Pacific.''

''Couldn't agree with you more,'' Anderson said, ''but it's what they're talking about.''

''How long have I got?'' LeMay asked, realizing now with gratitude that Anderson had made this trip expressly as an act of friendship, to give him a chance to get away before the fateful orders arrived.

''That I don't know,'' Anderson said.

''Well for Christ's sake,'' LeMay pleaded, ''stall 'em as long as you can.''

About two minutes after ushering Anderson out of his office, LeMay ushered in his closest aides—de Russy, Preston, Fulkrod, Cohen, and several others.

''Our original orders,'' LeMay said, ''are to proceed to Prestwick, Scotland, the moment we're ready to go. But unless we get the hell out of here, and fast, proceeding on those original orders, we're going to get some new orders. And we'll find ourselves grinding away toward the Pacific without any ground crews, without any equipment, even without a lot of our personal belongings.''

He looked around to find a roomful of bewildered faces gaping at him. ''We've now got how many of our planes?'' he asked. ''What's the latest count?''

Someone said, ''Thirty-three. Two to go.''

''And when do we get those two?''

''Tomorrow morning, they say.''

''Okay, there's only one thing we can do,'' LeMay said. ''Button up and button up fast. Get to work on those airplanes. We've got to shake off the flu germs of Syracuse before they change those orders.''

Three days later, the group was as ready to go as anyone could expect it to be. The pilots had never seen the north Atlantic, of course; they knew nothing about ocean flying and very little about the dangers of icing on their wings. But LeMay had flown the route himself many times during the B-24 shuttle project and he spent several hours telling the pilots what to expect. Likewise, the navigators had never been asked to find their way to any place farther than Florida, which was hard to miss if you followed the coastline. There was no such guide across the Atlantic. Some of LeMay's aides were so worried about navigators getting lost that they suggested a formation flight across the ocean, even though the gasoline use would be almost prohibitive and it would be extremely difficult, perhaps impossible, to maintain a formation with green pilots on that long a flight. LeMay, aware of all this, vetoed the idea.

"These boys are now supposed to be navigators," he said. "They've got to take off, one by one, and get themselves over there."

On the chilly morning of October 23, before the first plane took off, LeMay gathered his men for some last words. He reminded the pilots of the dangers ahead. He reminded the navigators of everything he had told them about finding their way into Presque Isle, then Gander, then Prestwick. And he reminded all of his men that they would be representing their country, the United States of America. They better hadn't disgrace it. They were going to England to fight a war. But they should bear well in mind that the British were not the enemy.

"If you go into their pubs," he said, "don't get into any fights with them. But if you do, make sure you win."[8]

CHAPTER THREE

To the amazement of Curtis LeMay, all thirty-five of the crews in his 305th "rabble" made the first legs of their long journey—Presque Isle and Gander—without serious incident. But at Gander one of them was overtaken by a mishap so ludicrous it sharply reminded LeMay he was still leading a children's crusade. The airfield at Gander in those days had runways that looked at first glance almost as wide as they were long. One of the pilots unfortunately believed his first glance and took off, not down the runway, but across it. Though no one was injured, the plane was banged up and the crew had to wait at Gander for another plane to replace it.

On the next leg, the long ocean leap to Scotland, many of the planes had trouble with runaway propellers. One of them lost a prop shortly after takeoff and turned back toward Gander only to find that bad weather had gotten there ahead of him and the field was socked in tight. He could do nothing but go on to Nova Scotia, where he was again defeated by the weather. He finally did get under the clouds, managed to locate the coastline, and ditched beautifully in the water, so close to the shore his crew hardly even got wet leaping off onto the sand. Another plane lost two propellers in mid-Atlantic but limped the rest of the way to Scotland after the crew threw overboard everything that wasn't attached. This was a useful lesson for the whole group. And it also showed what a good friend even a crippled B-17 could be if handled with some delicacy and understanding.

The navigators gave LeMay a pleasant surprise. For the first half of the flight, everyone had to fly by the compass, dead reckoning, because the heavy clouds prevented celestial navigation. But in mid-Atlantic, the clouds broke slightly. It became possible to get a few celestial shots and LeMay discovered his plane had drifted about one hundred miles south of its course. When he informed the other ships of this by radio, he was amazed and pleased to learn that all of his navigators had either discovered it already or were in the process of doing so. Maybe they were a better bunch than he had supposed.

When he called the roll at Prestwick October 26, he was as relieved as he was surprised to learn that, despite the mishaps, thirty-three of his thirty-five crews responded. And the other two would soon arrive in replacement planes. The 305th had made the Atlantic flight without tragedy.

But now what? Here they were in England at last, yet there was no sign that Hitler was ready to surrender at news of their arrival. What could they do to help convince him he must? How did a brand-new bomb group, fresh and green, go about fighting the Germans? LeMay could teach them to fly their planes, but as for fighting, he had no more experience than anyone else in his group. He needed to find someone who had done some fighting and ask him how to go about it.

As it happened, he didn't have to look far. He spotted, across the room from him at the Prestwick air base, Col. Frank Armstrong, a member of Gen. Ira C. Eaker's six-man staff that had arrived in England the previous February.[1] Eaker and his aides had come in civilian clothes on a civilian airline, with nothing but some paper clips, rubber bands, and letters of introduction, to launch the operations of the infant Eighth Air Force Bomber Command. Eventually, the B-17 groups had begun arriving and on August 17, 1942, Colonel Armstrong had flown the lead plane in the first American mission of the war against German-occupied Europe—a pathetic little twelve-bomber foray aimed at the railway yards in Rouen. Armstrong had since flown several other, more significant missions and was now the commander of the Ninety-seventh Bomb Group. Could there be anyone better able to tell these boys of the 305th how it was done? As LeMay said later, ''Here was somebody who'd been shot at.''

He hurried across the room and shook hands with this combat veteran, who was simply passing through Prestwick and preparing at the moment to get into his plane and depart.

''Don't leave yet,'' LeMay pleaded. ''You've got to talk to us.''

Armstrong was gracious. Though he was in a great hurry, he would spare a few minutes. LeMay gathered his pilots and the questions began. Armstrong stayed as long as possible and gave them the benefit of his experience on every subject that came to their minds. But on one subject he was more eloquent and more emphatic than any other. German antiaircraft fire, he said, was really terrific. If you flew straight and level for as long as ten seconds, he warned them, the Germans were certain to shoot you down.

LeMay, who had listened with admiration to much of what Armstrong said, now found himself bewildered and disturbed. Armstrong ought to know what he was talking about. He had seen it all with his own eyes. He had watched the flak burst around him and felt the jolting concussion when the shells exploded. But if he was right, if you didn't dare fly straight and level for even ten seconds, how could you bomb with any accuracy? What would you do during the bomb run when the flak, protecting the target, was likely to be heavier than at any other time? He knew from personal observation that the best bombardiers in the peacetime Air Corps, men of great skill and long experience, would not be able to hit even an undefended target after a ten-second bomb run. The standard operating procedure called for a bomb run of fifteen to thirty miles, which meant straight-and-level flight toward the target for the last five or ten minutes before the bombs were released.

LeMay was still racking his brain over this question when someone handed him travel orders. The 305th was to proceed at once to a field at Grafton-Underwood, about sixty miles northwest of London, where its ground echelon was waiting for it. After a Royal Air Force briefing on how to get there, and how to avoid hitting other aircraft in the crowded wartime skies over England, LeMay and his crews climbed back into their planes and flew south to their new nest. At last, it seemed, they had found a permanent home.

The euphoria wore off, however, as soon as the men of the 305th got acquainted with this new "home." The runways pointed in almost useless directions because they had been built without regard for the prevailing winds. But it began to look as if that didn't matter because the fog kept arriving day after day in time to keep the airplanes on the ground. And with the fog came a damp cold that made the men wish they could huddle around the coal stoves in their overcrowded, underheated barracks. But LeMay wouldn't even let them do that. Nor would he let them off the base so they could go take their first look at London. There was work to be done, he said, even if they couldn't fly. They had to learn British radio procedures and the British navigational beam system. They had to study the few available strike photos of missions other groups had flown. And they had to study aircraft identification to make sure they could tell enemy planes from friendly ones. Old Iron Ass gave them so little time to themselves they could cheerfully have strangled him. For three full weeks he restricted them to the base despite the fact that only twice during that time did the weather permit them to fly.

On the first of these two group flights, the purpose of which was to learn and practice the formation LeMay wanted them to use in combat, he made the mistake of flying the lead plane.[2] From his pilot's seat, he couldn't see well enough to know precisely what was happening behind him. But he could look back and see enough to realize the whole group was nothing but a disorderly mob of airplanes, sliding perilously all over the sky. They were supposed to be flying what was called a group stagger formation with elements of six planes each, one directly behind the other and at slightly descending altitudes. It was a formation calculated to give a maximum number of the group's gunners an unobstructed view of enemy planes approaching from any direction. But as the 305th flew it that day, it gave their gunners a much-too-unobstructed view of friendly planes approaching from all directions. Flying Fortresses were everywhere except where they belonged. They were shifting back and forth, cutting in and out, dropping down, pulling up, and swinging wide to avoid collisions. Nobody could be safe back there with all those pilots trying to figure out where they belonged but lacking a clue as to how to get there. LeMay decided to call off the exercise before someone got killed.

It was another three days before the weather permitted the 305th to take off on its second practice flight over England. Meanwhile, LeMay agonized over what to teach his crews when he did get them back into the air. He decided it would be pointless to ask anyone for advice because a study of those few available strike photos convinced him that the group commanders who had already been in combat didn't know what they were doing either. The Eighth Bomber Command at this time had flown only fourteen missions, mostly short, easy raids into occupied France. All the commanders were still feeling their way along. In their postmission reconnaissance photos, LeMay could find signs of less than half the bombs they were said to have dropped. In other words, more than half of them were so wide of the mark they didn't even show in the pictures, and of those that did show very few had hit the targets. Why? Was it because of the formations they were flying? Or their less-than-ten-second bomb runs? Or both? He couldn't tell. All he knew was that he would have to try something different.

He had to face up to the evidence that he couldn't teach the group stagger. His pilots didn't have enough experience to master the spacings between the elements and the complicated cross-over turns. In that formation they were such a threat to each other they wouldn't need an enemy. And he realized that from the lead pilot's seat he couldn't teach them anything because all he could see from there was the horrendous confusion behind him. He couldn't point out and correct specific mistakes.

He was thinking about this as he retired to the cot in his Nissen hut the night after the disastrous first flight. Suddenly he sat up in bed and said to himself, "Top turret. That's where I belong."

Having determined the best vantage point from which to teach, he gradually decided what to teach. In his own mind he proceeded to change and modify the group stagger until he came up with something he thought his men might be able to master. What he now conceived was a formation of six-plane elements approximately abreast instead of one behind the other. With the lead element in front and the others only slightly behind, one on each side, the lead pilots in each of the wing elements would have a close, clear view of the lead plane in the group and could therefore react almost immediately to the group leader's slightest movements. In this configuration the group would not lose the protective features of the original stagger because the elements would still be at slightly descending or ascending altitudes, the element on one side above the leader, the element on the other side below him. The maximum number of guns could still come into play against an enemy plane approaching from any direction. To illustrate this new concept, LeMay drew a simple diagram:[3]

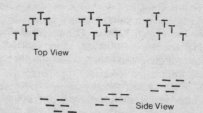

Top View

Side View

On the second practice flight he assigned another pilot to fly his lead plane while he took his position in the top turret where he could watch all the planes in the group and talk by radio to every pilot. This time he made certain all the planes were precisely where they belonged. He didn't stop chewing out the pilots until they had it right. And he resumed chewing each time he saw one of them begin to lag or fall away. He wanted them in as tight as possible so they could protect each other and he didn't let up on them until the crews, looking out their hatches, were close enough to read each other's worried expressions. But as the hours in the air continued, those worried faces began to relax. By God they actually could fly that close without sliding into each other. And there could be no doubt that they would thus offer a much more concentrated shower of .50 caliber bullets to an approaching enemy. They might need more practice before they got their modified-stagger combat box perfected, but it was begining to look as if it might work. At least in practice. The real test would come in combat.

After almost three weeks in England they were beginning to wonder if they would ever see combat. During that time the weather permitted the Eighth Bomber Command to fly only one mission—against German submarine pens at Brest—for which the 305th hadn't been deemed ready. Meanwhile, LeMay learned that his youngest brother, Leonard, now an engineering officer with Eisenhower's forces in the Mediterranean, had hit the beach November 14 in the North African invasion. Curt would never live down the fact that his kid brother had beaten him into combat.

Finally, on November 17 and 18, the 305th saw at last what might be called action if it is permissible to use the term loosely. They flew across the English Channel both days on diversion trips designed to draw attention from other groups which were going elsewhere on real business trips. The planes of the 305th carried no bombs; neither did they fool the enemy with their diversions. No German fighters deigned to pay the slightest bit of attention to them either day. The only satisfaction LeMay's crews derived from these "missions" was a chance to pretend they were in the war and a chance to practice their new formation.

On November 22 they flew as part of an actual mission to Lorient but again they carried no bombs. Not until the next day, November 23, did they actually get into the war. When they did, however, they won immediate notice, thanks to what they and everyone else in the Eighth Air Force could only regard as suicidal foolishness on the part of their commander.

Ever since his arrival in England, LeMay had been thinking about, and asking questions about, Frank Armstrong's belief that without evasive action during a bomb run, a plane was virtually certain to be shot down by German flak. He could find no one who disagreed with Armstrong though there were various estimates as to exactly how long a bomber dared continue in straight-and-level flight. The consensus seemed to be about forty-five seconds. Everyone agreed that to avoid destruction by flak it was absolutely necessary to keep zigzagging on the bomb run.

It depressed LeMay to hear this. The only point in going to the expense of building all these bombers and airfields, training all these crews and putting their lives at stake was to destroy enemy targets and thereby destroy the enemy's ability to make war. But you couldn't destroy a target unless you hit it, and you couldn't hit it, he was sure, unless you gave your bombardier a long enough straight-and-level run so he could line it up in his bombsight. To do so, you might have to pay, in casualties, a higher price of admission to the target. But you had to pay a certain price of admission to the target anyway. If you paid that price without damaging the target you were losing those lives to no purpose. And then you'd have to go back, time and again, on successive efforts, wasting more lives. In the end it would cost fewer lives to pay the extra price the first time and destroy the target so you wouldn't have to keep going back. Unless, of course, that initial price did indeed turn out to be prohibitive. Every one of the experienced commanders told him it would be, and they ought to know. All their groups used what was called "evasive action" on the bomb runs. At the same time, none of their groups had been able, so far, to put many bombs on their targets. LeMay couldn't overcome the belief that only the target was likely to benefit from "evasive action" by the bombers. But how could he be sure without accepting the risk of losing himself and his entire group on one disastrous mission?

As time passed before the 305th was called upon to fly its first mission, LeMay began to lose sleep over this question. Then one night, lying awake in his narrow cot, he remembered what would appear to have been the most useless thing he had brought with him to England—an old field artillery manual he had picked up during his college days in ROTC at Ohio State University. He had no idea why he had brought it. He didn't even remember putting it in his footlocker, but he had noticed it there when he unpacked.

Jumping out of bed, he closed the blackout curtains (the most essential items in any English building during those nights of German air raids), and began rummaging around in his footlocker. There was the old artillery manual, its cover soiled and discolored, its pages dog-eared. With notebook, pencil, and manual in hand, he jumped back into bed, put on a sweater and pulled the covers around him to keep warm, then turned to the section on the French .75 millimeter gun which had been a lifesaver to both the French and the Americans in World War I. LeMay was quite familiar with that old gun because in the 1920s it was still the best of its kind and his ROTC instructor, who had used it in World War I, spent a lot of time impressing upon his students its great virtues.

Needless to say, Hitler's antiaircraft guns were not old French .75s. They were new German .88s. But with what LeMay had learned from intelligence reports about the .88s, he could interpolate roughly the differences between the two guns.

"My challenge," he recalled later, "was the construction of a precision fire problem on a target the size of a B-17 sitting over there on an imaginary hillside, twenty-five thousand feet away."[4]

It was fifteen years since he had worked such a problem, yet it all came back to him quickly. He had won his degree in civil engineering. His pencil was soon spewing figures out onto the notebook paper. To the best of his ability, he took into account the number of guns the Germans might have in any one location and how much time they would have to aim and fire at a B-17 speeding through the sky. "They've got to lift a lot of rounds upstairs to get a hit on a target our size," he concluded.

What figure did his pencil give him?

Three hundred seventy-two.

If he had calculated correctly the Germans would have to fire 372 rounds with their .88s to be sure of hitting a B-17 flying straight and level toward a target. That was a lot of rounds. He was willing to take a chance, he decided, on odds like those.

The morning of November 23, when he briefed his crews for their first real mission, and told them that unlike the other four groups, the 305th would take "no evasive action" over the target at St. Nazaire, he didn't find any of his men sharing his confidence about the odds.[5] They, too, had been told by all the combat veterans they'd be dead ducks if they didn't zig and zag during their bomb runs. LeMay had always invited his men to speak up, during a briefing, about anything that might bother them. This morning he might almost have wished he had never extended that privilege because they didn't hesitate to tell him what they thought of his idea. Though there was no sign of open rebellion, the room was in an uproar of discontent and anxiety.

Finally, one of the men said flatly, "Sir, it just can't be done."

"Yes, it can," LeMay insisted, "and you'll see me do it first because I'll be flying the lead plane."

He learned a lesson that morning. If a commander is willing to do something himself, his men will go through hell to follow him. Without any more fuss, the men of the 305th got into their planes and prepared to fly.

Twenty fortresses of the 305th took off on schedule but four aborted and turned back on the way, leaving only sixteen to reach the target area.[6] That was considered very good during those early days of the air war over the Continent. The 306th Group, of which LeMay had been for a time the executive officer, was able to send up only eight; four of them aborted and one was shot down. The Ninety-first Group sent up ten; five aborted and all five of the others were shot down. It was not destined to be a pleasant day over St. Nazaire. LeMay knew that before his group-leading plane reached the target because three of the five groups on the mission were in front of him and he could see them catching hell from German fighters. It prompted him to draw his planes into an even tighter formation. That seemed to work. All sixteen of them were still in the air, clinging to each other like frightened children, when the submarine pens and railway yards at St. Nazaire came into view ahead of them.

LeMay's moment of decision had arrived. "Our bomb run," he had told his men, "will be from the time we see the target to the time the bombs are dropped."

Banking to fix a direct course, he leveled his wings and looked around to see what the rest of his group was doing. Not a single plane wavered, even when the flak came up to greet them. The nasty little black clouds began to burst above, below, and among them.

"After working out that artillery problem, I wasn't particularly bothered by the flak," LeMay later remarked. "But I didn't care for those flickering machine guns coming head-on at me.

You couldn't do much about it [though], except sit there and give your gunners a steady platform to shoot back."

He was making an unprecedented demand today, not only upon himself but upon the other men in his group, when he insisted all of them look into the muzzles of those machine guns and press forward with no evasive action. Not every man is capable of such cool courage, and he knew it. "Throughout history you've had assault troops and garrison troops," he has since observed. "The garrison troops only fight behind a stone wall, and then not very well. Some people can do it and some people can't. And even those that [can]—everybody I've come across with occasional exceptions—don't think much of fighting. That includes me. But you do it because it's your duty."

The men of the 305th apparently felt a strong sense of duty when they set out behind LeMay to try a new way of bombing at St. Nazaire that day. LeMay's own plane took a piece of shrapnel in the right wing, then another in the left. Five other planes also reported being hit but none went down. For seven minutes they continued, straight and level, toward the target. Six German fighters made passes at them but then moved on after doing only minor damage.

At one point, a British Beaufighter appeared suddenly from twelve o'clock low and LeMay's navigator, doubling as the nose gunner, found out it wasn't always easy to distinguish a friend from a foe. He opened up with his .50 caliber machine gun until the frightened Beaufighter pilot fired the colors of the day with his flare gun. As it happened, he needn't have been that frightened. The excited navigator's aim was no better than his identification. He hit nothing but air.

The bursts of flak were all around them at twenty-one thousand feet as the bombardiers took over and adjusted their bombsights, but the bombardiers continued their calculations and at 1340 (1:40 P.M.), the first bombs fell.

Two minutes later they were beyond the target. All sixteen planes were still in formation. Two of them had failed to release their two-ton bomb loads (due to mechanical difficulties) but none of the sixteen lagged behind or showed any sign of disability.

LeMay summoned the bombardier of his plane, Lt. P. V. Williams. "Well, how did you do?"

"Good run," Williams reported. "We got bombs on the target." He had dropped his bombs around the aiming point and he was convinced he had wiped out the north jetty, plus some machine shops.

"You sure of that?" LeMay asked.

"Yes, I'm sure of it," the rookie bombardier insisted. "It was a good run. But I could've done a little better if it hadn't been for those clouds. They kind of got in the way."

Though Williams didn't yet know it, the "clouds" he had seen were flak bursts. There were no other clouds in the sky that day.

LeMay's sixteen planes returned to England without further incident, landed at Davidow under instructions from First Wing headquarters, told their stories, and turned in their strike photos. It was two days before the photos could be analyzed by Eighth Air Force intelligence officers and the final results of the mission compiled. The 305th had put twice as many bombs on the target as any other group. And none of its planes had been shot down.

Within three weeks, every group in the Eighth Air Force was flying straight-and-level bomb runs, taking no evasive action over the targets.

CHAPTER FOUR

Shortly after the St. Nazaire mission, the 305th received what must have seemed like a reward for work well done. The group was moved from its cold, cramped, and badly constructed quarters at Grafton-Underwood to a base called Chelveston near the village of Higham Ferrers in Northampton, about thirty miles west of Cambridge. Actually, the move had nothing to do with rewards. The 305th had simply been placed in cold storage at Grafton-Underwood until work was completed on the enlargement and renovation of what had been an old RAF base at Higham Ferrers. After more than a month at Grafton-Underwood, the boys were delighted with their new quarters, though they were hardly luxurious except by comparison. Chelveston was to be the home of the 305th for the duration of its stay in England.

For many years thereafter, LeMay and the other men of that group would cherish bittersweet memories of the place. The early morning briefings and takeoffs into the foggy darkness. The return flights from the Continent with cold air whistling through the bullet holes in the fuselages, and the ambulances waiting at the end of the runway to carry off the blood-soaked, blanket-wrapped comrades who had caught those bullets. For those who didn't fly, there were the hours of anxious waiting for the crippled planes to come limping in on two or three engines, or with gaping holes in the wings, or with landing gears shot away. There were also less somber memories. The thin brown grass of winter; the little square church steeple of a nearby village; the British Land Girls, pressed into wartime service as farmworkers, pushing wheelbarrows in the fields, absorbing the hopeful stares and prurient suggestions of the more loose-mouthed Yank fliers. There was a haystack on the road to Bedford where, it was said, some of the more curious Land Girls were willing to investigate those suggestions.

But with LeMay running the group, there wasn't as much time for socializing as the boys would have liked. Though the weather permitted no more November missions after St. Nazaire on the 23rd, and only four more in all of December, he kept finding things for everyone to do. He himself led the group against Lille on December 6, and against submarine pens at Lorient on December 30 with mixed results. In a letter to his wife on January 3 he referred to the Lorient mission as "a little raid between Xmas and New Year's," but while he seemed to be playing it down, German opposition had been, in fact, surprisingly strong that day. For the first time he saw some of his men go down, and it impressed him. Though he was still far from satisfied with the skills of his men, he must have been pleased by their bravery. He recommended "a bucket full of medals to pass out to the boys," and he must have given some immediate thought, as he saw planes go down around him, to the precarious nature of the work he was doing.

"That's the first raid I've been on," he told Helen, "that I haven't written you a letter just before leaving and we ran into a hornet's nest so I guess I had better not forget any more."

After taking part personally in three missions, he was not yet ready to make any positive conclusions about the nature of combat operations against the Germans, but he did have some tentative observations:[1]

1. The 305th was attracting fewer fighter attacks than other groups.
2. They were using more ammunition than other groups but they weren't shooting down as many German planes.
3. They had a much lower loss rate than other groups. After six actual missions (not counting the first three dry runs) they had lost only two B-17s.

Why? After examining the data and impressions his intelligence section garnered from the crews, he came to some tentative conclusions which, he decided, were becoming "stronger with every mission":

1. The 305th usually had more ships in the air than any other group. Presumably, greater numbers provided greater protection.

2. Their stagger formation, in depth, gave them more fire-power against an approaching enemy.
3. They were shooting at longer ranges. LeMay was beginning to believe that if fighters were welcomed by bullets before they even came close, they were not so likely to come close.

The fighters and the flak were still coming too close for comfort, however, despite the fact that only two of LeMay's planes had gone down. (One had succumbed to propeller failure over France. The other simply disappeared into the clouds on the way home from a mission and was never seen again.) On the group's second visit to St. Nazaire, January 3, 1943 (without LeMay), nineteen of its twenty-two planes were hit, sustaining an average of fifteen holes. One B-17 had 150 holes in it when it returned to Chelveston. But it did return. That was an encouraging sign.

In a long letter January 12, 1943, to his one-time mentor, Gen. Robert Olds (now in the Training Command), LeMay showed for the first time some signs of qualified optimism about his situation: "In general I am proud of my group. It has given me a great deal of satisfaction to take people right out of schools and after such a short training period, take them into action against the best pursuit and antiaircraft defenses in the world. They have come off without turning a hair and while we have the greatest respect for the German fighting ability, we have no doubt of the final outcome. There are still Americans who can and are willing to fight. . . . Piloting ability is excellent. We have had no accidents since arriving at our station in England. . . . Such things as landing with engines shot out, controls and trim tabs shot off, flat tires, etc., are routine matters and are not even mentioned any more, except in a battle damage report. Takeoffs and landings are made at 30 second intervals. . . . I have long since ceased to worry about whether a 350-hour pilot can fly the airplane."

He was aware, however, that he and his group still had problems to solve and deep troubles ahead. They hadn't yet invaded the skies over Germany. The Germans were certain to defend the Fatherland much more fiercely than they defended occupied France and the Low Countries. Unless LeMay's group, and indeed the whole Eighth Air Force, improved dramatically, they were destined to catch hell when the real battle for Europe began.

His navigators, for instance, were better than he had expected. They had proven their ability to plot a celestial course on the flight across the Atlantic. But in Europe, pilotage (the ability to find your way by reading roads, towns, and landmarks on the ground) was essential. And pilotage was more difficult than in America because Europe was so crowded. "At home, a railroad, town, or river is a checkpoint," LeMay observed in his letter to Olds. "Here, the landscape is one jumbled mass of railroads, roads and towns and once you lose track of your position, it is almost impossible to find yourself again." In addition, visibility was usually poor in the winter months, rarely more than four miles, all of which meant the navigators had to combine pilotage with dead reckoning, and few of them had mastered this art.

While navigation wasn't yet any better than mediocre, the bombing, in LeMay's estimation, was considerably worse. "Sixty percent of the bombs dropped are not accounted for, less than one percent have hit the aiming point and about three percent within 500 feet. We have done considerably better than this but are still not good by any means."

He was beginning to think, though, that this wasn't the fault of the bombardiers. They often missed targets because they didn't know enough about them to recognize them. At the "specialized briefings" for navigators and bombardiers, they would see a photograph of the day's target on a screen, if a photograph was available. Otherwise they would see a drawing of it. And that was about as much target study as they were getting in those early months.

Besides the difficulty of recognizing a target, they faced, to be sure, another problem—the German fighter planes. "There is a lot of difference," LeMay told Olds, "between bombing an undefended target and running through a barrage of six-inch shell fire while a swarm of pursuits are working on you."

The gunners, who had the job of driving off the German pursuit planes, didn't seem to be doing any better than the bombardiers. "On our arrival here our gunners were very poorly trained. Most of them had not received enough shooting, especially at altitude, to even familiarize themselves with their equipment. We have over here a tow ship and one range for the Wing, but due to weather and missions, the only practice we have had so far is shooting at FW-190s and ME-109s. However, there isn't any better practice for rapidly improving the gunners' accuracy. On some raids I have had German pursuit try to break up our formation by flying through it from front to rear. We didn't bluff very well and as far as I could see, no one even moved his position an inch. However, they did get thru without being shot down by our gunners."

The situation was not hopeless, though. He saw some signs of improvement. "On the last two raids, every ship coming within two hundred yards was shot down. If we can push that out to five hundred yards we will have something."

LeMay's advice to Olds and the Training Command was, ironically, the same he had repeatedly received from Olds several years earlier: "More training." The men now in the various schools at home but destined to be sent to the European theater would have to be better prepared in every way. The gunners would have to have more shooting practice, not only at high altitude, but in formation. The bombardiers had to be taught to orient themselves quickly and locate targets despite poor visibility. The navigators needed "a good course in map reading, using English Aeronautical Charts, plus some pilotage problems with the windows covered to restrict the navigator's vision to one mile at normal altitudes." They should also learn "with the shields up to restrict visibility," how to identify camouflaged targets such as factories and airdromes. And the pilots should be taught "to fly formation on three engines and with the ship out of trim so they can stay in formation even though damaged by gunfire." It was true that formations usually slowed down to protect their cripples, but once a ship was hit and forced to leave the formation, it was "practically impossible" for it to get back in again. The Germans were always on the lookout for a cripple. They would "cut it out of formation and then shoot it down."

While this letter to Olds was being typed, LeMay and the other group commanders were summoned to headquarters by Gen. Laurence F. Kuter, the wing commander, for a conference on standardization of the combat formation. Convinced that his was the best formation so far developed, LeMay arrived with a set of B-17 models mounted on sticks of varying lengths, which he set up to demonstrate the increased firepower and self-protection afforded by his modified stagger. He argued hard, though with his usual minimum of words, for this formation, expecting opposition from the other commanders, each of whom was using some other formation. As he soon learned, however, his argument was almost superfluous. The deciding argument lay in the fact, already well known to Kuter, that the 305th Group was putting more bombs on the targets and suffering fewer losses (only two to date) than any other group. With some slight changes suggested, LeMay's modified stagger was officially adopted for use by the entire wing.[2] And on January 13, LeMay, at the head of his 305th Group, led the First Wing in a return mission against the steelworks at Lille. He described this mission in a postscript to his Olds letter:

. . . The [Wing] flew in the modified stagger one behind the other as close as possible, the interval varying from 500 to 1,000 yards. The 305th Group was in the lead at 22,000 feet and the succeeding groups stacked up in elevation. We had 22 ships in our [305th] formation disposed as follows:

The customary flak was encountered, moderate in intensity and not particularly accurate, it was not a factor in the mission. We were intercepted by 20 to 25 fighters over the targets and they were first sighted just short of the bomb release line and made their first attack just after the bombs were away.

This outfit seemed to be the most experienced and disciplined of any I have encountered so far. They flew a string formation of 5 or 6 airplanes; all attacks were made from dead ahead and on the same level.

During the second attack on the top squadron ships, "A" in the diagram was hit, pieces flew off #2 engine and it was definitely out. One other engine must have failed shortly after. After being hit he fell back about 150 yards. I immediately slowed down to 150 indicated [airspeed] and he was able to regain his place in formation. At about the same time ship "B" got a cannon shell through the windshield killing the Squadron Commander, who was flying the ship, and wounding the co-pilot. The ship went into a dive initially then pulled up diagonally across the formation, almost stalled, recovered and managed to get into the formation with the top squadron, [which] fell in around him to protect him.

The ship received attacks by 4 FW-190s while out of formation. At about this time ship "A" lost another engine and could not stay in formation. He was seen going into the clouds under control, but did not get home. Ship "C" was shot up and had the ball turret gunner wounded. Ship "D" received a few holes. Our group was the only one receiving any attention by pursuit. Two airplanes made one attack on the rest of the Wing. Our score on the pursuit was three destroyed, two probables and five damaged. We lost three, ours [from the 305th] shot down and two [from] the 306th [which] ran together in the air.

Almost as interesting as LeMay's description of the raid was the casual, laconic style in which he wrote about the experience. After flying personally on only four missions, he would appear to have become amazingly comfortable sitting in a B-17 while German shells and bullets whizzed past him. Many men who watched him at the time got the impression he had been born, not only without a panic button, but without even so much as a sense of fear. They thought so only because he was determined to make them think so. Since he was the group commander, he believed that, as an example to his men, he had to appear calm at all times. Looking back many years later, he could admit without hesitation that his stomach did as many flip-flops before a mission as any other stomach in the group. Once the mission started, though, he seemed able to find relief from tension in that remarkable cure-all upon which he had always depended—work.

Sometimes he would fly the plane, but just as often he would leave the flying to his copilot while he helped the navigator plot the course, or gave the bombardier extra instruction in the use of the Norden bombsight—an instrument with which he became familiar before the war when all the Air Corps practice bombing was done by pilots because there were no bombardiers. He knew not only how to navigate and how to bomb but also how to shoot, and several times on missions he replaced gunners to make sure he would have a full understanding of their problems and limitations when they tried to explain to him how hard it was to shoot down a four-hundred-miles-per-hour fighter plane.[3]

Some of his prewar colleagues, he later recalled, were not very interested in navigation or bombing or gunnery. "They were just interested in flying. That's all they did. I knew the airplane. I could navigate. And I could bomb. I made it a point to find out how to bomb from the best guys we had—J. B. Montgomery and Doug Kilpatrick. So I knew how to get bombs on the target. And we weren't doing it [at first] because we weren't doing certain things. I knew if we had a good tight formation where we could bring all the firepower to bear, we'd be better off. And also I had seven years in pursuit so I knew the fighter story. It really isn't much of a chore to shoot down a bomber, but if [the bombers] had sufficient firepower, it wasn't conducive to long life and happiness for the fighter pilot. We did have less losses than anyone else because I insisted on this tight formation. The gunnery was stinking, but if you're a German fighter pilot and you see this outfit tucked in tight with its guns all facing you, and you see this [other] one over here, straggling out in the wild blue yonder, you go over here.''[4]

It was a valid theory under ordinary circumstances, yet in the Rouen raid, as LeMay himself admitted, it didn't work. Though his group was presumably tucked in tighter than any other; it still absorbed the bulk of the fighter attention. According to his observation, only two of the German fighters attacked the rest of the wing, and each of them made only one pass. He was now learning that if you were leading the mission, the fighters were likely to come after you however well you were protecting yourself.

On January 27, 1943, the 305th took part in the first American mission against a target within the borders of Germany itself. The honor of leading the fleet of sixty-four flying fortresses and Liberators that day went understandably to Col. Frank Armstrong and the 306th Group, which he had recently reorganized. Armstrong, on the previous August 17, had led the first American mission of the war in Europe—against Rouen. After the Eighth Air Force had flown its first five missions of the war, General Eaker, the bomber commander, had written to his immediate superior, Gen. Carl Spaatz, an appreciation of Armstrong's work: ''It is not accidental that the three operations which Col. Armstrong has led were completely successful, while the two operations led by other officers resulted in one aborted mission and one with serious injuries to two aircraft.''[5]

Those first five missions were against targets in France, to be sure, and the ''success'' of which Eaker wrote could not be measured against the success that would be necessary to defeat Germany. But Armstrong had proven himself an excellent leader and he deserved the honor of being the first into Germany.

This premier invasion of German airspace January 27 was

aimed at a submarine-building yard on the Weser River near a little town called Vegesack, about thirty miles upstream from the North Sea. But the clouds over Vegesack were so thick Armstrong was forced to move on with his sixty-four bombers to a secondary target, the port of Wilhelmshaven, about twenty-five miles northwest, near the mouth of the Weser. The skies were broken there, allowing at least a partial view of the ships and wharves below. Fifty-eight of the bombers dropped their loads with results that were estimated to be, at best, "fair," even though no flak or fighters came up to disturb them.[6]

This less than gratifying result was understandable since no one in any of the bombers had ever before seen the target. But it left LeMay profoundly unhappy. And he became even more so on the way home when sixty German fighters finally did appear and shot down three of the bombers, while American gunners filled the air with lengthy, wasteful bursts of aimless bullets that sometimes hit the darting enemy but too often hit each other. After this mission, the gunners claimed officially to have shot down twenty-two fighters. LeMay realized this was a gross exaggeration. (German records captured at the end of the war showed a loss of seven fighters that day.)

LeMay could not concern himself with the other groups but as for his own, he was so dissatisfied that when they got home and landed, he took advantage of the relatively good weather in England to send his tired troops right back into the air for formation and gunnery practice. It might seem a cruel thing to do to these exhausted men who had just been dodging German bullets, but he was determined to continue doing it, after each mission, until they learned to do a better job of protecting themselves. He decided they were going to keep catching hell from him until they started giving it back to the Germans.

He had also developed by this time the practice of full-scale debriefing sessions after each mission.[7] Everybody connected with the mission gathered at the enlisted men's mess hall, the largest meeting place on the base. The doors were closed to keep everyone else out and to remind those inside that whatever was said in that room was not to leave that room. The rules at these sessions were quickly established. LeMay made it clear to all those present, from privates to colonels, that they could say anything they pleased about the performance of anyone.

"We've got a lot to learn," he told them at the beginning. "We want to know what went right, what went wrong, and why

it went wrong. And each of you is in the act. Everybody has his
say. If you think your group commander is a stupid son-of-a-
bitch, now is the time to say it. And why.''

This highly unusual invitation to his men to criticize him as
well as each other arose from the fact that his sense of responsibility for their lives and deaths was now bearing down hard on
him. He was feeling more deeply, day after day, the heavy burden that falls upon a military commander when he sends men
out to die. On every mission, some men were certain to be killed.
How does a commander, especially an inexperienced one like
himself, deal with that burden? He said later that his need to
deal with it ''was the basic reason why I started those critiques
following the missions.''

Like most people, he had been taught since childhood to grieve
at death and to abhor killing. As a career soldier, he was expected, theoretically, to be ready to kill whenever his country's
safety demanded it. But until now he had never been asked to do
so, nor had he ever been required to watch while his own
men were killed. In war, he had to do both, and he also had to
learn to cope with the anguish that naturally resulted.

''It used to be particularly vile,'' he recalled, ''when I realized that I'd lost someone, and felt that I shouldn't have lost him.
That's when it really comes home to you. I lost them because I
made a mistake or somebody else made a mistake.'' Hence, the
postmission critiques and the amazing invitation to his men to
pour out their gripes even against their group commander.

Col. Carl Norcross, an intelligence officer who flew some missions and attended some of LeMay's later postmission briefings,
was astonished to find that anyone actually could speak his mind.[8]
Norcross had known a lot of colonels and generals who talked
as if they wanted their men to speak up to them, but quickly put
the men down when they did so. With such commanders, the
men soon learned they had better figure out what the boss was
thinking and agree with him. But LeMay, supposedly the meanest, toughest commander in the Eighth Air Force, actually allowed his men to say anything they damned pleased about anyone
in the room including himself. And he didn't argue with them.
He sat there and listened until they were through. Then he might
say a few words. But he seldom said more than a few.

Among people who knew him only by reputation there was a
supposition that he demonstrated his toughness by shouting,
snarling, chewing his cigar and chewing the asses of everyone

around him. Even he himself, in later life, when asked one day about some harsh words he had delivered to a subordinate, remarked, "Hell, I used to chew out everyone." But people close enough to observe him say it was seldom so. He was too miserly with words to spend them on sermons or harangues. If he was displeased, which was often enough, he seemed able to show it convincingly with a glance, or a cold stare, or a devastating, "You can do better than that."

There were times, also, when he himself could have done "better than that." Lt. Russell Schleeh, one of his best pilots, who often flew on missions with him, has told an amusing story about a dark and foggy morning when they were taxiing out to the runway for takeoff. The fog was so thick they could see only a few feet in any direction. LeMay told Schleeh, who was in the copilot's seat, to keep his flashlight trained on the right-hand edge of the taxi strip. If they could stick close to that one side, they wouldn't have to worry about rolling off the narrow strip of pavement into the mud.

Schleeh concentrated all of his eyepower on that right-hand edge of the pavement, especially since theirs was the lead plane on the mission, and LeMay had made it clear that if any lead crew were to go off a runway, they'd catch hell from him personally. But alas, despite Schleeh's concentration, the plane suddenly rolled off the pavement and sank struts-deep into the mud.

LeMay, in seething fury, turned to his copilot. Before he had time to say anything, however, Schleeh said to him, "Damn it all, Colonel, you ran off on your side."[9]

At his postmission briefings LeMay was usually the last person to speak. And he usually spoke succinctly. If somebody had made a bad suggestion he would ignore it. If somebody made a good one he would approve it. If it became apparent that some new policy or procedure was needed, he would say, "From now on we'll do it that way." If a question had arisen that took more thought, he would leave it hanging. Later, perhaps in bed that night, he would mull it over. He might even call his staff into his office and get their ideas. Ultimately he would make the decision, but in the meantime, he would have made his men realize they were part of that decision. He wanted his men to feel the outfit was not his but theirs. "I never said 'I,'" he later recalled. "I always said 'we.'"

The postmission practice flights and the postmission briefings did nothing, however, to solve two vexing problems that had been bothering him ever since his arrival in England—the difficulties of his still-inexperienced navigators in finding the targets and the difficulties of his bombardiers in recognizing them even when they saw them. He had already concluded that neither the navigators nor the bombardiers could be blamed for this. They simply didn't know enough about the targets or the routes to them or the recognizable features surrounding them. And considering the number of targets there would be as the war progressed, there was no way any one navigator or bombardier could become thoroughly familiar with more than a few of them.

If each navigator-bombardier team, however, could become expert in recognition of one potential target and the route to it, that team would be ready to guide the whole group whenever the target they had studied was chosen for a mission.

As this idea took shape in LeMay's mind, he gathered his most trusted aides around him, particularly Joe Preston and John de Russy, and tried it out on them.

"We've got to have people who know their target area as well as they know their own backyards," he said. "Then when the guy comes up on that target, he won't be caught short. He'll know. Even though he can't see it, he'll see other checkpoints around there which he can recognize. If he sees that curve on the waterfront and those docks, he knows just how far the actual aiming point is, over there to the right. If he sees those big round gas tanks, or those long machine shops right there next to the Y of the railroad, he knows what lies to the north and south, to the east and the west. He knows the target. This is what we've got to make possible."

Since nobody disagreed (though LeMay was surprisingly tolerant of disagreement up to the moment an issue was decided), the staff of the 305th got to work immediately. (He was not very tolerant of waiting until the next day to do something.) On a map they divided the continental areas they would most likely be assigned to attack as the air war developed. Then they subdivided those areas, pinpointing the key targets within them, and sent aides scurrying all over England—to Eighth Air Force and Eighth Bomber Command headquarters, to the RAF Bomber Command headquarters, to the London newspapers, to bookstores, to the British Museum and every library they could find—looking for maps, ground and aerial photographs, travel books, articles, any items of information they could gather about every possible target. With this material they developed a few dozen of what they called target folders, each covering a small but important area within Hitler's Fortress Europe. Then they chose the best-qualified navigator-bombardier teams and assigned each of them to a concentrated study of one, two, or three of these areas.

"When that target was flashed on the screen at Briefing," LeMay later recalled, "it wasn't a surprise to at least one or two of those bombardier-navigator teams. They had soaked it up. They knew it well. They were the people who led the mission that day."[11]

This was the first step toward another LeMay innovation that developed into what were called lead crew schools.

It was now becoming more than ever imperative that LeMay improve and conserve his group. Since the Eighth Air Force had begun attacking Germany proper the losses were increasing sharply. Yet because of the demands of the North African campaign, which had begun in November 1942, the Eighth was not getting enough new planes and crews to replace its losses. He fully realized now how fortunate he was to have Ben Fulkrod as his chief engineeering officer. Besides being an expert on the workings of the B-17, Fulkrod was like the latter-day fictional wheeler-dealer, Milo Minderbinder of Joseph Heller's *Catch 22* in his ability to find, scrounge, or promote useful items. Before leaving the States, LeMay had sent his flight surgeons out to dig up several footlockers full of whatever medicines they thought might be useful but scarce in combat. And he himself had talked the Quartermaster Corps out of two truckloads of warm winter clothing. But neither he nor anyone else in the 305th had been able to match the scrounging power of Ben Fulkrod, who managed somehow to produce whole planeloads of scarce technical equipment. He got hold of every kind of tool that could possibly be useful in maintaining and repairing B-17s, including even a lathe with raw stock for duplicating parts and, most amazing of all, a set of wing reamers, which were absolutely essential to secure tight fits in replacing damaged wings. "Thanks to Fulkrod," LeMay has recalled, "we had the only set of wing reamers in the European theater. Where he got them I don't know. Before the war, we had to contact the Boeing people [manufacturers of the B-17] if we wanted to change a wing."[12]

With no replacements arriving and planes becoming more precious every day during those first months of 1943, Fulkrod and his tools performed miracles of maintenance to keep the 305th in the air. When word about him got out, he even had to make spare parts for other groups which didn't have the tools. Clever as he was, however, Fulkrod could hardly compensate for the fact that most of the replacement planes from home were going to North Africa, where the need was immediate and almost desperate. Nobody could do anything about this, including General Eaker, who had been promoted from bomber commander to the command of the entire Eighth Air Force. Eaker was trying desperately to stem and reverse the continuing depletion of his force. On February 26, he wrote to General Arnold in Washington deploring what appeared to be the gradual destruction of the Eighth due to the needs of the African operation:

> The two heavy groups we were supposed to get in February have, as you of course know, been sidetracked to the Twelfth Air Force [in Africa]. We have been told that there will be no shipping in March or April. This makes it appear that we are not to build up an increased force of heavy bombers to be available this spring. . . . There is only one thing that we require here to do a job—the job that will hurt the enemy most, and that is an adequate force. . . .
>
> We have to date received but 24 replacement crews and 63 replacement aircraft. We have lost 75 planes and crews in 2,206 sorties. We feel therefore obliged to save our force for days when we can deliver maximum effort under favorable conditions, until we can get a larger force, and until the flow of replacements matches expenditures. We never have and never will let one of these days pass without operating at maximum effort.

Eaker believed that one way to get a larger force was to let the people back home, especially the public officials, know exactly what the Eighth was doing to Germany, and how important it was to continue doing it. He had therefore invited six war correspondents to accompany his bombers on a mission that very day, February 26, 1943. The correspondents were Gladwin Hill of the Associated Press, William Wade of International News Service, Robert Post of the *New York Times* (who was shot down and killed on the mission), Walter Cronkite of the United Press, Homer Bigart of the *New York Herald Tribune* and Paul Manning of the Columbia Broadcasting System.

Hill, a big, unflappable New Englander who didn't believe anything until he saw it, was assigned to fly with LeMay's mission-leading 305th Group which that day was under the command of Maj. Joe Preston. In the evening, after the surviving planes returned home to Chelveston, Hill filed a remarkably descriptive dispatch for the fifteen hundred American newspapers that were members of the Associated Press:

At a U.S. Bomber Station Somewhere in England (AP): From the cockpit of the plane which led the American air armada in the third attack on Germany today I watched Flying Fortress bombs blast docks at Wilhelmshaven, one of the Nazis' prime naval bases.

It was the first time reporters—of whom there were six in the attacking planes—accompanied an American air raid in the European theater.

It was thrilling. Yet at the same time it was strangely prosaic in the business-like efficiency with which the raid was executed.

We were under attack by German fighter planes and a great barrage of flak for nearly two hours, one of the longest battles the Fortresses have encountered. Some of our ships went down, others were shot up badly, and we encountered handicapping clouds.

Yet I was standing a few inches from the officer directing the whole operation—Major Joseph Preston of Elgin, Minn.—and he was less spectacular, moving the control column and quietly enunciating decisions into his throat microphone, than an average conservative motorist out for a quiet drive in the United States. . . .

Your first view of an attacking German fighter has an odd impersonal quality like watching a visiting expert at an air show. Those German fighters can fly, and you're so preoccupied with their sweeps, twists and turns you forget they're trying to kill you.

It's only when you hear the rat-tat-tat of your own guns, sounding like a man knocking on the door with a pneumatic drill, and see the tracer bullets lofting down at the attacking planes like tennis balls—although actually going 2,700 feet a second—that you realize it's war.

Do you get scared going on a raid? The answer is No. You may have qualms if you stop and reflect on the possible hazards. But while it's happening, there's too much to do and see. . . .

The first big kick came when, after breakfast in the moonlit darkness at 4 A.M., we piled into the briefing building to learn the target and discover it was going to be a big-time raid.

Then two crammed hours while ground crews did the final tuning on engines and we climbed into several hundred pounds—it seemed—of paraphernalia necessary for high-altitude flights; fur-lined leather jacket, pants, boots and helmet, a "Mae West" life preserver, parachute harness, oxygen mask, earphones, throat mike.

The biggest kick of the whole trip was the moment of take-off when the pilot gunned the engines and said with finality, "We're going." Directional radio beeps on the earphones echoed it like the last words you hear when you go under ether: "We're going we're going we're going," as we zoomed off the runway. . . .

The first German fighter swooped up as we spotted a large convoy plowing along the Frisian Islands.

"Enemy aircraft at 2 o'clock," co-pilot Captain Clinton Breeding of Waco, Tex., stated matter-of-factly over the interphone, and our gunners trained on it until it came within range and then started banging.

From then on it sounded like a mouse-chase in a kitchen: "There's one! Get him! He's coming in at 9 o'clock. Let him have it, top-turret! . . ."

From the cockpit I saw about ten German fighters out of a force of about 25. The rest concentrated on the rear of the formation, and the exclamations of the gunners over the interphone sounded like a radio broadcast of a hockey game. . . .

Our crew didn't claim any fighters knocked down, but accomplished the more important aim of keeping them off. As Major Preston eased the formation over the target, the finger-like set of docks loomed up through the clouds just like in the aerial photographs.

Lead bombardier Lt. Charles Malec of Omaha drew a bead with his bombsight, and it wasn't until he called back to the major to resume full control of the ship that I realized our bombs had gone. The captain called back to the tail gunner to check the casualties in our group. Two ships had gone down, apparently under control. Three others, shot up, straggled back out of formation. . . .

[Back at the base] Lt. Harold O'Neill of Graceville, Minn., brought "Madame Butterfly" in despite a fire in one of her engines. Lt. Hugh Ashcraft of Charlotte, N.C., landed "Southern Comfort" in one piece with a third of his rudder shot clean away. The third of the stragglers had disappeared in the clouds over the North Sea. (This meant the group had lost three planes.)

It was a relief to climb out of that claustrophobic cockpit and shuck off all the equipment, which by now definitely weighed a full ton.

The station commandant Col. Curtis LeMay of Columbus, Ohio, walked up the runway and said to Major Preston, "Well, Joe, what happened?"

"Well," Preston said, as thoughtfully and laconically as a Vermont farmer, "we dropped some bombs on Wilhelmshaven."

It was a fascinating trip for a reporter, but as the boys discussed the casualties, contriving explanations of how the missing planes might have landed safely, it made you realize the vast difference between going on one raid and going on them all, week after week, sometimes day after day.

Anyone can go on one raid, and the averages say he'll get back safely. The solidity of our formation from the takeoff to the landing emphasized the strength of heavily armored, heavily armed, high-altitude daylight bombing.

But like roulette, if you play the wheel long enough, you can be [sure] a given number will come up. That's what these Fortress boys—ex-college boys, ex-farmhands, ex-truck drivers—face, week in and week out, willingly, cheerfully, enthusiastically.

That's what makes you realize it's an honor to ride with them.

Speaking many years later of his experience that day, Gladwin Hill still recalled the calm, casual tone in which Curtis LeMay, as he met his incoming fliers, said to Major Preston, "Well, Joe, what happened?"[13]

At that time, Hill hardly knew LeMay except by his unfavorable reputation. The word about him was getting around the Eighth Air Force, and the word was, stay away from him; he's the meanest bastard in all of England. There was a joke in circulation about men of the 305th hoping they'd be shot down and land in a German prison camp because they so desperately needed a vacation.

LeMay was undoubtedly concerned about the number of planes shot down and men lost on the mission to Wilhelmshaven, but that was not the question he was asking Preston and Preston knew it. On every mission it was likely that planes and men would be lost. A commander realized before he sent his men that some would die. But if they didn't hit the target, they would have died in vain. So the important question for LeMay was: Did you put your bombs on Wilhelmshaven? And he asked the question so calmly he seemed ruthlessly indifferent about that other question: How many men did you lose?

Most of the people near him were aware of this apparent coldness. It was one reason they called him Iron Ass. If he had any feelings about what was going on around him, the men of the 305th hadn't noticed it. Born in Ohio, the son of an itinerant laborer, he came from a poor family that had always refused to recognize its poverty, hardworking people who were accustomed to troubles and problems but not accustomed to talking about them—people who concealed their feelings almost to the point of pretending they didn't have any. He seemed to lack all feelings of warmth just as he seemed to lack a sense of fear.

There is evidence, however, that by the end of February 1943, LeMay had begun to share the admiration Gladwin Hill expressed so eloquently for the men of the 305th—the men LeMay had considered no better than a rabble when he led them to England the previous October. He might still be far from satisfied with their performance, yet he was gratified by their progress and their courage. While he either preferred to keep his deepest feelings hidden, or simply found it difficult and embarrassing to expose them, he revealed a surprising side of himself in a note to his wife in early March. The note was written beneath a copy of a letter found among the effects of one of his men who was shot down during a March 6 mission to Lorient.

The man's letter was addressed to a comrade he was thus designating as administrator of his estate in the event he was killed. The "estate" consisted of his uniforms and toilet articles, several photographs, a "heavy mackinaw," four pounds owed to him by another comrade, and the money in his wallet, enough to pay his only outstanding debt, his laundry bill.

He also had a wife and a two-month-old daughter whom, he hoped, his administrator might some day be able to pick up in his arms. Would he please tell her that her father loved her and that he wanted her to grow up to be exactly like her mother?

In conclusion, he hoped that, whatever happened to him, his comrades would continue giving the Nazis hell until the "last sparks" of their "barbaric tyranny" had been extinguished.

LeMay was so deeply touched by this letter he wanted his wife to see a copy of it. But the note he scribbled at the bottom said as much about him as it did about his fallen airman:

> This letter was left by one of my boys shot down over Lorient. I am constantly amazed at the heights these kids rise to when the big test comes. I sometimes wonder what I have ever done to deserve the command of an outfit like this. You have always complained about me not being sentimental enough. I think sometimes I'm too soft to properly fight a war. After training these kids from pups and leading them against the best pursuit and antiaircraft defenses in the world, and having them come thru the way they have, it hurts like hell to lose them.—Curt.

(There was, incidentally, a happy ending to the story of this man who was shot down, a lieutenant named Tom Mayo. He landed safely by parachute in France, was grabbed by the French underground, spirited to Spain, and returned through Gibraltar to England—all within two weeks. And the first thing he said to the "administrator of his estate" was "I suppose you've already drunk that bottle of gin I left.")

LeMay's increasing admiration for his men did not prompt him to let up on them. When they weren't flying missions they were in ground school, learning everything there was to learn about their airplanes, their guns, their bombs and bombsights, their navigational checkpoints, their targets. And when they came back from missions, if the weather permitted, up they went again into the sky over England to practice whatever he thought they hadn't yet mastered. Especially gunnery.

In March 1943, the only gunnery expert aside from LeMay himself in the 305th, Maj. Ralph Cohen, was requisitioned by Gen. Haywood Hansell of the Third Wing to begin a gunnery school. Though LeMay hated to lose Cohen he approved the plan because he had been arguing ever since his arrival for more gunnery instruction. One reason for the need became apparent when the general in charge of gunnery instruction in the States, plus the commanders of eighteen gunnery schools, arrived in England to see how their former students were doing. At a question-and-answer session with Major Cohen, the general asked, "What do you do if you have a ball turret view plate shot out?"[14]

Cohen said, "General, are you serious?"

"Yes, I'm serious," the general said. "That's what I want to know."

"All right," said Cohen. "You requisition a new gunner."

Twice it had happened and in both cases the gunner's head was shot off. After talking to the general and his eighteen "experts," Cohen could understand why the gunnery in the Eighth Air Force was so ragged. But he wasn't sure how much he and his school could do about it because he had very little ammunition to use in practice.

LeMay came to his rescue. He sent Cohen truckload after truckload of .50 caliber bullets that had gone out on missions but had not been used. And he also sent Cohen truckload after truckload of gunners who had gone out on missions but didn't yet know, to his satisfaction, how to hit anything with that ammunition.

At about this time, LeMay found himself in some unexpected trouble. An inspector general arrived from Washington to take a look at the operations of the Eighth Air Force, and in due course, visited Chelveston to see how the 305th was doing. When he found out how LeMay was running the outfit, he was so horrified he went back to London and turned in a very negative report to General Eaker.[15]

"This guy's not human," he said to Eaker. "After his gunners return from a long, hard mission, he sends them down to the range to practice gunnery."

Eaker didn't really know LeMay. Before the war they had met during preparations for a very venturesome flight of six B-17s from Washington all the way to Buenos Aires. But by early 1943, Eaker was beginning to think LeMay was one of the best group commanders he had. The inspector general alarmed him. As soon as he found time, Eaker flew to Chelveston to find out what was going on.

"Between puffs of [LeMay's] cigar," Eaker later recalled, his "philosophy" emerged. It ran something like this:

"Yesterday, German fighters flew by my plane so close I could have hit them with a Colt .45. My gunners must have fired a thousand rounds, but most of the ME-109s escaped. If we don't shoot better than that tomorrow, we won't come back. These crews are great kids and I want to bring them back alive. So this evening, the gunners are down at the range learning how to hit a moving target, and some of the pilots who flew raggedly on the mission today are now out practicing formation flying. I don't mind being called tough. In this racket it's the tough guys who lead the survivors.''

When Eaker returned to his headquarters, he said to the inspector general, who was packing to return to Washington, ''You may be right about LeMay. He may not be human, but when I can find a hundred other group commanders like him, we'll get on with this air war. We might even win it.''

CHAPTER FIVE

As the spring of 1943 approached, the American war effort on virtually all fronts was generating more impatience than progress. In the Pacific, the Japanese were solidifying their hold on China, Southeast Asia, and the Philippines while Gen. Douglas MacArthur's troops were making only slow and painful headway on Guadalcanal, a remote place previously unheard of by most Americans. The U.S. Navy's glorious victory at Midway had happened nine months earlier, and while it would one day be recognized as a pivotal event in the war against Japan, its importance in 1943 had been so obscured by subsequent events that the average American had virtually forgotten it.

On the other side of the world, the highly publicized second front in France had not materialized during 1942, and the American people couldn't figure out why. The only place American soldiers had faced German soldiers was in Africa, where they weren't faring very well. But what did Africa mean, anyway? Why weren't we fighting them in Europe? The North African invasion was apparently a project on which Winston Churchill had insisted. For what purpose? To keep open the route from England to her Middle East and Asian possessions? Had America joined the war merely to save the British empire, as many isolationists claimed? Whatever happened to President Roosevelt's crusade against Hitler and his brutal Nazi regime? The only direct acts of aggression America had yet launched against Hitler's Germany were those few small B-17 missions against submarine facilities at places like Wilhelmshaven and Vegesack. And a fat lot of good those raids were doing if one could believe the Berlin communiques on the Atlantic submarine war. The German High Command, which was much more reliable than Hitler's government, claimed that U-boats had sunk an average of six hundred thirty thousand tons of U.S.-British shipping per month in 1942. And while the Allies could quibble about the exact figures, they couldn't deny that shipping losses had been horrendous. The U.S. War Shipping Administration had announced in February that one out of every twenty-five American merchant sailors was now dead or missing after the first year of the submarine war. (In contrast, only one of every 133 members of the armed forces had been killed.)

A merchant sailor named Robert Weikart, who had so far survived the perils of the north Atlantic, gave a vivid account of the way some of his colleagues had died when two passenger-cargo ships were sunk by U-boats: "We got word that a ship had been sunk during the night. I was on the signal tower when we reached the spot, just as dawn was lighting the scene. We saw hundreds of bodies in the water and lifeboats full of men swirled about us. It took me awhile to figure out why we did not stop to pick any of them up—they were frozen to death at the oars of their lifeboats. I saw the sea dotted with bobbing heads in life jackets. I started counting but realized there were hundreds so I gave up."[1]

Americans, reading such descriptions, were shocked, perplexed, and restless despite the prosperity the war had brought. There was a feeling throughout the land that we weren't doing enough on the battlefronts. After all, we were Americans. It had taken us only seventeen months to settle the first World War. We had been in this one now for fifteen months, yet nothing seemed to be happening. Why hadn't Hitler and the Japanese been forced to surrender? Didn't they realize they were up against America? It was about time to make them realize it. This would surely be the year of decision. Everyone was certain of that. But not everyone remained so cocky about the road ahead. The *New York Times* said in an editorial: "This is the spring [our soldiers] have been waiting for. They must face it and so must we. The attack will not be easy or cheap. It will test this generation of youth as none has ever been tested."

Though the public, including the *New York Times*, didn't know it, the American government and the military command were aware that there would be no second front in 1943 either, despite the insistent urging of the nation's premier soldier, Gen. George Marshall, the Army chief of staff. Marshall had wanted to invade the Continent and open a second front in 1942, but Churchill had argued, persuasively, that it was too early. In 1943, Churchill was still arguing that it was too early, especially since so many troops were now committed to Africa, and he was still prevailing. Some American military men were convinced that he had insisted on the North African invasion to avoid having to invade the Continent. Some believed he intended never to open a second front, that he considered the Americans naïve in their hope of launching a successful invasion against the German army.

It was well known that Churchill considered the Americans naïve in their belief that the daylight precision-bombing campaign by B-17s would work against the German air defenses. In a secret letter of November 2, 1942, to his highest air officer, Air Chief Marshal Sir Charles Portal, Churchill was bitter about the efforts of the U.S. Eighth Air Force:

> The number of American Air Force personnel [in England] has risen to about 55,000. . . . So far the results have been pitifully small. . . . Far from dropping bombs on Germany, the daylight bombers have not ventured beyond Lille. . . . Meanwhile, the American public has been led to believe that a really serious contribution has been made by the American Air Force. It is not for us to undeceive them, but there can be no doubt that they will find out for themselves before very long. . . . Considering the American professional interests and high reputations which are engaged in this scheme, and the shock it would be to the American people and to the Administration if the policy proved a glaring failure, we must expect most obstinate perseverance in this method. . . . [That] leaves us in the position that for many months ahead large numbers of American air personnel will be here playing very little part in the war and, what is much graver, American air production will be cast ever more deeply into an unprofitable groove.

Churchill wanted the American aircraft factories to abandon the Flying Fortress, which carried only two tons of bombs, in favor of the British Lancaster bomber, which could carry eight or nine tons. He wanted the U.S. Eighth Air Force to convert from B-17s to Lancasters, and to abandon daylight precision bombing in favor of indiscriminate area bombing at night. And he did not limit his opinions in the matter to his correspondence with his own aides. He began telling President Roosevelt how he felt, and he came so close to foreclosing the American daylight bombing effort that only an impassioned argument by General Eaker at the Casablanca conference in January 1943 saved it.

By the spring of 1943, though the Americans had now begun direct attacks against Germany, Churchill was still unsold on the daylight precision-bombing strategy which had been for several years the basic tenet of American Air Force doctrine. On March 13, he sent a minute to Portal that said: "The real question is not whether 'the American heavy bombers can in fact penetrate into Germany by day without prohibitive losses,' but how often they can do it and what weight of bombs can they discharge for the vast mass of ground personnel and material [sic] involved."

While Eaker knew nothing about Churchill's secret correspondence with Portal and his other aides, and was beginning to believe Churchill had changed his mind in favor of daylight bombing, he was cagey enough to realize the prime minister might need reinforcement even if he had changed his mind. In an effort to make sure Churchill would not again wander off the reservation, Eaker staged a dinner in his honor March 26 at U.S. Bomber Command headquarters in High Wycombe near London.[2]

Curtis LeMay and all the other Eighth Air Force commanders attended this dinner, at which each of the group COs was awarded a Silver Star for leading missions against the Germans. In a March 28 letter to his wife, LeMay wrote, "we had a dinner at Bomber Command which all the brass hats and group and sq. [squadron] C.O.s attended. Prime Minister Churchill was the guest of honor and gave a very stirring speech."

LeMay was not aware at the time of the high-level military politics that had inspired the dinner. He was, of course, aware of the daylight precision-bombing doctrine of the U.S. Air Force, and he would have been shocked to learn that the guest of honor had very nearly managed to scuttle that doctrine. LeMay believed firmly in the well-armed, highly reliable B-17 and the daylight strategy the plane made possible. He had become convinced, however, that many more B-17s would have to appear on the scene if the American strategy was to prevail.

In the early months of 1943, the lack of replacement planes and crews had brought morale in the Eighth Air Force to an appalling low. LeMay had seen this even in his own 305th, where losses were lower than in other groups. As German fighters kept chipping away at the force, and it became a bit smaller, a bit more vulnerable with each mission, every crew member in the

Eighth became convinced that the inevitable and soon-to-be-realized eventuality was annihilation. Men were making bets and even organizing lotteries in their Nissen huts on who would be the next to fall. Since there was now an average loss of 8 percent per mission, it wouldn't be long before everyone was both a winner and a loser.

Eaker had tried to stave off this likelihood by careful target selection and less frequent raids, but in doing so, he was inviting even more of the criticism he had been getting from people like Churchill in London and his own notoriously impatient boss, Hap Arnold in Washington, both of whom wanted results rather than explanations. It was evident to Eaker, and to men under him like LeMay, that the only possible result was obliteration unless the Eighth Air Force could soon be both replenished and expanded.

During this period of depressing doldrums, LeMay and the 305th fell upon one stroke of good fortune, thanks to the group club officer. With the possible exception of letters from home, or girls in nearby towns, the factor most likely to raise the morale of unhappy soldiers is the availability of decent liquor. And this was especially true during the cold, dark, foggy English winter of 1942–43. But in England at that time, liquor was as scarce as warm barracks. So the officer got a truck from the motor pool and headed for Scotland, that mellow source of warmth and comfort for so many of the world's whiskey drinkers.

Stopping at the first distillery he could find, he described the plight of his depressed and thirsty Yank bomb group to the manager, who was properly sympathetic but unable to offer him any of the scotch he sought. Strict government regulations forbade the sale of whiskey at the distillery. He did, however, invite the Yank to stay for lunch.

After lunch, as the disappointed Yank was leaving, the manager casually remarked, ''By the way, I do have a few hogsheads of something sent over from America years ago. They wondered if we could duplicate it, but there was nothing we could do with it, and we don't want to sell it. Bourbon they call it. Could you use that?''

A few hours later, the officer was back at Chelveston with several hogsheads of bourbon, and the spirits of LeMay's men went up as the liquor went down.

But much more important were the indications in late spring that the badly needed new planes, and even whole new bomb groups, were about to arrive. One of those indications was the formation of a new provisional combat wing (the 102nd), which began as a paper organization, without planes or men, but with the expectation that the planes and crews were on their way. On May 18, General Eaker made manifest his admiration for Colonel LeMay by putting him in command of the newly created wing. This promotion, which made LeMay the first group commander in the theater to become a wing commander, moved him to the little village of Thurleigh, only eight miles away geographically from the men of the 305th at Chelveston, but much farther away substantively because the 305th was not a part of his new wing. The "rabble" of rookies he had brought to England was now, relatively, a veteran group, while he could expect that most of the men under him in the 102nd Wing would be a new "rabble" of rookies, just arriving from the States.[3]

During the 305th's first five months of combat under LeMay it had ranked second among Eighth Air Force groups in the number of sorties (375) flown against the Germans. It had sustained more battle damage than any other group, perhaps because its bomb runs were twice the average length. Yet it has sustained fewer than the average overall losses. And most important, it had placed twice as high a percentage of bombs on targets as any other group. But on May 17, the day before LeMay received his new assignment, there was an indication, ominous for the entire Eighth Air Force, that the Germans were beginning to marshal even more resistance to the American daylight bombing offensive. The 305th lost four planes that day when the German fighters attacked them with .37 millimeter cannons for the first time. "They stayed back about a thousand yards," LeMay observed, "and just shot hell out of us." At that range, the .50 caliber machine guns of the Flying Fortresses might as well have been slingshots. Then against Kiel two days later, the 305th lost four more planes when, in a colossal snafu, it had to attack the target without support from any other group and battled 150 German fighters for an hour and a half. As LeMay would soon learn, the struggle for the skies over Europe was just now getting warm.

Thurleigh, where LeMay established the headquarters of the new 102nd Wing, was a tiny hamlet of no more than two hundred people which dated back at least to the days of the Norman Conquest in the eleventh century, and had a lovely Norman church to prove it. There was one store, one pub, one garage, and several beautiful thatched cottages. This part of Bedfordshire was hedge country and the rolling hills on three sides of town were a patchwork of variegated green. To the west was a flat plateau on which the air base sat. It was a charming place but LeMay was not destined to get very well acquainted with it. In less than a month, on June 15, he was again promoted, not in rank but in responsibility. He took command of the Fourth Combat Wing, which was in the process of enlargement and was soon to be redesignated as the Third Air Division.[4]

Eaker was now promoting him faster than he might have wished. Command of the Third Division was intended to go to Brig. Gen. Nathan Bedford Forrest who had only recently arrived from the States, but Forrest was shot down on his first mission. The fact that LeMay was named to the post indicated Eaker's faith in him but also filled him with conflicting emotions—prideful expectation that he would soon be a general plus fearful uncertainty about handling such a big job.

LeMay was now approaching the realms of higher command for which Bob Olds had begun training him in 1937. But unfortunately, Olds would not be around to appreciate the progress of his protégé. On April 28, Olds died of heart disease at a sanitarium in Arizona. His death was not altogether unexpected. His health had been precarious for some time, which explained why he was in charge of the Training Command instead of overseas. It was generally agreed that he would have been a superb field commander if he had been healthy. But on February 24, he had written to LeMay what could only be regarded as a forerunner of more bad news: "Within the last 24 hours I have been relieved from command of the Second Air Force [Training Command] and hospitalized to try to get this damn rheumatism out of my joints. I will let you know what develops in the future."

Olds must have known even then that his great problem was not rheumatism and he had very little future. While LeMay sensed this, it did not lighten his feeling of loss at the news of Olds's death. Robert Olds had done more than any other man to prepare LeMay for the responsibilities he now faced.[5]

LeMay's uncommon abilities were beginning to attract attention even outside the Eighth Air Force. On May 22, Air Marshal Sir Arthur T. Harris, the RAF bomber commander, decorated him with a medal few Americans had ever received—the British Distinguished Flying Cross.[6] And after the ceremony, Harris said, not to LeMay but to Ira Eaker, "LeMay looks like a man you would like to have with you if you were sent out on a dangerous errand.''

When LeMay went to Fourth Wing headquarters at Elveden (in beautiful wooded country twenty-five miles northeast of Cambridge), he was replacing Brig. Gen. Nathan Bedford Forrest, who had replaced Brig. Gen. Fred Anderson, who had recently been promoted to become Eighth Air Force bomber commander. This was the same Fred Anderson who had warned LeMay in Syracuse the previous autumn that he had better fly his group to England in a hurry if he didn't want to be sent to the Pacific. Anderson was one of the most highly regarded young officers in the Air Force. Eaker had secured his transfer to England a few months earlier with the intention of making him bomber commander, and to prepare him for the job he had put him in charge of the Fourth Wing which was activated in May with the arrival of three new groups from the States. Though Anderson had led these groups on a few missions, they were still very green when LeMay got to Elveden in late June.

Col. Carl Norcross, then a captain, remembers the day LeMay arrived, bringing with him only Joe Preston and one other aide, Capt. T. E. Beckemeier. Norcross, as the wing intelligence officer, was delegated to show the new commander around his headquarters, a stunningly impressive building. It was called Elveden Hall and it was the country home of the earl of Iveagh, head of the vastly wealthy Guinness Brewery family. Situated on an estate of several thousand acres, the main building looked like a palace, with more than a hundred rooms, richly decorated and joined by marble corridors. LeMay would be living in the owner's suite, which offered a huge living room, bedroom, and private bath. Coming from the mud-spattered Nissen hut that was his previous headquarters, he was awestricken by such opulence. But he didn't say so. Norcross recalls that the first thing this tough-looking, cigar-chomping new boss said to him was, ''I want you to start target study classes in every group.''[7]

Norcross was taken aback by this sudden order, issued at a time when LeMay was getting his first look at the building. Was he so preoccupied by his job that he didn't even notice these plush surroundings? Norcross couldn't help feeling slightly uncomfortable in the presence of this strange, forbidding man. What he didn't know was that LeMay himself was just as uncomfortable. He was accustomed to the mud and the flimsy shacks at Chelveston. He was, after all, a soldier, and soldiers were supposed to accept primitive conditions. That was what it meant to be in the field.

"Now I found myself," he has recalled, "with a copper dome over my head and God knows how much 'richly veined marble' staring me in the face." His dominant thought as he looked around at all this luxury was, What the hell am I doing here?

"I reviewed my situation and found it about as comfortable as a barbed-wire fence. God Almighty! I had so little experience. I had commanded a squadron for only a short period of time—certainly not long enough to learn anything much. Next thing I knew, I had a group, and I was still engaged in learning the Commerce and Industry there when I got fired upstairs. In fact, I really hadn't learned it well yet. Hadn't been able to get going on the things I wanted to try out."[8]

The target study idea was one of those things. He had begun it in the 305th, but he hadn't been able to develop it fully. Here, he decided, he'd be able to do it right. Which explains his unexpected and abrupt order to Norcross. At least it explains the unexpectedness. As for the abruptness, that was something to which Norcross would become accustomed after he had been around LeMay for a while.

During the rest of their tour, LeMay said very little. Barely enough to be polite. Norcross, like many people before him, noticed quickly in LeMay the tendency to be silent and apparently remote, as if he considered himself above those around him and wanted to keep himself aloof from them. In the Elveden Hall dining room one table was reserved for the senior staff. LeMay ate at this table, with his aides, but he would often finish his entire meal without saying a word to anyone. Was it arrogance of command that prompted his silence? Was he choosing purposely to keep his subordinates in their place by insisting on being alone even when he was among them? Some people thought so, but only those who were unaware of an important aspect of his character—his uncertainty about his own qualifications, his fear of failure. He was much too unsure of himself to be arrogant. The habitual silence of the man, which appeared to be aloofness, was more likely to be preoccupation with problems and how to solve them. Each time he was assigned a new job, throughout his career, he was convinced he wasn't up to it. And he was further convinced that the only way he would ever bring himself up to it was through hard work. He almost never took a day off. His idea of a vacation from work, one of his aides said, was to get together with other commanders and talk about mutual problems. When he was silent during dinner, or any other time, it could be because he had such a limited fund of small talk and such a low opinion of it, but it was probably because he was working on something in his mind. Success meant work, which is why he considered work so essential for himself and why he demanded so much of it from the people around him. For his staffs, wherever he was, he would choose hardworking officers over brilliant ones. He once explained this in answer to a question about how he chose his subordinates.

"I'm a little suspicious of the genius," he said. "They can be used in proper spots but [they're] inclined to forget about the rest of the team, so that as long as they're around everything goes well, but once you lose them, you're liable to really fall to pieces. I'd much rather operate with a group of average individuals that were highly motivated. The first thing I expect of a man is that he's always on the job and it never enters my mind that he'd be anyplace except on the job. Then I expect him to work and work hard. I expect him to operate on the team. With this sort of a setup you can build an organization, not around any one individual, but around a whole team that will function and continue to function even though you lose some members. This is very important, I think, for a military organization. We've all seen units commanded by a very competent officer who did everything himself and everyone depended on him to do it, and when he was shot down or you lost him for some reason, the group really fell to pieces."[9]

Shortly after LeMay's arrival at the Fourth Wing, a new man joined his staff whom he didn't choose, but whom he was happy to have associated with him for many years thereafter. This was August Kissner, a colonel who had just arrived from the States and was sent up from London by Eaker to become LeMay's chief of staff. Kissner was a man of impeccable taste, one of the most gentlemanly, cultivated, precise, and punctilious officers LeMay had ever known; and in time he would prove to be one of the most loyal and reliable. He had been acquainted with LeMay since their days in flight school together. They had both graduated in the 1929 class at Kelly field, though Kissner, who had already graduated from West Point, was therefore senior in rank. They had also attended Tactical School at the same time—1939. But they had never known each other well enough to be friends, nor were they the types likely to be attracted to each other. Kissner would be at home in a drawing room where LeMay could never be comfortable; LeMay would be at home in a hangar or a garage, tinkering with an engine, while Kissner would always consider such a pastime thoroughly unsuitable for a high-ranking officer. LeMay was rough and ready; Kissner was highly polished. But they would find, in time, that they made an excellent team because each had something the other needed.

Kissner was a bachelor, and among Air Force wives with marriageable daughters he was considered the most eligible of bachelors, but he remained unmarried, perhaps because of a tragedy that overtook him in the early 1930s. During a tour of duty in the Philippines, he fell in love with the beautiful daughter of a colonel and they were engaged to be married as soon as they returned to the mainland. But on the ship en route home, the young lady contracted a strep infection and died. Kissner thereafter treated her parents almost as if they were his own. And he had never married.

LeMay, in retirement, would say of him, "Augie was the most polite individual I ever encountered. Never used a bad word or picked up the wrong fork. Helen would tell me about him coming around to talk to her [in postwar years] about the things I did which I shouldn't do. But he was a tower of strength. I had complete confidence in him. He took care of all the paper work, leaving me free [to concentrate on operations]."[10]

A Fourth Wing officer who closely observed both men has said that "some of LeMay's success was due to Kissner. He tried to relieve LeMay of the burden of many nonoperational functions. He might have been called the hatchet man if he hadn't been such a nice man. When he found someone at headquarters who was not doing his job, or who didn't behave himself after office hours, the man disappeared with great rapidity.

"He [Kissner] tried to think like LeMay. I remember once when LeMay did not go along with a Kissner recommendation and Kissner took it as a personal failure. He had not diagnosed LeMay's thinking correctly."

The three groups with which Gen. Fred Anderson had formed the Fourth Wing in May—the Ninety-fourth, Ninety-fifth, and Ninety-sixth—were still the only groups operational when LeMay and Kissner came to Elveden but two new groups, the One-hundredth and 388th, had arrived from the States and were training for their first mission. Under LeMay that training was to be tougher and more extensive than anyone had imagined. And it included the already operational groups as well as the new ones.

Carl Norcross's Intelligence Section launched its target study school as soon as the necessary photos and information could be gathered. Joe Preston began selecting the best candidates for a lead crew school. And LeMay put several men to work on what he called the Fourth Wing Tactical Doctrine File—a looseleaf notebook, kept up-to-date at all times, which set forth the constantly developing observations and most successful operational procedures of the men LeMay considered the best available experts on the subject of daylight precision bombing—the men in his crews.

Daylight bombing, though it had been a part of U.S. Air Force doctrine for several years, was still new in practice, and had not yet been fully developed or tested. ''[Our] crews knew more about [it] than anyone else in the world,'' LeMay once explained. ''The experts were right here and what they had to say was worth listening to. We gathered all that information together. We discussed it, thrashed it out, discarded some of it, kept what was good, then put it in writing in the form of a tactical document. It's in looseleaf form [so that] if something changes we throw away the old one and put in our new one.''

In addition to all this ground training, LeMay also intensified the flight training of the groups under him. They were already using the stagger formation he had devised in the 305th, but he made them learn to close it in even tighter. He made the gunners put in more hours of practice. He made all the crews accept the fact that they would have to reconcile themselves to longer, therefore more dangerous bomb runs. And he instituted another phase of training that was new to virtually all of them—instrument takeoffs to counteract the frequent morning fog. Though he didn't know it at the time, the bad-weather takeoff procedures he was teaching would soon become an important factor in one of the two greatest air battles the world had ever seen.

LeMay's insistence that his crews learn to protect themselves arose partly from the fact that up to this time, their fighter escorts were doing very little to protect them. The planes of the Eighth Air Force Fighter Command, mostly P-47 Thunderbolts, were clearing the way for the bombers only as far as Belgium or Holland, then returning home just when they were needed most. The German fighters, having caught on to this practice, would hang back until the P-47s turned for home; then they would close in on the bombers. This situation gave rise to a bitter joke among the B-17 crew members. As one of them said, "Now we have fighters with us all the way. Our P-47s take us as far as Aachen. The Messerschmitts and Focke-Wulfs take us to the target and back. Then the 47s pick us up again when we reach the Channel. If we reach the Channel."

It was a joke that produced no laughter from LeMay. At least not at the time. He later told a story about a mission he led during which one of his gunners fired at a P-47 that was moving in to escort the B-17s across the Channel. When they returned from the mission, LeMay cornered the guilty gunner.

"What the hell's the matter with you?" he demanded. "I saw you shoot at that Jug. You've studied aircraft identification as much as the rest of us."

"I didn't recognize it," the gunner said. "But anyway, I'd just as soon shoot at the son-of-a-bitch. Those Jugs aren't doing us any good"[11]

By early July, LeMay was as anxious as that gunner to do something about those Jugs. And so was Brig. Gen. Bob Williams, the mustached, swagger-stick-carrying commander of the First Bomb Division, who had lost an eye during a German air raid on London three years earlier, when he was in England as a U.S. Air Force observer. LeMay and Williams were so incensed at the lack of fighter support for their bombers that they confronted Brig. Gen. Frank Hunter, the Eighth Air Force Fighter Commander, during a meeting at First Division headquarters. Williams led the attack after learning about an extraordinary order Hunter had issued to his fighter pilots. If a fighter plane should become partially disabled during a mission, a second one was to detach from the formation and escort the cripple home. Williams found this kind of coddling unconscionable, and so did LeMay.

"Every time one of my boys loses an engine," LeMay reminded Hunter, "he has to go home alone. There's no one to cover him."

Hunter defended himself stoutly as Williams continued the attack. His pilots were inexperienced. Their planes were so limited in range they couldn't go any deeper than they were already going to help the bombers. And in any case, direct bomber escort wasn't the best tactic. In Hunter's opinion, the most sensible role of the fighters was to precede the bombers and sweep all enemy fighters out of the area so the bombers could advance unhindered. This was old Air Force fighter doctrine that LeMay could remember from the days when he was a pursuit pilot. But was it practical against the Germans who were clever enough to stay back and wait for the American fighters to complete their "sweep"? Neither LeMay no Williams thought so.

After listening to the argument as long as he could endure it, LeMay said to Hunter, "When you guys suffer the kind of losses we have, then I'll talk to you." And with that he stormed out of the meeting.[12]

Though LeMay and Williams may not have known it at the time, their arguments were destined to prevail over Hunter's because they had Ira Eaker on their side, and he was just as furious as they were. Like LeMay, Eaker had once been a fighter pilot himself, and he was so unhappy with the way his Eighth Air Force fighters were being used, he had already asked Hap Arnold to send him a replacement for Hunter.

The limited range of the American fighters, especially the P-47, was a problem that cried out for an immediate solution. But it would not be solved until a proper type of wing tank arrived from the States. Hunter could hardly be blamed for the lack of these auxiliary tanks, and neither could Eaker. For several months he had been sending messages to Washington about his desperate need for them, but so far to no avail. Meanwhile, however, there were other measures that might be taken in an effort to give the bombers at least a little more fighter support. It was over the usefulness of these measures that arguments arose.

Two less-than-ideal auxiliary fuel tanks were available immediately, for instance, both of which Eaker thought should be in use. One was a British-produced paper tank that Hunter disliked because it diminished the speed of his fighters and it didn't work very well at high altitudes. The other was a fuselage tank that Hunter disliked because it fitted into the plane right behind the pilot, making him a potential human torch. It also made the plane more difficult to handle by shifting its center of gravity.

Hunter was understandably reluctant to expose hip pilots to what he considered unacceptable risks. But as Eaker pointed out to him, it was the bombers, not the fighters, who were doing the most basic and necessary war work—destroying German targets. The bomber crews were accepting deadly risks on every mission, with no more protection than they could provide for themselves. If they were willing to take such risks, the fighter pilots simply had to do likewise. The only reason the fighters had been brought all the way to England was to protect the bombers.

Eaker ultimately won this argument, which meant that within a short time Hunter would be replaced by Maj. Gen. William Kepner, an able fighter expert with a more aggressive style. Eventually, a satisfactory wing tank for the fighters would also arrive. But not soon enough to save the bombers from some very bad days ahead.

Now that the Americans were bombing Germany rather than France and the Low Countries, the Germans were paying more attention to them. From August through December of 1942, before the Eighth Air Force had approached Germany proper, its average casualty rate per mission had been 4 percent lost and 34 percent damaged. During the first six months of 1943, when the B-17s began facing German fighters inside German borders, the bomber casualty rate had risen to 6.6 percent lost and 35.5 percent damaged.

The first mission in July came on the fourth, after a five-day weather delay. With casualty figures rising, it may not have been by accident that on this most important American national holiday, when the Germans might be ready for an attack against their Fatherland, the B-17s bombed instead three targets in France—La Palisse, Nantes, and LeMans. LeMay's Fourth Wing went that day to La Palisse on a mission more notable for its navigational accuracy than for anything else. It was such a long mission, to the very bottom of France, that the B-17s had to carry bomb bay tanks. Almost the entire route, from England to landfall near Bordeaux, was flown over water at low altitude, to avoid radar detection, and through an overcast at sea that made drift readings impossible. Despite all this, the bombers did find and attack the target, which seemed to indicate that the extra training was beginning to pay off. But no one bragged about the effectiveness of the bombing.

On July 10, the Fourth Wing was assigned an easy target—Le Bourget Airdrome outside Paris, where Charles Lindbergh had landed triumphantly after the first-ever transatlantic flight on May 21, 1927. As it happened, Lucky Lindy had better luck finding Le Bourget that night than the American B-17s had in daylight sixteen years later. They found nothing but clouds, and they left without even dropping their bombs, for fear they might hit the city. On July 14, France's most important national holiday, the

Fourth Wing was sent back to Le Bourget. This time, the B-17s at least dropped their loads.

On July 17 they went to Germany in the hope of bombing submarine plants at Hamburg, but the clouds were so heavy they couldn't locate the target. They weren't even sure they had located Hamburg. Another week passed with clouds protecting Germany every day, while the Eighth Air Force, more than doubled in size now with the addition of new groups, waited anxiously for the weather to clear. Eaker felt he was ready at last for a full-scale offensive against Hitler's heartland. But on July 24, Fred Anderson, the new bomber commander, became so impatient with the German weather he decided to go elsewhere once again. He dispatched 324 Fortresses that day against harbor installations and factories in German-occupied Norway. The Fourth Wing (now so close to division size that everyone had begun calling it by its soon-to-be official name, the Third Division) was divided into three "combat wings" for this raid. Two of them flew to Bergen and found the place so cloudy they took their bombs back home with them. But the third did considerable damage to ships, dry docks, and other installations at Trondheim. The general results of the mission were considered excellent and only one Fortress was lost.

This attack on Norway was not only the largest ever staged by the Eighth Air Force up to that time, it was also the beginning of an unprecedented and unforgettable seven-day, six-mission campaign that came to be known as "Blitz Week." Aside from the first mission, all were against targets in Germany. And LeMay's Third Division took part in each of them.

On July 25, Anderson sent his planes against Kiel, Hamburg, and Warnemunde, but the clouds were so heavy LeMay's division turned to its secondary target, Rostock, with "good" results, due partly to the target study to which the navigators and bombardiers had been subjected. Aside from the Rostock success, however, it was not a good day for the Eighth. German fighters shot down nineteen Fortresses in an impressive and deadly display of skill. Several of Germany's best fighter squadrons had been transferred back to the homeland from the Eastern Front to meet the growing threat of the American bombers. Fortress crews would see all too much of these squadrons in the days to come.

On July 26, 292 planes took off from England. Two hundred of them were so busy fending off German fighters they had no chance of locating their targets through the clouds. But ninety-two of LeMay's Third Division bombers were fortunate enough to find an opening in the sky above Hanover. They damaged a railway yard and registered twenty-one direct hits on a rubber factory.

The weather was so unpromising on July 27 that the crews were given a much-needed day of rest. But on July 28, the offensive was resumed. The Third Division hit a Focke-Wulf plant at Oschersleben that day, causing a month's loss of production.

On July 29, the Third Division hit Warnemunde while the First Division hit Kiel, each dropping about one hundred tons of bombs. And on July 30, the Focke-Wulf component factory at Kassel was the target. But only 186 Fortresses answered the call for that mission. And on the next day, no mission was scheduled, though the weather, at last, was perfectly clear. The Eighth Air Force could not continue the pace. It was, at least temporarily, exhausted. Its six missions in seven days had cost one hundred planes and one thousand men. The time had come to rest a while, to regroup and repair.[13]

An indication of the psychological stress created by the Blitz Week offensive can be found in the fact that seventy-five Eighth Air Force crewmen suffered emotional breakdowns in July of 1943. But the relentless pressure of German flak and fighter bullets was not the only cause of stress. Bomber crews in World War II—especially high-altitude bomber crews—were subjected to conditions unprecedented in the history of warfare.

The B-17 could not be heated during combat because its waist guns had to be fired through large open windows. And at twenty thousand feet or higher, the temperature could be between thirty and fifty degrees below zero. At the same time, the air was so thin oxygen masks were absolutely essential. Eighth Air Force flight surgeons estimated that more than half of all B-17 crewmen suffered some ill effects from lack of oxygen. Above twenty thousand feet, ice would form in the masks they wore, causing oxygen stoppage which might not be apparent to the victim until he was too weak to do anything about it. Sometimes the plane's main oxygen system would malfunction, perhaps after being damaged by gunfire, leaving crewmen dependent on bottles of oxygen, which didn't last very long. And when they ran short of oxygen, there was little they could do about it, because if the plane were to leave the protection of the formation and descend to an altitude where the air was breathable, it would be delivering itself over to German flak and fighters.

Even worse than the danger of oxygen shortage was the effect of several hours in thirty-to-fifty-below-zero weather. On every mission, despite the heavy, sheepskin-lined flight suits the men wore, several would suffer frostbite, in many cases so severe as to necessitate amputation.[14] Under such conditions it is surprising that any of these men were able to retain self-control, especially since they had to endure all these hardships in a state of close confinement. The B-17, considered large in its day, was insignificantly small compared to a modern airliner. The fuselage was only eight feet across at its widest point, and much of it was taken up by the bomb bay. If an infantry soldier can't stand what's happening around him at the front, he can, at least, run for the rear, accepting a court martial in preference to the carnage. But in a bomber under attack there is no place to run. At the end of the Eighth Air Force's Blitz Week, 80 percent of the flight surgeons reported ''undue fatigue'' among the men they had examined. What ''undue fatigue'' meant was fear. And it was a very rare man who didn't feel it.

Curtis LeMay himself flew on none of the Blitz Week missions because Fred Anderson had emphatically forbidden him to do so. But Anderson's order was not intended to save LeMay from any more combat. It was intended to save him for a special mission, already in the planning stage, one part of which General Eaker had decided LeMay should lead. He was destined to see enough combat on that one mission to make up for what he missed during Blitz Week.

CHAPTER SIX

It was an unusual visit. The Eighth Air Force commander sometimes came on inspection trips, but not very often did he simply drop in on a division or wing commander. If Ira Eaker wanted to see one of his subordinates, he had only to summon the man to his own headquarters. But here he was at LeMay's headquarters, Elveden Hall. Was he dissatisfied about something? No. There was no sign of that. He was here because he had something confidential to tell LeMay. Something he wanted to tell him in person.[1]

For some time, he explained, the Eighth Air Force planners had been working on an operation that might be one of the most important of the war. As LeMay was well aware, there was an immediate need to cut down German aircraft production. Unless the menace of German fighter planes could be sharply diminished, the fate of the American daylight bombing offensive was in grave doubt. What the Eighth Air Force was planning, therefore, in conjunction with the Fifteenth Air Force commanded by Gen. Carl Spaatz in Africa, was a massive two-pronged attack against Germany's most important fighter factories. Fifteenth Air Force bombers from Africa would hit the huge Focke-Wulf 190 plant at Wiener Neustadt in eastern Austria, while at the same time, the Eighth would be hitting the Messerschmitt 109 factory at Regensburg on the Danube River.

"And I want you, yourself, to lead the Regensburg mission," Eaker said to LeMay.

The main reason for attacking both facilities simultaneously was to spread thin the German defenses, preventing a concentration of fighters against either American armada. But Eaker didn't have to make a special trip to Elveden Hall to explain something as obvious as that. He was here because this mission was special in another way. It was to feature an intriguing experiment. After bombing the ME-109 plant at Regensburg, the Eighth Air Force Fortresses were scheduled to fly, not back to England but south to Africa on the first of what might be many shuttle runs. Then, returning home from Africa, they would bomb another target, someplace along the way. If the idea worked, it would force the Germans to defend an even larger part of the Continent, thus spreading their fighter defenses even thinner.

The B-17s would have no trouble reaching Africa. The question was where to land. It would have to be at an airfield that could provide fuel, food, bombs, repair facilities, and supplies for the return trip to England. By this time, American and British forces were in such firm control of North Africa they had moved on to invade Sicily. Had they left their African airfields well enough stocked to accommodate perhaps 150 bombers from England? LeMay decided he'd better fly to Tooey Spaatz's headquarters in Tunis and find out.

Col. Lauris Norstad, the handsome, blond Scandinavian whom Hap Arnold considered one of "the brains of the Air Force," was Spaatz's chief of staff at this time. When LeMay arrived in Africa and briefed Norstad on the needs of the projected mission, Norstad said, "Telergma [about sixty miles inland from Tunis] is your field. It's both a depot and a combat field. There you'll have supplies, extra mechanics—everything you need. That's the place to land. You can get well serviced there. All the parts you need. All the maintenance people and support."[3]

LeMay left Norstad feeling confident about everything but the weather, a commodity which inspired no confidence in Europe that summer. Perhaps he should have flown to Telergma to have a look for himself, but Norstad was a very bright and dependable fellow. If he said Telergma was the place, there was no reason to doubt it.

When LeMay returned to England, the seven bomb groups which now constituted his Third Division (94th, 95th, 96th, 100th, 385th, 388th, and 390th) were already preparing for a "special" mission, the target of which they didn't yet know and (except for the group commanders and lead crews) would not know until a few hours before takeoff.[3] Security about upcoming missions was as tight as Ira Eaker's staff could make it. For this reason, and because of weather uncertainty, official teletypes announcing missions would sometimes arrive so late that group and division commanders would become furious at Eighth Air Force headquarters. In the case of this mission, LeMay already knew the destination and requirements. What worried him most was the weather. He was so suspicious of it he ordered all the crews to concentrate their practice on instrument takeoffs. The procedure was hardly as sophisticated as it would be today, but it was the best that could be devised at the time.

"When ceiling and horizontal visibility were O.K.," as LeMay explained it, "I'd make our pilots take off on instruments—get the seat down and take off completely on instruments. Over in the right-hand seat the copilot would be ready to operate visually. If something went wrong, he could take over, and that would save the airplane and crew. But in the meantime, our pilot was training for an instrument takeoff in case he had to do that when the big day came. We held to this procedure all through the rest of the war."

Though his responsibility in the upcoming Regensburg mission must have been weighing heavily upon him by this time, there was little indication of it in his letters to his wife. On August 8 he wrote to Helen: "I suppose you are about to start your vacation. Don't get too sunburned on the beach." And in a lighthearted reference to one of his five-year-old daughter's flirtations with a little neighbor boy, he wrote: "It seems to me Janie is rather young for boy friends but I suppose she is taking after her mother."

As the days of early August passed, LeMay's distrust of the weather proved justified. Not until August 12 were his planes able to stage their first mission that month, and it was only a moderately successful foray against Wesseling and Bonn in western Germany. The clouds farther east, over Regensburg, continued thick day after day.

By August 13, Tooey Spaatz in Africa was tired of waiting for the Eighth to move against Regensburg. That day he sent his heavy bombers (including three B-24 groups) alone against the FW-190 plant at Wiener Neustadt, thus scrapping the two-pronged mission as it had been originally planned.

Still determined to split or confuse the German defenders, Eaker and his staff decided to stage a two-pronged attack of their own—LeMay's Third Division going to Regensburg, then Africa, as previously intended, while Bob Williams and his First Division hit another target which for some time had been uppermost in Eaker's mind—the concentration of German ball- and roller-bearing plants in the town of Schweinfurt. Clustered around the railroad yards in this small eastern Bavarian city were five huge factories which produced almost two-thirds of Germany's ball and roller bearings. If these plants could be totally destroyed, the output of German war machinery—indeed machinery of any kind—might be so diminished as to cripple the Nazi war effort. It is impossible to build an airplane, ship, submarine, artillery gun, tank, or vehicle of any kind without bearings.

Since the Germans knew this as well as the Americans, it would be at least as difficult to attack these plants as it would be to attack the Messerschmitt plant at Regensburg. Both would be fiercely defended. But again there was that intriguing notion that if both could be bombed at once, the Germans would have to spread their fighters so thin that neither could be effectively defended. Better yet, as someone pointed out, if LeMay and his Third Division were to go first and lure all the German fighter planes to Regensburg by making it look as if theirs was the day's only mission, the First Division might take off a half-hour later and find the route to Schweinfurt unobstructed. It was on the basis of this hope that the combined Regensburg-Schweinfurt mission was developed. If LeMay felt any uneasiness or resentment at being placed in the dangerous role of a decoy to attract German fighter planes, there is no record of it.

As the days of frustration passed, while eastern Europe remained hidden by clouds, the Eighth Air Force continued its missions to western Europe, where the skies were now clear. On August 15, LeMay sent 147 Fortresses against skimpily defended targets in France at Merville and Vendeville. On August 16, he sent sixty-six planes against Poix and Abbeville. This was a small operation, perhaps because on that day the weathermen were predicting clear skies over Regensburg and Schweinfurt the following day. The time had come for immediate preparations. LeMay scheduled a special briefing for the evening of the 16th and summoned to it all seven of his group commanders plus the lead crews they had chosen for this largest and most crucial mission the Eighth Air Force, indeed the entire U.S. Air Force, had ever undertaken.

Having thus set the stage, LeMay found himself with time on his hands that afternoon. His division was so fully organized by this time, and the duties of preparation so fully delegated, there wasn't much for him to do. As it happened, a young communications officer from Bomber Command, Edward D. Gray, had just arrived at Elveden Hall with an appointment to discuss a proposed experiment using a new, secret radar device. LeMay told one of his aides to usher Gray into his office.[4]

Gray, who was an assistant signal officer at Bomber Command headquarters, was so well aware of the upcoming Regensburg-Schweinfurt mission that when he reached Elveden Hall and realized it was scheduled for the following day, he lost all expectation of seeing LeMay on this day. But LeMay welcomed him promptly at the appointed time.

Though Gray expected to see signs of frantic, last-minute preparation, he saw none. For the next three-quarters of an hour, while he talked and LeMay listened, no one else entered the room and there were no telephone calls. LeMay, whose mind had to be full of the next day's mission, seemed to be devoting all of his attention to the radar gadget Gray was describing. LeMay said very little, but when he spoke it was usually to ask what Gray considered "sharply pertinent" questions about the gadget. LeMay's only small talk was, "That's a fine pen you're using. Better not leave it here or it will be mine."

As the commanders and lead crews gathered for their briefing that evening, the crowded room was deathly silent. These men already knew that tomorrow's mission was not like any other. Besides being the Eighth's biggest, it represented the deepest-ever penetration of Germany, against two targets certain to be as well defended as any in the Third Reich. But Gray, who had been invited to attend the briefing, "could never tell from the way LeMay went over details of the attack that here was anything except an important bombing mission to be done."

In a tone as casual as if he had been ordering lunch, LeMay concluded his remarks with one last warning: "Tell the boys to take field rations for a couple of days and prepare them for possible sleeping on the ground for a day or two. No Savoys or Claridges [two of London's finest hotels] in the north African desert, you know."

At the end of the briefing there were questions. He answered them all seriously, including some that Gray considered "damn foolish." When the meeting ended, with the men breaking up into small groups to discuss various details, LeMay tapped Gray on the shoulder. "Now then," he said to Gray, "don't you think it might be better to use a two-group combat wing with each group sixty percent equipped with your gadget rather than a three-group wing with one strongly equipped group unbalancing the other two?"

Gray, whose mind was now absorbed by the next day's mission, was so unprepared for such a question he was bewildered by it. Even when he stopped to think about it, he couldn't answer it. LeMay, while giving most of his thought to the next day's mission, had nevertheless come up with an idea about the radar gadget that had never occurred to Gray. That night in his bunk he gave it more thought. "For two hours I analyzed it," he later wrote. "LeMay was right."

Prospects for the mission did not look ideal when LeMay got out of bed shortly after three o'clock the morning of August 17; those prospects did not improve as he dressed and ate his breakfast. The clouds were low and getting lower throughout the eastern half of England. But there were indications of clear weather over the Continent. As long as the Fortresses could take off safely there was no reason why the mission shouldn't proceed as planned. LeMay felt pretty good about the fact that he had drilled his pilots on bad-weather, instrument takeoffs.

When the zero hour for takeoff approached, however, the low clouds had further descended to become thick fog. It was so thick as to prohibit taxiing. LeMay's pilots weren't skillful enough to take off safely in that soup. Finally, Fred Anderson at Bomber Command had to move up the Third Division zero hour one hour, then an hour-and-a-half. But that wouldn't change the basic plans since the First Division planes were also grounded by bad weather at their bases.

After almost an hour, LeMay decided that if his planes were preceded and guided by ground-crew men with flashlights, they ought to be able to taxi safely and find their way to the end of the runway. Was he therefore cleared for takeoff? Fred Anderson at Bomber Command said yes, he could go.

LeMay, who was still at his own headquarters when the approval came, grabbed his personal belongings and sped to nearby Snetterton Heath, where the planes of the Ninety-sixth Bomb Group were almost ready to fly. The minute the approval order came, the props had begun to turn. The Ninety-sixth was to lead the entire mission and LeMay was to fly in its lead plane, piloted by Capt. Thomas F. Kenny. It was on the runway, ready for takeoff, when his car, picking its way through the fog, came up behind it. LeMay was shoved into the back door of the plane, his belongings were thrown in on top of him, and away they went, up through two layers of overcast. When they finally broke into blue sky above the clouds, they would circle until the rest of the planes—146 of them today—also emerged and fell in be-hind them.

The process of assembly was in itself a remarkable feat. Each plane had to find the other two planes in its element. Then those three had to find their squadron. The squadron had to find the other two squadrons that constituted their group. This group had to find the groups that would constitute a combat wing. And the combat wings, three of them today, had to come together, in proper order, to constitute the division. To the uninitiated it could look like 150 reckless planes playing a risky game of tag. All over East Anglia, where the Eighth Air Force bases were con-centrated, people were awakened on mission mornings by the roar of B-17s assembling overhead. It took so long—sometimes an hour or more—that the Germans, with their sophisticated lis-tening devices, always knew when the Americans were coming. What they didn't know was where.

On this morning the assembly was relatively smooth, thanks partly to use of such shepherding devices as smoke signals and flares. The Third Division was soon ready to head east toward the Continent. But where were the eighteen squadrons of Amer-ican Thunderbolts and sixteen squadrons of British Spitfire fight-ers scheduled to escort them at least as far as Holland? And where was the First Division, which by now should have begun assembling its 230 planes for its mission to Schweinfurt. If the Third Division's function as a decoy was to work properly, the first would have to follow within at least a half to three-quarters of an hour. If it was any later, the German fighters would have time to attack the Third, then land at their nearby bases, rearm, refuel, and still take off in plenty of time to attack the First.

LeMay got on the radio to Fred Anderson and asked him what was going on.

The First Division, Anderson announced, hadn't yet been able to get off the ground. There were low clouds and fog at all the First Division fields.

LeMay was furious. There were low clouds and fog at his fields, too, but his planes got off the ground. Years later, he was still miffed about it.

"If the First Division had been concentrating on the same sort of bad-weather-instrument-takeoff procedure which we had been developing for a solid month," he insisted, "they might have been able to get off the ground. A few minutes late, perhaps; but still part of the originally planned show. And we couldn't horse around about this—return to our bases, sit on the ground, take off once more—even if weather permitted. We had to land in Africa before dark. It's a long way to Africa from England.''[5]

But despite his fury, he continued to circle, waiting for word that the First Division was on its way up to take its place behind him. The word didn't come. Fifteen minutes passed, then a half-hour. Each time he talked to Fred Anderson by radio the situation seemed more bleak. Finally it occurred to him that the entire mission was in danger of being scrapped. At any moment now, Anderson might order him to abort the whole operation. That would seem to him inexcusable. But fortunately, there was a way to prevent it. Suddenly, the radio in LeMay's lead bomber went dead.

Ira Eaker, on the ground with Anderson at Bomber Command headquarters, assumed immediately that LeMay had turned it off so he wouldn't hear any order to return to the ground.[6] But Eaker, surprisingly, wasn't upset about it. ''I might have done the same thing myself,'' he said later. ''And so would Anderson. It's such a job to get the bombers assembled it's destructive of morale to cancel because then you've got to do it again the next day.''

It is not entirely clear even now whether LeMay turned off his radio purposely. In any case, Anderson finally did get a message to him, perhaps through one of the other planes in his formation. The message was ''Go.'' So LeMay turned his armada eastward at about 9:30 A.M. and headed for the unfriendly Continent. The First Division was still on the ground. It was not destined to get into the air for another three hours, by which time the German fighters, having finished their business with LeMay's planes, would be ready for it.

Riding as copilot in Kenny's lead plane, LeMay searched the surrounding air space in vain for the thirty-four squadrons of fighter planes that were supposed to be escorting them at least to the limits of their short range. Today, it seemed, their range was shorter than ever. They apparently hadn't even made it out to the ends of their own runways.

The same could not be said for the German fighters. Lt. Col. Beirne Lay, a member of Ira Eaker's staff who was getting some extra combat experience today in preparation for taking command of a new heavy bomb wing, watched from one of the rearmost planes of the rearmost One-hundredth Group as the Focke-Wulf 190s began closing in over Diest, Belgium, about seventeen minutes after the Fortresses crossed the coast of the Continent.

Someone on the interplane radio said, "Fighters at two o'clock low!" A battle unprecedented in the history of aerial warfare was about to be joined.

When Lay first saw those radial-engined 190s he entertained a momentary hope they might be Thunderbolts, which were also powered by radial engines, but that hope was dashed when two of them raced through the formation at a closing speed of five hundred miles per hour—so fast that one of them nicked a pair of B-17s in passing. Smoke trailed from the wings of the stricken bombers but they remained in formation. The 190 was not so fortunate. Smoke was also trailing from its nose, and metal was flying from its wing, as it plunged downward.[7]

Within five minutes, whole squadrons of German fighters were climbing from below to engage them. By 10:40, when the tail-end One-hundredth Group was over Eupen, the sky around it was full of bullet-spitting ME-109s and FW-190s, but there were no Thunderbolts in sight. A twelve-ship squadron of 109s came in from twelve to two o'clock firing machine guns and .20 millimeter cannons. An exit door of one of the forward B-17s came hurtling through the formation, followed by a man who had apparently been sucked through that door when it was blown away. He was "clasping his knees to his head, revolving like a diver in a triple somersault."

A stricken B-17 fell gradually out of formation to the right, then moments later disintegrated in one giant explosion. As the fighters kept pressing their attacks, one plane after another felt their fury. Engine parts, wing tips, even tail assemblies were blasted free. Rearward planes had to fly through showers of exit doors, emergency hatches, sheets of metal, partially opened parachutes, and other debris, in addition to human bodies, some German, some American, some dead, some still alive and writhing. As more German fighters arrived and the battle intensified, there were so many disintegrating airplanes that "sixty 'chutes in the air at one time were hardly worth a second look." A man crawled out of the copilot's window of a Fortress engulfed in flames. He was the only person to emerge. Standing precariously on the wing, he reached back inside for his parachute—he could hardly have gotten through the window with his chute on—used one hand to get into the harness while he clung to the plane with the other, then dove off the wing for an apparently safe descent, only to be hit by the plane's onrushing horizontal stabilizer. His chute did not open.

"After we had been under constant attack for a solid hour," Lay reported, "it appeared certain that the One-hundredth Group was faced with annihilation. Seven of our group had been shot down, the sky was still mottled with rising fighters and it was only 1120 hours, with the target time still thirty-five minutes away. I doubt if a man in the group visualized the possibility of our getting much further without one-hundred percent loss. I know that I had long since mentally accepted the fact of death."

German fighters were swarming all over the armada but concentrating on the already battered and therefore more vulnerable second and third combat wings. Twin-engine ME-110s appeared on the scene to help the 109s and 190s. Some of them shot rockets from a distance. Others introduced a new tactic—aerial bombs dropped from above to explode in the midst of the Fortresses. Damaged, and therefore straggling, Fortresses were virtually doomed as whole German squadrons bore in on them.

The least damaged of the combat wings was the leading one in which LeMay was riding, an unusual circumstance because the Germans often zeroed in on the leaders. Today, however, the leading wing was composed of three groups, and therefore may have appeared less vulnerable to the Germans than the two-group wings that followed. Near Kaiserslautern the wing suffered its first loss when one of its planes fell out with its left wing in flames. The armada had now sustained more than two hundred attacks and had lost fifteen planes. Almost all the Fortresses had suffered some damage, yet they pressed on toward Regensburg, the survivors still holding their ranks, moving forward to fill in for their fallen comrades. Several were flying on two or three engines. Some had shell holes the size of doors.

Though LeMay knew that the men behind him had absorbed a vicious onslaught, there was no way for him to realize the extent of the damage. He had reason, in fact, to feel some satisfaction as the Fortresses reached the Initial Point from which they would begin their bomb run. Despite the onslaught, he had led his division to the target. And now, as if by miracle, the fighters were suddenly disappearing, apparently short of fuel and ammunition. The bombers still in formation could look through clear skies at the huge aircraft plant ahead which was their target. At 11:45 A.M., Lt. Dunstan T. Abel, the bombardier in LeMay's plane, dropped his load of explosives and incendiaries directly on the factory's buildings, and the rest of the planes in the group, releasing on his cue, did likewise. During the next twenty-two minutes, the planes of LeMay's task force dropped 303 tons of bombs on the Messerschmitt plant in what proved later to be one of the most accurate bombardments of the war.

The respite from fighter attack was not of long duration. Even before the Fortresses finished dropping their bombs, fifteen ME-110s and Junkers-88s caught up with the 94th and 385th Groups to continue their harassment as the task force flew south toward Africa. At the postbombing rally point, the Fortresses of the lead wing resumed their normal formation and continued south to a second rally point just north of the Alps, where LeMay's plane led them into two big circles to give the second and third wings time to catch them. By now the German fighters had disappeared but so had three more of the bombers. Two others, with no hope of reaching Africa, had headed toward Switzerland for sanctuary.

After circling twice at the north end of the Brenner Pass, the first wing had been joined by the second, but the third hadn't yet caught them and it would be foolish to wait any longer because a new problem was looming—shortage of fuel. The long wait over England for approval to launch the mission had used precious gasoline which would have given the bombers a comfortable reserve. Now they had no appreciable reserve. Some of the planes might not even have enough gas to reach Africa. LeMay gave the order and the first two wings moved on down the boot of Italy which, that day, was as bright and sunny as it is advertised to be. At an air base near Verona there were fighters on the ground but they must have been Italian. They did not come up to attack.

As the task force left the southern tip of Italy and headed across the Mediterranean, it began a slow, gradual descent to save gasoline. LeMay could sense a relaxation among his men at this point. Perhaps he himself was beginning to relax. He didn't even complain when he noticed the formation becoming sloppy. He realized that some planes might be forced to fall back to conserve what little gasoline they had left.

The lead navigator hit the African coast about eighteen miles off course (which didn't win him any congratulations from LeMay) but soon located the airfield at Telergma where the first forty-four planes landed, one right behind another at the shortest possible intervals, about 6 P.M. Those who couldn't make it to Telergma, some distance inland, found refuge on fields at equally desolate places near the coast called Bone and Berteaux. Four planes that couldn't make it even to Bone, came down in wheat fields and dry lake beds. Four that couldn't make it to the shore ditched in the Mediterranean. Two of the crews were saved by air-sea rescue units.

When LeMay's plane landed at Telergma and taxied toward the conglomeration of ramshackle structures around the operations tower, he was still expecting to find in those buildings "a B-17 parts depot" with "all the parts necessary plus 500 mechanics." What he found was a few housekeeping enlisted men on duty, no mechanics, and no parts depot. The war in Africa had moved on to Sicily, and with it all the parts and mechanics Lauris Norstad had described so glowingly when LeMay visited Africa a few weeks earlier. Even the project officer assigned to help the incoming B-17s was absent.

LeMay was still fuming about all this when Col. Beirne Lay arrived with the twelve planes of the rearmost One-hundredth Group which had somehow managed to survive. Lay, who had just flown through Armageddon, and had watched countless Fortresses fall, including nine from the One-hundredth alone, was amazed to find LeMay complaining, not about the losses, but about the conditions at Telergma. Didn't LeMay know what a beating his division had taken?

The plain fact was he did not know. This mission, like all others, had been flown in radio silence to avoid giving valuable information to the enemy. The leading Ninety-sixth Group with which he flew had lost no planes. He realized the air battle waged most intensely several miles behind him had been ferocious but he did not know how destructive it had been until Lay described it to him and, after all the planes had landed, he got the preliminary loss-damage report. Twenty-four of his 146 Fortresses had failed to make Africa. Most of those that did make it were damaged, many so severely they were not flyable. And here they were in Africa, without the mechanics or the parts essential for repair.

LeMay, aware that General Eaker expected him to bomb another target the next day on his way home, sent a message to England including the preliminary report of his task force's condition. Then he ate what he could find at a canteen built by the French when the base had been theirs, and finally, on this clear, star-filled desert night, settled down, like the other exhausted men he had brought to this depressing place, and fell asleep under the wing of his airplane, using his parachute as a pillow.

By the time Eaker received LeMay's alarming message, he already had the bad news about the Schweinfurt losses. Though the damage to the vital German ball-bearing plants had been, apparently, as great as he had hoped, thirty-six of the 230 fortresses in Gen. Bob Williams's First Division task force had been shot down. Added to LeMay's loss of twenty-four, this brought the day's toll to a disastrous sixty, without counting the many planes that were so badly damaged they might never fly again. Though Eaker had expected the day's casualties to be high, he had not expected to break all records. And he was especially worried about the condition of LeMay's force, because by this time he was well acquainted with LeMay. He had scheduled the Third Division for a mission the next day on the way back from Africa. It seemed apparent that the division was in no shape to fly so soon but LeMay was the kind of man who might attempt it anyway if he was committed to it. Eaker decided he'd better fly to Africa and find out for himself how badly the Third Division had been battered.

When Eaker reached Telergma the evening of August 19, he found that LeMay had set up headquarters in a tent, from which he was directing his own flight crews, since he had no qualified mechanics, in the repair of their bombers. They had already begun a giant cannibalizing operation, dismantling the hopelessly damaged Fortresses to use their parts in rebuilding the less damaged ones. Though most of the crewmen were poorly, if at all, qualified to do this work, they did have the advantage of advice and instruction from one mechanic among them who knew as much as anybody about the B-17—LeMay himself.

When Eaker landed at Telergma, his first question to LeMay was, "When will you be able to go back?"

LeMay's answer was, "As soon as we can hang some bombs and put some fuel in these crates."

But that would not be as soon as either of them would like. It would take time to finish cannibalizing the derelict bombers for the restoration of the merely crippled ones. And it would take almost as much time to refuel them because it would have to be done by hand from storage barrels. (It was four days before the men assigned to refueling were able to get the job done.)

Eaker, while depressed by the devastation he saw, was also amazed at LeMay. The man showed no signs of discouragement, nor did he waste any time complaining, even about Lauris Norstad, who had accompanied Eaker to Telergma to explain his bum steer about the facilities there. Though LeMay had been forced to delay his scheduled return to England, he still intended to bomb German facilities at Bordeaux on the way home.

Eaker, surveying the wreckage around him, shook his head and said, "No, Curt. There'll be no mission. Your men will not be subjected to hostilities on the return to England. We'll see to it that you go across north Africa and over the Bay of Biscay at night."

This was a kind and considerate offer, but LeMay had some powerful arguments against it. If he were to sneak around France at night, the Germans would conclude, quite properly, that they had defeated him. And worse than that, so would his own men. In a few days they would be ready to return proudly across France in broad daylight, bombing on the way and proving to the enemy that they were still a formidable force. These arguments prevailed and the Bordeaux mission was rescheduled for whatever date LeMay decided he was ready.

On August 24, exactly a week after the Regensburg mission, LeMay, having salvaged and repaired as many planes as possible under the almost impossible circumstances, was as ready as he could get for his homeward mission against Bordeaux. Recollections and even official reports differ as to the number of planes he was able to muster for this operation. LeMay himself recalls that he "came back with around 80 flyable B-17s." At a meeting with his group commanders August 28, 1943, four days after his return, he mentioned that they had managed to get "85 planes into commission" for the Bordeaux raid. But an Eighth Air Force Bomber Command report dated September 5, 1943, stated that "57 attacked Bordeaux on the 24th of August on their return to the U.K." The same report stated, however, that, as of that date, only "eleven of the aircraft dispatched to Regensburg are still in north Africa," which indicates that at least a score of Fortresses, while in no condition to take part in a mission, were nevertheless sufficiently repaired to fly home.

The best estimate is that of the 145 B-17s with which LeMay left England for Regensburg and Africa, at least half were either lost or would never fly another mission. But on August 24, most of the survivors "returned proudly across France in broad daylight," dropping 144 tons of bombs on the German-held air base at Bordeaux.

CHAPTER SEVEN

The Schweinfurt-Regensburg losses had been so far beyond imagination that Ira Eaker feared he would now feel renewed pressure, from Washington as well as London, to cancel the daylight precision-bombing offensive and adopt the British method of area bombing at night. The RAF had no choice but to bomb indiscriminately at night because their planes carried only a minimum of defensive armament and were not equipped with the remarkably accurate Norden bombsight. Eaker was still convinced that with proper fighter support the B-17 could conquer the daylight skies over Germany. It offered the only possible opportunity to destroy important pinpoint targets such as aircraft and ball-bearing factories, oil refineries, and submarine facilities. But when Hap Arnold read the loss figures, would he back away from the daylight strategy?[1]

Eaker, knowing Arnold as well as he did, shouldn't even have given a thought to such a possibility. Instead of backing away, Arnold demanded full speed ahead. Impatient as always, he reminded Eaker that the new B-17s were now arriving in England at a steady pace, and that he should therefore press on with the offensive as if there had been no losses at Schweinfurt and Regensburg.

To Eaker, this strategy, at the moment, was only slightly more feasible than the abandonment of the daylight offensive would have been. It was true that new B-17s were now arriving at a steady pace, but not yet at a very rapid pace. How could one press on as if nothing had happened after losing almost 150 bombers in one day's operation. The Eighth would have to stop, at least for a short time, to catch its breath. Not until August 27, ten days after Schweinfurt-Regensburg, was Eaker able to launch another full-scale operation, and it was only across the English

Channel to Calais, where the Germans were building concrete rocket-launch pads.

By this time, however, the new planes and crews were arriving much more rapidly. The B-17s still limited their bombings to relatively safe areas—on August 31, September 2, and September 3, they went to Paris. But on September 6, 338 of them, many with rookie crews, went to Stuttgart and soon wished they hadn't. In one of the worst missions of the war, forty-five Fortresses were shot down by German fighters without even the consolation of knowing they had done some good. Thanks to bad weather as well as the fighters, Stuttgart was as safe that day as if no American bombers had even come close to it. Once again the Eighth would have to slow its pace long enough to recoup its losses.

Despite the losses, LeMay, like Eaker, held steadfast to his belief that the daylight strategy was destined to work. Shortly after returning from Africa, he told an interviewer, "I think everybody is convinced now that four-engine bombers are here to stay, that they can't be stopped. We have never been turned back from a target and never will be turned back from a target."[2]

He realized, though, that for the big offensive which at this time had no more than begun, some changes would be needed. First of all, the fighters had to increase their range. The Stuttgart raid offered a perfect example of this need. One of his groups, the 388th, lost eleven of the twenty-one planes it sent out that day. "I visited that group," he told the interviewer, "as soon as I could get over there, to see how they were taking it. You know what they said? 'We're glad it was us that got hit so bad today instead of the 390th. They already lost nine.' "

LeMay was delighted to find that the 388th Group's morale remained so high, and that the men could show such concern for another stricken group despite their own losses, but he remained horrified at the continuing loss rate. Like most of his colleagues, he was convinced that if such losses were to be avoided, the fighters had to figure out how to accompany the bombers all the way to the target. The day after the Stuttgart raid, 185 Fortresses attacked three targets in Belgium and France, escorted all the way by P-47s, and suffered not one loss. "No bomber," he pointed out, "had an encounter that day with any enemy aircraft. The fighters kept them away."

He did not believe, however, that the bombers could simply sit and hope the fighter problems would soon be solved. The war wouldn't wait to be fought. The bombers had gone it alone so far. They might have to continue doing so in spite of the ever-intensifying German resistance. To survive, they would have to become even more cohesive. The units would have to get closer and closer together even as they grew in size.

"We are trying to weld them into one big fighting force and succeeding," he told his interviewer in September 1943. "The normal gunner on a crew knows his squadron; he sees some of the group activities, very little of the wing activities. Of the doings of the higher echelons he is more or less vague. In the forthcoming big formations we are going to fight as a combat wing; we are trying to get the crews to be loyal to the combat wing. The squadron is practically abolished on the stations. Three stations [groups] fight together to make a combat wing. So we are trying to fit them into the big picture, have a little rivalry between squadrons, something like that, but to think of the big team."

A football coach would have no trouble understanding LeMay. He never tired of talking about the importance of teams and teamwork. It was as much a cliché then as it is now, but it was also extremely pertinent to what he was trying to do. "Air warfare is getting so complicated," LeMay said in 1943, "that no one man can ever expect to know all the details of every job. . . . A normal bombing mission requires so much teamwork that unless your combat crews have mutual confidence and respect for every member of the team, you are not going to get good results. They've got to know just what everyone else is doing and why, and they must have confidence in the overall plan. I [try] to make my people feel . . . important in this war—and they [are]."

One way for a commander to increase teamwork, he believed, was to go on missions. His interviewer asked him about this: "I understand you've made as many as any, if not more. Your reputation is that you always take the lead in dangerous missions."

To LeMay that was a necessary element of combat leadership. His men, he said, "like to think the Old Man knows what he's doing. . . . We came into this war fresh; most of us hadn't had any actual combat. . . . How can any commanding officer send his people into combat when he knows nothing about it? So I started out leading all missions personally. Not only did I feel that I ought to lead the people fighting under me, but I had to find out things. . . . You have to get in there and fight to find out what it's all about." After the Regensburg-Bordeaux mission, however, he had again been forbidden by Anderson and

Eaker to "get in there and fight."[3] He had now to resume leading the Third Division from the ground. And to add to his embarrassment, not just from the ground, but from a sinfully comfortable country mansion.

On September 2, at Elveden Hall, he finally met for the first time a man of considerable importance to him—Gen. Henry H. "Hap" Arnold, the Air Force chief of staff. A few years earlier, LeMay had once visited Arnold's office, with several others, to receive a citation. But after fifteen years in the Air Force, he had not until now met the man on an individual basis.[4]

Arnold had come to England to see for himself what the Eighth Air Force was doing with all the B-17s he was sending, but perhaps also to get a look at some of the young commanders who were just emerging into prominence in the war against Germany. He had some deep worries on his mind, and among the most serious of them was a new bomber he was shepherding through the early stages of production—the enormous B-29, a plane half again as big as the B-17. When the B-29 was ready, he would need some dynamic and experienced combat commanders to get it into operation. And it wouldn't be an easy job because the B-29 was an airplane beset by problems so serious they threatened Arnold's reputation. He had virtually bet his career on the development of that plane, which, with its promised range and bomb load, offered the only hope of an effective air offensive against Japan. In the fall of 1943, it was beginning to look as if he had made a foolish bet. Several billion dollars had been spent rushing the B-29 into production in the hope, originally, that it could begin operating against Japan in the latter months of 1943. The schedule had been set back to the beginning of 1944, but Arnold now realized that deadline could not be met either. Boeing's production of air frames was proceeding satisfactorily; it was the delivery of the plane's newly designed Wright twenty-two-hundred-horsepower Duplex Cyclone engine that had failed to keep pace. These engines were crawling off the assembly lines. Only a hundred of them (enough for twenty-five planes) had yet been produced at a time when more than a thousand were due. Arnold's staff had prepared an impatient memo to Robert Lovett, assistant secretary of war for air, pleading for correction of this situation, but the memo was not impatient enough for Arnold.[5] He had scrawled across the top of the draft copy: "Poor presentation. What I want is a letter showing how our plans for B-29 units would be completed for early 1944 operation if it were not for lack of engines. H.H.A.''

Arnold, whose health was precarious at this time after two serious heart attacks, realized he might find himself prematurely retired if he didn't soon get the B-29 off the ground and on its way to Japan. From Eaker he had already received such exciting reports about LeMay that he may have made this trip to Elveden Hall with the special purpose of meeting the young fellow, but if so, he didn't mention it to LeMay. It wasn't Arnold's way. Indeed, he hadn't even seen fit as yet to promote LeMay, who was still a colonel, though he was doing a major general's job. That was an oversight, incidentally, that LeMay did not appreciate.[6]

"When I got to the Third Division," he later recalled, "there was an inspector general's report which said a commander of a unit not of the rank called for by the unit, if he was commanding 'at the direction of the president,' and if the unit had been commanded by an officer of the higher rank, and it was in combat, then that officer [of the lower rank] could draw the pay of the higher rank. There had been a brigadier general [Fred Anderson] commanding. I was commanding 'at the direction of the president' [because] there were a half dozen people [eligible for the job] who outranked me. [Ordinarily if an officer is placed in command above others who outrank him, the president, as commander-in-chief, must approve it.] So I was a colonel in a major general's job and we were in combat. I called in my finance officer [Capt. F. L. Greene] and said, 'Look at this. Get me a major general's pay.' He couldn't quite do that because the outfit was never commanded by a major general, but he got me a brigadier general's pay."

Finally, on September 28, less than four weeks after Arnold's visit to Elveden Hall, LeMay got the brigadier general's star to match the pay. But he hadn't forgotten or forgiven the unexplained delay in his promotion. "It was about time," he said to several staff members when they congratulated him.

For most of September 1943, the Eighth Air Force, while rebuilding its strength, husbanded its resources with relatively safe missions against France. After the September 6 Stuttgart fiasco it was three weeks before the Forts went back into Germany. During this time, LeMay was even more frustrated than his men because while they were flying minimally productive missions, he wasn't allowed to fly at all. Some of his excess nervous energy he was able to work off either hunting or shooting on the range. He was an expert marksman with both rifles and pistols. During the pheasant season, British landowners, by long established tradition, allowed hunters on their property with the provision that they would share the fallen birds. They extended special invitations to Americans stationed in the area because with many potential British hunters absent on war duty, or unable to get hold of ammunition, the birds were proliferating rapidly and eating more than their fair share of the crops. Shooting was one of LeMay's few recreations, especially since he actively disliked social events. He also played on the headquarters softball team, wearing a faded red baseball cap and an old summer flying suit, with his colonel's eagles still imprinted on the shoulders. He was one of the team's heaviest hitters.

On one occasion his intelligence officer, Carl Norcross, thinking a night out would do the commander some good, talked him into accepting a dinner invitation from some of the neighboring gentry. But the people at the dinner, especially the young British matrons, spoke in such a rapid, aristocratic garble that LeMay remained silent and looked miserable throughout the evening. On the way back to Elveden Hall, Norcross asked him if he had found it difficult to understand the ladies.

"Didn't get a damn word," he growled.

Though no longer allowed to fly missions himself, he continued to keep close surveillance over those who did. August Kissner, his chief of staff, recalls a morning when the 385th Group had trouble taking off for a mission because its airfield had just been hit by German bombs. The group commander, Col. Elliott Vandevanter, tried to reach his wing commander for advice but was told by an aide that the wing commander was asleep and not to be awakened. Vandevanter then called LeMay, who first told him what to do about his problem, then instructed Kissner to drive to the wing commander's headquarters immediately, wake him up, and fire him on the spot.[7]

Despite this example of how tough LeMay could be, Kissner did not agree that he deserved the "tough guy" reputation with which he had been tagged.

"He was always intensely serious rather than tough," Kissner insists. "His responsibility was so much on his mind every minute of the day that he wanted results from others in the earliest possible time. He never raised his voice, but by virtue of facial expression he could seem to be angered and adamant. He demanded results in a few words and [then] frequently walked away. To me he was never tough. He respected the ability of each of his contemporaries and felt they knew what they should do. His squadron and group commanders learned soon to put pressure on maintenance [and other sections] about details in readiness for the missions.''

LeMay himself has often indicated that a sense of his own lack of qualifications for the various jobs he was assigned, and a fear of failure, were the main driving forces behind his serious commitment to his work. Kissner suggests that his extraordinary sense of responsibility, not only for doing his job but for the safety of his men, was an equally important factor.

"At Elveden Hall," Kissner recalls, "he kept a batch of B-17 models on the ends of ramrod-stem stands of different heights, and [by shifting these models back and forth into various combinations, he would try] for hours to figure out a formation for reducing casualties and increasing the defense against German fighters. I don't know why he tried to be better than others in that duty but . . . his responsibility weighed on him and I think that's the explanation.''

On September 27, 1943, the bombers returned to Germany with a mission against the port of Emden. Results were so poor they had to repeat it five days later. But this was a fairly safe run because the distance was so short the P-47s, even with small drop tanks, could accompany them all the way. On October 4, when they lost their fighter protection at Aachen and had to go the rest of the way to Frankfurt alone, they saw twelve of their planes go down. On October 8, they lost another thirty in a mission to Bremen. The next day they caught the Germans by surprise with an attack on aircraft factories at Marienburg where they did so much damage that RAF chief Sir Charles Portal, after seeing the photos, declared it "the best high altitude bombing we have seen in this war." However, twenty-eight bombers were lost that day and thirty more fell at Munster the following day.

In LeMay's Third Division, the One-hundredth was the hardest hit group during this series of missions. At Bremen October 8, the One hundredth lost seven planes, which so depleted the group it was able to send only thirteen against Munster on October 10. Carl Norcross remembers vividly LeMay's postmission briefing on October 11 when, in the process of calling on the group leaders one after another, he came to "the One-hundredth Group."

Robert Rosenthal, a young lieutenant from Brooklyn, New York, arose from his chair. "The room quieted down," Norcross recalls. "We all realized that this was the pilot of the only [One-hundredth Group] plane that came back the day before." In an unrelenting seven-minute onslaught, German fighters had shot down twelve of its thirteen planes. Rosenthal's Fortress, riddled with bullets and both of its waist gunners wounded, dropped its bombs on Munster, then continued to fight off the Germans all the way back to the English Channel.

Though everyone had reason to be proud of Rosenthal and his crew, LeMay was far from happy with Rosenthal's boss, Col. Chick Harding, a one-time West Point football player who was the commander of the ill-fated group now known as "the Bloody One-hundredth." Harding was a convivial fellow, popular with his men partly because he was quick to defend them but not so quick to discipline them. John R. Nillson's history of the One-hundredth, *The Story of the Century,* describes a scene in the group's officers' club during which "Harding mirthfully strummed a base fiddle, while fist fights were fought between his men and uninvited visitors from the 95th [Group]."

LeMay was as aware of such incidents as he was of the One-hundredth's high casualty rate, but he had known Harding a long time and liked him so well he hated the thought of firing him. Still new as a division commander, LeMay hadn't yet faced up to the unpleasant responsibility of firing people, and especially people of such high rank. He had been a colonel himself until just recently. And until his promotion to brigadier general, Harding had outranked him by four years. So LeMay kept putting off the distasteful duty of replacing his old friend. And even forty years later, LeMay was still critical of himself for being too "soft-hearted" about the man.

"We had been together at Selfridge Field [in the early thirties]," LeMay said recently. "He wasn't doing very well [with the One-hundredth]. I knew I had to fire him but I just couldn't. I thought he'd snap out of it. Anyway, I should've fired him but I didn't. Then fate stepped in. He had a gall bladder problem or something. Had to go home for an operation. That taught me a lesson. It took time to get the One-hundredth back in shape."[8]

On October 14, 291 Fortresses of the Eighth Air Force fought their way to the ball-bearing factories in Schweinfurt again on a mission as rigorous and destructive to both sides as the famous Regensburg-Schweinfurt operation of August 17. These two op-

erations produced air battles which rank even today as the greatest of all time. The Third Division damage was relatively light
this time—15 of its 142 planes went down—while the First Division lost 45 of its 149. Once more, the German factories suffered enormous damage, but the American losses were
prohibitive. In spite of these losses, LeMay, for one, remained
optimistic.

"The First Division losses were severe yesterday," he told his
men at the postmission briefing on October 15. "We got it on
the Munster raid. It will swing back and forth. The fighters are
the last weapon the Germans have, but they will not stop us.
From our intelligence reports we get from Germany from underground sources, we are accomplishing our mission—to destroy the German war industries. We are doing it! We are going
to have to pay a price for it, but we are doing it. . . . They are
using four-engine planes and accurate reports state they are using
a lot of obsolete stuff. This could be a sign of desperation—
putting rocket guns on everything they can get their hands on. I
think we will find when they put rocket guns on old planes they
have nothing else . . . which means they are in bad shape."

It is difficult to say, in retrospect, whether LeMay was as optimistic as he sounded, or whether he was simply trying to buoy
the spirits of his men in the face of the ravages being visited
upon them, day after day. The loss of the sixty Fortresses shot
at Schweinfurt, plus the hundred or more others too badly damaged to fly again, was a matter of such concern to the Air Force
that Hap Arnold instituted an immediate press campaign, assuring the American public there was no need to worry.

"This attack on Schweinfurt," Arnold said in a statement on
October 15, "was not merely a spectacular air raid. It was an
engagement between large armies—a major campaign. In a period of a few hours we invaded German-held Europe to a depth
of five hundred miles, sacked and crippled one of her most vital
enterprises.

"We did it in daylight and we did it with precision, aiming
our explosives with the care and accuracy of a marksman firing
a rifle at a bullseye."

On the 15th, one day after the mission, it was a bit early for
Arnold to know whether his "marksmen" had been that accurate
(they were in fact quite accurate though not devastatingly precise), but it wasn't too early for him to know that the Air Force
might soon be under attack from Americans as well as Germans

unless he acted quickly to forestall criticism. Congressmen friendly to the Air Force made statements in support of the B-17 offensive. President Roosevelt at a press conference said (albeit reluctantly) that he wasn't worried about the losses. Ira Eaker described to the press the great damage done at Schweinfurt. And even LeMay received the war correspondents.

On October 15, he told a *New York Times* correspondent that by the spring of 1944, Allied air power would systematically destroy Nazi industry and neutralize Germany's ability to carry on the war. And on October 16, speaking again to the *Times* correspondent, he said, "the only real defense Germany can offer against our bombers is to destroy them on the ground or in the factories, and obviously she can't do either."

Public statements of this kind were so uncharacteristic of LeMay they seem most likely to have been part of a design he did not institute. Such remarks, coming within forty-eight hours after the Germans shot down sixty Fortresses in a single mission, must have sounded almost ludicrously optimistic to him even as he uttered them. But even if he didn't believe his own words literally, they reflected his continuing optimism about the outcome of the air war. He had lost none of his faith in the Air Force daylight precision-bombing doctrine.

Ira Eaker, in an effort to impart more of that faith to people on the home front, ordered LeMay to lead a delegation of combat officers back to the States for a few weeks in November to speak to training commanders and tell them what to emphasize in their schools. Aside from the opportunity it gave him to see his wife and daughter, LeMay had no enthusiasm for the assignment. He hated meetings and he hated to make speeches.[9]

Arriving in New York on the liner (now a troop ship) *Queen Elizabeth* (because the north Atlantic air route was closed by the weather), he and his companions hurried to Washington where Helen was waiting to greet him. He even wrangled a few days free to spend with her and their daughter, Janie, in Cleveland, but not until after he spent some time talking to Hap Arnold and his staff about the pressing needs of the Eighth Air Force, and reassuring them of its eventual success in destroying German industry.

Arnold, of course, shared LeMay's concern about the air war in Europe, but he was even more worried at this time about the air war against Japan, which hadn't yet begun, and wasn't likely ever to do so unless he could get some movement out of the

B-29. The plane had performed beautifully on its first test flight, September 21, 1942, but had been in trouble ever since. On February 18, 1943, the second B-29 test plane, flown by its original test pilot, Boeing's Eddie Allen, had crashed with an engine on fire. A faulty cooling system had caused the crash. Now, nine months later, B-29 engines still suffered from a faulty cooling system. And the automatic firing control system wasn't yet working right. And these were only two of the many problems still plaguing the aircraft. Most of them were caused by the speed with which it was being hastened into production. Every new plane has bugs which must be worked out. The B-29, because of its size and many original features, suffered from so many bugs it had forced Arnold, on October 11, to write what was for him a humiliating memorandum to President Roosevelt:

In connection with the bombing of Japan from China by B-29s, I regret exceedingly to have to inform you that there has been a holdup in production of engines. It looks now as if it will be impossible to get the required number of B-29s together in China to start bombing before the first of March, and with a possibility of not getting them there before the first of April. At this writing, I expect to have 150 B-29s in China by March 1st, of which 100 can be used against Japan.

But in fact, that last sentence was more of a hope than an expectation, and Roosevelt knew it. He wrote a sharp letter to General Marshall on October 15, expressing his displeasure about the continuing B-29 delays. Arnold, the plane's chief advocate, would be in serious trouble if he didn't soon get it moving. Perhaps with this in mind he let LeMay know he might soon be transferred to B-29s, but nothing definite was promised.

LeMay's fame had spread so rapidly that he discovered he was now something of a hero at the Pentagon, but he didn't create as much excitement there in November 1943, as did another hero—movie hero Clark Gable, who had also become, in the public mind, an Air Force hero. Captain Gable, a gunner with five missions over Europe to his credit, had been sent back to the States, an Air Medal and fifty thousand feet of film in hand, to produce a training film. General LeMay won some smiles and admiring glances as he walked through the Pentagon corridors. But Captain Gable found secretaries lined up ''six deep to watch him walk by,'' and to gasp at how ''marvelous'' he was. Gable was also modest about his combat accomplishments. Had he hit any German planes? No. What did he think of his Eighth Air Force colleagues? "I don't think I could put that in words. They're a pretty good bunch."

LeMay stayed in Washington only long enough to talk to Air Force people and to pick up the schedule for his tour. Then he and Helen flew to Cleveland where she and Janie were still living with her parents. LeMay's first duty there was to prove to Janie that she actually had a father and it was he. She had grown so much during his thirteen-month absence she "looked to me as if she was about ready for college." But to her he looked like someone whose existence she had begun to doubt. And even after she had convinced herself he was a real father, she wasn't quite satisfied.

"Daddy, let's go out on the porch," she suggested after dinner on his first day at home.

Since it was a cold November evening in suburban Cleveland, and he was basking in the luxury of central-heating for the first time in more than a year, he was less than enthusiastic about the idea. But when she insisted, they bundled up, went outside, and sat freezing on the porch swing for almost an hour.

Janie never did tell him why this was so important to her, but when they finally went back inside to thaw out, Helen explained it to him. The kids in the neighborhood had been telling her they didn't believe she had a father. She wanted them to know they were wrong.

It was a still uneasy America that LeMay saw on this trip home. The war, both in Europe and the Pacific, was proving painfully difficult to win. Twenty-three months after entering the conflict, the U.S. government announced that 23,592 of its men had been killed; 33,605 wounded; 32,556 were missing; and 26,130 were prisoners of the enemies. All this despite the fact that there had been no large engagement as yet between the armies. Nor was there even now a definite promise of an invasion of Hitler's Europe which would bring about such an engagement. As for our effort against Japan, we were still island hopping, more than two thousand miles from its homeland. And the gradual disclosures of the extent of the Pearl Harbor disaster made the public realize that our Pacific enemy was no pushover.

Most Americans, at the same time, were also uncomfortable about the wartime alliance with Josef Stalin's Soviet Communist regime, and the recent tendency of the American press to refer

to him as Russia's "premier" rather than its dictator. Still fresh
in many minds were his purge trials and his inhuman starvation
of five million Ukrainian peasants who defied his agricultural
edicts in the 1930s. Even fresher was his 1940 alliance of convenience with Adolf Hitler. To a majority of Americans, Stalin
seemed no better than Hitler, and probably more dangerous in
the long run.

As for the public attitude about the Air Force, it apparently
wasn't very positive or LeMay wouldn't have been sent home to
try to improve it. But at least the Air Force was striking some
blows against the German homeland. Where was the Army?
Bogged down in Italy. What good were they doing there? We
Americans didn't like Mussolini, but we weren't really mad at
the Italians, especially since they didn't really seem mad at us.
Or at anybody. Besides the fact that the Army looked as if it was
fighting in the wrong place, it was getting some less than favorable publicity because of what one of its officers had done to one
of its enlisted men. The truth was now emerging about an incident the previous August when Lieut. Gen. George S. Patton, a
tank commander, accused a hospitalized private of shirking his
duty and slapped the man.

On the home front, prices were going up rapidly but wages
weren't keeping pace. There was so much notoriety about fat,
cost-plus contracts awarded to war industries that labor unions
were demanding at least a bit of suet for their members. They
were staging strikes that the secure, government-financed em-
ployers were quick to call "un-American" and "treasonous."
President Roosevelt was walking the line between such factions,
but the combination of the domestic strife and the war seemed
to be affecting his health. He didn't look good on the rare occasions when he appeared in public. Besides, he was in his third
term. He wouldn't dare run for a fourth, would he? Or would
he? A lot of Republicans who didn't seem to think so were already warming up for the race to the White House. Though the
1944 election was still a year away, New York's little dandy Governor Thomas E. Dewey was already on the cover of *Time* magazine with a caption, "The next biggest job is good training for
the biggest." And Minnesota's former Governor Harold Stassen,
now a temporary lieutenant commander in the Navy, already had
an organization preparing for what would be the first of his endless attempts at the presidency.

The tour on which LeMay and his associates embarked that

fall included ten training schools plus several defense plants. The basic speech he made at each stop was a paean of praise for the men of the Eighth Air Force and an explanation of the importance of the job they were doing. By extension, therefore, it was also an explanation of the importance of the job these factory workers were doing, and these Air Force trainees would be doing if they were sent to England. It was a set speech he didn't even have to write. Sy Bartlett, a once-and-future screenwriter now on Eaker's staff (and the coauthor, with Beirne Lay, Jr., of *Twelve O'clock High*) wrote it for him. But for LeMay, who had never been called upon for such a public-relations venture, and who was always shy in public, it was a chore he was happy to put behind him. In mid-December he was back in Washington to receive the Distinguished Service Cross, and before Christmas he was back with his boys and his bombers in England, where he was more comfortable than he could ever be on the speaking circuit. Before leaving the States, however, he had received an order that he didn't dare to ignore. Janie, whose fifth birthday was approaching, had told her mother she wanted three things— a bicycle, a blue radio, and a baby sister.

"The man who makes bicycles has gone to war," Helen said, "and the man who makes blue radios has gone to war."

"And the man who makes baby sisters," Janie asked innocently, "has he gone to war?"[10]

He had, of course, but that didn't prevent him from making a blue radio. Because of the war, radios were difficult to find in the stores at that time, especially blue ones, so he set about building one, with the help of two radio technicians, as soon as he returned to England.

LeMay found some important changes in the Eighth Air Force on his return. Reinforcements were arriving at a rapid rate and his outfit was expanding into what would eventually become a fourteen-group division. Just after Christmas there was a wholesale rearrangement of command, sending Ira Eaker to the Mediterranean, bringing Tooey Spaatz and Jimmy Doolittle to England with Dwight Eisenhower. The preparation for the invasion of the Continent now began in earnest. But from the viewpoint of the Eighth Air Force there was another, even more important arrival. The long-range P-51 Mustang was coming to England, squadron after squadron, to escort the B-17s all the way to their targets and back. These slender, fast, durable, and deadly fighters, equipped now with Rolls-Royce Merlin engines, brought a dramatic change to the American daylight bombing offensive. When Hitler's air chief, Hermann Goering, was captured after the war, he told Tooey Spaatz that the day he saw the first P-51 over Germany he realized the war was decided. The Focke-Wulfs and Messerschmitts could not handle it.

The Fortresses had some more tough missions in the weeks to come, especially during their "Big Week" in late February when they dropped about five thousand tons of heavy metal on German aircraft plants, but even then they suffered only a 4 percent loss rate. Protected by the P-51s, they chewed away at those factories relentlessly. B-17 losses and German aircraft production both dropped so sharply that there was not one German fighter plane in the air over the Normandy beaches on June 6, 1944, the day of the Allied invasion.

By this time, Curtis LeMay's job with the Third Air Division was finished and his days in England were drawing to a close. But that didn't mean he was out of a job. It meant he was in for an even tougher one.

The first inkling of an impending transfer came March 3, 1944, when he was again promoted over the heads of several colleagues to become, at the age of thirty-seven, the youngest major general in the U.S. Army.[11] Shortly thereafter he heard a strong rumor about being sent to a new job, and quickly wrote a letter of thanks to General Eaker, who had recommended him for both the promotion and the job. Eaker, in the meantime, had taken command of all British and American air forces operating in the Mediterranean.

"I have just received notification of my promotion," LeMay wrote to Eaker March 11, "and I wish to thank you for your confidence in me. I hope that I will always be able to show that it has not been misplaced. . . . I believe I am returning to the States next month to take part in the B-29 program. While I am disappointed in not being able to see the finish of this phase of the war, the B-29 offers unlimited opportunity for experiment and I am sure the job will be interesting."

Within six weeks, he no longer believed he was on his way to the B-29s. On April 27, he wrote to his friend, Maj. Gen. Laurence F. Kuter, who had also been recently promoted:

Thank you very much for your note. We are happy to hear of your promotion. It is very good news to us over here. Auggie [Kissner] and the rest of the boys join me in extending congratulations.

I'm curious to know what happened to the B-29 plan now that I am remaining here. I hope it doesn't mean too radical a change. We all have high hopes for them and I expect we will hear big things from them soon.

Kuter was the obvious man to ask about the B-29. A protégé of General Marshall and a brilliant officer, he had become Hap Arnold's assistant chief of air staff for plans, and by this time, most of the Air Force plans evolved around the B-29. Within a short while, LeMay was informed definitely that he would not be remaining in England. He was going to the China-Burma-India theater to take over a job that had so far proved impossible for the man who was handling it. He would be in command of a contingent of B-29s that were trying to fly over the Himalayan hump and establish bases in China from which to attack the Japanese.

In mid-June, just before returning home to prepare for this unpromising job, he flew to Normandy for a look at the invasion progress. While he was there, he found out quickly how unpleasant ground fighting could be. He got a bitter taste of French soil when he had to hit the dirt during a German artillery barrage. Then he returned to England and Elveden Hall to say farewell to the people of the Third Air Division. He was pleased to notice that they seemed sorry to see him go. If he could have heard some of their remarks about him out of earshot, he would have been even more pleased.

One officer said of him, "Navigators will tell you he was the best damn navigator Third Division ever had. Bombardiers say he was the best bombardier. And pilots swear they've never ridden with a cagier pilot."[12]

A WAC who worked in headquarters said, "The best guy in the whole division is leaving." And a member of his staff said, "Any one of us would be happy to go with him." They all seemed to understand now why he had been so hard on them, why he had refused ever to let up on them.

CHAPTER EIGHT

Flying into Washington, Curt LeMay, a new major general, expected to have a long conference with Hap Arnold, who would tell him exactly what the B-29 situation was and what he would have to do about it. But there was a lot that he didn't know about Arnold. He didn't realize, for instance, that the Air Force chief was still recovering from his third major heart attack, which had knocked him down less than two months before, and that the B-29 problems, at every level, were serious enough to give him another heart attack at any moment.

When LeMay was ushered into his office, Arnold was preparing to attend a routine meeting, so he took LeMay along. Returning to Arnold's office after the meeting, LeMay presumed they would now sit down and discuss his new assignment at some length. It didn't occur to him that Arnold couldn't tell him what to do because Arnold, who had never been able to get any combat experience, didn't exactly know what to do about the operational problems of the B-29. That was why he needed LeMay. Instead of talking a lot of garbage to him, Arnold hung LeMay's second Distinguished Flying Cross around his neck, then told him to get out to India right away and replace Brig. Gen. K. B. Wolfe who was in charge of the Twentieth Bomber Command, the B-29 operation headquartered at Kharagpur, about ninety miles west of Calcutta.[1]

When Arnold told someone to do something right away, he meant Do it yesterday, but LeMay didn't yet know him well enough to be intimidated by him.

"If I'm going to command a bunch of airplanes that are strange to me," he said, "I'm going to learn to fly one of them first."

He persisted in this stubborn notion until Arnold and his staff finally agreed to set up a special course for him at a B-29 school near Grand Island, Nebraska.

Since he wasn't getting much enlightenment about the B-29 in Washington, perhaps because the situation was so depressing nobody wanted even to discuss it with him, he went to Cleveland for some rest and recreation with Helen and Janie. But he was just beginning to enjoy himself when, after only three or four days, the Air Force sent a plane to Cleveland to transport him to Grand Island. He being the only passenger, there was plenty of room on the plane. Why not take Helen and Janie with him? Yes indeed, why not? Helen, poor soul, was always packed and ready. And Grand Island could hardly be worse than some of the other luxurious resorts to which he had taken her during his military career—Pendleton, Oregon; Wendover, Utah; the Mojave Desert. So he ushered his two ladies into the airplane and off they flew to Grand Island, without any notion of what they might find there.

The first thing they found was a housing shortage. But then, by a stroke of luck, they also found Sy Bartlett, who had written LeMay's basic speech for his talking tour the previous November, and who was now, for some strange reason, stationed at Grand Island as an intelligence officer. Bartlett had a commodious cottage on a lake that was an offshoot of the Platte River. "Instead of trying to find a place for yourself, which you can't find," he said, "move in with me." So they did, much to Janie's delight. For many years thereafter she remembered with pleasure the happy summer days she had spent on the shore of this vast lake—until, as an adult, she visited it again and found it to be a long sandbar, with a bit of water out toward the middle of it.

Her father was not having such a happy time that summer of 1944 in Nebraska. "If you ever saw a buggy plane," he said of the B-29, "this was it. . . . Coming in to land, if you looked straight ahead, you'd wind up on the side of the runway because of the curve of the round nose."[2]

But that was among the least of the plane's problems. He could compensate for the distorting curve of the windshield by cocking his head to the left. The plane had other characteristics for which it wasn't so easy to compensate. "Those engines overheated, cylinder heads often blew out the moment an engine started turning over, ignition was faulty, oil leaked excessively, fuel transfer systems gave endless trouble. There were scores of other defects, either readily apparent or—worse—appearing insidiously when an aircraft was actually at work and at altitude."

Maj. Gen. Haywood S. Hansell, Jr., who also suffered through a tour of duty with the early B-29s, later described some of its other habits in those days: "The engines . . . had developed a very mean tendency to swallow valves and catch fire. The magnesium crank cases burned with a fury that defied all efforts to put them out. In addition, gun sighting blisters were either blowing out at high altitude or frosting up so badly that it was impossible to see through them."[3]

LeMay, after a month of learning to fly the airplane, and finding out things like this about it, decided it was time for him to hurry on over to India. He intended to fly a B-29 there, but perhaps fortunately for him, he had to abandon that plan. After sending Helen and Janie back to Ohio, he waited a week or more for his assigned plane to undergo some absolutely necessary modifications (even though it was brand new) but alas, the days continued to pass and it was still not ready. It became apparent that nobody knew when it would be ready, so he flew to India in a much more reliable Douglas C-54, arriving at Kharagpur on August 29, to take over the fledgling Twentieth Bomber Command.

The day after his arrival, in a letter to his wife, he described, with some amusement, his new way of life: "I am not too bad off for quarters here. Nothing like the last place but good enough. The plumbing is even more primitive than the British. . . . We have a conglomeration of servants to sweep the floor, do the laundry and various other jobs. . . . I have a bearer also to take care of my personal needs. I don't think he will take care of me as well as you do but he shows a lot more respect. Love, Curt."[4]

He was not as amused about the military situation in India. "Things were pretty much in an uproar," he later recalled. "Not bad from an administration standpoint. But they had no sound doctrine on the use of the airplane. [They flew] mostly at night. Small formations. Training was nonexistent. The situation was not as bad as the 305th when I took that over. They [the Twentieth Bomber Command] had a few people who'd been in combat. [Most of them] had a lot more flying time because they'd been instructors in flying schools. But that wasn't combat time. And they were not prepared to cope with the mountains. Nobody was prepared to cope with those mountains."

K. B. Wolfe, a matériel expert who had done an outstanding

job guiding the B-29 through its developmental phase, but lacked the experience to handle such a difficult combat assignment, had already returned to the States, leaving in charge an old friend of LeMay's and fellow student at flying school, Brig. Gen. Laverne G. "Blondie" Saunders. Saunders had no real authority because he was simply filling in until LeMay arrived, whereupon he planned to return to the States immediately and take command of a new B-29 wing. LeMay, valuing Saunders's advice about the bewildering situation in India and China, asked him to stay over for a while, and Saunders agreed, thereby, as it happened, almost sacrificing his life three weeks later.

LeMay was fortunate to find also at Kharagpur a one-time commercial pilot now in the Air Force, Maj. Alfred F. Kalberer, who was destined to serve under him on frequent occasions in the years to come. Kalberer, who had been stationed for some time in the Mediterranean, was especially useful here, as LeMay was quick to notice, because of his "encyclopedic knowledge of weather, terrain and nationals of the various countries—all gained through thousands of hours as a KLM [Dutch airline] pilot."

LeMay's headquarters was a walled compound that had once been a prison and his living quarters, outside the walls, had been the warden's house. A few staff officers lived with him but most of his men lived in Indian-style thatch-roofed huts, not on any defined military base but scattered about the area between the town and the airfield, some miles away. The weather was hot and sticky. The men were grumpy, which was not surprising. They had reason to bitch.

Even more exasperating than the weather and the living conditions was the problem of transportation and supplies. LeMay was pleasantly surprised, when he arrived in India, to find that one of the transportation officers there was his brother Lloyd, who had enlisted before the war and subsequently earned a commission. Lloyd was keenly aware of the supply problems in the China-Burma-India Theater, but there was no way that he or anybody else could actually overcome them.

The Twentieth Bomber Command, under Wolfe, had established eight bases in the Kharagpur area—four for the four B-29 groups already there, and four others for the C-109s (B-24s converted into flying tankers), which carried gasoline for the bombers to forward bases. All supplies, fuel, bombs, and ammunition had to be flown from India to the forward bases in China. These bases, from which the bombers took off on their missions against the Japanese, were situated around Chengtu in Szechuan Province, about thirteen hundred miles northeast of Kharagpur on the other side of the infamous Himalayan Hump. Chinese coolies, several thousand of them, had built the airstrips there by hand, just as Indian peasants had extended the already-established runways at Kharagpur. The B-29s, besides carrying in their own bombs, had also to help carry in gasoline. And it took seven trips back and forth across the Hump just to get enough gasoline to a forward base, for one mission for one plane. That is to say, seven successful trips. With all the overheating problems of the B-29, added to the altitude and weather factors across the Hump, the big bombers were, as LeMay noted, "going down over the Hump all the time, or they were busting up on the strips in India and China."

LeMay was so dismayed by these conditions that when Arnold's staff sent him a query as to whether he wanted more B-29 groups under his command in India, he said no. In his opinion, the entire notion of operating under these conditions was "basically unsound." He didn't have the resources to handle any more groups.

As usual when he took over a new organization, the first thing LeMay did was to institute a training program, for ground crews as well as air crews. There were some already-tested precautions that would at least minimize the danger of crashes: enforcement of standard procedures to hold down cylinder head temperatures before and during takeoff; more precise coordination among the members of the crews; more rigid maintenance and inspection; and on-the-spot engine modifications to increase cooling.

He also scrapped the four-plane diamond formation in use here, and instituted a twelve-plane grouping similar to the one he had used in Europe. And he began preparing his men for more frequent daylight precision attacks rather than the night missions to which they were becoming accustomed under Wolfe. To make sure the daylight attacks would be effective, he ordered each group to select six lead crews for special training in navigation and target familiarity.

It took him a while to manage all this. But with Arnold waiting impatiently in Washington, he could hardly delay his operations until he was sure he was ready. He continued preparations for a mission Saunders had scheduled for September 8 against a Japanese steel plant at Anshan, near Mukden in Manchuria. He had planned to lead that mission personally, but the air staff in Washington informed him he could not go. He immediately objected, heating up the wires between Kharagpur and the Pentagon. You can't have an outfit with a commander who doesn't fly combat, he insisted. A commander can't fly all the missions, but he's got to fly a mission when he thinks his unit needs it. Or when he himself needs it.

Finally, Washington compromised. He could fly one mission. So he chose the first one, nine days after his arrival, to Anshan, not only because it was the first but also because the Japanese were supposed to have their best fighters in that area, and he wanted to find out how good they were.[5] His strategy against the Japanese, including the number of gunners and the weight of armament his planes would have to carry, depended to some extent on the skill of the enemy fighter pilots and the danger they might present.

After almost a thousand cargo flights back and forth across the Hump from Kharagpur, carrying gasoline, bombs, and supplies, the Twentieth Bomber Command, on the morning of September 8, had 115 B-29s at Chengtu, loaded and ready for the mission to Anshan. LeMay himself arrived at Chengtu on one of the last of the supply flights and took his place in the lead plane. All but seven of the Superfortresses got off the ground that day and ninety-five reached the Anshan steel plant, where they dropped two hundred tons of bombs despite antiaircraft fire that perforated several planes, including LeMay's. Only four planes were lost on the mission. Photos later indicated that three coke ovens were so badly damaged it would take a year to restore them; three others would take six months. But to LeMay the most interesting aspect of the mission was what he learned about the Japanese fighter squadrons.

Flying north into Japanese-held territory, LeMay and his crews began watching for fighters. And as they approached Anshan, they suddenly found them, airborne, in squadron formation, poised to attack. LeMay, accustomed to facing German fighter squadrons in almost identical situations, expected now to get some answers to important questions in his mind. Not just how clever and relentless were the Japanese pilots, but how tough and resourceful were the men in this new outfit of his? How good were the B-29's power-driven gun turrets and central fire-control system?

As the fighters came into perfect position for attack, LeMay said to himself, ''Now we'll see what they can do.'' But their leader apparently misjudged the speed of the B-29s, which were cruising about 195 miles per hour at twenty-five thousand feet. The entire fighter formation turned the wrong way. Only the tail-end planes got so much as a chance to fire a few futile rounds at the huge American bombers. By the time the Japanese realized their mistake and turned themselves around, they were too far back to be able to close in for another attack. Most Japanese fighters, designed for optimum performance at about seventeen thousand feet, simply couldn't catch the B-29 at its higher altitudes.

When LeMay returned from the mission and Blondie Saunders asked him what he thought of Japanese fighters, he got an immediate one-word answer: "Stinkin'." LeMay was remembering his experiences in Europe. "My first impression," he added, "is that they won't be as tough as the Germans."

Despite the many favorable results of the Anshan raid, LeMay was not satisfied with the performances of his men, and he told them so. He gave them a long list of their shortcomings, but without blaming them. Their formations would have to be much tighter. They would have to learn more about conserving fuel. And to improve their bombing accuracy, they would have to learn to drop their loads, not individually, but on the signal of the lead bombardiers, as soon as these lead bombardiers were sufficiently trained to take the responsibility.

"You fellows are just getting your feet wet over here," he told them. They were still amateurs. They had a lot to learn. And there was only one way to teach them. He grounded the entire Twentieth Bomber Command for as long as it would take to retrain everyone, which meant the ground crews and support units as well as the air crews.

The purpose of the Twentieth B.C. was to fly combat missions. Everything else had to be subordinated to this end. To make sure it was done, he secured approval of a reorganization under which the commanders of his four combat groups, the 40th, 444th, 462nd, and 468th, would be the commanders of the bases on which these groups were stationed, thus making sure that the needs of the operational units would come first on those bases. This made it easier for him to combine and integrate all the ground support units.

Meanwhile, the "grounding" of the command didn't mean the cessation of flying. It meant only the cessation of missions. The aircrews now flew more than ever, learning to assemble efficiently after takeoffs, tighten their formations, save gasoline, avoid mountains, etc. Col. Alva L. Harvey, a long-time friend of LeMay who happened to be a B-29 group commander in India when LeMay arrived there, recalled later the problems presented by the Himalayas: "We didn't have reliable maps. We didn't know whether a mountain was 12,000 or 20,000 feet high. And we often had to fly between mountains. If you saw clouds ahead, you didn't take a chance. You started climbing as fast as you could. There was a saying among the pilots. 'Don't believe those maps. Add a couple thousand feet for yourself. Then add three thousand more for the wife and kids.' "[6]

While LeMay's command was going through reorganization and his men were being retrained, he decided he'd better pay some attention to the command structure above him, or parallel to him, as well as below him. "It was so confused," he later said, "that I tried one day to start from a squadron [level] and trace the way up to the theater commander, but someplace along the way I got lost in the shuffle. And I never did find out the relation between Mountbatten and Stilwell."

British Admiral of the Fleet Lord Louis Mountbatten, a cousin of the king, was in charge of the Allied Southeast Asia Command. Gen. Joseph W. "Vinegar Joe" Stilwell was in charge of the American China-Burma-India Theater, which would seem also to be at least partly under Mountbatten's jurisdiction, but even the two men themselves didn't act as if they were sure of that. And LeMay didn't feel he was actually under the command of either of them because Hap Arnold had secured for his B-29 units a unique operational status which put them outside the control of the theater commanders, wherever they might be.

Everyone in the war against Japan, including Gen. Douglas MacArthur, Chiang Kai-shek, and the U.S. Navy, had put in so many requisitions for B-29s that Arnold could envision them being divided up piecemeal, thus destroying the Air Force plan to keep them all together for a concerted air offensive against what had to be the most important of targets, the Japanese homeland. To save the Air Force plan, Arnold invented a scheme which would make him, as an agent for the Joint Chiefs of Staff, commander of all B-29 units worldwide, with headquarters in Washington, while subordinates like LeMay would command in the various theaters. By an amazing bit of sleight of hand, Arnold had managed to get the Joint Chiefs to approve this scheme. LeMay felt, therefore, that he had to answer only to Arnold. But being aware of the military courtesies, though not very adept at them, he decided he had better pay visits to Mountbatten and Stilwell.[7]

He flew first to New Delhi, where Stilwell was then head-quartered, but found when he arrived that Stilwell had gone into the jungle to solve some problem for a group of enlisted men. It was characteristic of Stilwell to go out of his way to help his men, but LeMay felt he should have been at his headquarters, taking care of bigger problems. On the other hand, LeMay was just as happy not to see him, having nothing important to say. He left a calling card and flew back to Kharagpur.

A few days later he flew to Kandy, Ceylon, to meet Mount-batten. He left early in the morning, hoping to return the same day, but when he arrived in Ceylon he was told Mountbatten couldn't see him until lunchtime the following day. Since he was already there, he decided to stay, which earned him, if nothing else, a splendid and sumptuous lunch. Mountbatten was living in a maharaja's palace on a mountaintop. He had excellent chefs and countless servants, including a crew who did nothing but wave a huge, hanging carpet back and forth behind the table to create a breeze.

After lunch, Mountbatten took him to what LeMay called "a ludicrous briefing" about an unsuccessful British attempt to knock out a Japanese machine-gun nest in Burma. After this subject was exhausted twice over, Mountbatten turned to LeMay and said, "I'm planning to invade Akyab Island on the Burma coast, and I want you to saturate the place [with bombs] before I go in."

As it happened, LeMay was familiar with Akyab because his crews had used it for bombing practice. Recent photos showed conclusively that the Japanese had evacuated it. There was no need to saturate it with bombs. That was all LeMay would have had to say. But he felt it was also important to make Mountbatten realize he had no control over the B-29s. He therefore, in his usual, undiplomatic way, made it very clear. "I can't help you on that," he said, "because it doesn't lie within my mission purview. But I've seen recent aerial photos of Akyab. There isn't a Jap on it. If you want it, send a rowboat down there with some troops and take it."

LeMay didn't feel, as he was leaving, that he had made him-self very popular with the British. He did not again see Mount-batten.

In the early morning hours of September 19, LeMay was awakened by an aide with some alarming news. Late the previous evening, Blondie Saunders, after a visit to the Twentieth B.C. base at Piardoba, about forty miles north of Kharagpur, had taken off in a B-25 to return to Kharagpur. But he was now several hours overdue and no one had heard from him. Not even a radio distress call.[8]

It would be useless to search the jungle in the dark, but LeMay issued an order that every available plane be used in an aerial search beginning with the first morning light. A thorough grid search covering every bit of the jungle between Kharagpur and Piardoba. But while he sent his men to scour the whole area, he himself began to think it most likely that Saunders had crashed right after takeoff, near the field at Piardoba. The lack of any radio contact intrigued him. If Saunders had time, he would surely have sent some kind of radio distress signal.

LeMay called in Kalberer and said, "Let's get a B-25 of our own and crank it up."

They took off from Kharagpur right away, in the dark, so that when the first morning light came, they were flying over the field at Piardoba, from which Saunders had taken off the previous night. Two minutes later, they realized that LeMay's hunch was right.

"Out there about three miles off the end of the runway," he recalled, "was a big gouge, a real rough gouge, cut right through the jungle. We went down and flew very low, practically brushing the trees as we examined the wreckage. It was a real mess." He couldn't conceive of anyone surviving it.

He called the Piardoba tower, reported the exact location of the fallen plane, and canceled the grid search. Then he said to Kalberer, "I don't think there's any use of our going in there. Let's go home."

But Kalberer said, "Nope. There just might be somebody alive. We just might be able to render a little bit of assistance."

They landed and went into the jungle on foot, following the needle of a hand compass through the dense foliage until they came upon the plane. "And there was old Blondie," LeMay recalled, "still inhabiting that wreckage, big as life. Did he give us hell for taking so long to get there. One of the engines was crushed down on his busted leg."

The only other survivor, the plane's crew chief, was walking around in a daze and talking incoherently despite a fist-sized hole

in his head. He died the next day, and everyone expected that
Blondie Saunders would soon follow him to the grave. LeMay
even began looking for a suitable place to bury him. But Blondie
refused to cooperate. After three years in military hospitals and
countless painful operations he returned to his hometown, Ab-
erdeen, South Dakota, and began a long, successful business
career as an automobile dealer.

While LeMay's decision to ground and retrain his men seemed
necessary to him, he didn't exactly expect Hap Arnold to ap-
plaud him for it. "Arnold was impatient and I knew it," he said
later. "But I didn't have a full appreciation [of his problems
until] I was chief of staff and found out how hard it was to get
something through. He had a new outfit which didn't get proper
training in the States. It got [into action] halfway around the
world with a plane not ready for combat. There were shortages.
And the command arrangement was not satisfactory. Yet I didn't
feel that Arnold was breathing down my neck."

If he didn't feel that, he was almost unique in the Air Force.
Though he didn't yet know Arnold very well, he had heard
enough stories about the man. Almost every career officer in the
Air Force had a "hurry up" story to tell about their chief.
LeMay's friend, Alva Harvey, who was now one of his B-29
group commanders, could give firsthand evidence of Arnold's
impatience.[9] In 1942, Arnold ordered Harvey to fly a B-17 from
Alaska to Russia because the Russians thought it would be practical for their pilots to do so in the lend-lease planes the United
States was offering them. Arnold doubted it. Harvey immediately
applied for Russian passports for himself and his crew but they
were delayed. Two days later, Arnold saw Harvey in the hall
outside his office and said, "Why aren't you in Russia?"

Harvey said, "We haven't yet got our passports, sir."

"Goddamn it, I don't care about passports," Arnold barked.
"I want you out of here in three hours."

Though Arnold never showed LeMay that kind of impatience,
he let him know very quickly, on September 22, 1944, to be
exact, that while he liked what he was doing, he wanted him to
hurry up and do more.

"I want to express again my appreciation for the fine work
you have done with the XX Bomber Command," Arnold wrote
to LeMay on the 22nd. Then, in the next paragraph, he got to
the real subject of the letter. He had heard by now about the

good results of the Anshan mission, but he apparently didn't like the fact that each plane carried only two tons of bombs.

"One of the questions which has been of deep concern to me," he wrote, "is the limited weight of bombs that we have been able to carry. . . . Our concept of the B-29 was an airplane that would carry very heavy bomb loads for very long range. We have attained some of the distances but we have not as yet obtained the bomb loads. . . . It is my desire that you give the bomb load problem a great deal of thought. . . ."

That same day, the 22nd, Arnold wrote a similar message to General Hansell who had taken over the Twenty-first Bomber Command, in training at Peterson Field, Colorado Springs. "We [the B-29s] have not carried any more bombs," he pointed out to Hansell, "and in most cases considerably less than the B-24s and B-17s carry. One of the greatest factors in the defeat of Japan will be the air effort. Consequently every bomb that is added to each airplane that takes off for Japan will directly affect the length of the war."

LeMay's letters to Arnold in the latter months of 1944 trace his progress in boosting the bomb load, but also offer a chilling picture of the problems of operating a new airplane in such remote countries as India and China. On September 26, his bombers returned to the steel plant at Anshan with some success, but on October 11, Arnold informed him that Manchurian steel mills were no longer important targets because the Japanese had lost so many ships they couldn't carry the steel home. Aircraft factories were now the top priority targets, so LeMay, on October 14, sent 130 of his bombers against an aircraft factory at Okayama. This time, each plane was able to carry 6.8 tons of bombs, more than tripling the previous record load. Cruising slowly to preserve gas in the newly learned box formations, 104 planes actually dropped their bombs on the factory, and in conjunction with naval carrier attacks, left only six buildings intact. Seven hangars and sixteen other buildings were destroyed, along with 116 airplanes parked outside.

Writing to Arnold five days later, October 19, LeMay didn't even deign to mention this accomplishment (aware, no doubt, that Arnold already knew about it), and only obliquely mentioned the bomb-load problem, which he was now on the way to solving by on-the-spot engine modifications, more economical use of fuel, cutting the ammunition allotment, and eliminating all unessential weight. He had also been forced to reconcile himself to a thin margin of safety, as he made clear to Arnold: "I have not been satisfied with the bomb loads we have carried in the past and have had several of my best staff officers working on the problem. To a large extent our bomb load is limited by gross takeoff load. This is in turn influenced by operating technique, runways, high free air temperature and power available. The take-off is a very serious problem with the B-29, and is the high point of any flight. All crews, in discussing a mission, invariably talk about their take-off and not about flak, fighters, or other enemy opposition. Even partial power loss from one engine almost invariably results in a crash from which there are very few survivors."

Having put himself in a strong position by virture of his initial successes, LeMay didn't hesitate to elaborate on the mess into which Arnold had thrust him. Among the other problems he wanted to impress upon Arnold was the continuing burden of supply. "Up to 1 Oct.," he pointed out, "thirty-five per cent of our total B-29 flying time was consumed in cargo operations to the Chengtu area." And the necessity to spend so much time carrying cargo had delayed his training program.

Fuel economy was difficult to regulate or even measure because "present fuel quantity gauges are practically useless." On the way home from a mission, a pilot could only guess whether he was running short of gas. He could not believe his indicator.

The B-29 feathering mechanism was dismally unreliable. (Propellers on dead or dying engines had to be "feathered" or tuned with the thin sides of their blades facing the air flow to reduce drag on the plane.) "On this airplane," LeMay wrote, "inability to feather almost always results in the loss of the ship."

But the worst villain confronting the Superfortress was still its own engine. "The B-29 airplane is capable of a considerably higher performance than the R-3350 engine now installed will permit, as the maximum gross operating weight is limited by the power available for take-off and climb. Until more power is available, we cannot fully capitalize on the capabilities of the airplane. Most of our difficulties center around the engine."

He described three plane losses on recent missions, all definitely due to mechanical failures.

"I am doing all I can by crew selection, training and education to eliminate this type accident, but they cannot be eliminated entirely until the engine is improved."

Nowhere in his letter did LeMay suggest that he might curtail his schedule of missions because of the problems he mentioned. One mission per week was about all he could hope to average under the circumstances; yet between October 24 and November 11, a period of eighteen days, he actually managed five.

On October 24, the B-29s returned to the same Okayama aircraft factory they had hit ten days earlier. The next day, he sent all he could muster on short notice—fifty-nine of them—against the aircraft factory at Omura on the Japanese home island of Kyushu. On November 3 his planes hit naval bases at Rangoon. Two days later, they traveled nineteen hundred miles to Singapore to bomb the largest dry dock in the Orient. And on November 11, they hit the aircraft factory at Omura once again.

The Rangoon and Singapore raids, directed against the Japanese navy, had been requested by the U.S. Navy. And when Arnold wrote to LeMay November 13, he extended the U.S. Navy's thanks for the help of the B-29s. "I have just received a letter from Admiral [Ernest] King [chief of naval operations], in which he expresses his appreciation for the fine work you did at Singapore, and indicates that he, too, is impressed with your ability to do a job."

Arnold's letter of the 13th began with some praise of his own. "I have told you in messages of my great satisfaction with the work that you are doing. . . . It was your task [in India-China] to operate the airplanes you had and they were not the latest models. I think the number of airplanes that you were able to keep in operating condition was impressive."

Then, in what appeared to be a recognition of the problems LeMay had mentioned in his letter of October 19, Arnold added, "I appreciate the difficulties that you must have encountered and know full well the problem must have been solved largely by the determination of you and your maintenance people."

Despite these congratulatory words, neither Arnold nor LeMay was so naïve as to think the basic problems of the B-29 operating from India and China—distance and supply—had actually been solved. The conclusion of Arnold's letter made that clear: "One of our major interests continues to be to get you out of China. I cannot at this time tell you where you will go or when your bases will be ready. In any event, you will have to operate under your present conditions for a matter of months."

By this time, Saipan, Tinian, and Guam had been taken from the Japanese. General Hansell's Twenty-first Bomber Command, with its brand-new B-29s, had already arrived on Saipan and was preparing for its first mission against Tokyo. Guam or Tinian might seem to be the logical place to send LeMay and his Twentieth Bomber Command, as soon as the bases on those islands were ready, but Arnold, at this time, didn't mention it.

Arnold was now beginning to regard LeMay as if he were something like a Messiah. Just two years earlier, the man had been obscure even in the Air Force. He had developed an excellent reputation as a navigator, but until America entered the war, he had never commanded anything—not even so much as a squadron. In the prewar Air Corps, he was one of only two thousand officers. Arnold knew most of them, but he didn't know LeMay, who was still a lieutenant until 1940. It was only because there were so few career officers available that he was given command of the 305th Bomb Group in 1942. Yet during twenty months in England, he had personally developed many of the tactics that were now standard in the Eighth Air Force. And during less than three months in India-China, he had apparently yanked the Twentieth B.C. off the ground across the Himalayas, and into significant action against Japan.

When Arnold sent LeMay to Asia, Arnold was in deep trouble. The B-29 was beginning to look as if it was destined to damage him more than it would ever damage the Japanese. Only a month later, on September 29, Arnold wrote in a letter to Tooey Spaatz: "With all due respect to [K. B.] Wolfe, he did his best, and he did a grand job, but LeMay's operations make Wolfe seem very amateurish."

In mid-November, Arnold was even more enthusiastic about his young subordinate. Arnold was a man more prone to criticize than praise, yet he was writing what could only be called fan letters to this fellow who had so suddenly popped up out of obscurity to get some good out of those exasperating bombers on which Arnold had staked so much of his reputation. Arnold hadn't been in Asia recently; he hadn't seen firsthand what LeMay was accomplishing, but he was receiving performance charts and aerial bomb damage photos which convinced him he had found the man he so desperately needed.

On November 17 he wrote a "Dear Curt" letter—the first time he had addressed LeMay by his given name—which began with more praise:

The progress you have been making in adding to your bomb load is most gratifying. . . . I have seen your bomb strike photos of Okayama and Omura . . . and I have proudly displayed them whenever opportunity arose. I don't recall any pictures of the European Theater which surpass those of Okayama for concentration of bombs and the damage resulting therefrom. . . . The fine work your people have been doing is providing a standard for the other B-29 units. We are passing to Hansell everything of interest from the XX Bomber Command, and he, in a recent letter here, stated that he would have to push his people pretty hard to stay in the same league with your Command.

General Hansell, another young officer, only three years older than LeMay, had already made a name for himself in the Air Force as a brilliant planner and administrator. He was one of the authors of the Air War Plan, an amazingly accurate projection of the course of the war and the needs of the Air Force in fighting it. But he was in a position now which no one would envy.

Having just recently arrived at the partially constructed bases on Saipan with his Twenty-first Bomber Command, he was preparing to launch his first mission against Tokyo, which promised to be the most fiercely defended target in all Japan since it was the home of the emperor and the government as well as the largest city. He had still to cope with all the B-29 deficiencies that had bedeviled LeMay. He was going into operations against the Japanese home islands with crews who had never flown this problem plane in combat. He had to send these crews fifteen hundred miles across water with only the Pacific Ocean for emergency landings. And on top of all that, he had an Air Force chief who was spreading the word that his other B-29 commander, LeMay, had already won the title as the Babe Ruth of Bombers.

In a November 29 letter to Arnold, LeMay mentioned another difficulty he had been anticipating for some time: "The weather in China has grown worse, and in addition, we have been forced to take off at night in order to bomb in daylight. This has increased operational losses."

More than a month earlier, in an October 19 letter, he had warned his boss about this approaching dilemma:

I am very much concerned about the effect of the weather on our operations out of the Chengtu area this winter. . . . I have enclosed a study I had made by the weather people on this Area and it presents a very bleak picture. . . . If we are to bomb during the middle of the day, when target conditions will probably be best, we must make take-offs and landings during the worst period at the bases. The ice problem will not be so bad for the let down [descent on the way home], but may be on the climb out [ascent after takeoff], with a heavily loaded ship. In addition to the hundred or so ships I will have coming back out of gas for an instrument approach, A.T.C. [Air Transport Command] runs a large volume of traffic into the area. Frankly I haven't a complete solution to this problem yet.

He got to work on the problem right away. What he needed primarily was reliable weather information. Since he wasn't getting enough of it from Chiang Kai-shek's Nationalist government, the principal U.S. ally in China, he turned for help to Chiang's mortal enemy, Mao Tse-tung, and his Communist government. The Communists, who controlled large sections of north and west China, plus some areas in east China, were fighting the Japanese invaders, as well as the Chinese nationalists, in a three-cornered war that offered small choice to an impartial viewer. Chiang's corruption, Mao's Communism, and Japan's militarism made it a war that one could only wish all three sides would lose. But wishing was a luxury no one had offered LeMay. Despite an abhorrence of Communism so virulent he has sometimes been ridiculed for it, he turned to Mao, not only for the weather service he needed, but also for help in rescuing and returning any B-29 crews who might go down in northern China. It had been almost impossible to develop reasonable working arrangements with our Russian Communist allies.

"We just didn't know how Mao would react," LeMay recalled. Actually, it was his concern about downed crews, rather than his need for weather information, that first prompted him to contact Mao. "I sent an officer from our Communications section right up to Mao's headquarters [in Yenan]. Sent him up in a Gooney Bird [C47] with all the radio equipment which would be needed; and we asked Mao if he and his followers would help in getting our people out of there when they went down. He agreed to assist."[10]

As soon as LeMay received that good news, he sent up another C-47, loaded with medical supplies. It was a calculated goodwill gesture. Chinese Communist medical supplies consisted primarily of splints and bandages, which they could make for themselves. They had very little access to anything more sophisticated. They were so short of medicines their doctors cried with happiness when they unloaded the airplane. They had never even seen such new "wonder drugs" as sulfa. But there was nothing unselfish in LeMay's generosity to the Communists. "I wanted to be damn sure that there were medical supplies in those areas when my own people came in, busted up or wounded. . . . Nor did I leave out of the picture the fact it would be bound to react favorably on our people when Mao Tse Tung found himself possessed of those supplies. He knew who'd given them to him."

Shortly after receiving the medical supplies, Mao sent LeMay a gift—a captured Japanese Samurai sword. And in return, LeMay sent him a pair of binoculars. Shortly after that, LeMay was able to set up his own private radio station in Yenan, with a small contingent of men stationed there to send him weather reports as well as any news there might be about fallen B-29s and their crews. This station, plus whatever could be garnered from the Chinese nationalists, plus occasional reports from a U.S. Navy station in the Gobi Desert, plus direct daily reports from his own far-ranging reconnaissance planes, eventually gave LeMay at least some notion of what weather to expect before scheduling missions.

Aerial photos taken November 17 illustrated why LeMay was so worried about the weather. These were photos of the aircraft factory at Omura, and they proved that the November 11 raid against it had been a dismal flop. Ninety-six planes had taken off from China, but due to a combination of bad weather and worse communications in the skies over Kyushu, only twenty-nine were even able to find the target, where they did zero damage. LeMay was not the Babe Ruth of Bombing that day. So his B-29s went back there November 21 in a raid that was conceived to coincide with Hansell's initial strike against Tokyo. But weather forced Hansell to postpone his mission until the 24th, and LeMay might as well have done likewise. The Omura results that day didn't do much to raise LeMay's bombing average. Of the 109 planes which launched the mission, sixty-one reached Omura and bombed through clouds by radar. Thirteen dropped their loads on Shanghai, the secondary target. And five others mistook nearby Omuta for Omura. The rest of the planes became even more hopelessly confused in the cloudy, stormy skies over Kyushu.

On November 27, LeMay's bombers went to Bangkok on another of what he called "training" missions, because it was against a weakly defended target, yet it gave his crews a chance to do some damage to Japanese installations while they were practicing and perfecting all the new techniques he had forced upon them. Like his B-17 crews in Europe, his B-29 crews in Asia were finding out that he never let up on training. And they didn't much like him for it. The grumbling continued. But so did the training and the retraining.

Another serious mission against the aircraft factory at Omura was set for December 3, but the depressing autumn in China had now turned into hideous winter, and it was even worse than LeMay had feared. On December 3, 4, 5, and 6, the B-29 crews huddled around their stoves in the bitter cold at Chengtu, waiting for the skies to clear over Kyushu. Finally LeMay received permission to hit Mukden, instead, on December 7. His bombers found no clouds there, but it was so cold they found a lot of ice on their windows. And outside those windows, obscured by the ice, they found a lot of Japanese fighters. They also found that these fighters were becoming more aggressive, if not more skillful. They made 247 individual passes at the B-29s, coming so close there were three midair collisions. All three of the fighters involved went down but only two of the B-29s. The third limped back home, luckily, with no more damage than a bent propeller. Still another B-29 was hit from above by a phosphorous bomb that became imbedded in a wing. The anxious crew watched that incendiary continue to burn all the way home, but the wing held and they made it.

LeMay by this time was engaged in an argument he wasn't destined to win, against Maj. Gen. Claire Chennault, the American in command of the Fourteenth U.S. Air Force and Chiang's nationalist air force; and Gen. Albert C. Wedemeyer, who had replaced Stilwell as China Theater commander.[11] Chennault, for some time, had wanted the Twentieth B.C.'s B-29s to stage an incendiary attack against Japan's biggest China supply base, at Hankow. LeMay had resisted this request and Arnold had supported him because, in their opinion, Chennault's Fourteenth Air Force could have done the job. There was strong suspicion among Americans in China that Chennault's planes spent more time smuggling prostitutes and other contraband for profit than they spent attacking the Japanese. When Wedemeyer arrived, he supported Chennault in the matter. He suggested that LeMay mount one full-scale attack on the Hankow supply dumps.

LeMay said no, and questioned Wedemeyer's authority to order the mission. But the Joint Chiefs had ruled previously that a theater commander could divert B-29s from their primary mission if the cause was sufficient. They now decided there was sufficient cause.

LeMay's B-29s, therefore, found themselves, on December 18, loaded with incendiaries and headed toward Hankow on a mission that turned out to be an important harbinger of things to come. Eighty-four planes dropped their fire bombs on Hankow, and the resultant conflagration was so devastating that Chennault said it "destroyed Hankow as a major base."

More important was the fact that it proved the efficacy of incendiary attacks against the predominantly wooden-structured, fire-prone cities of the Orient. Air Force planners had anticipated the possibility of adopting such a strategy, but not until the Hankow raid had anyone demonstrated how well it would work. LeMay himself would not soon forget what his planes did to Hankow, even though he had been reluctant to send them there.

While LeMay had disagreed with Wedemeyer on the Hankow mission, the two men were in basic accord on an even more important issue—the question of whether the Twentieth B.C. should be moved out of China. Wedemeyer argued that there simply wasn't enough gasoline arriving to support the B-29s, the Fourteenth Air Force, and the needs of Nationalist China.

"It was always a battle over gasoline," LeMay agreed. "We hauled gas and we chisled gas [from the Air Transport Command]. And Chennault was always trying to get us to help him out. . . . I had been recommending not to send any more B-29s because of logistics. I didn't say, 'Move them out.' [I said] 'Don't send anymore.' "

Wedemeyer, however, said to move them out. And LeMay did not disagree. While he continued his operations—Mukden December 21, Bangkok January 3, Omura January 6, etc.—he also alerted his groups to be ready to move. And on January 15, with Arnold's concurrence, the Joint Chiefs granted Wedemeyer's request. The Twentieth Bomber Command stepped up preparations for its move out of China. But Curt LeMay would not be there to see it.

CHAPTER NINE

In early January 1945, LeMay received orders from Washington to fly to Hansell's headquarters on Guam for a conference with him and with Gen. Lauris Norstad, now Twentieth Air Force chief of staff, which is to say, Hap Arnold's top aide and agent in matters concerning the B-29. LeMay hadn't an inkling as to the purpose of the meeting. "I thought," he said later, "it was [about] coordination between the two commands." His and Hansell's.[1]

With LeMay's orders came a directive that he was to fly around Japanese-held territory on his way to Guam. But when he realized he'd have to fly almost to Australia to do that, he decided to hell with it. He chose a copilot and four of five staff officers, piled them into a B-29, and flew across China, with one stop at Chengtu, on an almost straight line to Guam, skirting the southern coast of Japanese-held Formosa. He arrived safely January 19 to find an inscrutable Norstad and an uncomfortable Hansell waiting for him.

Though Hansell had done what any reasonable man would consider an excellent job so far with his fledgling Twenty-first Bomber Command, he had reason to be uncomfortable. Arnold, always impatient, was now even more so after three serious heart attacks and an endless succession of B-29 crises. Hansell, who knew him well, hadn't missed any of the nuances of his impatience. Like Norstad, Hansell was one of Arnold's "boys," that coterie of brilliant young officers—including Larry Kuter, Rosey O'Donnell, Charles Cabell, and others—who had served on his staff and were expected to make almost impossible jobs look almost easy.

It hadn't looked easy, nor had it been easy, for Hansell to bring his inexperienced crews to the half-finished bases in the newly captured Marianas (where Japanese remnants were still fighting), and get them directly into action. Delays were inevitable, and the first several came during preparation for the initial mission, which finally took place, against Tokyo, November 24. Hansell had reason to be disturbed by a December 7 letter from Norstad on this subject, even though it was meant to be reassuring:

> I knew you would worry about the Chiefs feelings at that time since you know him well enough to realize he would be very much keyed up until the first show was over. He was impatient, but his impatience was directed against the circumstances and not against you. You were not "on the pan" at any time. I think I can best illustrate his attitude by telling you his reaction to the fourth and fifth postponement. After he had indicated that he was disturbed, I made a statement to the effect that I didn't think it a good thing to put the heat on you under the circumstances. He replied, "Who said anything about putting the heat on Possum?"

Hansell's friends had always called him "Possum," though he did not, fortunately, look like one. He was a slender, handsome man with a kind and thoughtfully expressive face. Even he could not remember the origin of his nickname.[2] After all the postponements, the Tokyo raid was a qualified success. Two days later, his bombers returned to Tokyo with more success, but all of them came within minutes of being lost when a tropical storm enveloped the Marianas just as they were returning home, low on gas. Since the nearest American landing strip was at Kwajelein, twelve hundred miles away, they could do nothing but circle Saipan and hope the storm would pass, which, fortunately, it did after twenty-five anxious minutes, just in time for all but one of the bombers to land safely.

Even more serious problems ensued. Japanese fighter-bombers from Iwo Jima, 680 miles north, began appearing, night and day, to destroy B-29s on the ground. Arnold found that intolerable. On December 19, he wrote, "I cannot understand Jap planes coming over in the daytime and apparently making several passes at the field during a period of 45 minutes with no mention whatsoever made of our own fighters even attempting to prevent such strafing. . . . Just what do our fighters do out there?"

Within two weeks, the fighters of the Seventh Air Force eliminated this problem by eliminating the Japanese strafers. But then there were other difficulties. Because of the continuing mechanical deficiencies of the B-29, a certain number of the bombers kept going down into the Pacific between Japan and the Marianas. Needless to say, Arnold didn't like that, either.

> It seems to me that on every raid there are about three or four airplanes that go down, well on the return trip, with no definite cause being given. . . . We should find the causes and determine what we can do to prevent them. . . . The B-29 cannot be treated in the same way that we treat a fighter, a medium bomber, or even a Flying Fortress. We must consider the B-29 more in terms of a naval vessel, and we do not lose naval vessels in 3's or 4's without very thorough analysis of the causes.

But Hansell by that time had discovered an even more serious obstacle to be overcome—the winds aloft above Japan. Though he was a total believer in the Air Force doctrine of high-altitude, daylight precision bombing, he was finding that it didn't work as well in Japan as it did in Europe. The winds above Japan often blew at rates of two hundred miles per hour, and in shifting directions, making it impossible to bomb with any precision, especially since the targets were often obscured by clouds. He could explain this to Arnold, but he couldn't make the man happy about it. Arnold wanted the targets destroyed and he would accept nothing less.

In his December 19 letter to Hansell he wrote: "Your units out there have been doing a wonderful job." A pleasant opening, but Hansell knew Arnold too well to take it at face value. "It is regretted," Arnold continued, "that their strength is not such so that we could have complete destruction of the plants rather than just partial destruction."

And on December 27, Arnold wrote, "It is our purpose to destroy our targets. . . . We must accept the fact that we have a big obligation to meet. To fulfill this we must in fact destroy our targets and then we must show the results so the public can judge for itself as to the effectiveness of our operations."

That same day, Hansell gave a prepared statement to war correspondents in the Marianas reflecting his own, but perhaps also Arnold's, lack of satisfaction:

> I would say in summing up our accomplishments in the thirty days since we first bombed Tokyo that these first accom-

plishments have been encouraging but that they are far from the standards we are seeking. . . . The primary target is always a rather small section of enemy territory and it looks particularly small when seen from an altitude of something over five miles. Frequently you cannot see it because of clouds or overcast and must depend upon your instruments. We have not put all our bombs exactly where we wanted to put them, and therefore we are not by any means satisfied with what we have done so far. We are still in our early, experimental stages. We have much to learn and many operational and other technical problems to solve.

It is worthy of note that in the first draft of Arnold's letter of December 27—a letter that was not sent until the 30th—he had handwritten a postscript that was omitted from the final draft: ''I am not satisfied with the 'abortives' [planes scheduled to go on a mission that for one reason or another have to drop out]. On that one day—21—is far too many. We must not and cannot let this continue. I want to hear from you about this with reasons.''

That complaint reflected Arnold's dissatisfaction even more clearly than any of the letters he had sent Hansell. Why was the complaint not sent? Probably because, by that time, Arnold had decided to send his deputy. Norstad reached Guam a week later on January 7 (January 6 in the States) and announced to Hansell immediately that he was to be relieved of command. LeMay arrived the next day and stepped into an embarrassing situation. When he was a group commander in the Eighth Air Force, he had served for a while under Hansell. Now he was replacing him. It was a difficult meeting for all three men. Norstad and Hansell were long-time friends. They had served together on Arnold's staff for two or three years. Norstad later said about the meeting, ''Possum and myself . . . we see eye to eye. We're personal friends. We've done a lot of tough jobs together. And I'm the one that has to come out and tell Possum we're not letting him keep the best job in the Air Force today—the command of the Twenty-first Bomber Command. The reason is that General Arnold—and all of us, including, I think, Possum—now know that this LeMay is the best man in the Air Force right now for this particular job, the job of carrying out what Possum and the rest of us started. LeMay is an operator, the rest of us are planners. That's all there is to it. It's tough and it's right. And Possum is taking it the way Possum would.''

No one could have expected less from Hansell. Always a gentleman, he did his best to put Norstad and LeMay at ease. St. Clair McKelway, a highly respected writer for *The New Yorker*, who was during the war an Air Force lieutenant colonel and chief public relations officer for the Twenty-first Bomber Command, ran into Hansell shortly after LeMay's arrival. ''Mac, I think there's something you ought to know,'' Hansell said to him. For privacy, they went into the mission planning room and over to an unoccupied corner of it. While a dozen or more officers hurried back and forth a few feet from them, preparing a mission to the Kobe area, the two men perched on the edge of a table.

''LeMay is coming here,'' Hansell confided, ''to take over the command. I'm out. I'm leaving for the States as soon as LeMay has had time to fly back to China, wind up his business there, and fly back here. That's what Norstad came out to tell me.''[3]

McKelway, who, like most people, was very fond of Hansell, felt like shouting, ''Holy God, Possum! They can't do this to you!'' Instead, he said, ''Holy God, General, what is this all about?''

Hansell's answer said as much about him as it did about LeMay: ''I'm not entirely sure. I don't think''—he emphasized the word—''that they are dissatisfied with the way I've been running things. There is nothing to indicate that. Norstad brought the word personally from General Arnold, with the information that the boss wanted him to tell me the decision orally. I think what's happened is that the boss has decided LeMay is the best man to go on with this from here on out. I think that's really it. I think the boss considers LeMay as the big-time operator and me as the planner. There is no doubt whatever about LeMay's ability to do the job, although I can't be so hypocritical as to say I think he could do it better than I could do it. But LeMay is tops. He used to be a group commander in my division in the Eighth Air Force. I got him his promotion to brigadier general, and when he went up to major general, I was in a position, as deputy chief of staff of the Army Air Forces, to help that along. He may easily be the best combat commander today in the Army Air Forces for this particular job, all things considered, especially when you count in his combat experience with B-29s in China.''

If, as Hansell said, he helped secure LeMay's promotions to

brigadier, and then to major general, he thereby created an ironic situation for himself. As a colonel, he had outranked LeMay, but now he was a brigadier while LeMay was a major general. When LeMay was asked why, in his opinion, he had been thrust into Hansell's B-29 job, he pointed out that, with the impending consolidation of the Twentieth and Twenty-first Bomber Commands in the Marianas, only one commander would be needed there, and he outranked Hansell. When he said this, he may simply have been looking for a polite explanation. He knew as well as Hansell that Arnold was dissatisfied with the progress of the Twenty-first B.C. in the Marianas.

The men of the Twenty-first, taking a look at LeMay for the first time, weren't sure they liked what they saw. Part of his tough image lay in the fact that he looked tough. His piercing gaze, the defiant thrust of his jaw, and his skimpy rationing of smiles made him look like someone you wouldn't want to fight in a bar, or even meet in the dark. Most of the people he was now meeting for the first time knew almost nothing about him, but they were pretty sure they didn't want to work for him.

"His looks," McKelway observed, "had not helped us take a jolly view of the future. He was around a few days, said almost nothing to anybody, was what, by civilian standards, would be called rude to many people. He was a big, husky, healthy, rather stocky, full-faced, black-haired man, thirty-nine years old, from Columbus, Ohio. He apparently couldn't make himself heard even in a small room except when you bent all your ears in his direction, and when you did he appeared to evade your attempt to hear him. He did this by interposing a cigar or pipe among the words which were trying to escape through teeth that had obviously been pried open only with effort, an effort with which the speaker had no real sympathy, and to which he was unwilling to lend more than halfhearted assistance."

Brig. Gen. Roger Ramey, a classmate of LeMay's at flying school in 1929, and now Hansell's chief of staff in the Marianas, was chosen to replace LeMay in India, and the two men flew to Kharagpur together, LeMay to close out his affairs and Ramey to take command there. But before flying back to Guam on the 18th, LeMay helped Ramey get acquainted with his new job by staging two more missions—Formosa on the 14th and Shinchiku on the 16th.

On the 19th, when LeMay was taking over from Hansell after returning to Guam, Hap Arnold, in Washington, was falling victim to his fourth major heart attack—a fact which might be taken into account in any assessment of his growing lack of patience. It is a trait often observed in people who have suffered heart damage. Neither of the men on Guam realized at the time that their chief was again ill, but it would have made no difference if they had known. Hansell's fate was already decided.

McKelway, who attended a farewell ceremony for Hansell, his departing boss, spent much of his time in bemused observation of LeMay, his new boss. "It was not known whether LeMay would be there in time for the ceremony, but he was. I wanted a photograph of LeMay shaking hands with Hansell and I so informed LeMay. [He] seemed surprised that anybody would want such a thing. He had kept in the background at the ceremony, smoking a pipe and hiding it in his pants pocket when the band played 'The Star Spangled Banner' and the troops of the Twenty-first Bomber Command passed in review."

After the parade, when the time came for picture taking, LeMay stepped uncomfortably in front of the camera with the pipe in hand. He tried to get it back into his pants pocket where, it seemed to McKelway, he must have some hidden apparatus to prevent it from burning his pants and his leg.

"General, please let me hold your pipe," McKelway suggested. He handed McKelway the pipe and with what seemed like a look of "abject misery," said in a barely audible voice, "Where do you want me to stand?"

After the picture taking and all the day's ceremonies were over, including the presentation of a Distinguished Service Medal to Hansell, LeMay sought out McKelway, nudged him as if to remind him he was there, and spoke to him in a voice that "barely brushed the hairs" inside McKelway's ears.

"Better get some sleep," LeMay said. "Thanks for holding my pipe."

If this incident makes LeMay appear awkwardly self-effacing and even timid, it might surprise some people who knew him at the time. Awkward he could be, and reticent sometimes to the point of seeming rude and making people around him uneasy. But there is little evidence that he was ever very timid. Within a few days after his permanent arrival on Guam he was in contention with the Navy, an "enemy" he sometimes seemed to fight almost as fiercely as he fought the Germans and Japanese, though less effectively.

The conquest of the Marianas had been, basically, a triumph

of the Navy and its assault troops, the Marines. The Army had been active enough in it to suffer almost four thousand casualties (dead and wounded) but more than sixteen thousand Marines had fallen before the Japanese resistance was quelled. It was basically a Navy show, supported by naval gunfire plus carrier planes. And the Navy handled it with dispatch, securing Saipan July 9, Tinian August 7, and Guam August 10, 1944. But the purpose of taking the Marianas was nothing more nor less than to provide bases from which the Air Force B-29s could strike at the very center of Japan. And LeMay got mad at the Navy almost immediately after settling into his tent on Guam because he didn't think enough had been done, since the islands were secured, to facilitate that purpose.

His relations with the Navy on Guam began with a gesture of friendship by the theater commander, Admiral Chester W. Nimitz, who invited him to dinner.[5] LeMay was duly impressed by the spacious, comfortable house the admiral had arranged for his Seabee construction corps to build for him, the staff of Filipino mess boys, the immaculate uniforms of the naval officers and the mess boys (in contrast to his own wrinkled Air Force tans), the wide range of available cocktails, the splendid food, the brandy and cigars. It was pleasant to spend an evening in such luxurious surroundings at the top of the island's highest hill, instead of sitting on the cot in the tent he occupied down in the flat.

But a few days later, when he was invited to dinner by the island commander, who had built for himself another sumptuous house, with tennis courts, on the island's second highest hill, he began to wonder how all this could be, with the B-29 facilities still far from completed. And when he got a third naval invitation, from the Submarine Force commander, whose quarters turned out to be the Vanderbilt yacht, he decided he ought to study the way the Navy conducted its business. Since the Pacific Theater was under Navy control, it was the Navy's responsibility to provide all the necessary construction and supplies, not only for itself but for the Air Force. The Navy seemed to be doing only part of that job.

After making some discreet inquiries among the construction workers, LeMay managed to come up with a bootleg copy of the Navy's Construction Priority List for Guam. Not until he reached page 5 did he arrive at the needs of the Air Force and the B-29s.

He got back at his Navy friends first by inviting them down to his place for a dinner of the canned field rations the Air Force men were eating. Then he sent a copy of the Construction Priority List to Hap Arnold's office in Washington, and a speed-up soon began in construction of B-29 facilities. Meanwhile, he had found that he couldn't remain angry at the very charming and friendly Admiral Nimitz for dragging his feet. Though Nimitz was the theater commander, LeMay realized, he "had to give us his life's blood in logistics, in supply and support and so on." But at the same time he "had no operational control over the B-29s. Thus he was awarded no credit for anything they accomplished." When he took such considerations into account, LeMay was inclined to adopt a more tolerant attitude toward the Navy. For a while, at least.

Being an Air Force man, he was almost certain to find the Navy annoying. Since 1921, when the Air Service first sank a battleship, the airmen had been fighting with the Navy about the proper function of aircraft. But he had bigger immediate problems, and one of them was in the Air Force—Hap Arnold. An indication of what Arnold expected from him can be found in a memorandum, Arnold to Norstad, dated January 14, 1945, just a few days before the Air Force chief's fourth heart attack:

> . . . relative to the present status of the Twentieth Air Force . . . I am still worried—we have built up ideas in the Army, the Navy and among civilians of what we can do with our B-29s. We have all realized that in order to do considerable damage, large numbers of B-29s would have to deliver their loads of bombs against Japan continuously and consistently and yet in spite of the above, really and truly, our average daily delivery rate against Japan is very, very small. . . . The above should not be, because we have a total in excess of 200 airplanes in the Marianas alone. . . . Unless something drastic is done to change this condition soon, it will not be long before the B-29 is just another tactical airplane. . . . We are sending out to the Marianas B-29s at the rate of up to 8 to 10 a day. These airplanes are quite expensive and carry with them a crew of 12 men, and yet our results are far from what everyone else expects. . . .

LeMay began his new job, as he had begun so many previous jobs, with a retraining program. But after his first mission—January 23 against Nagoya—he realized he had another problem. One that had also frustrated Hansell and that no amount of training would solve. With very little weather information coming out of northern and central Asia, there was no way to predict the weather over Japan. And it would have provided scant comfort if he had been able to do so because Japan was one big cloud factory. During the best months of the year, he could count on no more than seven days when it would be possible to bomb visually. During some months there would be perhaps one day, perhaps none.

Worse than that, at the thirty-five-thousand-foot altitude for which the B-29 was designed, and from which Hansell's crews had been trying to bomb, the Pacific jet stream made accuracy impossible. "You could go on forever," LeMay discovered, "trying to get up to a target in such a wind. And if you went cross-wind, your bombsight wouldn't take care of the drift you had. If you came in downwind, you didn't have time to get a proper run on the target. This was really a tough proposition to lick."

He took a hard look at that thirty-five-thousand-foot operating altitude and decided the jet stream wasn't the only disadvantage it offered. He suspected the continuing high incidence of mechanical failure was also connected to it. The strain of climbing and flying that high might even equal the danger of fighters and flak at lower altitudes.

"I was convinced from my China experience," LeMay has observed, "that we were losing more planes to mechanical problems than to enemy action. So I brought them down ten thousand feet at the start. But we still hit that jet stream occasionally."[6]

On the January 23 Nagoya mission the weather was only part of the problem. To help defend the Tokyo-Nagoya corridor, the Japanese had deployed every available pursuit plane, and while they were not individually as formidable as the German fighters, their numbers created a hazard that couldn't be overlooked, especially since Japanese pilots didn't hesitate to ram their planes into the big invading bombers. On an attempted January 27 attack against a large aircraft plant in Musashino, near Tokyo, the clouds were again the target's main defense, but once more those Japanese fighters were there to get in the way, darting in and out, disrupting traffic, and making the air unsafe for the B-29s. The Superfortresses were subjected to "approximately 1,000 individual fighter attacks" that day.

The next day, LeMay suggested to the Pentagon that he should try some less hotly defended targets, at least temporarily, until his crews were better prepared, or until some long-range fighter support arrived. He suggested a Mitsubishi aircraft plant at Tamashima.

Because Arnold was now in Coral Gables, Florida, recovering from his latest heart attack, Norstad conferred about the matter with Lt. Gen. Barney Giles, the Air Force deputy commander. Giles informed Arnold in his January 30 report of the day's activities, "we are instructing LeMay to direct his efforts at more widely dispersed targets and to engage in night operations until our long-range fighters are available for employment, which should be in the latter part of February. From then on, the old maxim, 'The thicker the grass, the easier to mow,' should apply."

Norstad more specifically suggested to LeMay that he ignore Tamashima, which wasn't very important, and try instead a night firebombing raid on Kobe. Norstad had tried earlier to interest Hansell in firebombing because of the almost insurmountable difficulties of precision daylight bombing, and did induce him to make one inconclusive experiment. But Hansell, devoted to the Air Force precision doctrine, had not welcomed the idea, and his last mission, in daylight, had been, ironically, so successful it prompted LeMay to continue the same strategy.

LeMay, however, was always more practical than theoretical. When someone made a suggestion that sounded good, he was likely to try it without stopping to consider whether it fitted into his philosophy. One day a major in the aircraft maintenance section of the Twentieth Air Force went to headquarters to tell a superior officer he had figured out a better procedure of some kind.

"I was standing with my back to the door," he later recalled, "all wound up and going strong. I noticed that the man I was talking to sort of stiffened. I looked over my shoulder and there was LeMay. All he said was, 'Sounds like the major's got a good idea. Put it into practice.' "

In China, LeMay had conducted one firebombing mission (Hankow) successfully. He decided now to try it in Japan, where the predominantly wooden cities were thought to be equally combustible. In the years to come he would be criticized for using such a strategy on the grounds that it was inhumane. No doubt it was. All war is inhumane, despite its apparent popularity among humans. Fire is no fun, but neither are high explosives or shrapnel, or bullets. The Germans had begun the destruction of cities in World War II with Warsaw, then London and other English industrial centers. The Japanese had been leveling Chinese cities since their invasion of Manchuria in 1931. Beginning December 7, 1941, they had bombed Honolulu, then Manila, and would gladly have done likewise to San Francisco and Los Angeles if they had been able.

Since the industrial revolution, warring nations had accepted, in theory as well as fact, the notion that when they went to war, all of their citizens went to war. The farmers and factory workers on the home front, producing guns, tanks, aircraft, food, and equipment were as crucial to the war effort as the soldiers who fired the guns, ate the food, and used the equipment. To defeat a nation's army it was necessary to defeat the cities, towns, and ports that supplied that army. Like almost everyone else in the world of the 1940s, LeMay accepted this theory. And he accepted Norstad's suggestion. He scheduled the Kobe attack for February 4.

Kobe, a city of a million people about 275 miles southwest of Tokyo on Osaka Bay, was Japan's largest port and one of its largest industrial centers. Its heavy industries included shipbuilding, railroad equipment, munitions, and precision machinery. Its congested center, at which LeMay was aiming, adjoined the harbor and contained many of the large factories as well as businesses and residences. LeMay sent 129 planes there February 4. Only sixty-nine found their way to the target, and they dropped a disappointing 160 tons of incendiaries from about twenty-five thousand feet. To do so they had to fight off two hundred Japanese pursuit planes. But only one bomber was lost to enemy action while 1,039 buildings were destroyed or badly damaged. Five of the city's major industries had their output significantly curtailed. One shipyard lost half of its potential production and a synthetic rubber plant was totally eliminated. The results at Kobe, added to those earlier results at Hankow, gave LeMay something about which to think. But at the moment there were more pressing matters.

The Navy was now preparing to invade the little volcanic island of Iwo Jima, about halfway between Japan and the Marianas, and wanted B-29 bombardment support for the operation. LeMay was hardly in a position to refuse it flatly inasmuch as the major purpose of the exercise was to stop the harassment of the Marianas by Iwo-based Japanese fighters, and to provide a halfway haven for distressed B-29s on the way to and from Japan.

Six months earlier, Japan had only a few hundred men on Iwo. Perhaps the Navy should have taken it then, but it was too late now to speculate about that. The Japanese had since put so many thousand troops on Iwo, and had built up its defenses so alarmingly that the Navy, once indifferent about attacking it, was now quite enthusiastic about not doing so. Marine Gen. Holland M. "Howlin' Mad" Smith was predicting it could not be captured for less than fifteen thousand casualties. But that wasn't the only reason the Navy lacked enthusiasm for the enterprise. As it happened, the Navy, at that moment, had another, more pleasing project in mind.

For seven months, B-29s had been conducting missions against the Japanese homeland. They weren't always very effective, but they did bring the war home to Japan in the unpleasant form of falling bombs. And the Air Force, never bashful about blowing its own horn, had made sure everyone knew that only the Air Force was hitting the enemy directly, where he lived. The American newspapers and magazines were full of stories about this giant bomber that was going to bring Japan to its knees. And the Navy knew, as well as the Air Force, that favorable headlines in the papers were like money in the congressional bank when the time came for military budget allocations.

The Navy, even the Air Force would have to admit, had done much more than the Air Force so far toward bringing Japan to its knees. The Navy had virtually destroyed the Japanese navy in a series of remarkable and historic sea battles. And it had captured for the Air Force the very bases in the Marianas without which the B-29 would have only limited potential. But was the Navy getting credit for this? Not enough. Now that the Japanese fleet had been eliminated it was about time, the Navy decided, to show the American public that it, too, as well as the headline-hunting Air Force, was capable of direct attacks on Japan.

To this end, the Navy was now planning a series of strikes against Tokyo by the planes of a massive fleet called Task Force 58, which comprised sixteen carriers, eight battleships, seventeen cruisers, seventy-five destroyers and support ships in the hundreds. The only catch in the Navy plan was the well-known fact that land-based planes were more formidable and usually larger than carrier-based planes. This meant there was a significant danger of land-based Japanese planes sinking task-force carriers or battleships when they came close enough to Tokyo Bay.

Someone in the Navy offered a brilliant idea to prevent such a disaster. Why not get the B-29s to support the task-force strike against Tokyo by bombing Japanese air bases in the Tokyo area. That would keep Japanese land-based planes from attacking the task force.

With all these considerations in mind, Adm. Raymond A. Spruance, commander of the naval units assigned to capture Iwo Jima, invited LeMay to a conference on his flagship at the island of Ulithi in the Carolines.[9] The first question Spruance asked LeMay was whether he thought the capture of Iwo Jima was necessary.

LeMay said, "You're damned right it's necessary." He needed Iwo, not only as an emergency landing field for B-29s, but as a base for fighter escort planes and for air-sea rescue units assigned to pluck downed bomber crews out of the ocean.

The next logical question was whether he would be willing to support the invasion of Iwo by sending his B-29s on missions there? That was a tough question because LeMay was firmly convinced the B-29 should be used as a strategic rather than a tactical weapon. But since the Navy was getting ready to take the island almost entirely for the good of the B-29s, he could hardly refuse to help. He was willing, he said, to launch missions in direct support of the invasion when it was absolutely essential. But the best way for his planes to help the Navy at Iwo, he insisted, was to destroy key Japanese facilities in the home islands.

Surprisingly, Spruance and his staff failed to argue very strongly against this somewhat questionable reasoning, and LeMay soon found out why. Their most pressing priority at the moment was not the Iwo invasion but the attack by Task Force 58 against Tokyo. What they wanted most of all was a promise from LeMay that he would bomb Japanese airfields in the Tokyo area before and during the task-force foray.

LeMay, understanding now why this meeting had been called, pointed out that enemy airfields had not been included in the Joint Chiefs' target directive under which he commanded the B-29s because airfields as such were tactical rather than strategic targets. And it made no sense for B-29s to put a lot of holes in runways—holes that would be easy to patch—just to prevent a land-based attack on a naval task force. Those same B-29s, in the same amount of time, could put twice as many tons of bombs on important targets as the Navy task force could hope to do.

He offered instead to coordinate his missions against Japan with the Task Force 58 attacks. But he insisted he must strike only significant targets.

Apparently embarrassed at having to seek the help of the very source from which they were trying to siphon off publicity, the naval officers yielded. LeMay sent his B-29s to add their weight to the naval bombardment of Iwo Jima February 12 (five days before D-day there). Then, on February 15, 19, and 25, he synchronized B-29 missions against various targets with the Navy's missions against Tokyo.

There were two ironic results. The two-hundred-plus ships of Task Force 58, during 2,074 sorties against Tokyo on those three days, dropped 513 tons of bombs and rockets. They also destroyed 415 Japanese planes with a loss of 102 of their own 1,091 planes.

On those same three days, an average of 167 B-29s flew 439 sorties and dropped a total of 1,220 tons of bombs (two-and-a-half times as much as the task force) on the Japanese mainland. The B-29s shot down only forty-six planes but lost only five of their own.

The second ironic result of the Navy's elaborately staged strike against Tokyo was to make their own Marine general, "Howlin' Mad" Smith, howlin' mad. Though he said nothing publicly at the time, Smith told the whole world how he felt in a *Saturday Evening Post* article November 20, 1948, entitled, "Iwo Jima Cost Too Much." During the planning for the attack against Iwo Jima, Smith had asked the Navy to bombard its defenses for ten days before he sent his men ashore. Instead of ten days' worth, he got only three days', and he didn't like it:

> Limited, against our better judgment, to only three days' preliminary bombardment, there seemed nothing to do but make the best of the situation. . . .

> [But] our troubles were not at an end. Due to a change of plans by Spruance, the ships allocated to the pre-D-Day bombardment were unavailable and substitutions were made. We also were robbed of the services of the U.S.S. Washington and the U.S.S. North Carolina, two of our 16-inch gun ships originally assigned to the niggardly allotment of fire, but withdrawn at the last minute to join Task Force 58 and provide anti-aircraft fire. . . .

Spruance was apologetic for this disruption. He insisted that the importance of the strike was so great that he must give Task Force 58 all possible assistance to ensure a successful outcome. . . .

To me, naval insistence upon the priority of the strike against Japan at the cost of fire support for our assault on Iwo Jima was incomprehensible. It simply weakened the power we could use at Iwo Jima.

It should not be inferred, however, that during those few days the B-29s were accomplishing wonders over the Tokyo area while the Navy was simply playing around, making headlines, as Hap Arnold was quick to notice, and it did, perhaps, shirk its duties at Iwo, as Howlin' Mad Smith was quick to notice. But on the 17th, its carrier planes, at low altitude, created havoc at the aircraft plant in Musashino. Meanwhile, the B-29s were still trying to bomb with precision at high altitudes, and while they were dropping two-and-a-half times as many tons of bombs as the carrier planes, they were still wasting so much of their potential that LeMay was becoming more frustrated day by day.

So was Hap Arnold. He was recovering from his heart attack now, and as his health improved, his disposition worsened. When Giles informed him of the successful February 4 incendiary attack against Kobe by "over a hundred aircraft," his answer, scribbled across the Giles report, was, "Grand, but why not 150 or 200?"[10]

On February 16, after reading in the newspapers about the Navy's first strike against Tokyo, Arnold wrote Giles an "Eyes Only" letter just to let him know he wasn't any more excited about LeMay than he had been about Hansell:

I have been somewhat concerned over the number of B-29s actually employed in operations against Japan. This concern is more definitely brought to light as the result of two newspaper items which came out in the last couple days. One talked of the one thousandth B-29 being produced at Wichita. The other came out in this morning's paper and told of the Navy's fifteen hundred airplanes [other sources put the number at 1,091] hitting Japan proper. . . .

I know that you are going to be told that they must have X-hundred of these planes for training. I know that you will also be told that it is difficult to get them in the air from their bases in the Pacific. And I know that there are one thousand other reasons for not getting two, three or four hundred B-29s over Japan on every possible occasion. This cannot be done if we accept excuses and do not face the issue.

From my viewpoint down here [in Coral Gables], I would not be surprised any day to see the control of the 20th Air Force pass to either Nimitz or MacArthur.

Letters like that, though marked "Eyes Only," had ways of reaching the ears of the parties most likely to be affected by them. LeMay, who had been taking a crash course in Arnoldology during the last few months, was well aware of what his boss wanted and what might happen if he didn't soon get it. He also knew how those two great rivals in the Pacific, MacArthur and the Navy, both coveted the B-29s and the potential power they represented. He decided he had better forget precision bombing, at least for the moment, and try something daringly different. For February 25, he scheduled the biggest B-29 mission of the war to date—a high-altitude incendiary strike against the very heart of Tokyo, through the clouds if necessary.

CHAPTER TEN

The daylight precision-bombing strategy of the Twentieth Air Force against Japan was now under critical review, and Arnold was not the only critic. Admiral Nimitz and his Navy colleagues could very reasonably ask why they should have to invade fortified islands, lose thousands of men, build airfields, and ship in mountains of supplies for an Air Force that couldn't figure out how to use the weapon that supposedly justified this huge expense in lives and money. At the same time, Douglas MacArthur, a great general but also an emperor looking for an empire, and a self-publicist so effective he could sway his nation's political balance, had convinced a lot of influential Americans that this new weapon could achieve its potential only if it were placed under his control. LeMay, as much imbued with the Air Force doctrine of daylight precision bombing as was Hansell, had been scarcely more fortunate in making that doctrine work against Japan.

Among the least successful of LeMay's daylight precision missions was the one February 19 against the Nakajima aircraft factory at Musashino. Unable to find the target beneath thick layers of clouds, the 119 Superfortresses which reached the area finally dropped their bombs on metropolitan Tokyo by radar. But the radar operators at this time were so ill trained that depending on them was like depending on a hatpin to choose a horse in a race. The B-29s that day hit, by chance, a spinning mill, a railroad yard, and a bridge. And their failure was especially galling to LeMay because of the Navy's effective low-level mission, two days earlier, against the same Musashino target.

After the embarrassing February 19 raid, LeMay's operations officer, Col. John B. Montgomery, came to him and said, in effect, If we don't start hitting some targets, we'll soon be targets.[1] LeMay already knew that. He had at his disposal the most sophisticated airplane ever built. And by this time the worst of its bugs had been eliminated or at least alleviated. Its cabin areas were pressurized. Its engines were turbo-supercharged. Its guns were mechanized. And it was capable of operating at thirty-five thousand feet, above the effective altitude of Japanese flak and the best Japanese fighters. But in order to deliver only three tons of bombs to Tokyo at thirty-five thousand feet, it had to carry twenty-three tons of gasoline, several tons of which were devoted simply to getting the fully loaded plane that high and keeping it there.

Worse than that, it had no way of knowing precisely where to deliver that disappointingly small load of bombs when it got to its target since it couldn't see through clouds. After two thousand "precise" sorties over Japan, not one important target had been destroyed. The target that had attracted the most attention, the suburban Tokyo aircraft plant in Musashino, had suffered only 4 percent damage after seven missions against it.

Unless LeMay soon figured out how to make better use of this expensive weapon Arnold had entrusted to him, Norstad had bluntly informed him that his future would be as cloudy as the skies over Japan. If he didn't get results pretty soon, not only would he be fired; the strategic air offensive against Japan would probably be cast aside; the mass invasion would go on as scheduled in November, and perhaps a half million Americans would be killed in it.

LeMay had said to Norstad, "You know General Arnold. I don't know him. Does he ever go for a gamble? What do you think?"[2]

He didn't tell Norstad what kind of gamble he had in mind, nor did he get much of a reaction from Norstad except for a feeling that "being a little unorthodox was all right with Arnold."

LeMay had a high regard for Norstad, whom he had first met when they were both stationed at Wheeler Field in Hawaii during the 1930s. "He was one of those brilliant guys," LeMay once said of him. "A professional staff man. Somebody always latched onto him to do the paperwork and keep them out of trouble." But he wasn't quite ready to associate himself with whatever unorthodoxy LeMay might have in mind. "I didn't get much out of [him]. He never stuck his neck out."

All these matters were in LeMay's mind when he scheduled

the February 25 night incendiary mission against Tokyo. He no longer had time to figure out how to make daylight precision bombing work in Japan. He had to experiment with something new before Arnold decided to fire him.

He was so engrossed in this problem he gave only partial attention to an unusual visitor who appeared in his office one day— a scholarly-looking Army Engineers colonel who announced he was on a mission of extreme importance for something called the Manhattan District Project.[3]

LeMay had never heard of such an outfit, and the first thing he heard about it now was that he hadn't better let anyone else hear about it. This was no ordinary colonel. He had credentials that would impress the pope. And he had news about some kind of atomic device so secret that since LeMay now knew about it, he would never again be allowed to go on a mission. So secret that the crews that would eventually drop it didn't even know what it was, or for what purpose they were being trained. These crews were part of a B-29 unit, the 509th Composite Group, which would soon be coming to Tinian for further training on how to use the weapon, if the president of the United States decided to use it.

The colonel's job was to prepare an isolated area on Tinian where the 509th would be quartered in virtual quarantine, and to build the facilities the group would need there. This would include pits in which the weapon would be placed before loading onto a B-29. The plane would taxi over the pit, whereupon the weapon, apparently a large device, would be jacked up into the bomb bay. All of this would be done in absolute secrecy, with special security forces surrounding the area to make sure no one could watch. But LeMay would presumably be in command of the operation. At any rate, he was expected to set up a training program to familiarize the crews of the 509th with flying conditions in the Pacific and over Japan.

"I was told it was a nuclear weapon," LeMay later recalled, but "that didn't make too much of an impression: my college physics course was a long way behind. Generally speaking, I could understand what the Army man was talking about. We had a very powerful weapon. But it was late in the war and I was busy."

He sent the colonel up to Tinian with authorization to do whatever was necessary there. Then he decided he'd better send one of his own officers to Tinian to keep him in touch with whatever these atomic boys were planning to do.

He called in Col. Delmar Wilson, who had been with him in the 306th Group in 1942, and had been operations officer in the Twentieth Air Force until LeMay arrived on Guam. Since LeMay had brought along his own operations officer, Col. William H. "Butch" Blanchard, there wasn't much for Wilson to do on Guam.

LeMay said to him, "I want you to go up to the 313rd Wing [on Tinian] as deputy for operations. Take my airplane and go."

When Wilson arrived at Tinian, he found that the commanding officer, Brig. Gen. John "Skip" Davies, already had an operations officer he liked, and wasn't looking for another one. He and the rest of his staff seemed to resent Wilson's arrival.

"They looked on me as a spy for LeMay," he later recalled. "I had leprosy. They stuck me down at the end of the senior officers' tent row. They ignored me."[4]

One day, an Army colonel, E. E. Kirkpatrick, and a Navy captain, William S. Parsons, came to Wilson's tent. He had no idea who they were or what they wanted. LeMay had never made it clear to Wilson why he was sitting at Tinian with nothing to do.

One of Wilson's visitors said to him, "We can't talk to you here." They took him to another tent where Captain Parsons asked him, "Have you ever heard of an atom?"

Wilson had only a vague familiarity with such things as atoms and molecules and atomic physics.

Parsons produced a letter signed by Secretary of War Henry L. Stimson. It threatened a death penalty for anyone violating security about the subject to be discussed. After taking an oath of silence, Wilson learned about the atomic bomb. Suddenly he realized why, this time at least, LeMay had been so uncommunicative.

Meanwhile, LeMay himself had gotten back to his first order of business, which was the urgent need to get Hap Arnold off his back. On February 19, LeMay received a revised target directive from Washington which ordered him to continue strikes at aircraft plants in the Nagoya-Tokyo-Shizuoka areas, but which also placed increased emphasis on the importance of urban incendiary attacks. The Air Force, it seemed, was now officially abandoning its precision doctrine, at least in the Orient. And the fact that it hadn't worked was not the only excuse put forward.

In Japan's major industrial cities, it was explained, the crowded urban areas harbored tens of thousands of small shops that manufactured parts for the large assembly plants. And many of the large plants that were prime targets were also in these areas. If all these plants, large and small, were allowed to continue turning out guns, tanks, planes, etc., they would build up huge stocks of matériel for the Japanese army to use against the American invasion. By burning out large areas to get at the factories, the B-29s would no doubt be killing thousands of Japanese civilians, but they would also be saving the lives of thousands, perhaps hundreds of thousands of American soldiers who would soon be coming ashore to face the Japanese defenses.

New B-29 groups, plus replacement planes and crews, were now arriving in the Marianas at such a growing rate that the Command was able to get 231 Superfortresses aloft and on the way to Tokyo the evening of February 25, each loaded with three tons of incendiaries plus one five-hundred-pound high-explosive bomb to use against any specific target that might come into view. Only 172 planes reached Tokyo, but they dropped 453 tons of bombs, not throughout the city, but in one small section. LeMay had ordered them to concentrate their attack into a square mile or so.

As usual, there were clouds. Not enough to obscure the limits of the urban area, but enough to prevent the aerial cameras from taking strike photos. It was several days before pictures could be taken and the results of the mission determined. When LeMay saw the photos, he saw his future course in front of him. An entire square mile of Tokyo had been almost eliminated. (Tokyo police records later showed that 27,970 buildings had been destroyed that night.)

In the greater part of Tokyo at that time, 99 percent of the buildings were wooden. In the wealthier areas, 90 percent were wooden. The streets were so narrow small fires could leap them to ignite the buildings on the other side, and the city, like most others in Japan, had a long history of multiple-structure fires, even in peacetime. Under these circumstances, fire was a weapon the Americans could hardly ignore, especially since they now had a new kind of incendiary bomb—napalm, a combination of jellied gasoline and magnesium that stuck to almost any surface it hit and burned slowly at a high temperature.

LeMay staged one more daylight precision attack—another cloud-shrouded failure, March 4, against the Musashino aircraft plant—because he wasn't quite ready to try what he now had in mind, yet some effort was better than no effort. His mind, however, was on more daring plans. Arnold wanted a maximum effort in the weeks ahead, and he was going to get it.

For some time, LeMay had wondered about the uses of radar in finding a target. Until recently he hadn't paid much serious attention to it, partly because he had so many other things to do, partly because he had little faith in it. "Radar in England had been worthless," he later explained. "You could see a river and a shoreline and the ocean. Beyond that you couldn't see very much."[5] But during the almost eight months since he had left England, radar machinery had been improved, and a radar expert, a professor from the Massachusetts Institute of Technology, Dr. King Gould, had been assigned to his command. Why not use him?

He had called "Doc" Gould into his office and said to him, "Look, you go up [to Saipan] and pick out a couple of the stupidest radar operators they have, and Lord knows that's pretty stupid. You go up and fly with them and see if they can fly over this spit of land sticking out on the northern side of the island. That's a real good land-water contrast. Go see if they can do that."

After working for several days with the radar operators on Saipan, Doc Gould came back to Guam depressed at their inefficiency and lack of training. "I guess maybe they can do it," he told LeMay, "but they need a lot of training."

By late February they were getting this training, though mostly on the ground. They had developed at least a few glimmering ideas about how radar machines worked and how to read the "blips" on the screens. The time had arrived to begin testing them in the air. LeMay decided to make this test serve two purposes.

Off the coast of Saipan were several small islands, still strongly held by the Japanese, who had been bypassed and left stranded there when the Americans took the main islands of the Marianas. One of these small islands, Kito Iwo, included among its geographic features a tip of land similar to a protrusion at the mouth of Tokyo Bay. LeMay sent to Rosey O'Donnell, commander of the Seventy-third Wing on Saipan, an order for a radar training mission against Kito Iwo, scheduled for March 1, in which twelve B-29s—four columns of threes—were to use this tip of land as a target finder. There was nothing unusual about the order until it stipulated the altitude. The mission was to be flown at fifty feet above sea level.[6] Since most men entertained a lively fear of antiaircraft fire even at twenty-five thousand feet, LeMay did not expect Rosey or his crews to be overjoyed at the notion of flying in at fifty feet.

O'Donnell's acknowledgment of the order came back immediately: "Altitude in error. Two ciphers missing."

LeMay's answer was: "Altitude correct. Five zero feet."

An hour later, O'Donnell, having flown to Guam, burst in upon LeMay and several members of his staff.

"I cannot fly that mission," Rosey announced.

He wasn't a man to be taken lightly. In addition to being a highly regarded wing commander with a lot of experience (including leadership of the first B-29 mission against Tokyo), he was one of Hap Arnold's "boys." And just about the only one who dared talk back to the boss. A Brooklyn Irishman with an endless fund of funny stories, he seemed always able to make Arnold laugh. He had been for some time a member of Arnold's staff and had gotten into B-29s by making frequent pleas that Arnold send him out on a field assignment. One day in January 1944, Arnold got so tired of hearing these pleas he threw a paperweight at him. Rosey, who had been a West Point football player, caught it and threw it back at him. Rosey soon got his wish to go into B-29s, but he had not lost Arnold's affection, and everyone knew it.

LeMay and Rosey had known each other since 1928 when they became flying-school classmates, O'Donnell fresh out of West Point, LeMay fresh out of Ohio State. O'Donnell was a second lieutenant, LeMay an aviation cadet. "I had a high regard for Rosey," LeMay said later, "and I'm sure he did for me. I always liked to have him around. He was a party guy. No matter how tough things got, he could find a laugh in it someplace. In the back of my mind I always wondered, if something hit the fan, would Rosey be on the job or would he be down at the bar having a drink, [where] the party and the excitement would be? But he never was. Rosey was a first-class officer."

As the two men confronted each other over the question of this apparently insane mission at an altitude of fifty feet, LeMay's staff looked on with lively interest to see how he would handle Rosey's firm declaration.

LeMay raised his eyes and in that soft, almost inaudible voice, said, "You will fly it."

They stared at each other for a long moment but O'Donnell said no more. He flew the mission exactly as ordered and it proved exactly what LeMay had hoped. The radar operators could recognize that tip of land on their screens, and they could use it to find the target.

But why had he made them fly the mission at fifty feet? Simply because it fitted importantly into his plans to know whether, in spite of their griping, they would be willing and able to do so.

LeMay was not easy on O'Donnell, but he wasn't easy on anyone. He expected a lot, especially from his wing commanders and staff officers, and he got what he expected or else he got new officers. But by March 1945, he had men around him with whom he was very satisfied. Brig. Gen. John H. "Skippy" Davies, the handsome, boyish-looking commander of the 313th Wing on Tinian, had arisen out of obscurity on the strength of his ability, first as a pilot, then as a motivator and organizer. And Brig. Gen. Thomas S. Power of the new 314th Wing on Guam was a cold, hard, innovative commander who was not universally liked but who had proven in Europe that he could get results. When his wing arrived on Guam to find nothing but jungle where their quarters were supposed to be, he had put the men to work immediately, clearing the jungle with bolo knives. For the special mission LeMay was now planning, he figured he would need at least three hundred B-29s. He counted on O'Donnell's oldest wing to provide one hundred fifty, Davies's one hundred, and Power's at least fifty.

As his chief of staff, LeMay had now managed to procure the man who had served him so superbly in the same capacity in England—Brig. Gen. August Kissner, a tireless model of efficiency in handling administrative matters. His deputy chief of staff for operations, plans, and training, Colonel Montgomery, had been copilot of the plane LeMay navigated to intercept the Italian liner *Rex* in 1938. Before the war, Montgomery had made a special study of bombing techniques and was regarded by LeMay as one of the Air Corps' best bombardiers.

The oldest man on LeMay's staff, C. S. "Bill" Irvine, was still a colonel at forty-six because LeMay had not been able to secure promotions for him or for Montgomery. Irvine, as the officer in charge of maintenance and supply, was the one man who did more than any other to make sure the maximum number of B-29s were flyable every day.

One of Irvine's biggest problems was the replenishment of

spare parts. His daringly unorthodox way of handling it had gotten him into trouble with Army headquarters in Hawaii, through which all supply procurement was supposed to clear. Realizing how much delay this could cause, Irvine had somehow arranged with the Navy for the use of two ships that would do nothing but travel back and forth between Guam and the States, bypassing Hawaii to carry B-29 parts, especially engines, directly to the Marianas. But these ships were too slow to carry special emergency orders for other parts, and as the bomber fleet was growing, they couldn't even keep up with the demand for engines. So Irvine invented another scheme.

"I set up a big antenna on Guam pointed at Dayton, Ohio," he later admitted, "and then sent a man over to Dayton to build a similar one. Every night we would order supplies [from the Matériel Command in Dayton]. So every time we had a boat or a plane on the west coast we had stuff waiting on it. No one understood how we got such service."[8]

That last remark wasn't quite accurate. One man who unfortunately did understand was Lt. Gen. Robert C. Richardson in Hawaii, the Army commander for the entire Central Pacific. Already unhappy about the two supply ships that were bypassing his command, Richardson became furious when he found out about Irvine's private radio stations and private airline for parts. He arranged for the inspector general, Junius Jones, to look into this flagrant irregularity. There are two versions, not altogether inconsistent, of what happened next.

According to Irvine, "LeMay handled that. He went to the I.G. and said we had a war to fight. As far as information [to the enemy] was concerned, the Japs could get the tail number of every B-29 that passed over Kwajelein as they came in. LeMay said we tell the Japs what target we are going to hit the day after tomorrow so they [can] get the women and children out of the way. So they know that Bill Irvine is ordering 96 landing gears; what the hell are they going to do with that information?"

LeMay, trying years later to recall the incident, said, "I do remember some flak with Richardson about the supply situation." But he didn't remember how or whether he had "handled it." All he could recall was that Irvine had handled his end of it in a mysterious but exceedingly satisfactory way.

"I don't remember the details," LeMay said with a smile, "but at five o'clock in the morning, which was our reporting time for airplanes in commission, I'd have fifty planes out of commission for parts. And at eight o'clock a C-54 [four-engine transport] from Sacramento would land at a field next to our headquarters with parts. That afternoon, those fifty airplanes would take off.

"Bill Irvine was my A-4. He'd been in the Matériel Command and he knew the people in Sacramento [and Dayton] and I'm sure he fixed it. I didn't ask (him) any stupid questions. And I didn't ask him after the war, either."[9]

The success of O'Donnell's "fifty-foot" mission to Kito Iwo marked another step in LeMay's thinking toward a previously unthinkable decision. There was no doubt in his mind now about the necessity of conducting a serious incendiary campaign against the large industrial Japanese cities. And he expected no arguments about this, either from Washington or from his own men. But as for how to deliver those incendiaries, he had brewing in his mind an idea which, he knew, would scare the wits out of everybody.

The high-altitude fire raids against Tokyo, Nagoya, and Kobe had been effective. But he was still unsatisfied, not only with the lack of sufficient force to be decisive, but also with the lack of accuracy from twenty-five thousand feet. So he was now considering the practicality of lowering the attack altitude. What was so revolutionary or unthinkable about that? When he arrived in the Marianas he had lowered the bombing altitude from thirty-five thousand to twenty-five thousand feet without increasing the loss rate or unduly frightening the crews.

But this time he was thinking of lowering it not just five, ten, or even fifteen thousand feet. He was speculating on the feasibility of sending his bombers in at five or six thousand feet, and without any guns or ammunition.

"I expected," he said later, "that we would have less trouble with the airplane flying at low altitude—it wouldn't be such a strain on the engines and we would probably have less mechanical trouble. Also, all of the studies we'd made on the defenses of Japan indicated an absence of light flak or certainly not in the numbers that we found in Europe. I expected that if we went in at night at low altitude, say five thousand feet and up, we would surprise them and we would be able to get away with it, at least for a short period of time. . . . In Europe we couldn't have adopted these tactics at all, but in Japan, yes, I thought they would work."[10]

There were other factors in his thinking. The winds over Japan were much milder at the lower altitudes. And the savings in gas, which could amount to as much as sixty gallons per hour—nine hundred gallons on a fifteen-hour mission—would lighten the fuel load by as much as two and a half tons. Likewise, he would lighten the load by another two tons if he left all the guns, gunners, and ammunition at home. He would thereby also prevent his gunners from shooting at each other in the dark above Japan. But more important, by sending each plane out with four or five fewer tons of gas and gunnery, he could increase the bomb load by four or five tons.

But how would the B-29s protect themselves without guns? LeMay, who had a low opinion of Japanese fighter tactics, was convinced his planes wouldn't need much protection. Up to March 1, only seventy-eight B-29s had been lost over Japan on missions from the Marianas, and one-third of those were believed to have succumbed to their own mechanical failure. The loss of fifty-two planes to enemy attack in three months did not seem heavy to a man who could remember losing more than sixty planes on one mission against Germany. His intelligence reports indicated that the Japanese had one thousand fighters deployed to protect the cities of Honshu, the main island, but during recent missions there had been a sharp decline in the number of these planes rising to meet the B-29s. And all the available evidence indicated that the Japanese, expecting only daylight raids by the Americans, had just two groups trained as night fighters.

But what about the flak at five-to-seven thousand feet? Was it as sparse as he hoped? The Germans would wipe him out if he went in so low. There could be no argument about that. He could remember a low-level medium bomber (B-26) mission in Europe from which no planes returned. Would the Japanese low-level antiaircraft guns be that deadly? He called in his flak experts and asked them.

Yes indeed, they said. You'll lose up to 70 percent of your B-29s if you send them in that low.

He didn't believe them. He believed the studies that indicated a virtual absence of light flak. He didn't doubt that the Japanese would quickly install low-level antiaircraft guns when they realized the need. But until they did, he would conduct as many low-level missions as possible, as quickly as possible. He was convinced that, for a short time at least, he could get away with this daring plan.

All he had to do now was convince the men around him. A few days after the Kiwo Ito mission, he summoned his wing commanders—O'Donnell, Davies, and Power—to a meeting in the quonset hut on Guam that was his headquarters. To Tommy Power he had already leaked some indication of his plans and, surprisingly, Power had liked the idea. Liked it so well that LeMay decided Power would lead the first mission, since LeMay himself was now privy to a colossal secret that absolutely precluded any possibility that he might be allowed to lead it. But while Power no doubt sensed the purpose of this meeting, it was likely to be something of a shock to O'Donnell and Davies.

LeMay began by going through the reasons for switching from daylight-precision, high-explosive to night-incendiary bombing. Reasons they all knew well enough. Then he listed the primary targets of a new campaign—Tokyo, Nagoya, Osaka and Kobe. All obvious enough. He intended to burn down each of them as fast as possible, which meant a mission every other night with every possible plane. "I want to get in and out of the empire," he said, "before the Japs make things too costly for us." The three-hundred-or-so B-29s available weren't really enough, but he had a plan which might make them suffice by more than doubling their bomb loads. Finally, after a thorough analysis of the Japanese defenses and the prospects of resistance, he got to the big news. "I'm going to send you in," he said, "at five thousand feet. And without guns, gunners, or ammunition."

O'Donnell whistled. Davies simply sat and stared. Power, who was better prepared for the announcement, said he thought the plan would work. But now they'd all have to get busy preparing the men for it. And that wouldn't be easy.

There was one important person LeMay decided not to prepare—Hap Arnold. "If I do it," he had already decided, "I won't say a thing to General Arnold in advance. Why should I? He's on the hook, in order to get some results out of the B-29s. But if I set up this deal, and Arnold okays it beforehand, then he would have to assume some of the responsibility. And if I don't tell him, and it's all a failure, and I don't produce any results, then he can fire me. And he can put another commander in here, and still have a chance to make something out of the 29s."

The preparations went forward now in earnest despite doubts even among some of LeMay's own staff members. There was a lot of private shuddering about the probable rate of loss, but

LeMay guessed it would be no more than 5 percent and he was not swayed by arguments to the contrary. On March 6, two days after that last futile precision raid against the Musashino aircraft plant, he called in Colonel McKelway, the Twentieth Air Force public-relations officer, and sat him down. As usual, LeMay had a cigar in his mouth. A cigar, often half-chewed, had become such a feature of his face that the men around him had begun calling him "The Cigar."

"In the weeks that LeMay had been with us on Guam," McKelway later wrote, "I had learned, along with other staff officers, how to catch his soft and frequently arresting words, even when, characteristically, he mumbled them through his cigar."

On this occasion, the first thing LeMay mumbled was, "This outfit has been getting a lot of publicity without having really accomplished a hell of a lot in bombing results."

McKelway, taking the remark personally as if he were being accused of exaggerating to the war correspondents the results of recent missions, reacted with anger because, in fact, he had been trying to keep the B-29 publicity down until the plane did something truly worthy of advertisement. Instead of saying this, however, he controlled his anger and said there was "a long story attached to this matter." He could tell it if LeMay wanted to hear it, but that would be wasting the general's time.

LeMay made what "looked like a grimace of disgust," stared at the floor, shifted his cigar, and said. "Tell Monty [Colonel Montgomery] to fill you in on everything that's coming up. A lot of it can't be told until we know the Japs know what we're up to, but that's your baby. You see that what we don't want to get out doesn't get out."

McKelway said, "Yes, sir."

LeMay looked at him for another minute. "This B-29 is a wonderful airplane," he said. "Let me know if you have any troubles I need to know about."

About eleven o'clock that night, McKelway caught up with J. B. Montgomery at the operations officer's tent to find out from him just what LeMay was planning. Middle-aged McKelway and young Montgomery had become friends, perhaps because each admired the other's skills. "Monty looked on me," McKelway believed, "as an elderly, rather interesting, somewhat eccentric character with whom, at rare intervals, when both of us had nothing on our minds, he had discussed literature." It seemed to McKelway that the thirty-two-year-old colonel approached that subject "with the same natural, keen, get-to-the-bottom-of-it intelligence and lighthearted concentration" that he would apply to problems of aerial warfare.

In succinct terms, he told McKelway what LeMay was planning for the cities of Japan. "The four big pieces of news," McKelway decided "were (1) that the airplanes were going in at low level, at five to six thousand feet; (2) that they were carrying nothing but incendiary bombs; (3) that they were carrying around six tons of bombs per airplane; and (4) that the raids were to be staged every other night."

This information shook McKelway so profoundly he didn't sleep that night. The next day, by asking the right people and assuring them he had clearance to know, he found out that even the Pentagon was unaware of the radical aspects of LeMay's plan, and that while Power and Montgomery favored it, most of the people around headquarters who had been informed of it were shaking their heads with astonishment and apprehension.

McKelway by this time had formed some impressions of LeMay that were perceptive enough, but that also seemed to indicate that the man still puzzled him as he puzzled so many others. McKelway had come to think of him as "a very tough man" who had "the kind of toughness that comes from, or with, innate sensitivity, from, or with, innate goodness and hard, clear honesty." Not many others had used words like "sensitivity" in describing LeMay. McKelway observed also that the man had "the capacity to know the complex job of strategic bombardment up and down and in and out and . . . I think, the quality of leadership at its best." But when McKelway tried to define the peculiar quality of LeMay's leadership, he had as much trouble as others have had.

McKelway knew several staff officers who "at the mention of his name would say, 'Aw, Jesus, that guy's a pistol, a real pistol.' " Not a very expressive phrase, perhaps, but among the people at headquarters it seemed to have meaning. These officers, it appeared to McKelway, had "simply received LeMay's confidence and were breaking their necks to prove that his judgment was sound in trusting them to do their jobs."

For some, the cost of proving was high. McKelway knew one officer who worried so much about his job that he wasn't getting it done very well. When LeMay heard about this, he said he'd have a talk with the man. The talk, according to McKelway, was "brief and miraculous." LeMay listened to the man for about fifteen minutes, then said, simply, "Stop fooling around and get to work."

The next time McKelway saw the officer, he looked as if all his troubles had been swept away. And what did he have to say about LeMay, who had bestowed nothing but those seven uncomforting words upon him? "That guy's a pistol. A real pistol."

This was hardly an articulate explanation of LeMay's apparently profound effect upon the man, nor does the incident go very far toward explaining LeMay's ability to get men to break their asses for him. LeMay's unquestionable knack of extracting every ounce of effort from his men seemed to escape the articulation even of highly accomplished writers like McKelway. LeMay exuded some powerful kind of masculine, straight, demanding but honest, clear and simple aura to which other men responded almost hypnotically. When he talked to someone, he spent more time seeking information than giving it. And after he had digested this information, he spent very few words discussing it. Until he made up his mind about something, he was inclined to listen and say nothing. After he had made up his mind, he remained silent long enough to figure out how he could announce it in the fewest possible words. One or two sentences was his idea of a speech. Perhaps this paucity of words was by itself a factor in riveting the men around him. He had a way of sounding as if he had considered all the options, then chosen the only possible one. And by saying so in so few words, he seemed to convince everyone that, however surprising his decision might be, it was probably the right one.

McKelway took great pains in his effort to understand, define, and explain the man: "LeMay says things to people in a quiet, sometimes distinct, sometimes muffled voice, and always with sincerity. He says things with an effort, a straining to make not just his words but all that is behind his words fully understood. There is in his eyes at such times a tacit admission that he has been frequently disappointed in his wish to be fully understood, but his eyes also intimate that he still has an incurable faith in the ability of people to see things clearly and do a good job if they have half a chance. He keeps treating people this way day in and day out and it isn't long before he has transmitted his own anxiousness to get the job done and the war over."

None of LeMay's associates during the war has suggested that he was one of those strange soldiers who actually enjoyed it. He was as anxious as anyone to win it and go home, which provides perhaps the primary explanation for the firmness of his decision to launch what was destined to be the most destructive series of attacks in the history of mankind. In reconstructing his thoughts at the time, he later wrote: "No matter how you slice it, you're going to kill an awful lot of civilians. Thousands and thousands. But, if you don't destroy the Japanese industry, we're going to have to invade Japan. And how many Americans will be killed in an invasion of Japan? Some say a million.

"We're at war with Japan. We were attacked by Japan. Do you want to kill Japanese, or would you rather have Americans killed?"

Though preparations for the new incendiary campaign began immediately after LeMay made his announcement to the wing commanders, the field order for the first mission didn't go out to the wings until March 8, just after lunch, about thirty hours before the planes would take off: The target: ten square miles in the center of Tokyo. The assignment: not just to raise havoc in the area but to obliterate it. While this would hardly be a precision attack, it would feature two precision aspects. The ten-square-mile area was clearly defined to include the maximum number of industrial facilities. And certain particularly inflammable places within the area were designated to be hit first in the hope that they would become tinder spots for the desired widespread conflagration. Every detail of the mission was included in the telecom message which went to the wings on the 8th, but the crews were not informed until the pretakeoff briefing on March 9.

Glen W. Martin, then a colonel in command of the 504th Bomb Group, has described the reaction of the Tinian-based crews at the briefing for this historic mission: "The preamble . . . included some rather SOP [standard operating procedure] items such as standard air-sea rescue arrangements. Gradually the briefing schedule approached the operational phase and the target was announced: Tokyo. And then the map was uncovered and the route was shown and then finally, bearing in mind that we had been bombing around 30,000 feet, the bombing altitude was given, 8,000 feet. The tension and the interest on the part of those hundreds of people in that briefing room were truly remarkable. There was visible excitement and interest and eagerness."

The drama took a surprising turn when the announcement

came that the guns and gunners were to be left at home: "That was not entirely a satisfactory situation as far as the crews were concerned. It wasn't so much because of defense—they were quite prepared to rely on the command channel—they knew LeMay went over every mission in detail. They had a lot of confidence in LeMay and his staff and right on down through the wing and right on through the group and into the squadron. So there was no real concern about someone having made an error in what the enemy defenses would be likely to look like. But they wanted their crew integrity, and the gunners wanted to go with their crews."

On Guam, where LeMay himself attended the briefing for Tommy Power's 314th Wing, there were gasps of surprise when the crews were told they would go in at five or six thousand feet without guns, but there were no signs of revolt. At dusk, LeMay went to the flight line to watch the wing take off, plane after plane at one-minute intervals. To save gas they would fly the route individually, not in formation, but the early planes off the ground would fly at a slightly slower airspeed than the later ones so that the stream of bombers would be more condensed when they reached Tokyo, enabling all of them to get their bombs down in the shortest possible time. LeMay was convinced that the faster the fires got started, the harder it would be for the Japanese to cope with them.

In the book, *Mission with LeMay*, there was a mention of his fears about all the things that could go wrong, the calculations that might prove false, the defensive surprises the Japanese might have ready, the American mothers who might one day blame him for the stupid, needless loss of their sons.[11] Many years after the book was published, he recalled again his feelings at that time.

"I'll admit I walked the floor [during that mission]," he said, "because I couldn't go on it. I would have gone on it. I went on the mission [in Europe] when I said we'd go straight in [with no evasive action]. That's the time when the commander goes with his troops. A lot of people didn't like this five-thousand-feet-over-the-target. But I couldn't go. I might have argued for a few more missions if it weren't for [the expected arrival of the atomic bomb], but with that it was out of the question. So I picked Tommy Power to lead the mission. Not only lead it but get up there first, stay there until the last plane came through, and draw me pictures of the outline of the fire at intervals. I'll admit I was nervous about it. I made the decision. I had weighed the odds.

I knew the odds were in my favor. But still, it was something new. I could have lost a lot of people, appeared to be an idiot."[12]

Colonel McKelway, who spent much of that memorable night alone with LeMay, wrote shortly thereafter a more detailed account of how the general reacted.

In the afternoon, McKelway had summoned the war correspondents to a press conference at which Norstad (who had just flown in from Washington to find out what was going on) and LeMay briefed the newsmen. Then McKelway had taken the correspondents to North Field where they watched the incendiary-laden B-29s take off. After the planes were gone, the correspondents wrote their preliminary stories, which had to be turned in to McKelway, whose staff would censor them if necessary, then hold them until the first "bombs-away" messages arrived by radio from the planes over Tokyo.

About two o'clock in the morning of March 10, McKelway went to the operations control room to await these first bombs-away messages. Aside from the small overnight crew, the only other person there was LeMay. He had sent the rest of his staff to bed. And Norstad, who had just spent eighty or ninety hours in the air between Washington and Guam, was sacked out on a guest cot in LeMay's tent. LeMay was sitting on a wooden bench beneath the mission control boards, smoking a cigar as usual. Before coming to Guam he had alternated between pipes and cigars, but here the air was so damp that pipes and pipe tobacco would become moldy overnight, so he now smoked only cigars. He smiled at McKelway and asked him why he wasn't in bed. Then he said, "I'm sweating this one out myself. A lot could go wrong. I can't sleep. I usually can, but not tonight."

McKelway sat down on the bench, thinking a man in LeMay's position might get some relief from talking at a time like this, and he was right.

"If this raid works the way I think it will," LeMay said, "we can shorten this war. In a war, you've got to try to keep at least one punch ahead of the other guy all the time. A war is a very tough kind of proposition. If you don't get the enemy, he gets you. I think we've figured out a punch he's not expecting this time. I don't think he's got the right flak to combat this kind of raid and I don't think he can keep his cities from being burned down—wiped right off the map. He hasn't moved his industries to Manchuria yet, although he's starting to move them, and if we can destroy them before he can move them, we've got him.

I never think anything is going to work until I've seen the pictures after the raid, but if this one works, we will shorten this damned war out here.''

After looking at his watch, he said, "We won't get a bombs-away for another half-hour. Would you like a Coca-Cola? I can sneak in my quarters without waking up the other guys and get two Coca-Colas and we can drink them in my car. That'll kill most of the half-hour."

They sat in his staff car at the edge of the jungle that surrounded his headquarters and drank their Cokes while they talked about India, where both had been stationed. "The way all those people are in India gets you down," LeMay remarked with some irony, considering the way the people of Tokyo would be in an hour or so. "It makes you feel rotten."

A few minutes after they returned to the operations control room, the first bombs-away message arrived from the sky above Tokyo. It was quickly decoded and handed to LeMay.

"Bombing the primary target visually," it said. "Large fires observed. Flak moderate. Fighter opposition nil."

Shortly thereafter, the bombs-away messages from other formations began arriving. All of them reported "conflagration," with moderate flak and little or no fighter resistance.

Montgomery and other staff officers arrived in the operations room after napping for a few hours in their quarters. "It looks pretty good," LeMay told them. "But we can't really tell a damn thing about results until we get pictures tomorrow night. Anyway, there doesn't seem to have been much flak. We don't seem to have lost more than a few airplanes." He shifted his cigar and for the first time he smiled.

About nine o'clock the next morning, LeMay was at North Field to meet Tommy Power's returning plane. Though General Power was extremely tired, with dark circles under his eyes, he was also well satisfied.

"It was a hell of a good mission," he shouted down to LeMay from his cockpit seat. After releasing his own bombs, he had climbed to ten thousand feet, as LeMay had instructed, and circled the city for an hour, watching the other planes drop their deadly loads. At first there was a sprinkling of fires throughout the target area. Then these fires grew until they merged into one great conflagration. By the time Power turned for home, the center of Tokyo was an inferno.

Though all the other eye-witness reports confirmed Power's

observations, LeMay didn't have the conclusive results of the raid until about midnight of the 10th, when the first reconnaissance photos, taken that afternoon, were developed. These pictures were overwhelming. They showed that at least fifteen square miles of Tokyo had been obliterated.

The official Japanese figures, which took a month to compile, would eventually show that the catastrophe was even worse than the first aerial photos indicated. Actually, 16.8 square miles of Tokyo had been destroyed. There were 83,793 fatalities and 40,918 people were injured. (More than half the fatalities resulted from suffocation when the fire used up the oxygen in the air.) A million people were left homeless as 267,171 buildings were destroyed. But most important to the Allied war effort, 18 percent of Tokyo's industry was gone. The fire that engulfed Tokyo that night of March 9-10, 1945, was surpassed only by the 1923 earthquake, also in Tokyo, as the most horrendous disaster ever visited upon any city in the history of mankind. The great fires of San Francisco, Chicago, London, and ancient Rome were small by comparison. At the cost of only fourteen B-29s, LeMay had found out how to destroy Japan's capacity to make war.

CHAPTER ELEVEN

News of the unprecedented success of the Tokyo mission buoyed the spirits of Hap Arnold, who was in Coral Gables, Florida, at an Air Force hospital, recovering from his fourth major heart attack, which he had suffered January 17. While no one could say for sure that his B-29 worries had been a contributory cause, most of his close associates thought so. It seemed now that he could forget those worries. When the Tokyo results reached him, he sent LeMay a short wire: "Congratulations. This mission shows your crews have got the guts for anything."

Not until ten days later did he elaborate his feelings in a "My dear Curt" letter:

> As one of my first acts on returning to Washington after an absence of several weeks, I want to commend you and your Command on the superb operations you have conducted during the last month. . . . A study of the Tokyo attack of March 10 and knowledge of the fact that by July 1 you will have nearly a thousand B-29s under your control, leads one to conclusions which are impressive even to old hands at bombardment operations. Under reasonably favorable conditions you should then have the ability to destroy whole industrial cities should that be required.

LeMay was not waiting, however, for the thousand B-29s. A few minutes after his planes returned home from Tokyo the morning of March 10, he ordered his three wing commanders to get them ready for another mission that very evening, against Japan's largest aircraft center and third largest city—Nagoya.

"I saw," he later explained, "that if we were to achieve the maximum effect in this [Tokyo] attack, a second assault against

165

an enemy target should come immediately after the first. It would be possible, I thought, to knock out all of Japan's major industrial cities during the next ten nights."[1]

But his order for a Nagoya raid that very night was too unreasonable, even by LeMay standards. "My idea of what was humanly possible," he admitted, "sometimes did not coincide with the opinions of others." On this occasion, he surprisingly bowed to the opinions of others. But not for long. He postponed the Nagoya raid for only twenty-four hours.

LeMay ran into one other surprising human problem before the Nagoya mission was fully arranged. The gunners, fools that they were, still resented the fact that they had been left at home during the Tokyo mission. They wanted to go on the next one, even if it meant leaving some bombs at home. LeMay appreciated their eagerness, and he also realized that this time there might be a good reason to send at least some of them. The Japanese had been caught with their fighter planes down at Tokyo. In the missions to come, the B-29s might need self-protection, so he reinstalled some of the guns and some of the gunners for the Nagoya raid.

On the afternoon of March 11, 313 bombers took off for Nagoya, where they dropped more incendiaries that night than they had dropped on Tokyo two nights earlier. But partly because LeMay had made a mistaken assumption, they did less damage. "It seemed to me," he later explained, "that perhaps we had been concentrating our detonations at Tokyo more tightly than we actually needed to, and by scattering bombs more widely we could achieve the same results, but over a larger area. Nagoya showed how wrong I was."

Because the incendiaries were spaced one hundred feet apart, the fires at Nagoya did not merge into one general conflagration. Nevertheless, the mission was hardly a failure. Two square miles of the city were destroyed.

Osaka was next. On March 13, 301 Superfortresses dropped seventeen hundred tons of firebombs there at much closer intervals, and 8.1 square miles, including 119 large factories, were wiped out in the center of the city.

Three nights later, on March 16, the B-29s visited Kobe, where they destroyed three square miles. Then on March 19, they returned to Nagoya, where they destroyed another three square miles, though they had to bomb through the clouds by radar. In just ten nights, they had obliterated thirty-three square miles of

Japan's four most important industrial centers. But then came a sudden halt. They had run out of bombs.

LeMay did not suffer this circumstance gladly. He blamed the Navy, which was responsible for delivering bombs and other supplies to the Twentieth Air Force. Before launching his offensive, he had told Admiral Nimitz's staff what his incendiary needs would be, but his figures were so outlandish they had quite understandably refused to believe him.[2]

"We plan to fly these B-29s a hundred and twenty hours a month," he had announced.

The admirals had scoffed. "How're you going to fly a hundred and twenty hours a month out here in the boondocks," one of them asked, "when you only flew thirty hours a month in England?"

"We have a new maintenance system," LeMay had argued. "Better than we had in England. We feel we can do it and we're going to do it. If we run out of supplies, you explain it to the Joint Chiefs."

It must have sounded laughable when he said it. The admirals could be forgiven for doubting it, and they did doubt it until after those five massive firebomb missions during those ten days in March 1945. But it must be said for them, when they saw him use up his entire supply of incendiaries in that time, and burn the hearts out of four great Japanese cities, they were quickly converted. Orders went out immediately to increase the flow of bombs to the Marianas, and to hurry the ships. Meanwhile, LeMay had to return temporarily to the much less effective daylight-bombing strategy while he waited for the fire-bearing ships to arrive.

But first he had to suffer another defeat at the hands of the U.S. Navy. He was finding out it was easier to cope with the Japanese than with the Navy. This time the admirals wanted him to divert his efforts from the primary mission of the B-29—the destruction of Japanese industry—and devote a sizable portion of his planes instead to sowing mines in the mouths of Japan's harbors and its vitally important Inland Sea. Especially the Shimonoseki Strait, which was the narrow western entrance to the Inland Sea.

Ever since the B-29s began arriving in the Marianas, Admiral Nimitz had been trying to get at least some of them assigned to minelaying in those Japanese waters which were obvious shipping bottlenecks. Hap Arnold, jealously guarding his control of the B-29s, and determined to prevent the kind of diversion from their primary mission which had delayed the effectiveness of the B-17s in Europe, steadfastly resisted Nimitz's requests. Mine laying, Arnold insisted, was the Navy's job. Nimitz very reasonably pointed out that the Navy couldn't do the job because the Air Force was hoarding all the B-29s, and no other aircraft was capable of carrying large mines from the Marianas to the western shores of Japan.

From the time LeMay arrived in the Marianas, he had been, not surprisingly, espousing the Air Force rather than the Navy viewpoint. But the importance of corking the Japanese bottlenecks was so obvious that the Air Force position had gradually become less and less tenable until finally, by March 1945, the Navy had won over the Joint Chiefs of Staff and LeMay had to accept defeat in another interservice battle. But this was one battle he would eventually be glad he had lost.

To get the job over with as quickly as possible, LeMay assigned Skip Davies's entire 313th Wing to it. As usual, LeMay set up a training program, this time under the guidance of the Navy, which supplied mine-laying experts as well as the mines themselves. And on March 27, the 313th dropped by parachute into the Shimonoseki Strait a thousand of these one-ton magnetic and acoustic menaces to Japanese ships.[3] This was the beginning of a campaign in which not only the entrance to the Inland Sea, but all of Japan's major harbors, were to become deadly dangerous to Japanese vessels. Even after the 313th had completed its job and returned to its original mission, one of its groups, the 505th, continued resowing the waters which Japanese mine sweepers had managed to clear. The result was that in April, eighteen ships were sunk; in May, eighty-five; and in June, eighty-three. Altogether, the B-29s planted twelve thousand of these mines, sinking at least a half million tons of Japanese shipping and paralyzing hundreds of ships, either inside or outside of their harbors. Before the war ended, traffic through the Shimonoseki Strait was destined to be reduced to one-tenth of the volume when the mine-laying campaign began. The Navy deserved a lot of credit for forcing this great victory upon LeMay and the Air Force. But when it was over, the Navy was remarkably magnanimous. Admiral Nimitz graciously congratulated LeMay on the "phenomenal results."

About the time the mine-laying operation began, the Navy, in Washington, was prevailing over the Air Force on another issue—B-29 support of the amphibious invasion of Okinawa, the main island of the Ryukyu chain, 350 miles south of Kyushu. On March 31, Norstad, in a telephone conversation with LeMay, instructed him to tell Nimitz that the Twenty-first Bomber Command was at his disposal during the Okinawa operation ''whenever the B-29s could have a decisive effect, whether an emergency existed or not.''[4] As Air Force historians W. E. Craven and J. L. Cate have pointed out, this would, in effect, give Nimitz control of the B-29 effort until May 11.

In the beginning, LeMay did not resist or resent this temporary loss of control. ''An amphibious operation is the toughest military chore you can dream up,'' he later observed. ''And it's up to everybody to turn to and get the doughboys ashore. So we had a string of good weather and in seven days we had every airfield plastered.''

He was referring to every airfield on Kyushu from which planes might be launched against the April 1 Okinawa invasion. But after all these fields had been destroyed to LeMay's satisfaction, and the Navy insisted he keep bombing them anyway, his recurring annoyance at his ''webfooted'' friends came to the fore once more and he visited Admiral Nimitz to protest against the continuation of such a superfluous effort.

''All the facilities were flat,'' he later recalled. ''All the planes that weren't destroyed were off the fields, down the road someplace in the trees, where we couldn't get at them. Didn't know where they were. So we suggested [this was in the latter part of April] that we go back to our strategic bombing.

''Admiral Nimitz put his arm around my shoulder [and said], 'You've done a fine job for us, LeMay. Fine, fine, fine. But let's check with Sherman.' [Rear Adm. Forrest P. Sherman, Nimitz's chief of staff.]

''Sherman said, 'No. Keep it up.' So we kept it up and all we were doing was potholing the fields.''

Sherman was convinced that the raids had two more important functions in addition to destroying the airfields: they occupied Japanese fighter planes against the B-29s, thereby keeping them away from Okinawa; and they inhibited the kamikaze suicide attacks that were being launched from Kyushu. LeMay didn't think enough fighters, or enough kamikaze planes, were being launched from the ruined fields of Kyushu to justify the deployment of so many B-29s against them, especially since he had now proven, at least to his own satisfaction, how much more useful the huge bombers could be in destroying the Japanese ability to wage war.

Again LeMay visited Nimitz and again Sherman said, "Continue." LeMay then complained to Arnold, through Norstad, but even that didn't help. The Navy prevailed among the Joint Chiefs in Washington until finally, on May 11, Nimitz voluntarily relinquished his control with expressions of great appreciation for what the B-29s had done. "Personally, I don't think we should have received much in the way of thanks," LeMay has recalled with some bitterness. "The B-29 was not a tactical bomber and never pretended to be."

The success of the first major incendiary raids against Tokyo, Kobe, Osaka, and Nagoya in mid-March had convinced LeMay that the B-29, used in this way, could actually end the war. In late April he said in a message to Norstad, "I consider that for the first time strategic air bombardment faces a situation in which its strength is proportionate to the magnitude of its task. I feel that the destruction of Japan's ability to wage war lies within the capability of this command, provided its maximum capacity is exerted unstintingly during the next six months. . . ." He was itching to prove this, especially after the flow of firebombs from the States was resumed about April 12.

"As the ships came in," LeMay has recalled, "I'd get Seabees, Marines, anybody who'd get up in the morning to go and unload them, and haul the bombs directly to the hard-stands, where the planes were, and stack them up. You couldn't have done that if there was a chance of [air] attack, of course, but there was no chance [of it]. We operated without a blackout [this was in April 1945]. . . . We skipped the bomb dumps entirely. From then on, if the weather was good and I was sure it was going to be good, we would do some precision bombing. If the weather wasn't good, I'd fall back on hitting industrial areas [with firebombs by radar at night]. So if I got ready to run a mission, I could run it and not wait for the weather."[5]

Even when his planes were under Nimitz's control he could launch some missions of his own choice since the Navy didn't demand his services every day. He was able, therefore, to conduct about a half dozen daylight precision attacks. And on April 13, he got back to his firebombing with another attack against Tokyo. That night, 327 B-29s dropped 2,139 tons and wiped out another 11.4 square miles northwest of the Imperial Palace. Two nights later, 303 Superfortresses returned to the Tokyo Bay area with 1,930 tons of incendiaries destroying another six square miles of the capital, plus 3.6 square miles of Kawasaki and 1.5 square miles of Yokohama. But after these two missions, he got no more opportunities to continue the campaign until Nimitz gave him his freedom.

By this time, LeMay's force had grown impressively. New planes and crews (including many experienced and retrained B-17 crews) were arriving from the States in growing numbers. And Roger Ramey, who had replaced LeMay in China-India the previous January, had now brought his Fifty-eighth Wing to Tinian. On May 14, when LeMay ordered a daylight incendiary mission against Nagoya, 529 Superfortresses took off on the trip; 472 of them dropped 2,515 tons of bombs, destroying a large part of a Mitsubishi engine plant plus 3.6 square miles of the city. Two nights later, on May 16, 457 planes returned to Nagoya at a lower altitude which allowed larger bomb loads and dropped 3,609 tons, burning out another 3.8 square miles.

The Japanese were now so weakened by the pounding they had already taken that they could put up only feeble resistance against the pounding they were about to take. The statistics of destruction became almost monotonous: May 23—5.3 square miles of Tokyo; May 25—16.8 square miles of Tokyo; May 29—6.9 square miles of Yokohama; June 1—3.1 square miles of Osaka; June 5—4.3 square miles of Kobe; June 7—2.2 square miles of Osaka; June 15—2.4 square miles of Osaka.

By the middle of June 1945, the B-29s had wiped out 56.3 square miles of Tokyo; 12.4 square miles of Nagoya; 8.8 square miles of Kobe; 15.6 square miles of Osaka; 8.9 square miles of Yokohama; and 3.6 square miles of Kawasaki. A total of 105.6 square miles in these cities alone, not including vast damages elsewhere.

There was now no doubt about the eventual outcome of the war, unless it might have been in the minds of the Japanese generals, a group of men singularly isolated from reality. The Japanese admirals, those who still survived, were fully convinced of the outcome. Having lost almost their entire navy to the greatest fleet ever assembled in the history of mankind, they were sitting on the sidelines now, waiting for the final gun. The only hope any Japanese could muster was that the nature gods of the Shinto religion might intervene in their behalf. An hour after the June 1 attack on Osaka, nature did take a hand against the Americans. A flight of P-51 fighters, which had escorted the

B-29s to the target, got caught in a violent Pacific weather front during the return to base on Iwo Jima, and twenty-seven of the Mustangs were lost. But this boon to the Japanese was more than counterbalanced by the very fact that the P-51s, easily the greatest fighter planes of World War II, were now arriving in force from Europe. Though the storm had knocked down twenty-seven of them, there were plenty more where those came from. They would soon make the skies over Japan absolutely unsafe for any kind of Japanese plane, and the railroad tracks of Japan absolutely unsafe for any kind of Japanese train.

On June 15, Hap Arnold himself watched the B-29s take off from Guam on their way to Osaka. Arnold had arrived in Saipan on a Far East tour, one purpose of which was convalescence after his latest heart attack. In his mind was the notion that he could keep his blood pressure down by staying away from Washington, where his famous temper got too much exercise. At Saipan he was greeted by Lt. Gen. Barney Giles (now in command of the Pacific Ocean Area Air Force under Admiral Nimitz), LeMay, and Rosey O'Donnell.[6] The next day, Arnold had flown with LeMay and the others to Guam, where he was greeted by Admiral Nimitz, and also by a radiogram from Gen. George Marshall in Washington which chilled Arnold's reaction to Nimitz's warm welcome.

With the war in Europe at an end, Arnold was planning to send some of his most experienced generals there—notably Tooey Spaatz, Nathan Twining, and Jimmy Doolittle—to the Pacific. He intended to put Spaatz in charge of all strategic Air Force Pacific operations, with headquarters on Guam. But Marshall's message indicated the Navy didn't want Spaatz's headquarters on Guam. A lot of people on Nimitz's staff quite obviously didn't even want the B-29s on Guam, which was something of a Navy preserve. Though they could hardly get rid of the B-29s, they hoped, at least, to prevent any increased Air Force presence.

In addition, Nimitz's staff was again rationing the bombs to be delivered to LeMay. He had placed an order for a huge shipment—210,000 tons. Nimitz's men said it couldn't be filled because there wasn't enough storage space. LeMay found this argument intolerable because, in effect, it gave the Navy the power to tell the Air Force how many operations it could launch. He had pointed out that he didn't need storage space. He was stacking the bombs in hard-stands on the flight lines, and dropping them on Japan almost as quickly as they arrived. But LeMay, still a major general, didn't have enough rank to prevail against the Navy.

Arnold, who had the rank—five stars' worth of it—plus his well-advertised temper, could scarcely contain himself before confronting Nimitz at the latter's headquarters. But when the two men met, Arnold was pleasantly surprised. Nimitz agreed with all of his contentions. And LeMay was equally surprised. Why hadn't Nimitz agreed when he, LeMay, made the same arguments?

The bomb-delivery issue was especially important to LeMay because he was now convinced that the air offensive by itself could force Japan to surrender. Arnold surely shared this view, but to him, the important question was when. If the Air Force could bring on the collapse of Japan before the American invasion of Kyushu, which was scheduled for November, it would strengthen immeasurably the argument for establishing an independent air force after the war.

As LeMay recalled it, Arnold was "asking everyone [during his Pacific tour] the question, when is the war going to be over." LeMay had been so busy with day-to-day operations he hadn't given that specific question much thought. But now he did. He made a careful study of the target list.

"We looked at . . . what we had left to do and we couldn't find any targets that were going to be in existence after about the first of September. And we would have been purely on transportation after that, so we couldn't see much of a war going on after that time."

When Arnold, during a briefing at LeMay's headquarters, asked him the question he had been asking everyone else, LeMay said he still had to take care of some thirty to sixty industrial towns, large and small, but he would have Japan's industries destroyed by the first of October, and that ought to do the job. Arnold later wrote in the narrative of his tour, "So far on my trip across the Pacific, no one had hazarded the time for the defeat of Japan, except LeMay. Neither Admiral Nimitz nor General Richardson [in Hawaii], nor their staffs talked about when the war would be over."

Arnold believed LeMay, partly perhaps because he wanted to believe him. Since his arrival on Guam, he had been thinking about another message from Washington that awaited him there. This one informed him that Harry S. Truman, the new president, intended to meet with the Joint Chiefs of Staff June 18 to familiarize himself with the plans for the November invasion of Japan. Arnold was somewhat alarmed at this news because he himself would not be there for the meeting. He decided, therefore, to send LeMay to Washington on a hurry-up flight to convince the other chiefs—Marshall, Adm. William D. Leahy, and Adm. Ernest J. King—that there would be no need for an invasion.

LeMay and a few aides—experts in operations, logistics, and intelligence—took off from Guam in a B-29 on June 15 and flew nonstop, 3,780 miles, to Hawaii in fifteen hours and forty-three minutes. Then they made a record-breaking nonstop flight, Hawaii to Washington, 4,640 miles, in twenty hours and fifteen minutes. LeMay flew the plane during all the takeoffs and landings but shared the controls with his copilot during much of the flight. When they reached Washington at 11:43 P.M., June 16, the first thing he did was to call Helen in Cleveland. Still as ready as ever to chase around the country after her husband, she left the next morning for Washington by train because she couldn't get a priority to fly. It was not easy, in those wartime days, to get hold of airline tickets.[7]

Her husband, meanwhile, was appearing at a meeting of the Joint Chiefs, who had politely agreed to listen to him because Arnold had sent him. LeMay began with some general remarks about why he believed the war would end by October. Then he turned the presentation over to his aides. For their charts and drawings they used the only thing they had on Guam, a two-foot-wide roll of butcher's paper on a frame. Though their presentation seemed smooth enough, LeMay realized, when he looked around at General Marshall, that they had come on a bootless errand. The nation's most powerful military man was asleep.

"I didn't blame the old boy for sleeping through a dull briefing," LeMay said later. "Here were these dumb kids coming in, saying they were going to end the war for him."[8] By the time LeMay was ready to return to Guam, he realized that the whole general staff in Washington believed they had to invade Japan as they had invaded Europe.

Before leaving Washington, LeMay met with Maj. Gen. Leslie R. Groves, who was in charge of the Manhattan Project, for a briefing about the nuclear bomb that would soon be delivered to Guam. Groves wrote afterward: "This was my first meeting with LeMay and I was highly impressed with him. It was very evident that he was a man of outstanding ability. Our discussion lasted about an hour, and we parted with everything understood."[9]

Groves explained the bomb and the power it was expected to generate, but again, LeMay did not fully comprehend the magnitude of what was being described to him. "I took civil engineering [in college]," he later remarked. "Our course in physics was about structures and so forth. It wasn't nuclear physics. So I knew this would be a big bang, but I didn't know how big."

Groves estimated that the first bomb would arrive at Tinian around the end of July. The plan was to drop it, and each succeeding bomb, as soon as possible. He also talked about the size of the two types of bombs already developed. They were both so large they could be dropped only by B-29s with specially modified bomb bays. And he pointed out that they would have to be dropped from very high altitudes to ensure the safety of the men who released them. He informed LeMay that the operation would be "entirely under his [LeMay's] control, subject, of course, to any limitations that might be placed upon him by his instructions." These instructions would, of course, come from Washington. Perhaps from the president himself, but most likely from Groves.

LeMay, after asking a few questions, announced that he would want to send a single, unescorted plane on the bombing mission. A large fleet of bombers, all protecting one queen bomber somewhere in their midst, would attract attention and perhaps resistance. But one bomber alone, flying at a high altitude, would undoubtedly be taken for a weather or reconnaissance plane, and ignored. The Twentieth Air Force was now flying weather and recon planes over Japan on a daily basis. The Japanese had too many big problems on their hands to worry about individual planes overhead. All of this sounded reasonable to Groves and the two men parted in amicable agreement.

When Col. Paul Tibbets, commander of the especially trained 509th Composite Group, flew into Tinian in the last week of June, he found most of his men there ahead of him. The advanced air echelon had arrived May 20 to move into the semi-quarantine of the 509th compound. The others arrived either with or shortly after Tibbets so that by July 8, the group would be fully settled into its new quarters, ready for the training routine that had been arranged for them.

On June 27, Tibbets flew to Guam to report to LeMay and the two men had a conversation in which Tibbets may have been slightly uncomfortable because he was in an anomalous position. As the commander of this elite group which would receive its ultimate orders from Washington, he may have found it difficult to accept the authority of LeMay, who was, in the Marianas, his commander. LeMay himself recalls no uneasiness in their conversation, which is hardly surprising. Commanders are seldom uneasy talking to their subordinates.

"I don't remember any problem with Tibbets at all," LeMay said many years later. "He reported in just like everybody else and I had a training program set up. He may have had a little trouble with the staff. They were out there running the war and here he comes with a pretty high hand—what he's going to do and what he's not going to do. And they probably slapped him down a little bit, but I personally had no problem with him."[10]

The crews of the 509th, already trained at Wendover, Utah, in special procedures that hadn't yet been explained to them, began their final phase of training, in the requirements of combat operations against Japan, as soon as they arrived at Tinian. This included, first, the same one-week orientation LeMay required of all newly arriving B-29 crews, then three weeks of practice missions, mostly against bypassed, isolated islands like Truk, which were still occupied by Japanese troops. For these practice missions, a huge, conventional bomb had been invented, containing fifty-five hundred pounds of high explosives, and approximating the size of the atom bombs, which had not yet arrived. As a purposely misleading security measure, the Manhattan Project representatives at Tinian leaked the "information" that the special mission of the 509th was to drop these giant bombs, which were called "pumpkins." This campaign of deception was so successful that even the members of the 509th believed it (except for Tibbets and the handful of other key men who knew their real mission) and many of the crew members, in the belief that they had been training to drop some kind of colossal weapon, felt let down when they were told they had endured all that work just to deliver the kind of blockbuster the British had been dropping on Germany for two or three years.

While the 509th was preparing for a still-mysterious mission that was destined to alter the course of human history, the other units of the Twentieth Air Force continued their assault on Japan with such devastating effect that they came close to making the 509th superfluous. At least twice a week LeMay sent out his rapidly expanding force of B-29s. By the end of July, sixty Japanese cities, of large and medium size, had been virtually reduced to ashes by the one hundred fifty thousand tons of bombs the B-29s had dropped upon them.

By mid-July, however, LeMay was no longer officially in command of this holocaust. On July 10, Hap Arnold issued an order activating his planned reorganization of the Strategic Air Forces in the Pacific. LeMay, with only two stars, didn't have enough rank to command the huge armadas converging on Japan in preparation for the planned invasion. So Arnold sent four-starred Tooey Spaatz to fill that job, with LeMay as his chief of staff, three-starred Nathan Twining as commander of the Twentieth Air Force, and three-starred Jimmy Doolittle as commander of the Eighth, which was arriving from Europe.

When Spaatz flew into Guam July 20 and officially announced these changes, LeMay found himself surprisingly serene about his new subordinate role. He didn't think the changes would come to much. He told Spaatz he doubted that the fields would even get built for all these planes before the war ended. And many years later, he said, "I understood what went on. The war is over in Europe. Here's this winning team. May as well send 'em out, let's get it done in the Pacific."[11] So he took his new commanding officer on an inspection tour of the Twentieth Air Force facilities, then the two of them went to work together.

This meant, in effect, that LeMay went back to work as if nothing had happened. At least until Spaatz became familiar with operations in the Pacific, LeMay, as his chief of staff, would continue to run the entire B-29 show.

"I was happy enough," LeMay said later. "If that was the way they wanted it, that was fine. As far as I was concerned, the job was over and the war was won. I didn't feel insulted. I was kind of pleased that Spaatz would pick me for his chief of staff. Knowing Spaatz, I knew I would be running the whole damned thing anyway. He [liked to give] everyone the impression he was lazy. I've heard him on many occasions say, 'I'm lazy. If you think I'm going to do this work you're crazy. You're going to do it. Get out there and get busy.' He tried to give that impression. He had the ability to get people around him to do the things he wanted done." And since LeMay was already doing the job Spaatz wanted done, Tooey had the opportunity now to be as lazy as he pleased. All he had to do was sit back and watch.

Shortly after Spaatz's arrival in Guam, he handed over to LeMay the famous July 24 letter from the War Department, written by order of President Truman, authorizing the use of the atomic bombs that were soon to be delivered.[13] Spaatz gave the letter to LeMay without a word of comment. Like LeMay, he was a man who didn't waste words. But in truth, there wasn't much to say. LeMay had handled the preparations so far. Why shouldn't he finish the job? As for policy, neither man had any authority in such matters. Though the Air Force was to be the instrument through which the bomb would be used, none of the air generals, including even Hap Arnold, had any part in its development, and Arnold was the only airman whose opinion had been solicited as to whether it should be used. At Potsdam on the 24th, Truman had asked his Joint Chiefs for their views in the matter, but he had then made up his own mind.

Truman later wrote: "The final decision of where and when to use the atomic bomb was up to me. Let there be no mistake about it. I regarded the bomb as a military weapon and never had any doubt that it should be used. The top military advisers to the President recommended its use, and when I talked to Churchill he unhesitatingly told me he favored the use of the atomic bomb if it might aid to end the war."[13]

The fact that the Air Force had almost nothing to do with the decisions to build or use the bomb should not be taken to mean that the air generals disapproved of its use. In the world of 1945, very few people expressed any disapproval of its use, even after it had been dropped on two cities and its devastating effects were known to anyone who could read or understand pictures. LeMay, twenty years later, wrote, "I did not and do not decry the use of the bomb. Anything which will achieve the desired results should be employed. If those bombs shortened the war only by days, they rendered an inestimable service, and so did the men who were responsible for their construction and delivery."[14]

In 1945, however, LeMay, Arnold, and other airmen preferred not to use the bomb, simply because they were convinced it wasn't needed. "I think it was anticlimactic," LeMay later wrote, "in that the verdict was already rendered."

When LeMay received notice of the exact day the nuclear bombs would arrive at Tinian, he held another conference with Tibbets about the training program, which seemed to be proceeding satisfactorily. The 509th by this time had flown practice missions, not only over bypassed Japanese-held islands, but also over Japan itself. Tibbets believed, quite correctly, that he and his crews ought to be familiar with the Japanese mainland since that was where their ultimate mission would take them, but for key men like himself who knew about the bomb, it wasn't easy to get permission to fly over Japan. LeMay had forbidden it because of the rule banning bomb-informed people from flying over enemy territory where they might be taken prisoners. LeMay himself was a victim of this rule and he had no authority to exempt Tibbets from it. But when General Groves realized the importance of practice missions over Japan, he managed to get certain informed members of the 509th excused from the rule. And Tibbets, of course, was one of these.

When he and LeMay had their last talk before the initial atomic mission, LeMay said to him, "The bomb is coming now. Apparently it's pretty important. I want the best crew you've got to drop this first one. And that doesn't necessarily mean you."

But to Tibbets it quite understandably did mean him. He chose himself and his crew to fly their plane, the *Enola Gay,* on the world's first atomic mission. LeMay didn't blame him. "It was his prerogative to do it," LeMay said later. If LeMay had been in Tibbets's position, he would surely have done likewise.

The mission to Hiroshima took place August 6, 1945, a day the world will never forget. The next day, when LeMay saw photographs of the results and read the reports of damage to the city, he was almost as astonished as everyone else. "I knew it was a big bomb," he has said. "I didn't realize how big."

Nine days later, on August 15 (August 16 in the eastern Pacific), after one more atomic bomb fell on the city of Nagasaki, the Japanese finally surrendered. About 10 P.M. that night the news reached Guam that the war had finally come to an end. LeMay and members of his staff, after working late as usual, had just finished dinner and were sitting on the screened porch of his quarters when the good news was bellowed forth on the base loud-speaker system.

Some happy shouts arose from various directions. Two or three sentries fired off their guns. There was a bit of jubilant running around between buildings for about five minutes. Then, within a few more minutes, the lights went out, one by one, all over the base. During the last two months the aircrews had been flying 120 hours a month, as LeMay had predicted, and the ground crews had been working around the clock to keep the planes in the air. Here at last was a night when they could get some sleep, and they weren't about to miss the chance. They were too tired to celebrate.[15]

The next day, everyone was again at work, this time on the job of rescuing fallen comrades who were in Japanese prison camps. LeMay sent out reconnaissance planes immediately to pinpoint the locations of the camps. Then he launched an airlift to drop food and supplies for the imprisoned men. And finally, when Japanese airfields were secure for American planes, he launched another lift to bring the rescued prisoners out of Japan.

LeMay's job in the Pacific was essentially finished now. He flew a C-54 transport plane to Yokohama and attended the surrender ceremony September 1 aboard the U.S. battleship *Missouri*. Then he flew the same C-54 at a low altitude over all the bombed-out cities he could reach. He wanted to see for himself, for the first time, how effective his B-29s had been.

Finally, on September 18, LeMay, Barney Giles, and Rosey O'Donnell took off in three B-29s from Hokkaido, Japan, for what they hoped would be a world's record nonstop flight to Washington, demonstrating to the world the range of America's awesome Superfortress. Because they had unusual head winds all the way on their great circle route over the Aleutians and Alaska they ran short of gas and had to land in Chicago. After refueling, they flew on to Washington, where Hap Arnold was on hand to greet them. A captain only five years earlier, Curtis LeMay was now a major general and a war hero of such stature that the five-star chief of the Air Force had turned out to welcome him home.

Arnold's health was precarious after his heart attacks and he would soon be retiring from the Air Force. His apparent successor as chief was his old friend and protégé, Tooey Spaatz. As for LeMay's future in the Air Force, he had no idea what was in store, but he had one recommendation that wasn't likely to hurt his prospects. Spaatz, after observing LeMay's Twentieth Air Force operation in the Marianas, and watching LeMay work for three weeks, had sent a telegram to Washington August 7 that said:

HAVE HAD OPPORTUNITY TO CHECK UP ON BAKER TWO NINE OPERATIONS AND BELIEVE THIS IS THE BEST ORGANIZED AND MOST TECHNICALLY AND TACTICALLY PROFICIENT MILITARY ORGANIZATION THAT THE WORLD HAS SEEN TO DATE.[16]

PART II

PART II

CHAPTER TWELVE

Who was this suddenly famous but still perplexing and unexplained war hero whose fierce, unsmiling, cigar-speared face had begun appearing in all the newspapers and on the covers of magazines? If he was so remarkable, how come the public had begun to hear about him only recently? Until January 6, 1940, he was a flying lieutenant who had never commanded so much as a squadron of planes, or even a platoon of men. Five years later he was a general praised by military experts as the most innovative, determined, and triumphant air commander in World War II. Where did he come from? What kind of family? What kind of schools? How did he achieve his military skills?

Even in the Air Force, not many people could tell you. He had never been in any way a part of the air establishment. Few of the upper-level officers knew him before the war. And until seven months after America's entry into the war, at a time when there was a desperate need for qualified commanders, he was not chosen to command anything. Had he attended West Point? No. Command and General Staff School? No. Any of the staff colleges? No. Air Corps Tactical School? Yes, for a short time. Did he learn anything there? "Well, not too much," he later admitted.

When he was born, November 15, 1906, in a workman's cottage next to a grocery store on the east side of Columbus, Ohio, Curtis LeMay's prospects for success and fame could only be considered slightly better than dismal. His parents had both been raised on pitifully small, subsistence-level dirt farms near the town of Portland on the Ohio River at the bottom of the state, and had come to Columbus mostly because his father had developed the kind of wanderlust that grows out of relentless poverty. They had chosen Columbus, not because it was the state

183

capital or the site of the state university, but simply because Erving LeMay, twenty-two years old and trained only to work with his hands, had managed to find a railroad job there.

As his surname indicates, Erving LeMay's progenitors were French. A LeMay family genealogy published in Canada informs us that two LeMay brothers came there from France in the early nineteenth century, and among their listed descendants was: "Erving—married 1905 to Arizona Carpenter. Six children of whom Gen. LeMay was the first."[1]

The genealogy makes it clear that most of the LeMays were and are Roman Catholics, but the branch of the family that moved south into the United States apparently left its Catholicism in Canada. Erving LeMay was not a Catholic and his children do not remember him saying his parents had been Catholics.

Arizona LeMay was given her unique name because her father "didn't want his daughter to have an ordinary name."[2] Her family, the Carpenters, were people of English origin who had come from Virginia to Meigs County, Ohio, "in the early days." Probably not long after the American Revolution. In addition to farming, Arizona's father did some Methodist preaching in the country districts around Portland, but his religious beliefs did not make a compelling impression on his daughter. Neither Arizona nor Erving made religion a major issue in their own family. This is not to say they were short of ethical sensibility. As one of their daughters later remarked, "Right and wrong were the big issues."

Though both Erving and Arizona had been limited to eighth-grade educations, their parents had instilled in each of them a strong sense of duty, morality, and devotion to work. Arizona, despite her lack of formal training, had become a teacher by the time they met in 1902, and taught, in a country school, all eight of the grades that had been taught to her. Though petite in stature and almost frail in appearance, she was a tireless worker, cheerful, witty and well liked. She was fond of repeating the sayings she had learned as a child—sayings by which she lived: "Beg before you steal." "Where there's a will there's a way." "Learn to do two things at once." "You have a good name. Keep it that way."

Erving, six feet tall, strong and indefatigable, was more taciturn than his wife but equally devoted to work, duty, and family. In later years, his oldest son would remember him saying, "If you take something on, you should finish it. Don't do a sloppy job.'' During the hard years that followed the turn of the century, Erving couldn't always find jobs to take on but when he managed to earn money, he didn't dole out to his wife just what he thought she would need for the household. He turned over his whole paycheck.

The railroad job that attracted Erving LeMay and his pregnant wife to Columbus, Ohio, in 1906 had one thing in common with most of the other jobs he was destined to hold during his life— it didn't last. Shortly after their first child was born, and christened Curtis Emerson (because Arizona liked the sound of the name), the railroad job came to an end and so, for the next two or three years, did their residence in Columbus. They picked up all their belongings and the infant Curtis and moved about twenty miles south to a village called Lithopolis where Erving, continually scrounging for work, was able to find intermittent jobs as a carpenter, a house painter, or a general handyman.

It was in Lithopolis that their second son, Lloyd, was born, in 1908, and it was there that Curtis garnered his first boyhood memories, but they were sketchy. Family tradition has it that he was a habitual and persistent runaway during his toddling years at Lithopolis. And the book *Mission with LeMay* contains a detailed story about one of these unauthorized excursions. There is no reason to doubt the story but the information on which it was based must have come from some other member of the family because Curtis LeMay himself has no recollections of running away from home.

He does remember moving back to Columbus when he was about four years old and experiencing there one of the more exciting as well as significant incidents in his young life. During the winter between 1910 and 1911, or perhaps a year later—he's not sure—he was in the yard of the house the LeMays were then occupying near the western edge of Columbus, bundled up in winter duds and a red stocking cap, when, ''suddenly, in the air above me, appeared a flying machine. It came from nowhere. There it was, and I wanted to catch it. It would be a wonderful thing to possess—that mysterious fabrication which was chortling through the sky, its few cylinders popping in a way far different from any automobile or truck which went past our place.''

During later reflection, he surmised that it was a Wright Brothers' plane he had seen, since these two inventors of the flying machine were about the only people building them in Ohio at that time, and their factory and flying school were located on the edge of Dayton, a mere seventy miles from Columbus. Indeed it is conceivable that the pilot of the plane LeMay saw overhead that day could have been his future chief in the Air Force, Hap Arnold, who was then a student in the Wright Brothers' flying school. But needless to say, none of these considerations occurred to little Curtis at the time. The only thing he had in mind was catching that wonderful bird, the like of which he had never before seen, and making it his. So he "lit out" after it.

"Ran as fast as I could, across neighbors' lawns, across gardens and vacant lots, sometimes on the sidewalk, sometimes in the street. But the airplane was getting ahead of me. Try as I might I kept falling behind. It had been directly overhead; now it was far ahead, losing its strange crate-shape in the smoke of mid-winter, in a ragged horizon of chimneys and roofs."

He saw the wonderful creature disappear, finally, under the horizon, and it seemed to him it must have landed behind some trees about a half mile away. But when he got there it was no place to be seen.

"I set out for home in tears. . . . I had lost something unique and in a way divine. . . . I wanted it and hadn't been able to catch it, and was filled with a sense of exasperation and defeat. . . . I wanted not only the substance of the mysterious object, not only that part I could have touched with my hands. I wished also in vague yet unforgettable fashion for the drive and speed and energy of the creature. Also I needed to understand and possess the reason and purpose for this instrument—the Why of it as well as the What.

"I could not have spoken of these matters to anyone; yet they formed and circled in my mind like misshapen small aircraft of my own invention. . . . I have never erased from recollection the spectacle of that child in Ohio, trying to chase the aircraft and have it for his own. He stayed with me and sped beside me many times, later on, when it seemed often that I was trying to catch up with something that moved faster than I could run."

If the story of his earlier runaway attempts was true, perhaps it was a dream of unbounded freedom that attracted him so magnetically to the airplane. The dream of flight is thought to be a dream of freedom, of escape, and little Curtis, in those early years, seems to have been determined to escape from something.

When he was almost six years old Curtis went to school for the first time, and he quickly decided he didn't like it. He took vigorous exception to some idea the teacher was trying to propagate and headed for the door. Finding it locked, he then tried to get out the open window, but unfortunately, the teacher, being bigger and faster afoot, caught up to him in time to bring the lower window sash down firmly on his back when he was only halfway out. Since the boy's bottom was still inside, and thus inescapably vulnerable, he was in for a whaling he would never forget. This episode seems to have awakened little Curt LeMay from his dreams of escape, at least from school.

Shortly thereafter, the family again moved, from Lithopolis to Nez Percé, Montana, in the Bitter Root Mountains about sixty miles southwest of Butte. His father had been offered a job managing a fish hatchery there for a hunting and fishing club.

When the LeMays arrived in Montana, again with all their possessions (which now included two boys, Curtis and Lloyd, plus a baby girl, Velma), they found that the only way they could get from Butte to Nez Percé was by horse and wagon. For Erving LeMay this was neither a new nor forbidding prospect. When he was five years old, after his father was killed in a railroad accident, he drove a horse-drawn wagon from Ohio to Kansas under his grandfather's guidance. This family move in 1889, which was later reversed by a return to Ohio, indicates that the wanderlust in the LeMay family did not begin with Erving.

Aside from his displeasure at having to attend school, Curt LeMay enjoyed the family's stay in Montana. The trip west from Butte toward the mountains in a wagon was an adventure surpassed only by the realization when they reached Nez Percé that they would be living on a ranch. And even his parents' insistence that he go to school was somewhat relieved by the fact that he could ride to it on a horse.

There were three lakes at different levels around the ranch, with falling water between them, and where the water ran rapidly it did not freeze, so Curt could fish whenever he pleased. He remembers catching a trout and being so proud when he took it home that he went right back and caught another. But perhaps the most important aspect of the stay in Nez Percé was the chance it gave the boy to spend time with his father, whose job was right on the property rather than someplace to which he went in the morning and returned at night. They could go fishing and hunting together. It was at Nez Percé that Erving LeMay taught his oldest son how to handle a gun and how to shoot, thus fostering in the boy that reverence for guns and love of outdoor life shared by so many American males. And fostering in him also, as it happened, an appreciation of the profit motive. The first money Curt LeMay ever earned came from shooting sparrows for a neighbor lady's cat. With his first gun, a beebee gun, he managed to kill a sparrow every couple of days, for which the lady paid him a nickel a bird.

The LeMay family had been in Montana less than a year when the wanderlust again got the better of Curt's father. Erving LeMay received word from his brother Oscar in Emeryville, California (an Oakland suburb just across the bay from San Francisco), that a good job was waiting for him there. Once more the LeMays packed and headed west, even before little Curt had time to graduate from first grade. But when they reached Emeryville they found that the promised job was no longer waiting. And neither was Uncle Oscar. Erving wasn't the only LeMay who suffered from wanderlust. Oscar had enlisted in the Army and had already been shipped off to some camp or other for basic training.

Erving found lodging for his family in a tenement building and began again to scrounge for work, which he found in a cannery, then as a carpenter. Curt remembers watching his father at work on somebody's house, but a more vivid memory of Emeryville was another airplane flight. A prominent aviator named Lincoln Beachy performed exhibitions in connection with the San Francisco World's Fair in 1915, and Curt, now nine years old, saw one of them. It was only the second time he had seen a plane in the air. He didn't see the takeoff and he doesn't remember the details of Beachy's aerobatics, but he remembers well the sensations aroused by the sight of Beachy's machine flying past him overhead. While he didn't try to chase after this plane as he had the first one, he was sufficiently interested in it never to forget it. Nor did he ever forget what happened to Beachy a short time later when he was performing stunts in the air above San Francisco Bay. The aerodynamic stress was too great for the flimsy plane he was flying. Both wings fell off and Beachy, still strapped to his seat, plunged fatally into the water between two naval vessels.

Death almost became a more immediate reality for Curt while the family was in Emeryville. By this time they were living in a house next to a ballpark and not far from a racetrack. Curt, his younger brother Lloyd, and some other neighborhood kids were playing on the roof of a barn when Lloyd fell off into a pile of broken bottles. The blood spurted with such force from his wrist that he was in obvious danger of death if the flow could not be stanched. Curt grabbed the wrist and clamped his own boyish fingers down on the artery as tightly as possible. Then with the help of the other children, he pulled, pushed, and cajoled his howling brother to the home of a doctor who lived across the street from the local fire station. She sewed the wound but couldn't prevent Lloyd from developing tetanus, and he came close to death before recovering.

While almost losing a son, the LeMays gained a daughter during their stay in Emeryville. Their fourth child and second daughter, Methyll, was born there. How did she get that name? Her own explanation is that one of the LeMay cousins was named Ethyllm. Though Arizona LeMay was intrigued by this name, she thought it sounded too much like a gasoline, so she took the *M* from the end, affixed it to the beginning, then bestowed it upon her second daughter, thus preserving the family tradition of unique names.[3]

In 1916, when Curtis was ten, the family moved again, east this time to New Brighton, Pennsylvania, there being not much farther west they could go than the San Francisco Bay area. He does not remember what kind of work his father did in New Brighton but he himself very quickly managed to establish a paper route there. It was a job that took two hours each afternoon and he sold eight different newspapers, including those from nearby Pittsburgh, so he needed a wheelbarrow to carry all of them. As a profit of half a cent a copy he was in no danger of becoming wealthy but he was making enough to begin saving money for a bicycle. When his father learned this, he generously promised to match every dollar the boy saved. "But this turned out to be one of the disappointments of my life," LeMay recalled many years later. "I was working like hell for this bicycle and before we got enough money for it, before I got my half, my dad said to himself, 'Well, he's worked hard enough,' so he went down and got the bicycle and rode it home one night. This was the wrong thing for him to do. I wanted to go down and buy the bicycle, and pick out the one I wanted."[4]

In 1917, the family was in Wellsville, Ohio halfway between Youngstown to the north and Wheeling, West Virginia, to the south. Here, their fifth child, Leonard, was born. Erving was again working on the railroad, but again not for long. By 1918, in time to celebrate the World War I Armistice, they were back in New Brighton. And a year after that they were back in Columbus. Curtis had, by this time, lost any romantic enthusiasm he might once have felt for the family's many moves. In each place from which they departed he left a group of boyhood friends who had just begun to mean something to him. And in each new place he had to have one fight to establish himself with another group of friends.

"It didn't matter whether I won or lost," he soon learned. "After [one fight] I was accepted. But if you didn't fight you were in trouble so you might as well get the fight over with when you got there. Pick out somebody who wasn't too big. But I made some errors in judgment from time to time."

He and his brother Lloyd didn't really fight with each other, but they didn't exactly get along, either. Their sister, Methyll, recalls that "they argued about silly little things. I think Lloyd resented Curtis all his life." It was probably understandable. For many boys it wouldn't be easy to tolerate a big brother as dominant as Curtis LeMay. Methyll remembers Lloyd saying, "If we played horse and wagon, I always had to be the horse,"

Curtis says of Lloyd, "We never got along. I tried to guide him. I didn't think he had a sense of responsibility." As an adult, Lloyd proved that he did have a sense of responsibility by beginning an Army career as a private and working his way up to the rank of colonel, but the two brothers were never close. "The feeling we had as boys remained to some extent," Curtis recently admitted with what appeared to be a touch of regret. Lloyd is now dead.

All of the LeMay brothers and sisters seem to have enjoyed warm feelings for their parents. Though poverty and serious deprivation were seldom more than a day or two away, they never actually knew hunger, and so much self-respect was instilled in them that none of them recalls ever feeling poor.

"We didn't have much money, but we had no envy of the rich," Curtis recalls. "Our parents didn't talk about poverty. If we wanted something we had to save up for it, of course, but then we could go buy it."

Methyll recalls that "everyone we knew was poor. My mother always felt sorry for them. She'd give and give and give."

Methyll also recalls that her parents got along well with each other. "They never had squabbles." But Erving LeMay was strict, especially with his daughters. He also had a bad temper, yet it was not easily aroused and it didn't seem to create any problems.

"He'd get mad," Curtis recalls, "but after it was over he was fine. He treated mother well and he treated us kids well. After I got older, I felt he was—not exactly on the shiftless side [since] he was working all the time—but he was jumping around too much. He'd have done better to stay in one place. Still, he seemed happy [and] mother seemed happy."

In Columbus the LeMays rented a house they were destined to occupy longer than any other. "A narrow building, high roofed and covered with a shingle trim." The two older boys were assigned to the back bedroom on the second floor. "Lloyd and I fought all the time," Curtis recalls. "It wasn't a very harmonious roomful."

World War I, which had recently ended when the family moved back to Columbus, apparently made a minimal impression on twelve-year-old Curtis, except for the Armistice Day parade in New Brighton, which he has recalled with fond excitement. Columbus was the hometown of one of the most famous heroes of that war, easily the most famous air hero, Capt. Eddie Rickenbacker, the ace fighter pilot. But LeMay in later years said he didn't know much about Rickenbacker at that time. Throughout his childhood he was interested in airplanes and in learning to fly them, but he was not noticeably prone to hero worship.

In Columbus, where a building boom was now beginning, his father began establishing himself as a structural ironworker—what might today be called a "hard hat"—and he developed such skills that he was later said to have worked "on major projects in nearly every state of the Union." Among the Columbus projects on which he worked were the State Office Building, several buildings on the Ohio State University campus, and the city's tallest skyscraper—the 555-foot Lincoln-LeVeque Tower. While the steel skeleton of this structure was rising into the Ohio sky, Arizona LeMay used to go downtown and watch the construction.

"The men were so high up," she later recalled, "you could not recognize anyone, but Erving always told me where he was working and that way I could spot him." She also admitted that seeing her husband so high in the air on those slender steel girders "sometimes" worried her.[5]

Curtis began high school in Columbus, and from the start he was a serious student in those subjects that interested him. He especially liked mathematics and history, and he read a lot of historical novels but "didn't pay any attention to who wrote them.'' He got ''good grades in history and math, average grades in general.''

He said in later life, ''I don't recall coming into contact with anyone on the faculty who waved a flag of inspiration.''[6] But he does remember several who were good teachers and had constructive influences on him. There was his Spanish teacher, a Mr. McDonald. ''I don't know that he was a good Spanish teacher but he taught me a lot more than Spanish.'' And his English teacher, a Miss Tallent. ''She had been a nurse in the World War. Later she remembered me as the worst speller she ever had. I don't remember them inspiring me but they had an effect on me. In their classes I learned more than just the subjects they were supposed to teach.''[7]

Like most American boys of his generation he had a deep fascination with mechanical things, which was apparently due to the simple fact that he was born and raised in this country. His own explanation for it was that ''there was more machinery [in the United States] than in other parts of the world. . . . Most [Americans] were [originally] farmers. If there was machinery, you had to fix it and take care of it. Then the automobile came along. Every kid wanted to build his own.'' LeMay was like most other kids in that respect. His fascination with mechanics intensified as he approached the age when it became conceivable that he might have his own car.

Because money was so scarce, the purchase of a car was nothing more than a consummation devoutly to be wished until he was a senior at South High School in Columbus. Though one could buy a fairly good secondhand car for as little as seventy-five dollars in those days, one could not so easily come upon a sum that large. For LeMay, a seventy-five-dollar car would have been beyond his dreams, but because his mechanical skills were already impressive, he could look for an even cheaper one.

As it happened, a young man who was a friend of one of his friends had bought a 1917 Model T Ford touring car shortly before entering the Army and embarking for France to fight in the war. The car sat in his garage until 1919 awaiting his return, but when he got back he couldn't drive it because of a disabling wound he had sustained. The parents of Curt's friend had acquired the car, and after driving it four or five years, had bought a new one. Curt, with another friend, bought the Model T for twenty-five dollars, and shortly thereafter Curt got hold of twelve fifty with which to buy out his partner. The car was quite dilapidated. He had to take it apart and put it together again to make it run properly. But he was destined to keep it, and keep rebuilding it, until he was a senior in college.

It was, to a great extent, his desire to fly that lured him into college. There were then no college graduates in his immediate family. And his parents had never tried to make him feel that a college education was an essential part of his preparation for life. On the other hand, his parents did not discourage him when he announced his intention to enroll at Ohio State. The day he told them about his decision his father said, "That's fine. You can stay at home."

He had chosen Ohio State partly because it was right there, in his hometown, and partly because he couldn't get into West Point. "I think I always wanted to fly," he said later, "and about the only way you could get a first-class flying education in those days was through the military service." West Point was therefore his first choice, but one had to have a congressman's recommendation to get into the Military Academy and the LeMay family knew no congressman. He had heard that Ohio State graduates with ROTC commissions had at least some chance of being accepted as flying cadets in the Army Air Service. It was a chance he was willing to take.

After scrimping and saving for the entire summer of 1924, he had enough money to pay his freshman fees at Ohio State. He did not come close to having the $650 he figured he would need for a whole year in school, but he counted on finding part-time work here and there to see him through. He began with three primary aims: to find a job so he could stay in school, to earn a civil engineering degree, and to win the ROTC commission that he hoped would get him into the Army Air Service. He joined the ROTC immediately and he began to study more seriously than he ever had in high school. But finding a job looked much more difficult, even in this year of Coolidge prosperity, until one day a friend told him about a foundry in Columbus, the manager of which "had worked his way through college and was extremely sympathetic with people who were trying to do the same thing." Curt LeMay was in this man's office telling his story as fast as he could get there. And the man was indeed sympathetic, but there were no openings at the moment. If anything were to come up . . . LeMay had heard that kind of talk before. He went home discouraged. But by some miracle or other, a job did soon come up at that foundry, the Buckeye Steel Casting Company, and he began work there for the astonishingly high wage of thirty-five dollars a week. He had to work nine hours a day, six days a week (5 P.M. to 2 or 3 A.M.), but for that kind of money, who wouldn't? In 1924, you could raise a family comfortably for thirty-five dollars a week. Millions of Americans were getting by on less.

Those millions were not, however, taking a full course load at a university. LeMay was single and could now "make his money jingle" in the words of a popular 1920s song, but he didn't have much time to enjoy spending it. Besides his studies, he still had responsibilities at home, especially when his father took jobs out of town, which happened quite frequently. On such excursions Erving LeMay often took his wife, leaving Curtis in charge of house and family until one or both of them returned. This was not easy for Lloyd to endure but the two girls, Velma and Methyll, and little Leonard, didn't mind it. Methyll remembers her oldest brother studying most of the time. "He was a very serious person." Leonard's memories of him in those days are almost identical. "He had a drawing board set up in the living room. He was studying much of the time. He was very dedicated. Knew what he wanted to do."[8]

In those days when her parents were absent, Curtis became a father figure for Methyll, though she did not realize it. "Dad was gone so much," she later recalled, "and he never took that much interest in what we were doing, as far as school was concerned. But Curtis would say, 'Let me see your grade card.' One day I asked him to help me with a math problem. He said, 'I'll show you this just once.' I never asked him again. We toed the mark when he was the boss. Lloyd had trouble with that."

Lloyd had quit high school at the age of sixteen, much to the disgust of Curtis, who was then a freshman in college and a passionate advocate of the need for education. He often argued with his younger brother about going back to school but Lloyd was determined "to go to work and get things [for himself] quickly." Lloyd was apparently the equal of Curtis as a mechanic. He soon had a good job, a car, and plenty of money in his pockets. "He was going strong while I was struggling through school," Curtis recalls, "and he'd say to me, 'You see, this is what you should be doing.'" Lloyd may have been at a disadvantage in age and size, but he knew how to get under his big brother's skin in a way that few people could do during Curtis LeMay's military career. Perhaps in his failure to cope with

Lloyd, he learned a few things that would help him to manage other men in later years.

One of the great advantages of college life that Curtis LeMay seldom had the pleasure of enjoying was the company of women. Male engineering students have always suffered some handicap in this respect because few women take engineering courses, so there are few girls in their classrooms. But LeMay had other handicaps. His tendency to look stern and remain virtually silent, whether with men or women, is probably more disturbing to women than to men. It may have put off some coeds who might otherwise have become interested in him and encouraged his attentions. He did, after all, own a car, that beat-up Model T that he had painted scarlet and gray, the Ohio State colors. In the 1920s, many a coed flapper would find this, by itself, almost irresistible. He even became a frat man, joining Theta Tau, an engineering fraternity, but this coveted badge of social acceptability didn't seem to draw any flocks of sorority women. His own explanation for his lack of social life in college is that he simply had no time or money for it.

"I was shy," he admits, "and not too much interested in girls, [but I] was not antisocial. I simply had to work too much." He was not indifferent to his deprivation. He felt keenly the melancholy it often brought upon him. "Sometimes when boys and girls were arranging a party or a picnic or some such merrymaking, I became aware that they were saying, in effect, 'Shall we invite Curt? Hell no. No use inviting him because he has to work.' When I was invited I would go if I could. I wasn't essentially a lone wolf, nor was I a social outcast.'"[9]

At one time during his college career his father took a job in Youngstown and the prospects of its permanence were so good that the entire family again moved, leaving Curtis alone in Columbus. On this occasion he moved into the fraternity house and, to the extent that it was possible for a student of Curt LeMay's serious disposition, began living the life of Joe College. In the summer of 1927, before his senior year, he and a fraternity brother named Bob Kalb went to ROTC camp together, then, for several weeks, to Kalb's home in Bradford, Pennsylvania. During the last week of summer vacation, on Thursday night, a big, spectacular fire broke out in Bradford, leaving a car dealer's garage in ruins and destroying countless cars.

Next morning, LeMay and his friend Kalb dropped around to survey the remains and found, in an extension off the main building, a Model T Ford touring car, perhaps three years old, which would make it about six years newer than the decrepit Model T LeMay had been driving and repairing and patching and repatching since his senior year in high school.

The car in the burned-out garage was so thoroughly demolished it's not easy to imagine why LeMay even gave it a second glance. The wheels, tires, and most of the body, except for the metal fenders, had been burned away. But the dashboard and foot pedals remained, and it had one of those marvels of the age—a self-starter. The self-starter was still the talk of every town. If your car had one, you didn't have to crank it. But most cars, especially Fords, didn't have self-starters. Here was one that did. LeMay, out of curiosity, stepped on it, and behold, the engine turned over.

The two young men looked knowingly at each other. They both realized what this meant. The wheels and body might be gone, but the fire hadn't damaged the steel chassis or the drive shaft, and apparently it hadn't damaged the engine, the battery, or anything under the hood. If LeMay could get the insurance company to sell him this skeleton for twenty-five dollars or so, he could put on it the wheels and tires from his old Model T, plus the body from some car he could find in a junkyard, and for less than fifty dollars, he could have the equivalent of a three-year-old car. But alas, this was Friday. On Sunday, he and Kalb had to drive to Columbus, where the school term was to begin Monday morning.

Most young men would decide under the circumstances that the whole project was too complicated and impractical even to consider seriously. And for a young man like Curt LeMay, who had established almost no record of success in life, this would seem to be especially true. As he often admitted in later years, he felt unqualified for just about every job he ever attempted. Yet no one ever accused him of backing away from an attempt. Even as a college student he seems to have been imbued with the notion that you didn't know whether you could do something until you tried it. And the time to try it was immediately. So on that Friday morning in September 1927, he immediately undertook the virtually impossible and certifiably foolish project of buying the burned-out hulk from the insurance company; trading his old Model T, minus wheels and tires, to a junk dealer in exchange for the body of a fairly new Ford coupe plus a steering wheel, lights, and several yards of electric wire; attaching the coupe body to the touring-car frame; making the mechanical connections and adjustments, and having it ready to drive to Columbus by Sunday afternoon.

The fact that he managed to accomplish all this demonstrates the single-minded, stubborn persistence that has always driven Curt LeMay and explains some of his unexpected accomplishments during his long career. It might also explain some of his failures. When he got an idea in his head he was likely to pursue it despite all advice to the contrary, even despite the disapproval of his most trusted friends and advisers. He might be wrong, he might even be afraid that he was wrong or that he would fail, but if he was convinced of something, he seemed always ready to plow fixedly ahead to try to prove his point.

During his last year at Ohio State, the rest of the family returned to Columbus from Youngstown, where another of Erving LeMay's jobs had expired. Arizona LeMay was expecting another baby—her seventh pregnancy in twenty-two years, one child having been stillborn. This seventh pregnancy produced a healthy baby girl who has traveled through life with another in the long series of unusual LeMay names.

There are several versions within the family of how she was named.[10] Mother Arizona's explanation, as filtered through her son, Curtis, is that he arrived home from class a few days after the little girl's birth and said, "I've got the baby's name."

"What is it to be?" his mother asked.

"Vernice Patericha."

"Patericha? Don't you mean 'Patricia'?"

"Nope. Vernice Patericha."

"Well, where did you get that name?"

"I just got it. Don't you like it?"

Everybody said they did, so the baby was named Vernice Patericha. That's the story, at least, as Curtis LeMay remembers his mother telling it. One trouble with this version is that the baby was not named Vernice Patericha. Not quite.

LeMay himself, after recounting his mother's version, has also discounted it, substituting his own: "I named her Patricia, and that was that. I don't remember anything about the Vernice Patericha nonsense, and don't believe it ever happened that way."

But there's also one trouble with his version. The baby was not named Patricia either. Not quite.

Helen LeMay, his wife, has offered another, slightly different explanation which, she recalls, originated with his mother. According to this version, Arizona LeMay told her son he could name the baby. And he decided on the name Patricia, but he didn't know how to spell it, so he spelled it "Patarica."[11]

This version has the beauty of agreeing with what his high-school English teacher once said about him—that he was "the worst speller she ever had." And it also has the beauty of agreeing with the actual legal name which was bestowed upon his youngest sister—Vernice Patarica. Well, almost anyway. Where from did the Vernice come? Oh, that's easy to explain. Erving LeMay, the child's father, wanted to name her "Vernis."

As LeMay approached the end of his fourth year at Ohio State, he realized his hopes for an Army Air Corps commission were threatened by a problem that had overtaken him in his first two years. His foundry job at the Buckeye Steel Casting Company, which had kept him up until 3 A.M. six nights a week, had also made it impossible for him to remain awake with any consistency during his early morning classes. And in one of those classes, an engineering course entitled Railroad Curves, he could hardly stay awake at all. He found those curves so soporific he flunked the course two semesters in a row. Since he hadn't had a chance to make up this deficiency, he approached the end of his senior year fifteen credits short of what he needed to graduate.

He did have one accomplishment in his favor. He was an honor graduate in ROTC. And sometimes honor graduates could win regular Army commissions after which they could apply for whatever branch of the Army they might prefer. In his case, the Air Corps. But this year there were no vacancies for commissions in the Army. Especially for someone who hadn't earned his college degree. Because he had won honors in ROTC, he was awarded a reserve commission on June 14, 1928. It was hard to see, however, what good that would do him. Reserve officers, he was told, ranked seventh on the priority list for entrance into the Air Corps flying cadet schools. It looked as if the time had come for him to wake up and shake off his long-held dream of becoming an Air Corps pilot.

Then one day he found out that while Reserve officers were seventh on the flying-school priority list, National Guard members, officers or enlisted men, were second on the same list. And the Ohio commander of the National Guard had his office right there in Columbus, across the street from the capitol. He had once met this man, "a nice old brigadier general," at an ROTC ceremony. Though he didn't expect a brigadier general to remember him, he hurried down to his office anyway and offered to enlist as a private in the Guard. Why? He put it straight to the general. "I want to get up on the eligibility list, to get into the Air Corps flying school."

The general was apparently refreshed by this bit of honesty. He also remembered seeing LeMay at the ROTC ceremony. After ascertaining that the young man already had a Reserve commission, he offered to take him into the Guard, not as a private, but as an ammunition officer—second lieutenant. "Why don't you take that?"

"Sir, I should feel honored," LeMay said. "But actually I'd be perfectly satisfied just to enlist, in order to get up on the priority list. Because I'm determined to go to flying school."

The general obviously had a high regard for qualities like determination. "All right," he said. "We'll fix it up."

The two of them walked across the street to the State House where LeMay forthwith received a commission as a second lieutenant in the National Guard, and a lesson on how to get things done in the Army. To accept the National Guard commission he had to resign his Reserve commission. But as a result of having a National Guard commission, he soon got another Reserve commission. And he had won himself a chance to lose both commissions by acceptance in the Air Corps as a flying cadet. All he had to do now was figure out how to get the Air Corps interested in him.

"My application as a National Guard officer applying for admission to the Army Air Corps flying school went in just as fast as it could be processed. Then ensued the deadly business of waiting."

From June to September he waited, not patiently but quietly. His determination to get into the Air Corps, almost an obsession now, is difficult to explain in light of the fact that until that summer he had flown in an airplane only once in his life, on a five-minute "joyride" for which he and a friend had paid two fifty each. It was hardly a compelling experience. He did still cherish, of course, the romantic image of that first flying machine he had ever seen overhead when he was about five. And during his summer of waiting he managed to wangle a few short flights with a Reserve pilot at Norton Field, near Columbus. But all of these factors added together would seem inadequate to explain the fixed ambition he had carried through childhood, and then the four years of devotion he had given in college to an

ROTC program which had nothing to do with the Air Corps except as a vaguely promising means of entry. He obviously enjoyed his ROTC experience. It seems likely he would have joined the ROTC and enjoyed it even if he had never heard of such a thing as an airplane. Is it possible that if the airplane had never been invented, he might have chosen to pursue a career in some other branch of the service? How important was his father's wanderlust and insecure life-style in prompting him to choose the security and permanence of a career in the military? Such a factor can never be measured precisely, but it is worthy of note that he had taken a leave of absence from the National Guard for the summer to pursue his Air Corps ambition. He had not resigned from the Guard. The old general had suggested he take a leave. Even if he failed to get into flying school, he intended to pursue a military career of some kind. He later recalled that even after he got into flying school, ''I was always extending my leave for three months, time after time.'' Always holding onto the military career he had in hand in case the one for which he was reaching should slip away from him.

As that summer of 1928 wore on, LeMay became less confident day by day that he would ever get into flying school. From the Air Corps he heard not a word. Had his application been lost? Had he been rejected? Was this how the Air Corps was accustomed to treating its applicants for cadet training? Didn't those people in Washington realize how much this meant to him? A new cadet class was scheduled to begin in November. If he wasn't chosen for it, he intended not only to activate his National Guard career, but also to resume his studies at Ohio State and make up the credits he needed for a degree. But it was now September and he would have to register by the 28th or 29th if he wanted to take the necessary courses during the fall term. He couldn't afford to put down the money for his fees if he was going to be there for only a month or so.

The time came when he could wait no longer. He went to the Western Union Office and sent ''an expensive Night Letter'' to Washington explaining his dilemma and asking flatly—was he or was he not on the list for the November cadet class?

At Air Corps headquarters, someone must have admired his guts. He soon got a telegram from the War Department that said: ''This authorizes you to enlist as a flying cadet at the nearest army station.'' He would then be expected at March Field, Riverside, California, but not until November.

The nearest Army station was Fort Hayes, a small post right in Columbus, the only Regular Army post in the entire area. LeMay went there immediately.

He hurried into the headquarters building, waved his telegram at a sergeant, and announced he was there to enlist as a flying cadet.

The sergeant had never heard the term, "flying cadet," but he was eager to take this healthy-looking college boy in as an enlistee. The Regular Army, in those days between World Wars I and II, was able to enlist even fewer healthy-looking college boys than it does today. Almost before he knew what was happening to him, LeMay was in the Army. Much to his surprise, they were assigning him to a barracks and sending him to the quartermaster depot to draw a khaki private's uniform.

When he realized where he was headed, he resumed waving his telegram from the War Department. This time almost frantically. "No, Sergeant, no! I want to go home. I don't want to stay here tonight. There's no point in it. I'm going to flying school."

Eventually the sergeant took this smart-ass college boy to a lieutenant, and the lieutenant took him to a captain who was experienced enough to know that the best thing to do with a problem like this was to get rid of it. The captain put LeMay on leave until the day he was to report to flying school in California.

Bursting with pride in his new rank, LeMay drove his Ford directly to the Ohio State campus. Now that he was a flying cadet, he couldn't resist selling the flying business to several other ROTC members who had expressed some interest in it. One of them was a fellow member of the class of 1928, a commerce and journalism major named Francis H. Griswold, who had also failed to graduate the previous June because he had missed one semester.

Griswold, known to his friends as "Grizzy," was only an acquaintance to LeMay. The two didn't yet know each other well enough to be friends, which explains why LeMay was unaware until now that Griswold had also wanted to become a flying cadet, had even passed the physical exam, sent in his application and had been approved. But he had sent back his regrets because he had changed his mind about the whole thing. At the urging of his parents, he had decided to make up his lost semester and get his university degree.

When LeMay learned all this, he "called me a couple of

words," Griswold later recalled, "and said, 'I can take care of that.' "[12]

Before Griswold had time to think about it he was in LeMay's Model T on the way to Fort Hayes. LeMay marched him in to meet the same sergeant with whom he had negotiated.

Pointing to Griswold, LeMay said to the sergeant, "This guy had an approved application to be a flying cadet and said no. He sent it back. But now he wants to be one."

The sergeant, no doubt remembering the complications LeMay had caused him, decided to make it simple this time. "Well, hell, that ain't no problem," he said. 'just sign here."

A few minutes later, Griswold, having taken the oath in the captain's office, was on leave, like LeMay, awaiting the day when the two of them would board a train west.

About two weeks before they were to report to March Field, LeMay and Griswold were back at Fort Hayes to arrange transportation. The captain sent them this time to the first sergeant, who was obviously puzzled by this pair of college boys in civilian clothes.

"What are you?" he wanted to know.

"Flying cadets."

"What's a flying cadet? I never heard of a flying cadet."

Griswold, who must have had an inborn sense of how to simplify Army situations, said, "I don't know what it is, but we're supposed to go to California to the flying school at March Field."

By neglecting to answer the sergeant's question, he had reduced the sergeant's problem to a matter of transportation, which was something the sergeant understood very well. When you've got troublemakers, you simply ship them out. Every sergeant knows that.

"Okay," he said, "I'll issue you transportation requests, and in about a week you'll leave."

"Don't you want us to report to you?" Griswold asked.

"Oh no," the wise old sergeant said. "I don't care what happens to you."

Now came another week or so of waiting. "I used to wake up at night," LeMay has recalled, "and think about washing out. Just twenty-five percent of the would-be cadets were making it at that time."

When they boarded the westbound train in Columbus, they found that the "very generous" Army had paid for just one berth, which the two of them were supposed to share. Fortunately they encountered a kind and friendly conductor, who gave them a second berth.

When they got off the train at Riverside and entered the station they found to their surprise and dismay that the Air Corps had sent no one to meet them and drive them to the field.

LeMay said to Griswold, "Why don't you call March and tell them to send a car for us."

One might almost have expected Griswold to say, in the immortal words of the already popular Oliver Hardy, "Another fine mess you've got us into." But Griswold, a man always ready to see the lighter and brighter side of things, simply laughed and made the call. After announcing himself over the phone, he said, "Cadet LeMay and myself are here and we want transportation to the base."

The man at the other end of the line said, "If you go downtown you'll see a building with a flag on it. That's the post office. You hang around there, and if a truck comes in that says March Field on it, and takes mail, you get on the truck too and come on out."

In due time, such a truck did arrive at the post office. LeMay and Griswold climbed aboard at the rear and settled down on top of the mail bags. At last they were getting their first taste of the glamorous life of flying cadets.

CHAPTER THIRTEEN

If it seems strange that the Army Air Corps didn't provide transportation for new cadets from the Riverside railroad station to March Field in 1928, consider how much money the Corps had to spend in those days. For fiscal 1928: $25,097,594; for fiscal 1929: $24,630,268. Not enough to buy one fighter plane today. The entire corps in 1928 consisted of fewer than eleven thousand officers and men. Why didn't March Field send a car for cadets LeMay and Griswold? Maybe there wasn't a car to spare. Or anyone to drive it.

The Air Corps was not the only branch of service short of money in those days. The entire Army budget for 1928 was $390 million; the entire Navy budget, $331 million. Enough to buy less than one-half of a submarine today. There were one hundred thirty-four thousand American soldiers in 1928; ninety-five thousand sailors. The United States, in reaction to World War I, was a strongly isolationist country throughout the 1920s. Americans were convinced that George Washington was right. We had to avoid all foreign entanglements. The Great War had taught us what seemed to be a sensible lesson. Let the Europeans fight as much as they pleased. We must never again be drawn into any of their stupid conflicts.

In addition to peace, what interested most Americans in 1928 was prosperity—making money and having fun. The prosperity of the postwar era was in full bloom, although a lot of people were still poor. About two and a half million were unemployed in a nation of one hundred million and wages were low. But many other people were wealthier than ever before. They were eating, drinking, and making merry despite Prohibition. In 1928, Americans spent about $5 billion on bootleg booze, the equivalent of perhaps $20 billion today. They were driving their Graham-Paiges, Hupmobiles, and Stutz Bearcats to speakeasies and roadhouses everywhere. They were listening to popular new songs like "Ol' Man River," "You're the Cream in My Coffee," "Makin' Whoopee," and "Only Make Believe." They were seeing silent movies like Charlie Chaplin's *The Circus*, Gloria Swanson in *Rain*, Janet Gaynor and Charles Farrell in *The Street Angel*, Gary Cooper and Colleen Moore in *Lilac Time*.

In the presidential campaign of 1928, the American people had to choose between the governor of New York, Alfred E. Smith, and the secretary of commerce, Herbert Hoover. A majority of them found it an easy choice. Al Smith, a Democrat and a Roman Catholic, was running in the face of "Republican" prosperity and deeply imbedded religious bigotry. Hoover won handily, 21 million votes to 15 million.

Young Curtis LeMay, voting in a presidential election for the first time at the age of nine-days-less-than twenty-two years, found the choice as easy as did most people, but not for the same reasons. "I had no political feelings," he later recalled. "I voted for Hoover because Hoover was a fraternity brother."[1] The "Great Engineer," a Stanford graduate, had also belonged to the Theta Tau engineering fraternity. But it seemed likely that LeMay would have voted for him anyway. It may be true that he had no well-defined political feelings, yet like many young men who choose military careers, his political attitudes were basically conservative, even at an early age. He has also recalled that he used to argue with his father at the dinner table because his father, an impecunious working man, quite naturally espoused a more liberal, labor-union point of view.

However, it was largely the Ohio environment in which he spent his formative years that shaped LeMay's political attitudes. A youngster who thinks of himself as having "no political feelings" is prone to accept and absorb, without much questioning or debate, the political ideas and values of the people around him and the newspapers he reads. In Ohio, most of the people around him except his father, plus most of the newspapers, were persuasively Republican. And it was a nineteenth-century Republicanism they shared.

Ohio in the 1920s was still considered the very heartland of conservatism. It was a state dedicated to the virtues of business and the sanctity of free enterprise. It had already produced seven presidents of the United States—Ulysses S. Grant, Rutherford B. Hayes, James Garfield, Benjamin Harrison, William McKinley,

William Howard Taft, and Warren G. Harding. All were Republicans. Harding, who was elected president in 1920, when LeMay was fourteen years old, had been the editor of the local newspaper in the small town of Marion, Ohio, only twenty-five miles from Columbus. His political creed was one he didn't have to preach to his fellow Ohioans. Most of them already professed it. Harding was for America, first, last, and always, and like most Republicans, he was as absolutely opposed to the nation's "foreign entanglement" in the newly formed League of Nations as he was to that menacing foreign ideology, communism, which might soon come leaping across the Atlantic from Russia. Historian Frederick Lewis Allen wrote of him, "Harding looked back with longing eyes to the good old days when the government didn't bother businessmen with unnecessary regulations, but provided them with fat tariffs."

The political orthodoxy LeMay absorbed as a boy in Ohio included quite naturally a strong disapproval of communism and made him receptive to the growing rage against it exemplified by Attorney General A. Mitchell Palmer's "red scare" of 1919. Like the Joe McCarthy "red scare" of the early 1950s, the 1919 campaign against subversives failed to uncover many American Communists, but it did fill millions of Americans with a permanent fear and loathing of communism. As social commentator Mark Sullivan wrote, here was a new conception of society and government. And a fearsome one. "In Russia, some aggressive exponents of new thought . . . imposed on that country a conception of government that not only was novel but ran counter to every pattern of society the world had ever experienced. The new ideal of society denied most of the things which governments are founded to secure; it denied the right of the individual to own property; it denied practically every right of the individual . . . it denied the validity of many of the social and family relationships that in other countries were sanctified; it denied religion . . ."

Such a concept was, of course, abhorrent to most Americans, and especially to conservatives like LeMay who had never doubted the sanctity of the American system. It seems that only his father had ever seriously challenged him with questions about social inequity in America. (If there were any liberal or radical professors on the Ohio State faculty at the time, they were not likely to be in the engineering school.) And however persuasively his father might point out the social injustice and poverty in America (a poverty under which the LeMay family had lived), he could not deny that his son, by working his way through the university, was already positioning himself to take advantage of the country's unparalleled opportunities. Since young men in their teens are inclined to be skeptical of their fathers' views, it must have been easy for Curtis LeMay to reject the workingman's opinions of Erving LeMay, which meant, ironically, that when they argued politics, the younger LeMay was expressing the conservative orthodoxy most often associated with fathers, while his dad was expressing the liberal orthodoxy most often associated with sons. LeMay entered the Army Air Corps, therefore, already devoted to the conservative views he would find among most of his colleagues there.

The first month of aviation cadet life was no more fun in 1928 than it is today. And in some ways it was even less fun. At March Field, for instance, there were the tents in which the fledglings were lodged. They had wooden floors and sides but pyramidal canvas roofs that provided a novel type of ventilation. Sparks and embers from their Sibley stoves, and from the stoves of neighboring tents, would settle on the canvas and burn holes of various size in it. This meant the cadets got plenty of fresh air at all times, and during California's rainy winter months, there were times when they hardly needed baths.

Lest the lower classmen become too comfortable in these tents, there was always the hazing by the upper classmen, who were eager to visit revenge upon their juniors for the indignities their now-departed seniors had previously visited upon them. But what bothered the new cadets more than any of this was a deprivation they had not expected. Almost the first thing they saw when they arrived at March, and certainly the first thing that riveted their attention, was the long row of shiny airplanes on the flight line. Consolidated PT-3s, with Wright Whirlwind engines. They were only primary trainers, but to eager young cadets who had seldom if ever been off the ground, they looked as hot as fighter planes. The thought of flying them in a couple of days was as exciting as the thought of a beautiful girl saying yes. But alas, the first thing the boys learned about these planes was that they wouldn't get near them for the first month.

It was a month full of tent inspections, close order drill, ground school, and hazing, interrupted only by meal after meal of almost inedible food. The Army, apparently aware of how badly most of these fellows' mothers cooked at home, had established schools where mess trainees were taught to cook even worse. LeMay at that time was a very slender fellow who weighed only 135 pounds, due partly, perhaps, to the daily fare in the March Field cadet mess hall, but he was sustained through that first month by the sight of those planes on the flight line.

When the time came to fly, LeMay and his tentmate, Griswold, were both ready, and they found the early stages quite simple. Both of them soloed after about six hours of instruction. But as the days and weeks wore on, LeMay encountered a stumbling block he had not anticipated. However hard he tried, he didn't seem able to learn much from his instructor, a marvelously talented pilot named Peewee Wheeler. The more LeMay listened to Wheeler, the more the man's message seemed to fade. LeMay was beginning to doubt his own powers of perception and concentration when, eventually, it dawned on him that Peewee Wheeler's other students weren't reaping much knowledge from him either. Within a fairly short time, four of them had washed out. He was the only one left of Wheeler's five original students. Then three more students were assigned to Wheeler, and all three of them washed out. The man was undoubtedly a fine pilot, but he seemed to be a hopelessly incompetent teacher. LeMay thought of asking for a different instructor but then thought better of it. He had never heard of anyone getting through flying cadet school by bitching about his instructor, so he continued plugging along under Peewee's wing, with almost disastrous results.

By the time LeMay took the final check ride that would decide whether he was to wash out or go on to larger aircraft (DeHavillands or Douglas 0-2s), he realized he was in more than a little trouble. He still felt he wasn't learning much from his instructor. And unfortunately he found himself assigned, for that fateful flying examination, to the toughest check pilot on the base. His Air Corps future was in the balance and, as it happened, that ride proceeded so badly it could hardly have done much to swing the balance in his favor. Out of ignorance, he made the wrong decisions on two or three forced-landing approaches, and when he was told to do a snap roll to the left, he had to admit he didn't know how. Finally the check pilot got tired of chewing his ass and told him to go in for a landing, whereupon LeMay misjudged the wind and the angle of glide, bringing the plane to earth smoothly, but too far down the field.

"It wasn't one of my better days," LeMay later recalled. "I

could just hear that train tooting dismally through the mountains and prairies once more, carrying a brand new washout back to Columbus, Ohio.''

But while it wasn't one of his better days, it was one of his luckiest. After this crucial ride, the exasperated check pilot said to him, ''By Jesus Christ, I don't know whether to wash you out, or give you a chance and send you on. I guess I'll send you on after all, but I'll keep my eye on you.''

During his next phase of training, LeMay quickly began to do better, having been assigned to a different instructor, a World War I pilot named Joe Dawson who knew how to make his students understand him. In LeMay's opinion Dawson didn't have ''the technique or the skills which Wheeler had,'' but ''he could tell you what you were doing wrong. . . . In two weeks I learned more from Joe Dawson than I had all the rest of the time I'd been at March.'' He was the first in his class to solo in the DeHavilland, and two months later he was the first to solo in the Douglas 0-2s.

On June 14, 1929, however, about two weeks before his class was scheduled to leave March for advanced training at Kelly Field in San Antonio, LeMay and an 0-2 he was piloting suffered a mishap that must have caused him a few sleepless nights.[2] He had taxied out onto the field from the flight line, parallel to the line and parallel to another cadet on his left wing. When this cadet turned left to take his position in a formation, his propeller blew so much dust into the air behind him that LeMay and his plane were quickly engulfed in a cloud of it. Before he could come to a stop, his propeller was chewing its way into the wing of a third cadet's PT-3.

The investigating officer concluded in his report that the reason for the accident was the same one assigned to almost every accident involving a cadet—pilot error. The Air Corps believed in putting every one of its cadets on notice that if he were to get himself killed, his epitaph would be ''Pilot Error.'' (The investigating officer, incidentally, was First Lt. Barney M. Giles, and the base commander, who also signed the report, was Maj. Millard F. ''Miff'' Harmon. Both men would be, for short periods, colleagues of LeMay's in the Pacific sixteen years later.)

With so many cadets washing out (only half of LeMay's class graduated, even though it later proved to be an exceptionally outstanding group), one might suppose that LeMay's accident alone would be enough to eliminate him, but while the Air Corps liked to place official blame on cadets for accidents, the actual evaluation of a cadet's work was much more broadly based. It is even possible that his superiors, considering the circumstances, might hold him blameless for an accident, but that wouldn't mean they'd tell him so. In the Air Corps, blame was part of the learning process. So LeMay was sent on to Texas with the rest of the survivors. Though still a fledgling, he knew now what he had gotten himself into. He had to his credit about 150 hours in the air. And they were serious hours. Flying was not fun for LeMay. It was work. About his flight training he has admitted, "It didn't come easy. I really worked at it. . . . I'd wanted to have a joyride ever since that first two-dollar-and-a-half flight at Columbus; but I wasn't about to undertake it in this year of 1929. I didn't sneak off. I didn't joyride. If I was supposed to practice Eights, then by God I practiced Eights. I told myself, night and morning, that I must do exactly what I was ordered to do. The one thing that I wanted to do more than anything else was just to go up and take a ride in an airplane. Never did."

Here was an example of what seems a rather sad aspect of LeMay's life. He had his pleasures. He loved to hunt and fish and practice his marksmanship. He loved the outdoors and he loved to smoke. He began smoking, in fact, when he was a flying cadet. But pleasure always seemed to be something far in the background of his life. He didn't appear to have as much fun as other people. Unless he considered work to be fun.

Cadet life in advanced training at Kelly was much more relaxed than life in primary at March. Almost all of the cadets who were destined to wash out had already done so. And the remaining cadets were now joined by remaining officers from another primary class at Brooks Field in San Antonio. These officers were West Point graduates who had subsequently been sent to Brooks after opting for flight training. The fact that the cadets were now fellow students of officers, and that they had survived the most rigorous part of their training, prompted the Air Corps to consider them more mature now and to treat them with a little more leniency. The food at Kelly was excellent. Most of the weekends were free, and the flying was easy. It was amazingly simple compared to advanced flight training today. There were PT-9s, AT-11s, and P-1s, but there wasn't a lot of difference among them.

"They were all single-seaters," LeMay recalls. "All had the

same thing: a stabilizer, a stick, a rudder, a throttle, a spark control. That was it. You just got in and flew.''

There were no checklists to run through before taking off, and no brakes when you landed. You simply made sure there was room to coast to a stop. There was also no instrument flying because there were very few instruments. And therefore there was no bad-weather flying. There was some night flying, though only on clear nights and only in assigned sectors where you couldn't run into another cadet.

It seems ludicrous now to think of the young men in LeMay's class as qualified Air Corps pilots on the day they were given their wings—October 12, 1929. They had only about 270 hours apiece in the air at that time. Yet they were already among the better aircraft pilots in the world of 1929 because, primitive as their training had been, it was nevertheless about the best available anywhere. Even a partial list of the eventually distinguished airmen among the 117 officers and cadets who graduated in that class indicates there must have been something good about their training: Emmett ''Rosey'' O'Donnell, Laverne ''Blondie'' Saunders, Samuel Anderson, Norris Harbold, Arthur Woodley, Nathan Bedford Forrest, Robert Travis, Stuart McLennan, Arthur Meehan, George Brinton McClellan, Roger Ramey, William H. Tunner, John K. Gerhart, Fred Anderson, August Kissner, George Mundy, Frank Everest, Jr., Francis ''Grizzy'' Griswold, and LeMay himself, to name a few.

Second Lieutenants LeMay and Griswold, who had been together throughout their training, remained together after graduation when they were both sent to the Twenty-seventh Pursuit Squadron of the First Pursuit Group, stationed at Selfridge Field, Michigan, near the town of Mount Clemons. Selfridge was a small fighter base, activated during World War I and named after Lt. Thomas E. Selfridge, the first Army officer to fly an airplane and the first to be killed in one.

On September 17, 1908, Orville Wright gave a demonstration flight for Army officials at Fort Myer, across the Potomac River from Washington. The purpose of the flight was to sell the Army some of the planes the Wright brothers were building, but Orville didn't do a very good selling job that day. With Selfridge riding as a passenger, Wright's plane crashed after some of the wing wires came loose. Wright was badly injured but eventually recovered. Selfridge was killed, thus helping to launch the Air Corps custom of naming its fields after its fallen fliers.

Presumably the First Pursuit Group of the Army Air Corps was an operational unit, but if so, the country was fortunate not to be involved in a war at that time. There were three squadrons, supposedly with twenty-five planes in each. Actually there were enough planes for only one squadron. LeMay recalls that on an average day "the work consisted mostly of climbing up as high as you could get, and then diving at the hangar line. This was the way we strove to make the Team: to be considered combat ready."

As for training, the new pilots simply had to learn from the veterans, which meant, primarily, that they had to take a certain amount of postgraduate abuse from them. It was important for the older, hotter pilots to remind the younger ones that they were not so hot. The one other aspect of training was a week each year at a gunnery and bombing range above the waters of Lake Huron near Oscoda in northern Michigan. LeMay did well enough there to be included on the Selfridge team at the national gunnery matches, but this had little to do with the quality of the training. He simply happened to be remarkably accurate with weapons.

When they weren't flying, LeMay was a mess officer and Griswold was a maintenance officer, but like the rest of the pilots on the base, they didn't have enough work to keep them busy. With another pilot, Sid Nelson, they rented a house in town. They didn't seem to have much excitement there, either. Griswold recalls that there was never a woman in that house. The most exciting incident he can remember happened one winter day when LeMay put some newspapers in the fireplace. They plugged up the flue and almost burned the house down.

Lt. Gen. Glenn Barcus, who was also at Selfridge in those days, has aptly described duty there: "I will be perfectly honest with you. The mission was to fly at cities and fly at airshows mostly. We did quite a bit of it, and we had a grand old time doing it. We would indulge in maneuvers occasionally. That was still pretty much in the way of an airshow."[3] The entire Air Corps, in those days, shared the mission of selling the public on the importance of air power.

LeMay recalls some of the junkets the Selfridge squadrons took "to open up airports." Lindbergh's historic flight across the Atlantic in 1927 had made Americans so air-conscious that towns and cities throughout the country were building airports.

And all of them wanted Air Corps squadrons to attend and perform at their dedication ceremonies.

"Naturally, the Air Corps snapped at the opportunity to advertise the Air Corps," LeMay recalls. "We would do formation flying, put on a show, and then some individual acrobatics. If it was one of the large municipal ports that was being saluted, we sent enough airplanes to make up our eighteen-ship formation. Smaller airports, they would send perhaps a flight."

He recalls also that to be included on one of these dedicatory excursions, a pilot "had to be qualified for cross-country." It is difficult to imagine now that there were full-fledged Air Corps pilots in those days who were not yet qualified for cross-country flights. Especially when one considers how little it took to qualify. There wasn't much more to learn than how to read a compass, how to read a road map, and what to do if the weather looked bad. What did you do? You stayed on the ground. Almost all flying was by visual navigation, which meant you flew below the clouds, followed roads and rivers, and tried to identify towns as you passed over them. To go from Selfridge to St. Louis, for example, one took off and flew directly toward a large, prominent smokestack in south Chicago.

General Griswold in retirement recalls a dedicatory excursion which he, LeMay, and several other pilots flew to Bradford, Ontario, to take part in a ceremony opening a stretch of road. It was as a result of this excursion that LeMay's colleagues began calling him "The Diplomat," in recognition of his inability to be tactful when there was an opportunity to be blunt and truthful.

The Royal Canadian Air Force at the time was even more poorly equipped than the American. The Canadians were represented at the ceremony by a squadron of World War fighters, whereas the boys from Selfridge were flying shiny P-12s. After the air show, the Canadian commander, resplendent in a blue cape with red lining, invited the U.S. pilots to inspect his planes. And while they were doing so, he made the mistake of asking LeMay, "What do you think of them?"

Without thinking twice, LeMay said, "Jesus Christ, aren't they lousy!" He would eventually become famous for that kind of diplomacy.

LeMay survived two aerial mishaps while stationed at Selfridge. On the morning of August 15, 1930, he was flying the number-two plane, a Curtis P-1B, on the leader's right wing in the last element of a formation when he was hit by the prop wash of the preceding element. His plane was thrown at the lead plane by the turbulent airstream, his top wing hitting the lead plane's horizontal stabilizer. While the lead plane was undamaged, the upper wing of LeMay's biplane "was so damaged that the ailerons were jammed." He was able to land it safely, however, by using the rudder to turn it.[4]

On March 28, 1931, he took a young lady friend up for a ride in a PT-3, with the group commander's permission, and was cruising around at five hundred feet, showing her the local countryside, when the engine quit. He thought at first she had unknowingly turned off the magneto switch in the rear cockpit. It was later determined that the right magneto shaft had broken, and the carburetor had been clogged by bits of rubber. There was no way for LeMay to discover this, or do anything about it, at the time. All he knew was that there were high-tension wires straight ahead and an open field to the right. Needless to say he chose the open field, sliced the plane in, ran through a fence, washing out the landing gear, and slid to a stop in a manure pile.[5]

Neither he nor the girl was injured and the plane was easily repairable. The most interesting aspect of the incident was that the girl was with him. Now that he had a lieutenant's paycheck of $125 a month coming in, plus flight pay, his wallet had thickened slightly and he was becoming more active socially. This young lady had been his date at a party on the base the previous night.

Another interesting aspect of the incident was that the accident report says he had no passenger with him. The officers signing the report seem to have understood that in the Army, what isn't said doesn't have to be explained. No doubt they sympathized with LeMay. They, too, might sometime like to take a girl up for a ride.

After this incident, LeMay didn't see much more of his lady passenger. Perhaps she didn't enjoy impromptu landings in manure piles. In any case, his own interests turned sharply in another direction that spring when he met another young lady, Helen Maitland, a University of Michigan coed who was the daughter of a Cleveland corporation lawyer.[6]

The story of their first meeting, as LeMay tells it, is simple, straightforward, and, as usual, "diplomatic." One of his colleagues at Selfridge, Lt. Herb Tellman, had been a classmate at

Kelly, and was now a friend. "He was engaged to a girl at the University of Michigan," LeMay recalls. "They were having an ROTC party at Ann Arbor and his girl talked a couple of us into going, with a couple of her friends, which we did, without much enthusiasm. That's when I met Helen."

As Helen LeMay tells the story, it is apparent that she was no more eager to meet him than he was to meet her: "The first of May was the Military Ball. It was a big thing. This friend of mine, Helene Strong, was dating an officer, Herb Tellman. She said, 'Wouldn't you like a date with a real Army officer?' Big deal. I said, 'Not particularly. I already have a date with somebody I like. He's a good dancer. And I don't go on blind dates.'

"She said, 'You don't have to go on a blind date. Herb will bring a couple of fellows over the weekend before, and we'll go to dinner or a show. You can look out the window and choose.'

"There was this other cute girl who was going out with us, so we looked out the window as they came up the walk. Curt was not fat at that time but this other officer was very slender. So I said, 'I'll take the fat one.' "

LeMay admits that "I was attracted to her from the start. I liked her wild blue eyes and her hair. Don't know whether you'd call it dark blond or light brown. Kind of curly and wiry. She talked plenty. Couldn't seem to stop. And it was all in a bubbling effusion which I found myself rather enjoying. She'd skip from one topic to another like a dancer just hitting the high points. Often you couldn't get a word in edgewise."

Since Helen was so outgoing and effusive, and Curt was a man who seldom even wanted to get a word in, they were ideally matched from the beginning. Though there was no talk of marriage, they began seeing each other frequently on weekends. He liked her company and he was impressed by her education. She had studied at Western Reserve in Cleveland and was now working for her degree in dental hygiene at the University of Michigan. Her accomplishments made him think about completing his own college work and earning his degree at Ohio State.

The country was now in the throes of the Great Depression, however, and while he was making a tidy sum—$187 a month including flight pay—he had to send home even more money than usual because it was not easy, in those hard times, for his father to find work.

Curt LeMay at this time felt the financial pinch so severely that he considered leaving the service to take a job with the Ford

Motor Company as a pilot. Ford was then manufacturing its famous trimotor airliner for the growing passenger industry. Each time the company sold a plane to an airline, it would provide a trained pilot as part of the equipment, so to speak. For this purpose Ford was hiring Air Corps pilots at twelve hundred dollars a month—a staggering wage—and teaching them to fly the trimotor.

When LeMay heard about this, he went to the Ford plant in Detroit and applied. He was quickly accepted and actually took the job. Then he began to wonder if he really wanted to give up his Air Corps career. He asked the people at Ford to "give me a couple of days to think it over," went back to Selfridge, and began asking his friends what they thought he should do.

Career expectations for Army officers were not very promising in those days. During the twenties and thirties, a lieutenant could wait as long as seventeen years before he became a captain. (As it happened, LeMay was destined to become a captain after eleven years, only because of World War II.)

"We could look forward to retiring as lieutenant colonels at the end of thirty years," he recalls. "We had a seniority list and the only way you got promoted [was when] someone died or left the service or retired and created a vacancy."

In spite of all this, he decided to turn down the job with Ford and remain in the Air Corps. "I stayed," he said later, "because I liked the people in the Air Corps. They had pride and they believed in what they were doing. Also, I had found I could go to a bank, sign a note, and get money just because I was an Army officer. This impressed me. It wasn't because of my shiny face. It was the reputation a long line of Army officers had built up before me."[7]

Having decided to stay in the service, he also decided, with some prompting from Helen Maitland, to find a way to go back to Ohio State, as a student officer, and get that civil engineering degree. But if he hoped to do so, he would have to come up with a plan his commanding officer might swallow.

The commander at Selfridge, Maj. George H. Brett, was not an easy man to get around. He was an able and ambitious officer who, before the end of the decade, would compete, though unsuccessfully, with Hap Arnold for the job of Air Force chief. LeMay went in to see him, explained that he wanted to finish work for his degree at Ohio State, and had figured out how to do it without shortchanging the Army. How? Well, first of all, he would need five months and twenty-nine days of detached duty at Norton Field in Columbus. If he wanted any more than that, as Brett knew, he would have to ask for a permanent change of station, but he didn't want to leave Selfridge permanently.

He had ascertained that there was only one regular officer on duty at Norton, and this man needed help, especially with the reserve training program. LeMay assured Brett he could easily put in full time at Norton and still complete the necessary courses at Ohio State on a part-time schedule. The school had assured him of that. And because the two quarters would actually take several days more than the six-months-minus-one-day he hoped the Army would allot him, he had also asked for and received a promise from the university that he could arrive a few days late and leave a few days early, as long as he completed his work.

In the official report of LeMay's August 15, 1930, accident at Selfridge, Brett had rated him only an "average" pilot with "average" skills, but he apparently admired him now for his desire to complete his education, and for the painstaking plan he had worked out to make it possible. He granted his approval and LeMay was off to Columbus, a few days late, but still early enough for the quarter that began the first of October.[8]

While he was in Columbus, during the autumn and winter of 1931-32, he shared an apartment with a friend named Cale Osborne whom he had known during his previous undergraduate days. He was bringing in almost $250 a month now, with base and flight pay, quarters and ration allowances. And the price for everything was so low, thanks to the Depression, that he remembers one married couple, with a baby, complaining because they couldn't keep their grocery budget below a dollar a day. LeMay and Osborne, who was working for the State Highway Department while he, too, made up some courses toward a degree, both had money to burn.

"Cale and I had the world by the tail in more ways than one," LeMay recalls. "We were in good health; we had work and we had ambition . . . we were bubbling with it. And I owned a good car. For the first time in my life I seemed to know what it was like to be young and alive, to be intent, and yet at the same time not self-disciplined to the point of crucifixion."

Even his schoolwork was easier now that he was older and more mature. He went to classes in civilian clothes each morning, then to Norton Field in his uniform each afternoon. And for his thesis he teamed up with Osborne in a convenient blending of aviation with engineering. Since he had an airplane at his disposal, he created an "aerial mosaic," a photographic map of the Columbus area, and Osborne wrote the report for it. They got only a B for the project because that was the highest grade the professor ever gave for a thesis, but in general, LeMay got better grades now than he ever had before. When he returned to Selfridge toward the end of March, his civil engineering degree from Ohio State followed him in the mail a few days later.

The Depression continued to deepen during 1932, boding ill for the political fortunes of President Hoover and for the economic fortunes of millions of Americans, including, especially, the LeMay family. Jobs were now so scarce that Erving and Arizona LeMay finally moved again, this time from Columbus back down to her family's homestead farm near Portland, which she had inherited from her parents. Four-year-old Patarica went with them but Methyll, now seventeen, and Leonard, fifteen, remained in Columbus because the high schools were better there. One of Leonard's more vivid memories of Curtis was his repeated advice to "get an education." Methyll and Leonard lived with the families of friends and paid their way with what Curt could give them plus whatever they could earn from part-time jobs. Curt was also helping his parents, and they needed it.

Patarica, though only a toddler at the time, remembers that move. The farmhouse had been abandoned when they arrived. The weeds were overgrown around it and it needed repairs. "There was a barrel of pickled sweet corn and beans in the cellar. Also a can of lard. We didn't have anything so we ate the corn and beans. They were delicious. And in the winter, we had potatoes."[9]

At least twice while his parents were living there, LeMay flew down to see them. During one of his visits he took his parents up for their first plane rides—separately, of course. The Army planes he flew at the time had room for only one passenger. His father had a tendency to get airsick, but his mother loved every minute in the air, including the acrobatics. She had always been a bit of a daredevil. Leonard recalls that a cousin used to take her for rides on his motorcycle. Curtis recalls that "I made a pretty good pilot of my mother. She took to it."

In the presidential election of 1932, LeMay was spared the duty of choosing between his fraternity brother, the incumbent Herbert Hoover, and the patrician Democratic alternative, Gov-

ernor Franklin D. Roosevelt of New York. That year, and for
many years thereafter, LeMay abstained from voting, as did most
American military officers. The duty of the military, in the minds
of these officers, was to uphold and protect the legally constituted government, not to select it. As for 1932, it wouldn't have
mattered whether or how the military voted. Roosevelt swamped
Hoover, who was almost universally blamed, not for creating the
Depression, but for failing to alleviate it.

Roosevelt wasted no time before instituting programs of relief,
banking reforms, business incentives, and public works to get
the economy moving again. One of his measures, the Civilian
Conservation Corps, soon became a source of inconvenience and
distraction to military officers like LeMay. Right after Roosevelt
took office in March 1933, he activated the CCC to provide jobs
for the throngs of young men all over the country who couldn't
find work. And he ordered the Army to assign about five thousand officers, regulars and reserves, to run the several hundred
camps designated to house the men.

LeMay was one of those unfortunate officers. He was assigned
to manage the mess hall, among other things, at a camp near the
town of Brethren, Michigan, more than two hundred miles
northwest of Selfridge Field. He qualified almost inevitably for
this highly undesirable duty by being still near the bottom of the
seniority list, and still a bachelor.

The Brethren camp was full of mostly Polish, working-class
brethren from Hamtramck, an industrial suburb of Detroit. They
were tough, and they were unhappy about the conditions that
had displaced them from their familiar Hamtramck surroundings, only to dump them up here in this wilderness. They would
as soon fight as eat, and if there was no one else to fight, they
would gladly fight each other. Since they were civilians, not
subject to regular Army discipline, and since there were no police of any kind in the camp, LeMay and his colleagues had to
devise some thoughtfully persuasive methods of keeping them in
line. LeMay had to admit later that he had learned from the
experience a few things about leadership that would eventually
prove useful. But all in all, it was a dull assignment and he didn't
like it.[10]

He had, however, two consolations. The first arose from Major Brett's annoyance at seeing his pilots sent out into the sticks
on assignments that could hardly be expected to maintain their
flying efficiency. He offered them planes to take along if they

could find suitable fields in which to land and take off. After LeMay found a farmer amenable to this cattle-scaring disruption of his property, he could occasionally fly away from that god-forsaken place. His second consolation was that he wouldn't have to stay very long with his Brethren brethren. Before leaving Selfridge, he had gotten himself on the list for the September class in the Air Corps Communication School at Chanute Field, Illinois. This hope of salvation seemed to fade away one day when he read in a newspaper that the communication school had burned down. But the communication system in the Army being what it was in those days, the authorities at Selfridge never heard about the fire at Chanute, and LeMay had no intention of telling them about it. In late August 1933, he was ordered back to Selfridge, apparently on the way to Chanute. While he knew he wasn't going there, he had no idea where, if anyplace, he might be going. But one thing he did know. He was glad to be leaving Brethren.

When he reached Selfridge, they weren't expecting him. They had canceled his orders to return, but, in another communications failure, had forgotten to inform him. So they had him on their hands with no place to put him at the moment.

He had been at Selfridge for a week or so when an order arrived from Washington. They were to send a pilot to some kind of new Air Corps experiment—a navigation school at Langley Field in Virginia, near Washington. Since LeMay was sitting around with nothing to do, they asked him if he wanted to go. He said, "That's for me." This bit of luck was destined to add an important dimension to his career.

As previously noted, the Air Corps hadn't paid much attention before this time to the notion of precise, calculated navigation. Its planes were so small, and had such short range, that navigation wasn't yet a serious problem. The Air Corps had encouraged manufacturers to develop various navigational instruments, and had even made a few tentative efforts to launch navigation schools, but it wasn't until February 5, 1932, at the instigation of a pioneer navigator, Lt. A. F. Hegenberger, that a serious attempt was made to launch a permanent school. And even then, it was designated as "a small experimental detachment."[11]

Hegenberger, who had been harping since 1919 on the need for airplanes to know exactly where they were going, had also suggested that the Air Corps hire a civilian expert, Harold Gatty, who had been the navigator for the famous one-eyed flier, Wiley

Post, on his highly publicized 1931 flight around the world. (This was four years before Post and Will Rogers died together on a flight to Alaska.) In 1932, Gatty was finally hired and work began on establishment of a school with two branches—one at Rockwell Field in San Diego, the other at Langley Field. It wasn't until October 1933 that the first students reported at Langley. LeMay was among them.

Gatty was one of the instructors. So was Lt. Norris "Skip" Harbold, a member of LeMay's class at Kelly Field. Skip had also been a colleague of LeMay's at Selfridge until he was assigned to the Frontier Defense Research Unit, a group activated in 1932 to work on navigational developments and other problems. Harbold was chosen for this assignment partly because he had studied astronomy at West Point. The job was also destined to add a dimension to his career. He became, eventually, one of the foremost authorities on aerial navigation.

Harbold spent most of his time at the school's Rockwell Field branch. Gatty was the principal instructor at Langley. He familiarized his students with such instruments as gyroscopes, artificial horizons, and periodic compasses. He put them "under the hood" for simulated instrument flight. And he tried to teach them celestial navigation, but with only qualified success.

"Actually, Gatty wasn't too much of a teacher," LeMay recalls. "We didn't get a lot out of that." But LeMay's experience in that first class at the Langley navigation school did whet his curiosity about the subject. Especially the time he spent under the hood.

"It's not too astonishing to record that we were learning to fly straight and level, hold courses, get out of spins—all under the hood. I should say that the average was about twenty-five hours apiece of instrument training under these conditions. In my own case, I was told later that I had achieved more time under the hood than anyone else in the entire Air Corps. I think it was about twenty-seven hours. The program fascinated me. I hung around and pestered my instructors, and managed to rack up that extra time just because I was so hot-and-bothered about the whole thing." He returned to Selfridge in December well aware that with the anticipated development of long-range, multiengine aircraft, navigation was destined to become a vital aspect of flying.

Resumption of duty at Selfridge also gave him the opportunity to intensify his romance with Helen Maitland, which has been sorely interrupted by his detachment, first to the CCC camp, then to Langley. Shortly after they met, she had taken a job with the Firestone Company in Akron, which meant that whenever someone had to fly from Selfridge to Akron, LeMay would volunteer. "My commanding officers used to be amazed at how willing I was to go to Akron." But while he was at the CCC camp and at Langley, he didn't get much chance to go to Akron.

After finishing navigation school, he was entitled to a short leave, which he decided to spend in Cleveland. Though Helen was still working in Akron, she happened at the time to be at her parents' home in the Cleveland suburb of Lakewood. LeMay arrived there with high hopes of resuming their romance, only to find it had developed a serious snag. A lot of other young men were just as interested as he was in Helen Maitland, and she was, in his words, "a terrific flirt." She announced to him shortly after his arrival that she was engaged. And not just to one man, but to two. So she said.

This didn't mean she had lost interest in Curt. Not at all. She was as friendly and affectionate as ever. But he wasn't as modern as she was. He announced that he was leaving.

As he remembers it, she said, "Well, Curt, when are you coming back?"

"Not coming back," he said, in his usual flowery style.

"You're not?"

"Nope." And away he went.

Whether it was his sudden and firm resolve that eventually smoothed out the course of their true love has never quite been established. Even today they don't exactly agree on the specifics that brought them back together. In due course, he says, "she talked me into coming to her sister's wedding. By that time she had shaken those other two characters, or she said she had, anyway. I don't know exactly when we got engaged."

Helen LeMay insists, on the other hand, that he came running back to her very quickly. She broke off her other engagements because they weren't serious anyway, whereupon she and Curt decided right then to get married as soon as possible.[12]

Before they could get around to it, however, President Roosevelt again intervened. Maybe that's why Curtis LeMay has remained such a dedicated conservative Republican. It seems that for most of his career, Democratic presidents—whether Roosevelt, Truman, or Kennedy—kept interrupting or altering his plans.

In early 1934, Roosevelt, unsatisfied with the government's mail-carrying contract with the airlines, asked Maj. Gen. Benjamin Foulois, then Air Corps chief of staff, if his pilots could do the job. Foulois made the mistake of saying yes. He forgot to notice that Air Corps pilots lacked the right airplanes, the navigational skills, and the necessary cross-country experience. He simply said yes and Roosevelt took him up on it. Then, testifying before Congress, Foulois compounded his blunder by saying, "We have had a great deal of experience in flying at night, and in flying in fogs and bad weather, in blind flying and in flying under all conditions."

Thus began, on February 19, 1934, one of the great fiascoes in the history of the Army Air Corps. Though Foulois's pilots had no such experience as he claimed, they soon would have. And twelve of them would be dead as a result.

LeMay, who was assigned to the Richmond, Virginia-Greensboro, North Carolina, route, suffered no accidents though he was forced down once by bad weather. His training at navigation school, where he had more time under the hood than anyone else, gave him an advantage over most of his colleagues.[13] But he was as happy as all the others when the president, and even Benny Foulois, finally realized the Air Corps was not equipped to fly the mail.

On June 1, 1934, the airlines resumed the job, after sixty-five of the Air Corps' totally unsuitable planes had crashed in the attempt to replace them. And the twelve dead pilots plus the smashed aircraft were not the only Air Corps losses. The public humiliation and ridicule was so great it would not be fully overcome until World War II.

CHAPTER FOURTEEN

During the great air mail experiment of 1934, Helen Maitland waited impatiently to find out when she could schedule her wedding. Though her husband-to-be sometimes joked about this pending event as if it were more like a sentencing, he was almost as deeply involved in the plans as she was. She saw to that. He even went so far as to manipulate himself into a trip to Washington to find out whether there might be a change of station in his immediate future. He had been at Selfridge a long time. Four and a half years. It would be silly to buy a houseful of furniture for his new bride, and rent a house in which to put it, if he was about to be sent elsewhere.[1]

"The Army," he has observed, "displayed diabolical efficiency in dealing with such matters. It was as if a witchlike Board sat in some haunted cavern, looked over the lists, and said, 'Now who's nicely settled down in some new quarters? Let's put him on the list for this far-distant assignment—and immediately.' "

As soon as LeMay reached Washington, therefore, he repaired to the Army Personnel Office in the Munitions Building and asked if there were any plans to transfer him.

The answer: "Relax, Lieutenant. Nothing in sight for you. Nothing whatever."

He was able to relax thereafter about the prospects of being dislocated, but not about the details of the wedding. "Never before had I realized that there was so much to the mere mechanical process of getting married. For complication, the airmail wasn't in it. Whenever I was in touch with Helen—which was as frequently as could be managed—I was notified concerning major crises which ensued about every two hours, and minor ones every five minutes."

Who could blame the poor woman? She was making plans for a wedding and didn't even know when it would be. She'd look silly alone in front of that altar while he was up in the clouds someplace, delivering somebody's dull, boring mail. She had reason to rejoice, therefore, when the president released her fiancé from that odious duty. Now if only the Army Air Corps would cooperate and give him a leave in June. He had ten days coming to him.

"I'll take five days before the ceremony and five days after it," she told him on the phone one night, "but see to it you're here." She seemed, even before her marriage, to know about the frustrations of an Army wife trying to make her plans mesh with her husband's duties. But this time it worked. His leave was from June 4 to 14, so the wedding was scheduled for June 9.

From the beginning, Lieutenant LeMay stipulated that it was not to be a big wedding. "I'm not going to have anyone singing 'O Promise Me,' " he decreed, "and I'm not going to do any kneeling." He didn't consider himself a religious person. As a child he had gone to Sunday school, but as an adult he "wasn't quite settled" on religion. "I believe in a Supreme Being," he once said, "but I don't feel that I need some other character to advise me on how to conduct myself to please this Supreme Being." It seemed to him that Helen shared these sentiments, but when it comes to a wedding ceremony, it's hard to guess how a woman might feel. Hence his firm decrees.

Given the force of Curtis LeMay's personality, one might assume these decrees were final. Unless one were aware of the force of Helen Maitland's personality. Shortly after LeMay arrived in Cleveland for the upcoming nuptials, she announced that they would both be expected at a church rehearsal the day before the ceremony. For the short, simple ceremony he had ordained, he saw no reason to rehearse.

"Any stupid person can get married," he said.

Surprisingly, she didn't bother to argue with him. It seemed she didn't really care whether he came to the rehearsal. So he stayed at her parents' home and played cards with her father while she and her mother rehearsed at the Episcopal church to which the Maitlands belonged. "I got along just great with Helen's father," LeMay has said. "I think her mother looked upon me with dark suspicion, because I was an impecunious youngster in the fly business; and in common sense, the mother thought her daughter could do better."

The next day, with LeMay still mumbling that they could as easily have "gone down to the courthouse and got married," they arrived instead at the church to find it packed, with an overflow of people crowding around the doors, trying to get inside. Six of his fellow officers were there as ushers while at least an equal number of Helen's friends were there, dressed in sumptuous finery, as bridesmaids. Helen herself was wearing a gown designed by Jay Thorpe, pink in color and festooned with lace. At the pew assigned to the bridal couple there were pink pillows on the kneeling benches. The ceremony with "no kneeling" was turning out to be a high church Episcopal mass. Before he knew it, the organ began to play and LeMay heard another friend of Helen's singing "Oh promise me . . ."

He gave his bride-to-be a side glance of pure fury. She simply looked away.

A few minutes later, when the priest said to them, "You will kneel," LeMay gave Helen another glance of renewed fury.

The priest repeated, "You will kneel."

Helen kicked Curt in the shins and they both knelt.

As soon as they were alone after the ceremony, LeMay said to his bride, "I thought I told you . . ."

That was as far as he got. "You didn't come to the rehearsal," she reminded him. "You got what you had coming."

Reminiscing recently about this wedding incident, Helen LeMay turned with a mischievous smile to her daughter, Patricia Jane, and said, "That sort of has to be our mode of living, isn't it, Janie. We sort of try to do what we please without telling him. If it isn't too bad, we can get by with it."

After the wedding festivities, the newlyweds drove to a downtown hotel where they had reserved a suite. With only five days of freedom, and not much money, they had decided to forego a honeymoon trip. What money they did have they wanted to spend on the embellishments they would need for their first permanent home. They had "a lovely big brick house" awaiting them and had spent most of their reserves buying furniture for it, but they would also be needing curtains, linens, and so forth. Helen was so eager to make that house a home she couldn't wait. After two days in downtown Cleveland, they hurried north to Selfridge Field and began settling into their permanent love nest.

It was a lovely house. The happy couple could hardly have asked for anything more. Each day, when Curt went to the flight line to take off into the wild blue yonder, his loving bride would clean and sew and arrange and change until, after ten or twelve weeks, their first permanent home was just about perfect.

Then one day the adjutant called Curt into his office. An hour later, he arrived at their enchanting cottage with an announcement for Helen: ''We are assigned to the Sixth Pursuit Squadron at Schofield Barracks, Wheeler Field, Hawaii. Just in case you hadn't noticed, Helen LeMay, you're in the Army now.'' In ten days they were completely packed, from furniture to incidentals, and on their way to New York, where they boarded an Army transport, the *Republic,* for an unexpected two-year Hawaiian ''honeymoon.'' Curt made Helen stand and watch with bated breath while their car was lowered into the hold. It was a new, cream-colored Auburn sports coupe with orange wheels. Not the kind of jalopy one would want to see scratched. Curt LeMay had come a long way from his first Model T Ford.

When they arrived at Wheeler Field, they were not surprised to learn that quarters were assigned according to rank, of which Curt LeMay didn't have much. They were among six couples arriving together who couldn't get housing on the base. They found a one-bedroom cottage right on the beach, which served them well enough. It had no hot water, but that was less of an inconvenience than Helen feared it would be. She couldn't use the shower anyway. There was a huge spider in residence on top of it. But some neighbors had hot water so she took her showers at their house. Or she'd go into the ocean, which was always warm.

At Wheeler, in addition to flying, LeMay had a succession of other jobs—communication, engineering, mess, operations—but his most satisfying assignment was the role he helped invent for himself in the establishment of a navigation school. Shortly after arriving in Hawaii, he ran into a Kelly cadet classmate, Lt. John Egan, who had taken, at Rockwell, the same navigation course LeMay completed at Langley. When they got to talking about navigation training in Hawaii, they found themselves in a short conversation. Air Corps pilots out there in the middle of the Pacific Ocean, where one might consider navigation fairly important, were getting no more instruction on the subject than one-hour lectures each week in ground school.

LeMay and Egan didn't delude themselves that they knew a lot about navigation, but they were sure that, having at least taken a course in the subject, they knew more than most of their colleagues, so they went to the Air Corps department commander, Col. Delos C. Emmons, and asked for permission to start a school. He told them to go ahead and even assigned them an amphibious plane for practice. They soon had a full-time school in operations, with about a dozen students, whom they divided into two groups. While LeMay and his six practiced in the air, on flights to Niihau (Bird Island) near Kauai, about 150 miles west of Oahu, Egan's group studied in the classroom. And after both groups were dismissed for the day, another phase of the schoolwork would begin—LeMay and Egan studying every book and chart they could find on the subject of navigation to make sure they could at least stay ahead of their students. For LeMay, at least, the most important aspect of this school was not what he taught but what he learned from it. His next six years in the Air Corps would be shaped largely by that experience.

Shortly before Christmas 1936, he was rotated back to the mainland as a first lieutenant, having won his promotion in March 1935, and was soon assigned, surprisingly, to the Second Bomb Group of the General Headquarters Air Force at Langley Field. During the whole seven years of his career he had been in pursuit. Now he was transferring to bombardment.

How did this switch come about? The process began with LeMay himself. Or did it? While he was in Hawaii, it dawned on him that from a far-seeing airman's point of view, bombers had to be more important than fighters. The fighter could never be much more than a defensive weapon. The bomber was by its very nature an offensive weapon. And there were bombers on the way—the B-17 in particular—which promised to be dominant offensive weapons. Defense was important but it was offense that won wars. If there was to be another war, it was the bomber that would take the real challenge to the enemy. It was the bomber that would have the job of destroying the enemy's ability to fight.

With all this in mind, LeMay, on his return to the mainland, applied for a transfer to bombardment. And he was astonished to learn that his request was immediately granted.[2] So were all his friends. That wasn't the way the Air Corps usually did business. When you asked for something, you expected to have to wait for it. But that was when your request was simply your own idea. In this case, as LeMay soon learned, it was also the Air Corps' idea. When he reported to Langley, after a Christmas-and-New-Year's leave, the personnel officer of the Second Bomb Group told him exactly why he was there. He was to start a navigation school for the group. The GHQ Air Force was aware that he had graduated from the Langley navigation school, and that he and Egan had run a school of their own creation in Hawaii.

Was LeMay happy to hear this news? Not by any means. He didn't want to run another navigation school. It was ironic that this transfer into the GHQ Air Force, where he hoped to learn about bombardment, was now offering him nothing more than a repetition of something he had already done, something he felt he already knew. When the personnel officer told him what was apparently in store for him, LeMay began doing something he supposedly doesn't do very well. He talked and he talked and he talked—about how little information he actually had on the subject of navigation, about his limitations as a teacher, about the great teaching skills of Lieutenant Egan, who would be returning to the mainland shortly, and about his own eagerness to begin learning about bombardment.

When LeMay had finished reciting his entire prayer, he stopped to catch his breath. And he was astonished to hear the personnel officer say, "Well, okay." The establishment of a group navigation school was left to Egan, who did, in due time, return to the mainland and join the GHQ Air Force. LeMay was assigned to the Forty-ninth Squadron of the Second Bomb Group as assistant operations officer.

It was in this job that LeMay encountered Lt. Col. Robert Olds, the man who was to influence his development and shape his military thinking more than any other. If there was a man alive who knew the bombardment business, it was Bob Olds, the commander of the Second Bomb Group. He had been in the business for more than twenty years. He flew a bomber against the Germans in World War I. After the war, he became an aide to General Billy Mitchell, the maverick airman who was eventually banished from the Army for his strident advocacy of air power. Olds was a dedicated disciple of Mitchell's doctrine that air supremacy would be the key to military success in any future war. To him, as to other Air Corps theorists of the time, air supremacy meant large fleets of four-engine, long-range bombers. And specifically, it meant the B-17 Flying Fortress, the first of which the Boeing Company was about to deliver to the Air Corps. But more than a theorist, Olds was an operations man. He believed in combat readiness at all times, which meant he believed in constant, intense training in preparation for any emergency that might develop. In this latter belief he was probably more passionate than any of his predecessors or contemporaries. He demanded of any outfit he commanded that it be ready to fight at a moment's notice. Whoever wishes to understand Curtis LeMay should begin by studying Bob Olds. LeMay modeled himself after Olds almost from the moment he joined the Second Bomb Group of the GHQ Air Force.

"I can't imagine any experience more demanding and more valuable to a young officer," LeMay has written,

> than a tour of duty serving under Bob Olds. In my own case he was the first man I'd ever come in contact with who really penetrated my thick skull with a sense of urgency in getting things done. . . . The whole purpose of the Air Corps was to fly and fight in a war, and to be ready to fly and fight in that war at any given moment if the war should come. That capability was what Olds required of his equipment and his people. Any individual or any ideal which worked toward an increased state of efficiency in his organization was welcomed. Anything which mitigated against that efficiency was not tolerated. Life was just as simple as that; and thus life was made inspiring.[3]

It is easy enough to understand why a man like Curtis LeMay would be inspired and intensely motivated working for a man like Olds. LeMay seems always to feel most comfortable when he is able to reduce an issue or a problem to its simplest possible terms. The same was true of Olds. When LeMay first came under Olds's authority, however, he was not so comfortable about his new boss. He soon found out that working for this fellow was not like working for anyone else.

"He was the one who shook me up as to what we were in business for. After I became squadron operations officer, the group operations officer took sick, so I was brought up to the group while he was gone. My office was on the ground floor [of one of the hangars] and the commander's office was right above it. I found out I'd better be in my office when Olds came to work in the morning. And he didn't come when everyone else did at eight o'clock. It was more like seven, and I'd better be there."

When Olds arrived he would always stop at Operations and ask a few questions. "LeMay, what's the weather in San Antonio this morning?"

In the beginning, LeMay was simply puzzled by such demands for what seemed like useless information. The weather in San Antonio? At that hour, he was hardly even aware of the weather there at Langley. "I don't know," he would say.

"You should know. Your planes can fly that far."

The next morning, Olds might ask, "How many planes have you got in commission to fly today?"

Such information didn't reach the Operations desk until the engineering officer came to work. Then why didn't the engineering officer come to work earlier? The operations officer should know the status of his force at all times.

After hitting LeMay with a few such questions, and embarrassing him about his lack of answers, Olds would begin talking about projects he had in mind, and he would assign his acting operations officer enough jobs to keep him busy for two or three days. Then he would go upstairs to his own office and think of more jobs to assign the next day.

"I began to get a feeling of what operating a military unit was all about," LeMay recalled recently, "and what I ought to be doing about it. Our job was to get the outfit ready for war. This hadn't dawned on me before."

During the 1920s and early 1930s, very few Americans thought seriously about the possibility of another war. And that included American military men. Hadn't the war of 1914–18 made the world safe for democracy? "We knew about Hitler," LeMay recalls, "but it hadn't sunk through to me at least that we were headed for war."

In 1937, the job of getting any Air Corps outfit ready for war was far beyond the ambitions and dedication even of men like Olds and LeMay. The best American bombers, the twin-engined Martin B-10s and Douglas B-18s, were not comparable to what the Germans, or even the British, were producing at that time. The B-17 was promising but the first one off the ground in 1935 had crashed, and the War Department was only grudgingly allowing the Air Corps to buy a few more. Money was so scarce it seemed foolish even to dream of making long-term plans. The entire Air Corps still consisted of fewer than twenty thousand men. And wages were so low—twenty-one dollars a month for privates—that it was difficult to attract qualified recruits.

LeMay tells a story about two tough street boys from Brooklyn who enlisted in the Air Corps and were sent directly to Langley without basic training. Before long, there was a series of thefts

in the barracks. Eventually the two were caught stealing someone's wallet and asked to explain themselves.

"What do you expect us to do?" one of them asked indig-
nantly. "You don't pay us enough to buy our meals." They had
been eating off the base every day. Nobody had told them about
the mess hall.

But even though the Air Corps was so drastically short of men,
money, and equipment, everyone in it was imbued with high
hopes. Despite the stinginess of the War Department and Congress, the B-17 was finally coming, and this was the plane that
would prove all the Air Corps theories about the importance of
air power.

"You couldn't approach any conversational group of bombardment people in those days," LeMay recalls, "without hearing B-17 all over the place. . . . The oncoming Fortresses would
offer new concepts in training, new concepts of use of airplanes
for strategic purposes. We were hazarding and speculating constantly."

On March 1, 1937, the first Flying Fortress was flown into
Langley from the Seattle Boeing plant by Maj. Barney Giles,
and it was destined for the Second Bomb Group. But that didn't
mean LeMay was about to become a B-17 pilot. Even the following June, when seven more were delivered, he was far down
the list. All of the original B-17 first pilots were at least captains.
It would be a while before he got a chance to take the controls.
Meanwhile, however, there was his old specialty, and Bob Olds
was aware of it. Before LeMay knew it, he was again a navigator.

Many years later, when asked whether Olds took a special
interest in him, LeMay said he didn't think so. But in August
1937, when the Air Corps was grudgingly allowed to take part
in an important exercise with the Navy, Olds chose LeMay as
the navigator in the lead plane. By that time, the Air Corps was
itching for a chance to flex the muscles of its new B-17s in an
effort to prove to the U.S. Navy, the U.S. Army, and the nation
at large that big, land-based, long-range airplanes could sink
approaching enemy battleships far out at sea, and could therefore
play a major role in the defense of our shores. Whether the Navy
brass believed this or not, they didn't want to take the risk of
testing it. Neither did the Army brass, except for the airmen.
The Army General Staff at the time was absolutely committed
to the belief that the only practical use of airplanes was in close

support of troops on the ground. It was for this reason that the War Department had been willing to order only eight (plus a supplemental five) Flying Fortresses for its Air Corps. The concept they represented—mass attacks against an enemy's heartland, against the industrial sources of his military power—was foreign to the thinking of ground-force generals. And also of admirals, who so deeply resented the threat of airplanes against their ships that they insisted no such threat existed. (Even after World War II, indeed, even today, there are admirals who argue that the airplane hasn't hurt the Navy.) These admirals, together with the ground force generals, had no trouble convincing Congress. But they did not convince those hotheads in the Air Corps who were still spouting the gospel according to Saint Billy Mitchell.

Ironically, it was because of the ground-force resistance to air power that the General Headquarters Air Force existed. It was apparently hoped that the thrust of the Mitchellites might be weakened if they were divided. Accordingly, the Air Corps was split into two parts. Most of it, comprising the administrative, procurement, supply-and-training arm, continued to function basically as a service unit, while the operational or fighting arm, which would be called the General Headquarters Air Force, would function under the direct control of the Army General Staff. But this plan of weakening the air-power zealots hadn't worked because, through some inadvertence, one of the most zealous of the zealots, Maj. Gen. Frank M. Andrews, had been put in command of the GHQ Air Force. And he was such a bright, articulate, persuasive, and dynamic personality nobody had yet figured out how to cope with him.

Thanks to his persistence, the Air Corps was given a chance to prove its outlandish theories in a maneuver called Joint Air Exercise Number Four, scheduled to take place from precisely noon on August 12 to precisely noon on August 13, 1937.

During the daylight hours within that twenty-four-hour period, the Air Corps would be allowed to seek out the battleship *Utah*, somewhere in the Pacific Ocean within three hundred nautical miles of the California coast, roughly between the latitudes of San Francisco and Los Angeles. An area covering about one hundred twenty thousand square miles. If the Air Corps bombers managed to find the battleship, they would be entitled to try to hit it with harmless water bombs. But the Air Corps would not be allowed to conduct its own reconnaissance in search of the ship. It would have to depend on Navy reports of the ship's position. And in August, it would then, in all probability, have to penetrate heavy clouds to find the ship because August happens to be a foggy month in the eastern Pacific.

The Air Corps contingent, led by the eight Flying Fortresses of the GHQ's Second Bomb Group, flew to California in early August and settled in at the Oakland Airport, which was about as close as they could get to the ocean. There were also some B-10s, B-18s, and other planes in the task force, but they didn't have the range to be signficant factors in the exercise. It would be a B-17 show or no show at all.[4]

Maj. Caleb V. Haynes, a big, rough, tough North Carolinian, was the pilot of the lead plane but Olds would also be riding in it as commander of the task force. And LeMay would be sitting behind them at the navigator's table. All the crews were ready long before noon on the 12th, waiting for the order to take off; the hours passed and no order came because Olds was pacing back and forth in the operations building awaiting word from the Navy reconnaissance people, either by radio or by phone, as to the *Utah's* location. Since that day's exercise was to end with darkness, in accordance with the rigid rules laid down, Olds finally decided he hadn't better wait any longer for a message from the Navy. If a message were to come, it could be relayed by radio. He gave the word and his planes took off across the cloud-covered Pacific in the general direction of the area where the *Utah* seemed most likely to be.

Shortly before dark, the Navy sent a message to the Oakland Airport, where the Air Corps planes were presumably still waiting on the ground. The message included a position report on the *Utah* that was immediately radioed to the B-17s flying around above the water, looking for holes in the clouds.

When the report of the *Utah's* location reached the lead plane, navigator LeMay immediately plotted its position and decided they weren't far from it. As soon as they reached the spot, Haynes sent the lead plane carefully down through the clouds and fortunately got beneath the overcast about six hundred feet above the water. Neither the *Utah* nor any of its support ships was in sight. LeMay worked out a square search (a method of flying ever-larger square patterns) but still there were no naval vessels to be seen. When darkness fell, which meant the day's exercise had to end, Haynes wearily pointed the plane up through the clouds and the whole task force headed back toward Oakland.

Olds, angry and frustrated, came back from the cockpit to the navigator's table. "LeMay, why didn't we find the fleet?"

LeMay, who wasn't very happy about it either, said, "I don't know, sir. I think we got to where they were supposed to be. I'm in the process of checking it out. I just now took some celestial shots."

After finishing his calculations he announced, "We weren't very far off. Maybe two or three miles."

"How do you know that's right?"

"If it's right," he said, pointing to his chart, "here's where we are now. And we're headed straight for San Francisco."

Olds, far from satisfied, mumbled to himself, "Well, there's still tomorrow morning." Then with fierce determination he turned to LeMay. "I want the *Utah*. You'd better find it for me. You were selected to fly lead navigator because I thought you were the best in the group." Still angry, he swung on his heel and went back to the cockpit.

After making one more celestial observation and rechecking his figures, LeMay wrote on a piece of paper his estimated time of arrival over San Francisco and took it forward to Olds. He glanced at it and said, "I hope you're right."

LeMay was a nervous navigator when he went back to sit at his table, but about ten minutes before his ETA for San Francisco, he returned to the cockpit and stood waiting behind Haynes and Olds, who was in the copilot's seat. With all the fog, they wouldn't actually see San Francisco, but if he was correct and they passed directly over it, they would at least see through the gloom the vast expanse of city lights.

As the ten minutes were about to elapse, there, just ahead, the glow of San Francisco lights slowly began to appear. Olds glanced again at the paper with LeMay's ETA, rolled it into a ball and tossed it at him. "By God, you were right," he said. "Then why didn't we find the *Utah*?"

"Maybe," LeMay suggested, "they gave us the wrong position."

Because the Oakland Airport was socked in, they flew on to Sacramento, where LeMay tried to sleep while Olds spent most of the night on the telephone. At dawn, Olds came into the hangar where LeMay was dozing, on the floor beneath the wing of their plane, and kicked him in the ribs. "The Navy now admits they were one degree off on the position they sent us," he said.

"One degree! That's sixty miles. No wonder we couldn't find the son-of-a-bitch. Come on, let's have a cup of coffee."

Again on that morning of August 13 they waited for the Navy to send a position report, but this time they didn't wait as long. Once more Olds put his planes in the air and flew out to sea. But once more, the only thing they could do out there was to fly around above the clouds, looking for open spaces.

Finally the *Utah's* position report from the Navy arrived at the Sacramento Airport and was relayed to Olds by radio. What time was it now? After eleven o'clock. Less than an hour before the exercise was to end.

LeMay plotted a course and all eight B-17s headed toward the target. But when he worked the interception problem, he came up with bad news for Olds. They couldn't possibly get to the *Utah's* position before the noon deadline.

Spirits sagged, but, having nothing better to do, they plodded on anyway. And since there was no chance of seeing a ship from above the clouds, Olds decided that all eight planes should go down through the overcast, spread out as far as possible without losing sight of each other, and continue on course, hoping they would at least find the *Utah,* even if they were too late to drop their water bombs on it.

At about ten minutes before noon, as the spread-out formation was droning along, six hundred feet above the water, with all eyes focused on the gloomy sea ahead, the superstructure of a huge ship suddenly came into view. A battleship. No question about that. But was it the *Utah?* According to LeMay's calculation they were still fifty or sixty miles from where the *Utah* was supposed to be. The men on this ship didn't look as if they were alerted against even a mock attack. They were lounging on the deck, taking it easy. Could this be the *Utah?* It had to be. The bombardier on the lead plane prepared his mechanism.

"I'm going to bomb it," he said to Olds, "unless you tell me not to."

What if it turned out to be some other battleship? How could they tell? One battleship looked like another to these Navy-hating airmen. But the *Utah* was supposed to be flying something called the International Preparatory Flag. Blue with a yellow cross. LeMay had never seen one but he had looked it up. Through his binoculars he scanned every mast on the ship. And as the lead plane began to close in, he spotted the yellow cross.

"Okay, that's it," he shouted to the bombardier.

Curtis LeMay as a young lieutenant in the United States Army Air Corps shortly after winning his wings. (*National Air and Space Museum*)

State of the art in U.S. bombers (shown here flying over Staten Island, New York, May 27, 1931) at the time LeMay began his career. (*National Air and Space Museum*)

Interception at sea of the Italian liner *Rex,* May 1938. (*National Air and Space Museum*)

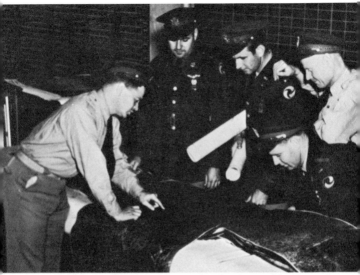

LeMay, "the best damn navigator in the Army Air Corps," plans a long-range flight with other officers. (*National Air and Space Museum*)

First Lieutenant LeMay (*rear, second from left*) with fellow crew members, standing in front of the B-17 that left Miami on August 5, 1938, at 3:08 A.M. and arrived at Bogotá, Colombia, at 11:27 A.M. Average speed: 180 mph. (*National Air and Space Museum*)

Pre-war series B-17s in formation, flying over an America at peace. (*National Air and Space Museum*)

B-17s make contrails as they fly over Germany through "the most fiercely defended skies in history." (*National Air and Space Museum*)

Brig. Gen. Haywood S. Hansell, Jr., and Colonel LeMay next to a B-17 of the 305th Bomb Group in England. (*National Air and Space Museum*)

Above
Schweinfurt, damage assessment photo. (*National Air ‹
Space Museum*)

Below, right
LeMay (*left*) just after assuming command of the Twer
first Bomber Command, relieving Brig. Gen. Haywood
Hansell, Jr. (*center*). At right is Brig. Gen. Roger M. Ram
chief of staff for General Hansell, who was named to succ
General LeMay as commanding general of the XX Bom
Command in China. (*National Air and Space Museum*)

Last-minute discussion at an advance base in China, just before takeoff for a November 11, 1944, bombing raid on Omura, Japan, and simultaneous attacks on Nanking and Shanghai. Left to right: Lt. Col. P. M. Hoisington, Maj. Gen. Curtis E. LeMay (commanding general XX Bomber Command), and Graham Barrow, British war correspondent for Reuters. (*National Air and Space Museum*)

B-29s from LeMay's command dropping bombs over Japan
(*National Air and Space Museum*)

LeMay at Templehof during the Berlin Airlift. (*National Air and Space Museum*)

Gen. George C. Kenney (*seated*), former commander of the Strategic Air Command, and Lt. Gen. Curtis E. LeMay, chief of SAC, confer at the House Armed Services Committee hearing on purchases of B-36 bombers after LeMay told Congress that the B-36 could drop an atomic bomb on "any potential target in the world and return." (*National Air and Space Museum*)

Above, right
A B-36, the interim strategic bomber that filled the gap between the B-29 and the all-jet-engine bombers that would follow. (*National Air and Space Museum*)

Right
A B-47 with Sabrejet escort. (*National Air and Space Museum*)

Below
LeMay, while vice chief of staff, talks with F-104B pilot Maj. Milton E. Nelson after an orientation flight in the new fighter. (*USAF photo, Department of Defense*)

LeMay is sworn in as vice chief of staff by Maj. Gen. Reginald Harmon, Air Force Judge Advocate General, during ceremonies in the Pentagon, July 1, 1957. Secretary of the Air Force James Douglas officiated. (*USAF photo, Department of Defense*)

LeMay with Secretary of the Air Force Eugene M. Zuckert in the secretary's office just after the announcement of General LeMay's nomination for chief of staff, May 22, 1961. (*USAF photo, Department of Defense*)

Left
LeMay, while chief of staff, in the cockpit of a C-135.   (*USAF photo, Department of Defense*)

Below, left
LeMay getting in a round of golf during a break in the annual Commander's Conference at Ramey AFB in Puerto Rico in January 1965. (*USAF photo, Department of Defense*)

Below
General LeMay's official photograph as chief of staff.   (*USAF photo, Department of Defense*)

At a ceremony held in the Pentagon, LeMay accepts a portrait of himself from the artist, Sandor Klein. (*USAF photo, Department of Defense*)

During General LeMay's trip to Vietnam in April 1962, Brig. Gen. Ton That Dinh explains how a native weapon can be used in guerrilla warfare. (*USAF photo, Department of Defense*)

The last day of active duty in a career that began when Curtis E. LeMay earned his pilot's wings at Kelly Field, Texas, in October 1929. Here at his retirement ceremonies, which took place first at the White House and then at Andrews AFB on February 1, 1965, General LeMay rests his hand on the prop of a Consolidated P-1 "Trusty" (*above*), the same type of aircraft he flew during his first tour of active duty at Selfridge Field, and stands before a B-17 (*right*) with the markings of his old 305th Bomb Group. (*USAF photo, Department of Defense*)

General and Mrs. LeMay standing beside a bust of the general, donated to the Air Force Academy after his retirement. (*USAF photo, Department of Defense*)

It was five minutes before twelve as they bore down on the *Utah*. The sailors on deck were now scurrying for cover, but some of them were still exposed when the cylindrical water bombs began to fall, spattering the deck with water and fragments of tin or some such metal. There were rumors later that a few sailors were injured, but the Navy never announced it. The Navy never announced anything about the events of this day.

By the time the eight Fortresses finished their bomb runs, they had three direct hits on the *Utah* plus several near misses. The task force pulled back up through the clouds and headed happily toward the California coast.

Olds said to LeMay, "Can we get to March Field from here?"

They had used a lot of gas but LeMay said, "We can make it." He figured the course to March (near Riverside) from where he believed they were. Then he made some other calculations, which he invited Olds to inspect.

"Remember when I told you the *Utah* was too far away and we couldn't get there by noon?" he asked.

"Yeah."

"Well, we ran over it, as you just observed, and it was sixty miles from where it was supposed to be. They gave us that old business of one degree off again."

"Are you sure?"

"Here's where I think we are," LeMay said, pointing to his chart. "If I'm right, we'll be about twenty miles off Point Conception [west of Santa Barbara] when we approach the coast. If I'm wrong, we'll be off course by sixty miles."

As he predicted, Point Conception was about twenty miles to their left when they passed it. Everyone in the task force was intoxicated with victory as they landed at March Field. But their elation didn't last long. An order had already arrived from Washington. There was to be absolutely no publicity about Joint Air Exercise Number Four. Those who participated did, of course, turn in records and reports about it. These went into the Air Corps Central Record Files. But they didn't stay there long. All mention of the exercise quickly disappeared from the files except for a brief notation that it did take place.

The silent treatment of the *Utah* water bombing did not discourage the Air Corps in its effort to get public attention for its air-power campaign and the new plane, which was expected to prove the usefulness of long-range bombers. All kinds of projects were now suggested to win publicity for the B-17. In early

1938, the news from South America provided an idea that would be difficult for the Army General Staff to veto. A newly elected president of Argentina was to be inaugurated February 20. Why not send a flight of Fortresses to Buenos Aires as a goodwill gesture that would at the same time show the world what a powerful air weapon the Americans had developed?

The project was approved, Olds was named to carry it out, and he again chose LeMay as his lead navigator. Then the two of them hurried to the Munitions Building in search of any maps of South America that might be useful. While they were there, Colonel Olds introduced Lieutenant LeMay to Col. Ira C. Eaker, who was then the Air Corps chief of information. Olds and Eaker were old friends. During their conversation, Olds sent LeMay to the Army Map Room to begin his search.

After he was gone, Eaker said to Olds, "You know, Bob, this is an important mission you're undertaking. It's designed to demonstrate the overseas, intercontinental range of our new bomber. If you're successful, the General Staff and the Congress may give us some more of them. How can you entrust your navigation to a young lieutenant?"

"Lieutenant LeMay," Olds replied, "happens to be the best damned navigator in the Army Air Corps."[5]

The "best damned navigator in the Army Air Corps" couldn't find any useful maps of South America in the U.S. Army Map Room, which says something, perhaps, about the general condition of the U.S. Army in 1938. But he did, in due course, find his way south along the west coast of South America, then through the Andes to Buenos Aires as the lead navigator in a six-plane flight of Fortresses. Such a flight is now a daily occurrence, but in 1938 it was a pioneering project, especially the crossing of the Andes, which were only vaguely charted at the time. What did LeMay use to guide him through the mountain passes? *National Geographic* magazine maps. But all six of the B-17s arrived safely in the Argentine capital, and all six returned safely to Washington, where everyone in the Air Corps was dreaming up ideas for the next dramatic demonstration of the B-17's capabilities.

Once again, the Navy inadvertently provided an occasion. The admirals, in an effort to impress Congress with the need for a bigger fleet, were planning an extensive war game, and the Air Corps was invited to participate, but not in the Pacific where most of the naval vessels would be maneuvering. If the Air Corps boys wanted to stage some kind of defensive demonstration it should be in the Atlantic, where they couldn't do any harm.

The fertile brain of Ira Eaker went to work on this project and he came up with a gimmick that was certain to get favorable publicity if it worked. An Italian luxury liner, the *Rex*, would be approaching New York on one of its regular runs in mid-May, when the maneuvers were scheduled to take place. With the approval of the steamship line, Eaker got permission to send a flight of B-17s out into the Atlantic in an attempt to intercept the *Rex* while it was more than seven hundred miles at sea. The planes would then dip their wings in salute to the passengers and photographically "bomb" the liner, bringing back the pictures as evidence that B-17s, in wartime, would be able to find and destroy enemy ships even that far from American shores. And to make sure the U.S. Press got full coverage of the stunt, reporters and radio newsmen were invited along as passenger-observers. LeMay was again chosen lead navigator in a plane flown by Major Haynes. The winds were blowing and the clouds were overflowing at Mitchel Field, Long Island, as the three-plane flight of B-17s prepared to take off on the morning of May 12. And the weather did not improve as they rattled and bounced their way out into the Atlantic.

"I have been in a great deal of turbulence through some thirteen thousand hours of military flying," LeMay has observed. "I doubt that we ever flew in worse turbulence than on that twelfth of May."

The chances of finding the *Rex* seemed almost nil. Besides the storm they were enduring, they faced the cold, dark wall of a fierce Atlantic weather front. And to make matters worse, the NBC correspondent aboard was planning a live, coast-to-coast broadcast at 12:25, the time LeMay had estimated the interception would take place. Fortunately they got through the front, unscathed though shaken, and came out into bright sunshine. The minutes passed. At 12:21, new clouds enfolded them and the sun vanished. Then at 12:23 the sky opened again. And at 12:25, they were staring straight ahead at the big Italian liner.

Eighteen years later, LeMay received a letter from a man named John F. Royal who was a passenger on the *Rex* that day. "When I boarded the *Rex*," he wrote, "a dozen or more leading Fascists were present. . . . As we sailed on there were whispers about the proposed meeting of the planes and ship. They scoffed and sneered. . . . Came the day! I was on the bridge with the

Fascists. When the bombers dropped through the clouds in perfect formation at sea I thrilled at the sight. . . . They were speechless and not a word was heard from them for the remainder of the trip. Every Yankee yelled and screamed and went to the bar—it was glorious.''[6]

On August 5, 1938, LeMay was in the air once more with the Air Corps' flying publicity seekers, this time on the way to Bogotá, Colombia. By now his reputation as a navigator was well established within the Air Corps. And that was all to the good except in one respect. The Air Corps was the private preserve not of navigators but of pilots. Though LeMay was a pilot, he was still only a lieutenant, and he was not a B-17 pilot. Being the best navigator in the Air Corps, if indeed he was, might be compared in a way with being the best mechanic. You performed an important function, and you might even be praised for your skill, but you weren't necessarily going to be promoted for it. And it wouldn't necessarily convince the right people that you could do anything else. Under ordinary circumstances, LeMay could have looked forward to another six or seven years as a first lieutenant. Then maybe he'd become a captain and perhaps the first pilot of a Flying Fortress if the Air Corps was allowed to buy the plane in any quantity. But this was 1938, and in 1938, circumstances were far from ordinary.

On March 11, German troops had crossed the border of Austria and swallowed up that country without a battle. Then on October 1, after British Prime Minister Neville Chamberlain's fatal capitulation to Adolf Hitler in Munich, German troops crossed the Czechoslovakian border and soon took that country without a battle.

By this time, many Americans, including President Roosevelt, had begun to realize that the country would almost certainly have to become involved in stopping Hitler if he was to be stopped. The expansion of all American armed forces began. Hap Arnold became Army Air Corps chief of staff and people highly placed in the government, men like Roosevelt adviser Harry Hopkins, aware now of Hitler's growing air power, began listening to those hotheads in the Air Corps who had been preaching the gospel of air supremacy.

In 1939, Curtis LeMay began to feel seriously the effects of Air Corps expansion. But first he had a very happy personal experience for which he had been trying since the day he was married. On February 8, 1939, his daughter, Patricia Jane, was born at Langley Field after Helen had miscarried during two previous pregnancies. LeMay, still fond of the name he had meant to give his youngest sister, managed even to spell it correctly on the birth certificate.

He didn't get much time to beam with pride over his new baby. From May to September 1939, he was at the Air Corps Tactical School, Maxwell Field, Alabama, where, as he has remarked, he learned "not much." He graduated from the tactical school September 12, just twelve days after Hitler's air force bombed Poland and his troops invaded that country to begin World War II.

When LeMay returned to his Forty-ninth Bomb Squadron at Langley Field, the Air Corps was already buying, and the Boeing Company delivering, B-17s at an increasing rate. As a result, he had the unexpected experience of becoming, while still a lieutenant, a first pilot of one of the brand-new bombers. But in November he was again a navigator on a flight of seven Fortresses to Rio de Janeiro—a flight with a greater purpose than publicity now that the south Atlantic route might soon become an important link with western Europe.

In January 1940, he was promoted to captain and a month later he was transferred to the Forty-first Reconnaissance Squadron, still at Langley, as operations and intelligence officer. In March 1941, he was finally given the first command assignment of his entire twelve-year career—a squadron in the Thirty-fourth Bomb Group, stationed first at Langley, then at Westover Air Base in Springfield, Mass. But that command didn't last long. Because of his experience in B-17s, he was soon named group operations officer. It was just a few weeks later that he was relieved of this assignment and summoned to Canada by C. V. Haynes on that peculiar and furtive job of flying B-24s to England. It was another four months after that, in September, when their ferrying mission was complete, that Haynes and LeMay teamed up again for their route-finding, information-gathering, 24,700-mile flight to Brazil and Africa.

That fateful Sunday, December 7, 1941, came not long after LeMay's return to the Thirty-fourth Bomb Group at Springfield. On March 21, he had become a major, under temporary appointment. In less than two years he had been promoted twice. But this was hardly an indication that the Air Corps thought of him as anything more than a good, conscientious officer. It was no indication that he was considered promising as a commander.

With the unprecedented Air Corps expansion, all the regular officers were winning rapid promotions. And the promising ones were taking command of the new units in the process of organization. LeMay had once commanded a squadron for about two months and had then been transferred out of it. He was an operations officer with an excellent reputation as a navigator. He worked hard and his record was clean. But he was not a part of the Air Corps establishment. And he was not one of the boys. He spent his spare time with his wife and child, or puttering with automobiles. He drank occasionally, though less than most of his colleagues. He had few funny stories to offer at the officers' club and almost no small talk. He seemed constitutionally opposed to unnecessary speech, and when he did talk, he was so notoriously blunt that he had earned the nickname The Diplomat. If anyone in the Air Corps had suggested on December 7, 1941, that this man would become the outstanding air commander of World War II, he would have provoked derisive laughter.

PART III

PART III

CHAPTER FIFTEEN

After the ball is over,
After the break of dawn,
After the dancers leaving,
After the stars are gone;
Many a heart is aching . . .
After the ball.

To a surprising extent, that was America's mood after World War II. The war was no ball. The survivors will testify to that. Most of us insist we hate war, and no doubt we do. But it has seductive attractions that many people miss when it comes to an end. Not just the excitement, the travel, the higher wages and profits, the lower social barriers, the relaxation of behavior, the rush to have fun today against an uncertain tomorrow. There is also, at least during a war generally accepted as necessary, a feeling of dedication and sacrifice to a cause larger than self, a sense of common purpose and accomplishment.

After World War II was over, there was the immediate celebration, the intoxication with victory. There was the realization of righteous triumph over an evil power. There was sudden freedom from a heavy burden. There was relief at the cessation of bombing and fighting and bloodshed. But then, all too soon, a vague suggestion of emptiness began to dispel the euphoria and difficult questions arose. Where do we go from here? What is our purpose now?

It soon became apparent what our first national purpose was going to be: to demobilize. Bring the boys home. Get them out of uniforms and back to their families, their jobs, their schools. Of the twelve million men and women in the Armed Forces when the war ended, more than ten million scooted away to civilian

245

freedom as if they were convicts and someone had knocked down the prison walls.

For these ex-servicemen and just about everyone else, the next national purpose was to regain and surpass America's prewar standard of living. They were tired of wartime rationing and shortages. They wanted new cars, new refrigerators, new clothes, new homes. To meet these demands and win the expected profits, manufacturers hastened to convert their war plants to the production of civilian goods. And working people, to make sure their wages would be high enough to let them buy those goods, began striking for a larger share of the expected profits.

In September 1945, the Ford Motor Company temporarily halted all production and laid off fifty thousand workers because of strikes against smaller companies supplying Ford with parts. In October, U.S. Steel rejected a union demand for a two-dollar-a-day increase in wages. Both General Motors and Chrysler rejected demands for 30 percent wage increases. The public clamor for the first new cars since 1942 was so great that General Motors counterproposed a forty-five-hour week, but with only six percent wage increase. It began to look as if the labor-management war would replace the World War. All over the country, in almost all industries, strikes were breaking out.

By the early months of 1946, a lot of people were blaming international communism for these strikes, as if Americans in both labor and management lacked sufficient greed to start their own battles. Then on March 5, 1946, Winston Churchill, on a visit to America, suggested to an audience in Fulton, Missouri, that the English-speaking nations should join in an alliance against Communist Russia, which had unquestionably divided Europe with an ''Iron Curtain'' from the Baltic to the Adriatic.

It was a speech that struck a responsive chord with millions of people. The vast majority of Americans had been imbued with a fear and loathing of communism long before World War II—a fear and loathing softened only slightly by the fact that Russia was our ally during the war. Many people even believed that, having defeated Germany in 1945, our armies should have continued the march eastward to conquer Russia. Nobody could deny that Josef Stalin was as vicious a tyrant as Adolf Hitler. And many of these same people were convinced that the vague malaise and restlessness afflicting the United States was inspired purposely by the American agents of Russian communism. To these people the new national purpose, the new war, became the

Cold War against encroaching Russian aggression and its insidious companion, international communism.

In the weeks and months after Japan's surrender and his return to the United States, Maj. Gen. Curtis LeMay, a staunch conservative and opponent of communism since boyhood, was perhaps even more alarmed than most people about the spread of Russian power because he was privy to a lot of restricted information about Russian strength. He was sure that as the American Army diminished its presence in Europe, there would be little more than the threat of the atomic bomb (of which we had very few) to prevent Russia's huge army, still at full strength, from marching westward, all the way to the Atlantic. And he knew also that Russia had done very well in the scramble to capture German scientists and technicians, thereby facilitating the development of new, sophisticated weapons. Perhaps even its own atomic bombs. The Americans had been able to grab a few German scientists, but the Russians had grabbed whole batches of them, and had taken them back home together with their intact laboratories. To LeMay, therefore, it seemed that some of our postwar national purposes conflicted with others. By bringing the boys home in a rapid demobilization and converting most of our war plants to the manufacture of consumer goods, we were weakening our ability to cope with the rising tide of Russian communism.

He was sufficiently alarmed to consider seriously an offer to get into politics at a high level. On September 18, 1945, the day LeMay, Barney Giles, and Rosey O'Donnell flew back to the United States from Japan, President Harry Truman, though a Democrat, appointed Sen. Harold H. Burton, an Ohio Republican, to the Supreme Court, leaving a Senate vacancy to be filled by Ohio's Governor Frank Lausche. It apparently occurred to Lausche, also a Democrat, that the appointment of an Ohio war hero to that seat would be a popular move. Though Lausche was himself a conservative Democrat, it's doubtful that he realized exactly how conservative LeMay might be. He would have had a lot of explaining to do to his fellow Democrats when "Senator Curtis LeMay's" voting record began to emerge. Nevertheless, he offered the Senate seat to the general, and LeMay wanted to accept it, partly because it would be for only a year or so.[1] The Burton term that he would be completing was due to expire in 1947. If LeMay could get a one-year leave from the Air Force, he would have the U.S. Senate floor, during that time, as a platform from which to voice his conservative political views, his concern about rapid disarmament, and his belief in the necessity for a strong Air Force. At the end of that year, rather than running for reelection, he would then resign and return to the Air Force.

The prospect seemed flawless until he went to Washington and discussed it with Robert Patterson, whom Truman had appointed secretary of war on the same day he appointed Burton to the Supreme Court.

Patterson told him, LeMay said later, "that I should read the Constitution." A commissioned military officer could hold a seat in the House of Representatives but not in the Senate.

It was the end of that dream. Much as LeMay would have enjoyed a year in the Senate, he was not willing to resign his commission for it. Which meant there was nothing for him to do now but settle down and wait for the Air Force to decide what to do with him and with hundreds of other highly qualified, battle-wise career officers; where to find places for all of them in the rapidly shrinking organization.

While he was in Washington in 1945, LeMay talked to Tooey Spaatz, Hap Arnold's heir apparent as Air Force chief, and a lot of possibilities were discussed but no promises were made. Spaatz, as it happened, had a possibility in mind that he didn't immediately discuss with LeMay, but which he did discuss with two other members of an exploratory board he had formed at Arnold's behest. The board was charged with studying the long-term effects of the atomic bomb on Air Force strategy and organization. Among the recommendations made by Spaatz and his two colleagues on the board—Lauris Norstad and Hoyt Vandenberg—in their October 23 report to Arnold was that he establish a new job, deputy chief of staff for research and development, and that "an officer of the caliber of Major General Curtis LeMay" be appointed to fill it.[2]

This was an extraordinary recommendation in that it named a specific officer for the job. It was apparently another indication of Spaatz's high regard for LeMay's accomplishments in the Pacific. But Hap Arnold was not the kind of man who would let even an old friend like Tooey make his appointments for him. On October 5, Secretary of the Air Force Robert Lovett had suggested to Arnold the establishment of another new job—air comptroller general.[3] The man who filled this job would, under the direction of the chief, control the Air Force purse strings.

And Arnold was inclined to give the post to LeMay. He was so strongly inclined, in fact, that he had Ira Eaker send memos to Lovett and LeMay on November 7, informing them that LeMay would head the Office of the Air Comptroller General.[4]

Arnold was, at the same time, quite capable of changing his own mind, even though he didn't allow many people to change it for him. Within ten days he had decided that Rosey O'Donnell, an old favorite of his, would take charge of the research-and-development staff in Washington. And as for LeMay, he would not get his hands on the purse strings after all. He would take charge of research and development at Wright Field in Dayton, where much of the R&D work would be centered.

This arrangement actually went into effect, much to O'Donnell's dismay because he hated staff work in Washington, and much to LeMay's satisfaction because he felt the same way. "He [Rosey] was going to have to buy a house; and all I'd have to do was breeze out there to Ohio and move into a nice set of quarters." Helen was also happy about the appointment. They were both Ohioans. They were going—almost—home.

They did, in fact, go "almost home" to Dayton, about November 20, but they stayed only ten days. By that time Arnold had changed his mind again. At a staff meeting November 29, he announced that LeMay would return to Washington as deputy chief of staff for research and development—the very job Tooey Spaatz had suggested for him. Perhaps Tooey had gotten his way after all. But LeMay seems to think his own lack of qualification for the Wright Field job may have accounted for his recall to Washington.

"There was a lot of discussion [about using World War II experience] in building the new Air Force. That's probably why I got sent to Wright Field. But lo and behold, I was a senior officer and I didn't know anything about building an airplane or procurement or that end of the business. There were better people to do it. It took about ten days to realize that. Ben Chidlaw was out there and he was far more knowledgeable. [Benjamin W. Chidlaw was the Air Force's ranking expert in aeronautical engineering.] He was older than myself but I ranked him. He had ranked me before the war."

If, as LeMay indicates, his lack of technical qualifications made him unsuitable for the Wright Field research-and-development job, then why did Arnold decide to put him in charge of the entire research-and-development program? It could not have been a matter of playing favorites. If he had been inclined to play favorites, he would have made Rosey O'Donnell the R&D chief. He had a genuine affection for Rosey (as did most people) and everyone knew it. Yet once more, as he had done in the Pacific during the war, he lifted LeMay over Rosey's head. Arnold seems to have sensed in LeMay a quality he possessed himself—an ability to simplify issues. This was a knack that might be useful in the detailed projects at Wright Field, but might be even more useful on the much broader problems of preparation for an as yet only vaguely imagined future.

It was Arnold himself who had conceived the role he now assigned to LeMay. Arnold had virtually conceived the whole idea of research and development as it applied to the Air Force. Before the war, the Army Air Corps planners, always strapped for funds, could do little more than wait for civilian companies or individuals to invent new equipment in aeronautics, or design new planes, then hope the War Department would be willing to approve the purchase of these latest technological developments. And the ground-oriented War Department was not always willing. The long struggle to procure the Flying Fortress illustrated that. (This was one of the arguments Air Force people marshaled during the postwar campaign, beginning in late 1945, to establish a separate Air Force.) Arnold had believed for a long time that the Air Force, required as it was to cope with the ever-improving air forces of other countries, should lead the aeronautical industry toward advanced technology rather than waiting for civilian agencies, on their own and with limited resources, to produce the kinds of machines that might be needed in the highly complex world of the future. In the 1930s, Air Corps research was so pitifully rudimentary that Gen. Donald Putt, its director, once told Curt LeMay the prewar budget for research on propellers would not buy one set of B-29 propellers at the end of the war.[5] In 1939, Arnold, cognizant of this situation, asked the National Advisory Committee on Aeronautics to institute more research projects. Then he began picking the brain of a California Institute of Technology physicist and aeronautical engineer, Dr. Theodore von Karman, on the subject of advanced research for the Air Force.

In 1940, von Karman designed and supervised the construction of a twenty-foot, forty-thousand-horsepower wind tunnel at Wright Field. And in 1944, Arnold asked him to establish a scientific advisory board for the Air Force, composed of first-rate men from all the pertinent disciplines. This board, which included such distinguished men as Frank Wattendorf, Nathan Newmark, Lee DuBridge, Detlev Bronk, William Pickering, Fritz Zwicky, Enrico Fermi, and von Karman himself, was already at work when, on December 5, 1945, LeMay assumed his newly created post as deputy chief of staff for research and development. Several of its members had accompanied von Karman on a trip to Germany right after V-E Day, and they came back with some frightening discoveries about how far they were behind the German scientists and technologists in air developments. It was they who also brought back the sobering news that the Russians had captured the major share of those German scientists, as well as their laboratories. LeMay realized immediately that he had again been dumped in over his head. He could add one more to the growing list of jobs he had faced with the conviction that he was unqualified. A bachelor engineering degree at Ohio State and three years of combat command didn't seem like adequate preparation for the sophisticated scientific decisions he might be called upon to make. But this time he was not alone in being unprepared for the job ahead. The country wasn't ready for it, and neither was the Air Force.

The United States in 1945 and 1946 was not thinking of any future wars. Hadn't we once again saved the world for democracy? We had the most powerful Army, Navy, and Air Force the world had ever seen. The Air Force, for example, had something like seventy-two thousand planes at the end of the war. No one knew exactly. Who was counting? And besides everything else, we had the atomic bomb. No one would dare attack us as long as we had that. Certainly not the Russians. They weren't dumb enough to challenge the atomic bomb. And they weren't smart enough to invent one of their own. So why should we spend a lot of taxpayers' money on esoteric projects like Air Force research? The subject wasn't a bit popular with Army or congressional budget makers. And if the budget makers weren't willing to pay for research, the Air Force was in no condition to push on alone, especially since it was then engulfed in another job.

"Research was something that people knew we had to do something about," LeMay said later, "but all these general housekeeping chores were taking first priority." Primary among these "chores" was the demobilization of excess personnel and disposal of surplus property, including a majority of the seventy-two thousand or so planes, dozens of bases all over the world, and mountains of neatly stacked matériel. "There was this general and complete chaos, public clamor to disband the military establishment, get the boys home. No one [in the Air Force] was getting much done except some administrative work, closing up bases, discharging people, trying to take care of the vast amount of property scattered around all over the world."[6]

LeMay began his assignment by talking to people. Not only the members of the Scientific Advisory Board, but also the members of his own hastily assembled staff. "We had some people who had been in [research]. I relied on them very much. We spent a lot of time sitting around, talking about what we ought to be doing."

Ten years behind in technology, and limited in budget, they decided the best thing they could do, during those early postwar years, was to assemble the personnel and the tools with which to launch a significant program when and if the money for it was forthcoming. So where did they begin looking for personnel? Not just among American scientists but in Germany, where there were still a lot of highly skilled people trying to avoid capture by the Russians. But how could the Air Force get State Department clearances to bring these very recent enemies into the United States?

"The only way we could get them over was as prisoners of war," LeMay has explained. "Even our scientific people didn't want them over here. They fought tooth and nail to keep them from coming but we finally got some to come over as prisoners of war. We had quite a time convincing them that although they were prisoners we were going to take care of their families in Germany and see that they were fed and housed properly. I even found some of these people actually behind barbed wire after they got over here. Well, you know, you can stand over a prisoner of war with a club and say dig a ditch here and make him do it, but you can't stand over a scientist with a club and say invent this. So we had our problems in getting going and getting these people out of the prisoner of war stockades and into laboratories."

One such "laboratory" was a private company for which Hap Arnold had managed to provide $10 million out of the Air Force budget in the fall of 1945. Its original name was Research and Development Corporation and it was located in Santa Monica, California. It has long since become famous under the abbreviated name: RAND. Why should the Air Force finance what was unquestionably a private company?

"We had a few technical people in the Air Force," LeMay explains. "A few Ph.D.s and a few civil servants who were qualified [for advanced scientific research]. But not near enough of them to do the job. And we couldn't attract people like that into the Air Force." Scientists could make much more money in private industry than the Air Force would be allowed by law to pay them. "So the organization [RAND] was a gimmick. The Air Force would give RAND a contract to do certain things, then RAND would hire the talent necessary to do the job at the going [civilian] rate."[7]

This subterfuge could be hidden in the budget and go unnoticed because, for an organization as big as the Air Force, it did not represent a very large expense. But the whole Air Force research-and-development program, as Arnold and then LeMay envisaged it, would take large sums of money. And with both Congress and the War Department indifferent to it, that kind of money was not to be found. For this reason, LeMay was far from happy about his accomplishments during his almost two years in command of the program.

"I guess about the only thing I got done," he said later, "was to forget about research-and-development programs and try to put all the money that we could lay hands on into the basic tools that we would need for a big research-and-development program. At that time we had no supersonic tunnels, no really big wind tunnels, for instance. The Germans had developed some of these tools (tunnels, rockets, etc.) which were necessary to conduct a program leading to intercontinental missiles and supersonic airplanes, but we didn't have them. So that is what we concentrated on during the time that I was there."

He also had other things to occupy him during this frustrating tour of duty at the Pentagon. On January 3, 1946, he testified before the War Department Equipment Board that an atomic attack against the United States would be impossible to stop.

"Our only defense," he said, "is a striking-power-in-being of such size that it is capable of delivering a stronger blow than any of our potential enemies."[8]

This sounds in retrospect almost like an advance notice of something that happened two and a half months later. On March 21, 1946, Tooey Spaatz, Air Force chief of staff since the retirement of Hap Arnold in January, announced the establishment of what was intended to be the very kind of "striking-power-in-being" LeMay had mentioned—the Strategic Air Command. But Spaatz did not put LeMay in charge of it. He selected an older officer, Gen. George C. Kenney, who had been Douglas MacArthur's air commander in the south Pacific during the war.

In June 1946, LeMay flew to the Pacific for his first on-the-spot (though fortunately several miles from the spot) view of an atomic bomb explosion. The Navy was in charge of this well-advertised test which was conducted June 30 at Bikini Atoll, but LeMay was responsible for supplying the required aircraft, including the B-29 which dropped the bomb. And he offered his opinion as to the deployment of the seventy-three elderly ships anchored off the atoll which were to be the targets. The Navy, still eager to prove that it could survive even atomic bombs dropped from airplanes, wanted to position all the ships bow-on to the explosion, and empty of cargo, thus diminishing their vulnerability. LeMay said later, "I wanted some empty, some full, some bow-on, some broadside." It was a Navy show. They did it their way and they had reason to be content with the results. Only three ships were sunk and the battleship *Nevada*, the primary target, "suffered negligible damage."[9]

During LeMay's tour in Washington, he and Helen and Janie lived in a house they had found in Arlington, not far from the Pentagon, and at his insistence, they kept a low social profile. He hated the Washington social scene, but he was so prominent now he could not completely avoid it. He appeared at his share of obligatory dinner parties, though not gladly. Women who were seated next to him at such parties, some of whom he had known for years, wives of his friends, have recalled that he was quite capable of sitting through an entire dinner without saying a word.

About the only social event he unequivocally enjoyed during this period was the celebration provoked by the establishment, on July 26, 1947, of the new U.S. Air Force, independent at last from the Army. LeMay recalls that he got drunk that night. Whether this unusual relaxation of control was altogether due to his pleasure at the enhanced status of the Air Force, or whether some of it was prompted by personal frustration in his research-and-development assignment, he has never said. In any case, the frustration of that staff job in Washington was about to end. On October 1, 1947, LeMay received his third star. He was now the youngest lieutenant general in the Air

Force, and, as he also learned, he was on his way to Germany, not with a planeload of bombs this time. His job now would be, not to conquer Germany, but to save it from the Russians.

CHAPTER SIXTEEN

Lt. Gen. Curtis LeMay's assignment in October 1947, as Commander of the U.S. Air Forces in Europe, was not as impressive as it would have been in 1943 or 1944. The entire force, which included 2.4 million men and women in 1944, had been reduced to three hundred twenty-four thousand by 1947. On paper it had only thirty-eight combat groups. In the air, actually operational, it had eleven. And that was its worldwide strength. LeMay had at his disposal in Europe only a fraction of it. Yet these circumstances, ironically, instead of making his job smaller, made it bigger. While the Americans had reduced their military strength, the Russians had not. And nobody knew what the Russians were planning to do in Europe. Whatever it might be, very few people believed it would be friendly. The Russians hadn't been exactly cordial even during the war, when they were our allies. On the other hand, neither had we. Since the German surrender, the atmosphere of suspicion and hostility between Russia and the Western powers had deepened so sharply that occupied Germany, dissected into French, British, American, and Russian zones, looked as if it could again become a battlefront at any moment. But if it did, what would the Western powers use as weapons? They had only one that was certain to stop the Russians, and neither Curt LeMay nor anyone else was eager to use that.

All of these considerations were rumbling around in LeMay's mind when he arrived in Germany, wearing the three stars Helen had pinned on his shoulders a few days earlier. Since he had very little air power with which to threaten anybody, maybe he'd have to practice some diplomacy. That was a scary prospect. Diplomacy was an art in which no one had ever accused him of displaying talent. He soon found, fortunately, that there were other American officials in place to handle relations, at least with the Germans, French, and English. Whether they could handle the Russians remained to be seen.

That question became more than ever acute in his mind when he moved Helen and Janie into their Wiesbaden quarters. It was just ten miles west of Frankfurt; more important, it was only seventy-five miles west of the Russian zone. And while there were American occupation forces between Wiesbaden and the border, there were no combat units. But that was true in most places he might be headquartered in Europe, so they might as well put it from their minds and get settled into their new quarters.

It is perhaps ludicrous to refer to their Wiesbaden home as "quarters." They were moving into the 102-room mansion of Otto Henkel, a prominent champagne dealer whose daughter, Anna, had married Joachim von Ribbentrop, Germany's foreign minister during the Hitler regime. Like her husband, Anna was an avid admirer of Hitler, calling him "a marvelous man, a true gentleman," all of which must have been profitable for the family champagne business while the Nazis were in power, but hadn't done it much good since the defeat of Germany. Even the family mansion was now in the hands of one of those American fliers who, only four years before, had been dropping bombs all around it.

By the time the LeMays arrived, the Henkels would probably not have recognized the interior of their beautiful house because a lot of other American soldiers had passed through since the Allied invasion of Germany, and some of them proved that the Germans weren't the only "Huns" in the war. They had carted away whole truckloads of the exquisite Henkel furniture. There was still plenty of furniture left when Helen LeMay first inspected the place (some of it having been recovered from the men who "liberated" it), and there were thirty-eight servants to take care of it, but there were things about the house that she didn't like. One was the cost of paying thirty-eight servants. The LeMays, who were to receive an expense-account allowance of only three thousand dollars a year, simply couldn't afford them. "We hired and fired until we got [it down to] eighteen servants,"[1] Mrs. LeMay recalls.

Another thing she didn't like was the way the place had been managed under the previous commander, Gen. Idwal Edwards. "He let the bachelor [officers] live there. They ran it like a club.

When you do that, you draw rations per person so it never costs you anything except your own ration. And Idwal liked people around. When we got there, the upstairs maid was pregnant. The housekeeper had been one of Goebbels's people. She was very friendly with one of the officers and her ten-year-old son was living in the house. I said, 'I'm not going to have this. We have an eight-year-old daughter and I'm not having any of this.' So we lived in the house by ourselves.''

But they soon found that they had a constant flow of military visitors, not only from the United States but from the western European countries, which meant that whether they liked it or not, they were virtually running a hotel. ''We had to keep thirteen suites made up at all times.'' And most of their guests were people of such importance that, much to her husband's displeasure, they had to be entertained formally. ''Three or four times a week we had formal dinner parties. I budgeted very carefully. We couldn't buy from the German economy.'' That was partly because the Occupation Forces had rules against it, but mostly because there was hardly any German economy in existence at the time. The German people, still strictly rationed, showed unmistakable signs of malnutrition. ''A big German shepherd was there when we got there. Then it disappeared. You never saw dogs or cats.'' Most of the LeMay food came from their own rations at the post exchange. But much of the meat came from Curt's hunting trips into the forests. ''He shot a lot. That was the only way we could have much meat. German boar is marvelous. It's pork but it's more like beef.'' As for other items: ''I ordered from Sears Roebuck and from S.S. Pierce in Boston. And I had to order for the servants, too, there were so many things they couldn't get [in Germany]. They were limited to one pair of leather and one pair of wooden shoes. And we had to supply their uniforms.''

Janie LeMay [now Mrs. James Lodge] recalls an incident that illustrates another way people managed to come by a bit of meat once in awhile. They raised animals for slaughter: ''One of the butlers, Henry, got hold of a goose to fatten it. I was nine years old and I thought it was a pet. And we had this Scottie dog. Well, the day of the slaughter arrived. Mother was gone. Henry said he was going to do something to the goose. I didn't understand so I went with him to the chicken coop, and so did our Scottie. All of a sudden Henry's got this hatchet and he chops the head off the goose. Here's the head on the ground and the body running around. I thought it was horrible. The dog took one look at it and from that day forward, he would go nowhere near Henry. As for me, when my mother came home, I told her I thought Henry was cruel to his pets."[2]

Henry had a disturbing habit of listening through the door and it wasn't easy to conceal family secrets from him because he understood and spoke several languages—sometimes rather colorfully. Shortly after the LeMays arrived, he announced to Helen, "Madam, I am an American bastard."

She said, "Henry! That's a horrible word. What do you mean?"

"I am an unborn baby," he insisted.

"You can't be. That's ridiculous."

"My father was American," he explained. "My mother was German and they were never married." His father had come to Germany on a business trip before World War I and had met a German girl. Henry was the result. It wasn't always easy to predict what he would say or do, but he was resourceful, and he knew how to run a household. The LeMays considered themselves fortunate to have him.

LeMay, in his first staff meeting, tried to give his new subordinates some idea of what they could expect from him: "I want to see all my key staff officers at least once a week. Don't bother to knock. Just walk in. If I'm busy I'll tell you to get out. I want men of action in my organization who can make their own decisions. If you make an occasional wrong one, I'll back you up."[3]

But his big problem was that he didn't have much with which to back up anyone. He knew it and the Russians knew it. "Spaatz and Vandenberg came over on a visit," he recently recalled. "They looked at everything we had over there and they were apparently satisifed that I was doing everything I could. I really didn't have anything with which to do much."

On December 15, 1947, a Four Power Foreign Ministers' Conference in London was shattered by Soviet demands for $10 billion in war reparations from Germany. This was simply the last of several unpleasant developments during the conference. A few days earlier, the usually unflappable Gen. George C. Marshall, at that time U.S. secretary of state, became so exasperated he said that Soviet foreign minister, Vyacheslav Molotov, was making it "difficult to inspire respect for the dignity of the Soviet government." Prospects for a happy Christmas in Germany, already dim, were suddenly even dimmer. The rumble from the East was now so ominous that Christmas Eve found LeMay's entire command on alert. He held a staff meeting at his house until 1 A.M. that night, trying to make sure everything had been done that could be done to counter a possible Russian move. It was fortunate that the Russians didn't move because LeMay's staff meeting developed no promising ideas. Neither the American air or ground forces in Europe had the resources to put up very strong resistance.

The early winter months of 1948 passed in uneasy expectation. On January 3, British Prime Minister Clement Attlee accused the Soviet Union of launching a new "ideological, economic, and strategic" imperialism that threatened world peace. Four days later, the British and Americans announced a plan that would, in effect, help the German economy to recover from the devastation of war by creating economic unity within their two occupation zones. The Russians, still angry at the Germans for fomenting the war, and afraid that recovery might give the Germans a chance to "do it again," did not take kindly to the Anglo-American plan. There was also the additional reason that they were still busy stripping Germany of every kind of useful asset they could cart home to Russia. On January 11, a Russian army newspaper in Berlin protested against the Allied plan. And it included in its protest a reminder that Berlin, though governed jointly by Russia, France, England, and the United States, was completely within the Russian zone.

"There is no room in Berlin for adherents of the partition of Germany," the paper warned. The Anglo-American plan would "lead to a change in the occupation status of Berlin." On January 20, the Soviet commander in Berlin declared that the plan would violate the Potsdam Treaty. It was clear now that the Soviets intended to use their apparent stranglehold on Berlin to get what they wanted in the rest of Germany.

On February 25, Communists in Czechoslovakia overthrew the democratic government of President Edvard Beneš. And two days later, Josef Stalin sent a note to Finland inviting that country to join in a "mutual defense treaty" with Russia—a curious suggestion inasmuch as Russia was the only nation from which Finland needed to be defended. Stalin seemed to be reminding the world that, although Hitler was dead, there was still someone around who had learned much from him, and was eager to take his place, indeed to surpass him, in the field of conquest.

On March 20, the Soviet delegation to the Allied Control Council in Berlin walked out of a meeting to protest the economic merger plan for the American and English zones. The Russians by this time were also insisting that they alone had the authority to govern Berlin, since it was within their zone.

On April 1, they dramatized this insistence by announcing restrictions on all train and road traffic through their zone between Berlin and the Western zones. Freight would have to be cleared, baggage inspected, and personnel identified. For military freight, permits would be required.

The gauntlet was now down and Gen. Lucius D. Clay, the American military governor, had to take it up, even though he didn't quite know what to do with it. He began by putting in a phone call to LeMay. Could the Air Force haul some coal up to Berlin?

"We can haul almost anything up there," LeMay assured him. "How much coal do you want?"[4]

Clay didn't really know how much. "Just haul some," he said.

"Can you have it delivered in sacks?" LeMay asked. "And can you bring it to the Rhine-Main Airport?" It was there that LeMay's one group of DC-3 transport planes was stationed. Aside from a few other DC-3s that he used for administrative purposes, these were the only transports he had. He also had one well-trained fighter group under the command of Col. G. T. "Curly" Edwinson. This constituted just about all the useful air power LeMay could muster.

Clay rushed several truckloads of sacked coal to the Rhine-Main Airport, and the LeMay Coal and Feed Company was in business, though not on a very large scale. What Clay had delivered amounted to only two planeloads. But a few days later, Clay called LeMay again.

"Could you haul some more coal?"

LeMay assured him he could.

"Then put on more planes and more crews."

LeMay responded by putting on all the transports he had, including the few DC-3s he had been using for administration. Within less than two weeks, after the DC-3s had flown no more than three hundred tons of coal and other supplies into Berlin, the Russians relaxed their demands. Surface routes were opened again. The war scare seemed to abate, but not entirely. There was no way of knowing what the Russians would do next. LeMay, remembering with a shudder the abrupt banishment of Gen. Walter Short and Adm. Husband E. Kimmel, the two American commanders victimized by the surprise Japanese attack against Hawaii, had decided he'd better do at least whatever could be done in preparation for a Russian attack. He had requested that Washington send him as many B-29s as possible. On April 15, twenty-eight of them landed in Munich after a flight from Salina, Kansas.

"They had no atomic capability," LeMay recalls. "As a matter of fact, they didn't have the capacity of much of anything." But their very presence in Europe might possibly bluff the Russians. So LeMay sent them to England, where they would be less vulnerable to Russian attack on the ground, and where they could at least appear to present a deadly threat against the cities of Russia.

The Russians, unfortunately, proved difficult to bluff. Maybe they, too, knew that those B-29s had no atomic capability. On April 22, the Russians stopped all passenger-train travel from Berlin through their zone to the Western zones. Clay informed them on April 24 that American planes would continue to fly in and out of Berlin whether they liked it or not. This was followed by a slight lull in the argument punctuated only by a surprise announcement on May 10 that Molotov had sent a note to the U.S. ambassador in Moscow suggesting an improvement in relations between the two countries. But by this time the Russians had made so many meaningless gestures toward improving relations that Molotov's note was rather like the repeated assurances of Lucy in the "Peanuts" comic strip that she won't pull the football away from Charlie Brown's foot.

In June, when the Western powers introduced a new currency, the deutschemark, to help breathe life into the paralyzed German economy, all talk about improving U.S. Soviet relations was quickly forgotten. The Russians took such umbrage at this seemingly innocent measure that on the 22nd they instituted a complete road and rail blockade of Berlin. Once again the American airlift was on, this time in earnest. And now, for the first time since his arrival the previous October, LeMay became involved in a serious, immediate plan of military action.

LeMay was convinced, and Lt. Gen. Arthur G. Trudeau, commander of the American Constabulary Force, obviously agreed with him, that if they were to run an armored column up the Autobahn through the Russian zone to Berlin, the Russians, in

LeMay's words, "would back off." With that hope in mind, they plotted a course. Whether General Clay gave his approval to the scheme is not clear. In any case, Trudeau and LeMay worked out the details.[5]

Trudeau had at his disposal in the Constabulary one full Army division and "the equivalent of another." He was prepared to drive a portion of this force up the great German highway with himself in the lead, watching for Russian reaction. At the same time, LeMay would have his lone fighter group at nearby fields, ready to defend the column, while the B-29s would hover farther west, outside Russian radar range, loaded with conventional bombs.

"He [Trudeau] would have to make a decision whether he was getting all-out or token opposition," LeMay recalled many years later. "If the decision was fight, we [the bombers and fighters] would have hit the Russian air with everything we had, which wasn't too much."

It was enough, however, to make him think the idea would work. He told historian John T. Bolen in 1971, ". . . We planned to enfilade their radar positions so that we could hit the airdromes in Germany where all the Russian [planes] were lined up wing tip to wing tip. We probably could have done a good job of cleaning out their air force with one blow with what we had, using the B-29s as well as the fighters."

When the details of this plan were complete, they presented it to General Clay, "and he, I suppose, presented it to Washington," LeMay said later. But the plan was vetoed.

"I think, Monday morning quarterbacking after it was all over," LeMay remarked to Bolen, "that if we had done it we would have gone right up there and opened it up and there would have been no resistance."

This is exactly how one would expect Curtis LeMay to look at the matter. No one ever accused him of backing away from an issue. But the plan does raise some difficult questions. How long would all those Russian airplanes continue to be lined up, wing tip to wing tip, after the Russians heard about that American armored column rolling up the Autobahn? Surely those planes would have taken to the air as quickly as possible. But whether they would actually have engaged the Americans in battle is another question, the answer to which would have depended on old Joe Stalin and how he felt about the atomic bomb. The Russians didn't yet have it. They knew we had it and they knew we were willing to use it. We had already done so twice against the Japanese. And the American people were almost as hostile now to the Russians as they had been to the Japanese when those first two A-bombs fell. Stalin was realistic enough to know how eager some Americans might be to drop a selection of those bombs on him and his regime. It seems likely in retrospect that he would have backed away if faced with that immediate prospect. LeMay and Trudeau might very well have bluffed the Russians and saved the Western powers a lot of hard, expensive work in the year to come if they had been allowed to take their trip up the Autobahn. But Stalin was so tough, ruthless, and indifferent to the sufferings of even his own people (as he proved in the late thirties when he let five million Ukrainians starve to death because they had ignored one of his edicts), that official Washington couldn't predict with any certainty what he would do. So the LeMay-Trudeau plan, which might have frightened the Russians into more reasonable behavior, but which on the other hand might have led to a cataclysmic confrontation, was disapproved in favor of a less dangerous strategy—the resumption of the airlift on a larger scale.

Even then, however, no one realized what an enormous operation the Berlin Airlift was destined to become. "Finally it began to dawn on me what was going on," LeMay recalls, "so I said [to Clay], 'Look, if you really want to haul stuff up there, we've got to have more airplanes. Some DC-4s [four-engine Douglas planes that were then the largest available transports]. Let's really open up an operation.' "

In the beginning, LeMay's headquarters ran the entire project, and it soon became so complicated he had more than the Russians with whom to deal. Before he knew it he found himself in the diplomacy business, for which he had considered himself so ill suited.

"It was perfectly apparent that I had to have some airdromes back behind the Rhine [in case] we were going to have to fight. But this was peacetime and the laws of France and Belgium stipulated that no foreign troops could be stationed on French or Belgian soil in peacetime."

He made a discreet visit to the chief of staff of the French Army and explained his dilemma. Fortunately he found a sympathetic ear. The French, so recently overrun by the Germans, were not eager to be overrun by the Russians. LeMay soon had permission to stock several French airfields with fuel, ammunition and other supplies, as long as no one found out about it. If it became public knowledge, the French Communist Party, which was quite popular and powerful at the time, would build it into a *cause célèbre.*

LeMay then went to Belgium and got the same kind of agreement. All he had to do now was make sure he kept the whole project secret. "I talked to our Army quartermaster and ordnance officers. We decided to load up a bunch of trains [with fuel and supplies] right away and start shuttling them around in France and Belgium. We had not only to elude enemy observation [there was plenty of that: their espionage system was plugged in all over the landscape]. We had to fool the civilian populations—our late allies, the French and the Belgians—because of the extralegality of the whole procedure."

The American military personnel involved in this great train shuffle were dressed as civilians, and they were helped by reliable Frenchmen and Belgians who knew what was happening. "We zigzagged our trains from hell to breakfast," LeMay has recalled. "We wanted to lose them and we did. We wanted to get them back in a far different area from the one in which we'd lost them. . . . They would send a train to one town, and it would sit on a siding for a while; and then they would gather it up on another train, and take it someplace else and let it sit there . . . another bill of lading would be made out . . . and then another, in another location, then another. Whole trainloads could be lost in the shuffle this way, and that was what we wanted."

Out of all this confusion, LeMay's people, with the help of the French and Belgians, built an orderly supply system in France and Belgium. And not a word of publicity about it ever emerged. Meanwhile, the Berlin Airlift grew as more planes arrived from the States to take their place in the continuous stream to and from the three Berlin airdromes—Templehof, Gatow, and Tegel. LeMay himself made several trips to the beleaguered city. He even delivered some coal. The LeMay Coal and Feed Company was now engaged in a monopoly business. The Russians had made certain of that by cutting off all other sources of supply to the people of West Berlin. When the serious phase of the airlift began, the Russians, on June 24, had stopped the supply of fresh milk to the American sector. The next day, they had stopped all food shipments to the three Western sectors. The Western powers, in retaliation, had then banned all food shipments to the

Russian sector. The deadly game of tit for tat had begun with Russia at least a six-point favorite because the notion of supplying more than half of a city the size of Berlin by means of air transport alone seemed preposterous.

LeMay, however, didn't think it impossible. He asked for help from the Air Transport Command and from the British. On July 12, the American Military Government, with German labor, began building a new airstrip at Templehof which would increase the field's traffic capacity by one third. The next day, U.S. officials announced that 426 American and British transport sorties into Berlin had already brought 2,047 tons of cargo, increasing to four weeks the Western sectors' reserve food and fuel supplies. On July 15, Soviet fighters began to buzz and harass the transports en route to Berlin, but the flow of supplies continued.

By early October, American and British transports were carrying five thousand tons of food and supplies daily to Berlin despite constant harassment by Soviet fighters. And reserves were so high that on October 8, food rations in the three Western sectors were increased two hundred calories per day. There was no doubt now that the Berlin Airlift had proven successful. But by this time Curt LeMay was no longer running it. He had turned it over to Gen. William H. Tunner of the Air Transport Command, whom LeMay considered "the transportation expert to end all transportation experts."

LeMay was now thinking about something that might prove to be an even larger challenge than the Berlin Airlift. It was a challenge for which the airlift and the Berlin crisis were at least partially responsible. The troubles created by the Russians in Berlin had awakened American military authorities to the woeful condition of our own Armed Forces, which had been deteriorating steadily since the end of World War II. The Air Force, as LeMay had often observed, was in dreadful shape. The United States had atomic bombs. And we had the Strategic Air Command which Tooey Spaatz had established in 1946 as a "striking-power" capable of delivering the bombs in the event such an extreme measure should ever become necessary. But in October 1948, Gen. Hoyt Vandenberg, who had replaced the retiring Spaatz as Air Force chief, was not convinced that the Strategic Air Command, as then constituted, was capable of delivering the bomb, or even of frightening a potential enemy. He ordered LeMay to return to the States and see what he could do about getting SAC into useful shape.

LeMay could hardly be expected to feel any regrets at leaving Germany. His year there, among the hungry, beaten people in that battered country, had been marked by many frustrations. But the Berlin Airlift, at least, was one operation from which he derived great satisfaction. Not until September 1949 did the Russians relent and reopen the ground access to Berlin. During the year and a half of the Russian blockade, British and American transport planes flew 2,343,315 tons of food and supplies into the besieged city.

"A lot of us folks who worked hard on the Lift," LeMay later wrote, "found a kind of tonic in the enterprise. We had knocked the place down; had battered it, burned it, slain or mutilated many of the inhabitants. Now we were doing just the opposite. We were feeding and healing."[6]

CHAPTER SEVENTEEN

When the LeMays returned home from Germany in mid-October 1948, they found a self-satisfied country in its fourth year of peace and enjoying every minute of it. One could feel the prosperity in the way people carried themselves. The rest of the world was still poor in the wake of the worst war in human history, but America was wealthier than ever. New postwar cars were filling up the streets, the highways, and the drive-in theaters, where the passengers, unless they had something more exciting to do, could watch movies like *Treasure of Sierra Madre,* with Humphrey Bogart and Walter Huston (directed by his son, John); *Hamlet,* with Laurence Olivier; *Johnny Belinda,* with Jane Wyman (then Mrs. Ronald Reagan).

On the radio, Jack Benny, Fred Allen, and Bob Hope kept people laughing. Bing Crosby was singing "Now Is the Hour"; Margaret Whiting, "A Tree in the Meadow"; Peggy Lee, "Mañana"; and Frank Sinatra, "Once in Love with Amy." On Broadway, Ray Bolger was starring in *Where's Charley,* in which "Amy" was one of the hit songs. Also on Broadway were *Kiss Me Kate, Look Ma, I'm Dancin',* and *Inside U.S.A.*

Some women had fallen for the "New Look," an attempt by cloth makers and fashion designers to lengthen skirts, but the scheme was doomed to failure because those with pretty legs were in no mood to hide them. Some men (especially gangsters) had taken to wearing double-breasted suits, but that fad was also fading.

As for sporting news, the Cleveland Indians, from the LeMays' beloved Ohio, had just defeated the Boston Braves in the World Series, four games to two. Notre Dame, North Carolina, and Michigan were still undefeated after the first half of the football season. LeMay's alma mater, Ohio State, had lost one game, to Iowa. In politics, also at the midseason mark, President Harry Truman was struggling mightily against Republican nominee Thomas E. Dewey, but nobody seemed to pay much attention because this was one contest in which almost everyone, except Truman, agreed on the outcome. Truman didn't have a chance.

In Congress, the big sport was hunting "reds." Anyone who looked even slightly pink was fair game for the House of Representatives' Un-American Activities Committee. But other people in Congress, as well as President Truman, were beginning to worry more about the immediate "red" threat—the armies of Russia. The Berlin Blockade was awakening many Americans to the dangers posed by Stalin's ambitious and relentless regime. The president's Air Policy Commission and the Congressional Aviation Policy Board agreed, in separate reports, that the Air Force had to be rebuilt, and the budget had to be increased to get the job done. There was a general feeling throughout the country that the Air Force had become our first line of defense. Hadn't it flattened Germany and destroyed Japan? The American people weren't yet aware what a weak line it was now putting up, just three years and two months after war's end.

President Truman knew how dangerous the Soviet Union had become. In March 1948, he called Russia the principal threat to world peace. And he knew the Air Force needed new planes, new techniques to counter that threat. But he was also so concerned about the danger of inflation that his original 1949 budget provided only $700 million for new aircraft. He and the Congress both decided, however, that this sum was not nearly enough. Eventually the figure was almost tripled to slightly less than $2 billion, and Air Force people began to feel they might be getting back into business.

The most pressing item of business in the fall of 1948 was the reconstruction of the Strategic Air Command, which, after two years in being, couldn't yet come close to fulfilling its mission. On the previous May 16, for instance, more than 180 SAC B-29s undertook what was to be a "maximum effort" simulated air raid against New York City. Only 101 of them even got off the ground and made the trip.

When LeMay landed at Andrews Air Force Base in suburban Washington, where SAC was headquartered at that time, he didn't even unpack his belongings because the command was already in the process of moving to Offutt Air Force Base just outside

Omaha, Nebraska, where its distance from U.S. borders made it less vulnerable to attack, and where its distance from Washington might make the nation's capital at least a slightly less inviting target. LeMay was at Andrews only long enough to watch the outfit move, but that by itself was enough to convince him he was inheriting a mess. He had a tendency throughout his career to think badly of each succeeding outfit at the time he inherited it, perhaps because his standards were so exacting, and SAC was no exception, but his low opinion of SAC in 1948 would soon prove to be justified. Meanwhile, the more he saw of the outfit, the less congenial he became. By the time he left Andrews, he was not exactly a pleasant fellow with whom to talk. Newspaper reporters in Omaha found that out when he arrived there to get his first look at his new headquarters. As he walked from his plane to his car, the reporters tagged along, firing questions at him. He managed to ignore most of them, but one newsman came up with a question he was in no mood to ignore.

Referring to the boom in the local economy that the arrival of SAC was expected to create, the man asked, "General, don't you think this will be a great thing for Omaha?"

"It doesn't mean a damned thing to Omaha," LeMay was reported to have replied, "and it doesn't mean a damned thing to me."[1] It seemed to him, he later recalled, that the reporter had nothing on his mind but the money Omaha might get out of SAC. This was what didn't "mean a damned thing" to him.

The Diplomat had wasted no time before introducing himself. He must have made the people of Omaha wonder what kind of dude this was, marching into their town with a cigar in his mouth and a scowl on his face. It would take a while for them and LeMay to get used to each other. At the moment he was much too worried about SAC to worry about Omaha.

He had indicated his vision of what SAC ought to be when he told the War Department Equipment Board, in January 1946, that our only defense against an atomic attack would be "a striking power in being of such size that it is capable of delivering a stronger blow than any of our potential enemies."[2]

From time to time, after taking command of SAC, he restated his views on what it ought to be, perhaps never more precisely than on April 30, 1956, when he testified before a U.S. Senate subcommittee. He said that day:

Strategic Air Command is the long-range atomic striking force of the United States. It is responsible to the Joint Chiefs of Staff through the chief of staff of the United States Air Force as the executive agent. [Its] mission . . . is to train and maintain an effective and secure nuclear air offensive force . . . to become and remain sufficiently strong to deter aggression during a cold war and, in cooperation with other United States and allied forces, to win the decisive air power battle in a general war should it occur. . . . All responsible airmen agree that it is impossible to provide an airtight defense against a well-coordinated and properly executed atomic bombing attack. . . . A substantial part of the offensive force will always get through the defenses. Therefore the primary defensive force becomes the offensive atomic strike capability of sufficient effectiveness to provide a deterrent force.

A deterrent force is an effective nuclear offensive force which is secure from destruction by the enemy regardless of what offensive and defensive action he takes against it.

Judged by this standard, the Strategic Air Command, when LeMay took charge of it, was, in the language of World War II, a very sad SAC.[3]

"One of the first things I did," he recalls, "was to take a look at what we had." From the SAC operations staff he heard an impressive story. George Kenney and his deputy commander, Maj. Gen. Clements McMullen, had embarked on a cross-training program in which crew members were to learn each other's jobs so they could replace each other in the event of disabling emergencies. They had begun an aerial refueling experiment to lengthen the range of their B-29s and the new B-36s which were now arriving. They had conducted a series of simulated bombing attacks on metropolitan areas. They had helped map Greenland. They had opened bases in Alaska, Japan, and England. And their crews were recording phenomenally high scores in their practice bombing missions.

"Kenney was gone when I got there," LeMay recalls. "I never met him. McMullen was there. I started in checking on bombing accuracy. I found they were not doing any realistic training at all. Radar bombing was at a radar reflector on a raft anchored off Eglin Field [Florida, in the Gulf of Mexico.] They were not flying altitude missions. It was medium altitude, fifteen thousand feet. They had trouble [at higher altitudes] because the radar wasn't pressurized. And also, McMullen was [the] advocate of cross-training everybody so that anyone could fill in on most any position. Consequently, none of them were any good at anything. The personnel situation was sorry. No group was properly manned. Fighter mechanics were with the bombers and vice versa. Supplies at the bases didn't match needs. Nobody knew what was there. The whole thing was in a state of confusion.''

LeMay was not alone in his dismal appraisal of SAC at the time he took charge. Another Air Force general, Frederic H. Smith, Jr., felt that George Kenney was more interested in becoming commander of an anticipated United Nations Air Force than he was in his duties at SAC. And when McMullen came in as his deputy, ''then a deterioration really started.''[4]

Brig. Gen. Noel Parrish also blamed McMullen. Parrish believed that Kenney was expecting to be the next Air Force chief of staff. Having been Douglas MacArthur's air chief during World War II, he was MacArthur's candidate to take over the Air Force when MacArthur became president, presumably in 1952. Meanwhile, Kenney simply didn't have his mind on SAC. He allowed McMullen to run it.

''McMullen was a fanatic in trying to eliminate from the Air Force everybody who wasn't a pilot,'' Parrish told historian James C. Hasdorff in 1974. ''[He] was running [SAC] completely off the ground. . . . Several officers had come in to see General Vandenberg and arranged for a meeting with him to try to get McMullen removed. [But] the decision had already been made by Vandenberg, [Air Force Secretary Stuart] Symington and others, particularly Symington. . . . So Kenney was relieved.''[5]

Col. C. S. ''Bill'' Irvine, who had been LeMay's maintenance expert in the Pacific during the war, and became a group commander in SAC after the war, also had difficulties with McMullen. ''I got into a lot of trouble before LeMay came,'' he told Air Force historian Robert Kipp in 1970. ''General McMullen said, 'Well, you have all these stupid ideas, why don't you go out and bust your ass and try to make them work.' ''[6] Since many of Irvine's ''stupid ideas'' had been developed when he was under LeMay in the Pacific, he was delighted to see LeMay arrive at SAC.

Kenney said in his own defense several years later, ''The business of building SAC up to where it could be termed a striking force was a tough one. Money was short and Congress was in one of its economy moods. As more B-29s came out of overhaul or mothballs, it was impossible to get personnel assigned to the new groups I was activating, so we robbed all USAF headquarters, including our own, to get bodies to maintain and fly the aircraft. Another complication was that the B-29s came to me with carburetor engines which had a bad fire record when used at high altitudes. I refused to accept them and insisted on fuel injection engines. I got them, though this delayed the formation of new units.''

Looking back from a perspective of several years, Kenney was also gracious in his appraisal of LeMay's eventual accomplishments with the Command. ''SAC at that time was of course nowhere near as efficient or well trained for its mission as the present force which has had years of intensive preparation under the leadership of a real commander—LeMay—and with excellent support from USAF headquarters which finally decided to give it the priority it needed in assignment of personnel, bases, equipment, and funds.''[7]

LeMay would be the first to agree that all of these problems were slightly easier for him than for Kenney to solve because he took over the Command at a time when the president and Congress were coming to the realization it had to be rebuilt. But he was dismayed to learn he would have to start rebuilding at such a low level. This may have accounted at least partially for his rude remarks to the press the day he arrived in Omaha.

Offutt Field, into which SAC moved on arrival in Omaha, was a nineteenth-century (1888) Cavalry station, originally named Fort Crook, where, it was said, enlisted men were once forbidden to shoot buffalo from the barracks windows. No such prohibitions were decreed about Indians, however. Camp Crook was established during the Indian campaigns of the West. The original Cavalry parade grounds were still there in 1948. So were the original officers' houses and three barracks built during World War II but subsequently abandoned. The dominant features of the base when the SAC people arrived, however, were the pervasive, oppressive odors from the nearby Omaha stockyards, and a group of huge factory buildings in which the Glenn Martin Company had assembled aircraft during World War II. LeMay was to move his people into the houses and barracks, and operate the Command from these factory buildings.

There were rumors that the political influence of Nebraska's powerful Republican senator, Kenneth S. Wherry, had been responsible for the selection of Omaha as the permanent headquarters of SAC, but the site was chosen while LeMay was in Europe and he could only guess at the factors involved.

"My first reaction was, this is a helluva place to be going," he told historian John T. Bolen in 1971. "There wasn't anything out there except an Indian-fighting post. I wondered how it came about, but the orders were out and there wasn't any use in fiddling around, finding out what went on. But I think it was to a large extent political, although as it turned out it wasn't too bad. It was a pretty good communications hub. It was the center of the country where we could get to our outfits which were scattered all over the country and later all over the world, a central point. [And] the people of Omaha were the best I ever had run across as far as cooperation was concerned."

It would be a while before he found this out. In the meantime, he moved in his men, planes, and equipment and, on November 9, 1948, opened his new, makeshift headquarters. Even his own office was nondescript, with just a desk, a chair, and a few pieces of "meager furnishings," but that didn't matter because he wasn't planning to spend much time there, at least in the foreseeable future.

Without even waiting for his men to get settled in, he undertook to educate his subordinate commanders "to the fact that we had a helluva job and they weren't worth a damn to start with, completely worthless. . . . I have a strong recollection of looking at the reports and records of what the training had been and coming to the conclusion myself that they weren't worth a goddamn. There wasn't one single professional crew in the outfit, not one, and in talking to people about this, they all became insulted. They thought they were pretty good, actually thought they were pretty good. So my first chore was to convince them they weren't."

Some of them were soon convinced. Others were soon elsewhere, and LeMay was replacing them with a group of old reliables who had worked for him at other times in other places. As his deputy commander he chose Tom Power, a man so cold, hard, and demanding that several of his colleagues and subordinates have flatly described him as sadistic. LeMay himself, when asked if Power was actually a sadist, has said, "He was. He was sort of an autocratic bastard. But he was the best wing commander I had on Guam. He got things done."[8]

Some people who watched Power work under LeMay have

also suggested that one of Power's functions was as a hatchet-man, that he did the unpleasant things LeMay didn't like to do. LeMay denies that. "I don't think I dodged any nasty stuff," he insists. "I never asked anyone to do anything I wouldn't do my-self. Maybe Tommy made things nasty that actually weren't. He wasn't all that bad, though. The only fault I could find with him—he was a little too autocratic. Always, 'Goddamn it, I want this done and you have to do it. Go do it. Get your ass out there right now.' I always maintained, 'We're a team. We have to do this. Your part of it is this. Get going.' "

When LeMay put out the call for him, Power was about to leave for London as the air attaché in the American embassy there. "He had already bought all of his stiff shirts demanded by protocol. I got him snaked out of that."

For his chief of staff, LeMay didn't have far to look. The smooth, impeccable, and ever loyal Augie Kissner, who had been with him in England, then the Pacific during the war, and again in Germany after the war, was ready for his fourth assignment to the same job under the same commander.

As his operations officer, LeMay chose J. B. Montgomery, whom he had known since GHQ Air Force days at Langley Field in 1937. Just out of flying school, Montgomery was assigned to the same squadron as LeMay and soon became an expert bom-bardier as well as pilot. "We nicknamed him 'Jackpot,' " LeMay recalls. "Every time we had to give an exhibition, he hit the target. He wouldn't always hit it in practice, but when the chips were down, he always did it." When Montgomery came to SAC, it was for his second stint as operations officer under LeMay. He had handled the same job during the war with the Twenty-first Bomber Command on Guam.

As director of plans, LeMay chose another Twentieth Air Force man, W. C. "Cam" Sweeney. And as public information officer, an unenviable job under a "diplomat" like LeMay, he brought in Al Kalberer, who had been his partner in locating and res-cuing the badly injured Blondie Saunders the morning after Saunders crashed in India during the war. LeMay has admitted that Kalberer had a tough job improving his public image. "He worked hard at whittling me down to size, or whatever metaphor you want to use. At least he taught me to put a little padding on the blunt mallet."

The more trustworthy old acquaintances he brought in, the more comfortable LeMay felt about his staff. But his staff was only a small part of SAC. He couldn't, and didn't even want to, replace everyone. What he felt he had to do, first of all, was to show his crews how incompetent they would be to perform the combat mission assigned to them if the country should suddenly find itself at war. Or, better than showing them, he wanted them to show themselves. He was convinced that, once they realized how bad they were, they would quickly become amenable to the training they needed. As soon as Montgomery was aboard and well briefed on the situation, LeMay decided the time had come for his dramatic demonstration. It would come to be known in SAC as the Dayton Mission, and it hasn't yet been forgotten in SAC, even though there is no one now in SAC who was there when it took place.

"Let's play out a problem," LeMay said to Montgomery. "Have 'em attack Wright [Field]. The whole damn command. By radar."[9]

It was to be a real combat mission. Maximum effort. Every crew, every airplane, flying at combat altitude against an anti-aircraft radar target at Wright, where operators on the ground could plot the approaching planes. They could even plot the descent of the radio signal "bombs" as they "dropped" and pinpoint with a high degree of accuracy where those "bombs" would have hit if they had been real.

LeMay had made a bet with himself that most of the crews, as then constituted, would register abysmally low scores. He realized he would look foolish if they did well, but he wasn't worried about that possibility. "They were not accustomed to flying at altitude. Neither were the airplanes. Most of the pressurization wouldn't work, and the oxygen wouldn't work. Nobody seemed to know what life was like upstairs."

The weather that night conspired with LeMay to help him prove his point. "There were thunderstorms in the area [of Dayton], for which I was glad." But he didn't really need the thunderstorms. Mechanical failures kept many of the planes on the ground, and sent others back to their bases after they were airborne. His predictions about high-altitude problems proved accurate, and his assessment of the command's bombing skills proved charitable. Not one airplane in the entire Strategic Air Command was able to complete its assignment on that short and relatively simple mission. This was an operation so ragged that all the details about it had to be classified immediately. It was an operation that would have made the Russians chortle with glee.

What did LeMay say to the boys the next day, after their return to their bases?

He didn't have to say much. "What a sorry operation. I've been telling you we were in bad shape. We are in bad shape. Now let's get busy and get this fixed."

CHAPTER EIGHTEEN

Based on LeMay's evaluation, the best of a bad lot of bomb groups in the Strategic Air Command at the beginning of 1949 was the 509th, the group which, during World War II, had dropped the first atomic bomb. Even this group LeMay pronounced to be in sorry shape. The personnel turnover in the four years since the war had been almost complete and every aspect of its operation had suffered. Yet in LeMay's view it was still better than any of his other groups, perhaps because it was under the command of Bill Irvine, who had proven his worth to LeMay as the Twentieth Air Force maintenance chief during the war.

Lacking both the men and the money to improve the entire command at the same time, LeMay chose the 509th, stationed at Roswell, New Mexico, as the first group to be put in what he considered proper condition. With the ruthlessness for which he was famous, he replaced the people he didn't think could be brought up to his standards. He revised the entire system of supply. He replaced the old crew-chief maintenance methods with an assembly-line operation. He got the airplanes into shape so they could fly long missions at combat altitude. And, as usual, he imposed an endlessly tiresome retraining program on everyone, especially the crews. Then he instituted tough, demanding evaluation procedures for those crews, and, as soon as they were ready, reopened the lead crew schools he had established during the war. He dearly loved that lead crew system.

"My personal goal," he told an interviewer in 1971, "was to get a real strong and efficient outfit, but you couldn't do it with a peace-as-usual atmosphere around the place. Every group I saw go into action during the war tied up its first mission something awful, complete failure, without exception. . . . So I felt that with atomic weapons and the type of warfare that we were going to have to fight, we had to be ready to go to war not next week, not tomorrow, but this afternoon, today; and you couldn't switch that quick from peacetime methods to wartime methods and expect them to work. In other words, we had to operate every day as if we were at war, so if the whistle actually blew we would be doing the same things that we were doing yesterday with the same people and the same methods. So what we tried to do was put SAC on a wartime basis and get going. The 509th had been assigned the so-called atomic mission at the time, and was better manned and better equipped than any of them, and even they weren't fully manned and fully equipped. All right, let's get one outfit fully manned, fully equipped, get them training and get them ready. Then let's keep them that way"[1]

As the upgrading of the 509th progressed, LeMay decided there was one other thing he wanted to do for it—promote its commander, Bill Irvine, from colonel to brigadier general. He may have felt guilty about Irvine. He had tried to get him promoted during the war but had failed because Gen. Robert C. Richardson, the Army theater commander stationed in Hawaii, refused to approve. Richardson apparently disliked Irvine because it was he who had made the deal with the Navy to circumvent the Hawaii supply channels in bringing B-29 parts to the Marianas. But Richardson was out of the picture in 1949, so LeMay again submitted Irvine's name for promotion. Alas, it was again rejected.

"The president knocked me off," Irvine recalls. "I was fifth on a list of four. Curt called me and told me to come up to [Omaha], and remember this is the tough LeMay, and when I got out of the airplane he bent over and picked up my bag. I asked him what he was doing.

"He said: 'For one thing, I'm younger than you, and for another, if I can't get you promoted I can at least carry your bag.' When you got through all that crust, LeMay was really a soft touch."[2]

By March 1949, four months after he took command, LeMay was beginning to feel he had made some progress. In a lecture to the students of the Air War College at Maxwell Field, Alabama, he assessed the current condition of SAC with reservations, but also with some optimism.

"The Strategic Air Command now has the capability of delivering [a decisive attack] in a matter of days," he said, "and we intend to reduce the time factor to a matter of hours."[3]

Both of the Air Forces within SAC were now under the command of men who worked for LeMay in the Pacific. Rosey O'Donnell was running the Fifteenth out of his headquarters in Colorado Springs and Roger Ramey had taken charge of the Eighth, headquartered at Fort Worth. Both were now major generals.

The Eighth, of which the 509th Wing [formerly group] was a part, would be expected to "furnish the main elements of the striking force and direct the early attacks." The Fifteenth, which was not yet up to LeMay's standards, would "provide units for the striking force and replacement crews." He now felt his organization could make at least some showing if called upon in a war emergency. But he was still far from satisfied.

"We hope someday to be able to bring all units up to a very high standard," he told his Air War College audience, "but this will depend on the availability of aircraft, personnel, and equipment."

In other words, it would depend on money. Here was a problem new to LeMay. He had fought a lot of battles during his career, but he was now engaged in one of the most difficult he had ever faced the Battle of the Budget. It was a battle that didn't end, even if or when you won it. You had to be ready to fight it again the following year. And people familiar with LeMay's diplomatic or political skills had to wonder whether he could ever win even a skirmish in that kind of conflict. For the next sixteen years they were destined, depending on their point of view, to be entertained, frustrated, pleased or infuriated by his efforts. And so was he.

"I was thinking," he recalls, "of a fighting force so good and strong no one would attack us. That took more money for everything. Bases, supplies, training. I laid out a program of what I was trying. First I had to get it into the Air Force budget. Then through the Department of Defense, then the Budget Bureau, then Congress." He would find out, first of all, how the rest of the Air Force liked it when SAC asked for the lion's share of the Air Force budget. And then how the Army and Navy liked it when their budgets were threatened to compensate for SAC's growing monetary appetite.

The budget process was a field of endeavor almost entirely new to him. During the short time he was in research and development, he had done some staff work connected with the meager pittance that enterprise had the temerity to request. But now, as commander of the most important operational arm of the Air Force, and potentially the most important element in the nation's entire system of defense, he would have to persuade the administration and the Congress, in peacetime, to give him each year a wartime army's worth of money.

Within the Air Force he found that he had the support of the chief of staff, General Vandenberg, who had, after all, assigned him to the job he was trying to do. And within the Department of Defense, he received the help of Stuart Symington, secretary of the Air Force, who was as convinced as anyone that SAC had to be rebuilt and enlarged. Symington had the ear of President Truman, which didn't hurt. But it was Congress that voted on the budget, so it was toward Congress that LeMay aimed his strongest weapons. He marshaled every argument within reach to convince congressmen that the only viable defense against Russian aggression was an atomic force so big and strong and well prepared that it could strike at almost a moment's notice.

"I began to appear more frequently before congressional committees," he recalled in *Mission with LeMay,*

> and with more at stake than I had ever owned before; and with more people dependent on me. . . . At first I'd considered that some of the questions put to me by the congressmen were captious or even silly. Were these people deliberately trying to pick at me, to needle me? Or, in more overt fashion, to beat my brains out? . . . I was, you might say, frightened initially.
>
> But not for too long. It soon became apparent that the members of that committee had been around for a long, long time. . . . They weren't being captious or silly. . . . As well as I, they had a responsibility to provide for the defense of our country. . . . As soon as this fact penetrated my thick skull, the whole ordeal became easier.[4]

Some of the men in Congress he found most helpful were Carl Vinson of Georgia in the House and Richard Russell, also of Georgia, in the Senate. But they were not the only people on Capitol Hill who were receptive. He began to realize he had a lot of friends there, and he did his best to cultivate those friendships. He even invited entire congressional committees to Omaha to see for themselves what SAC was trying to accomplish, and he got some individual congressmen to make the trip. He never did get a whole committee to visit him on his own grounds, but he did, with the help of the international circumstances and the support of the administration, score a smashing victory in his first Battle of the Budget. In 1949, the Air Force received the then considerable sum of $5 billion in appropriations, more than either the Army or the Navy.

The apparent ease with which this was accomplished may have given LeMay a false notion that henceforth it would not be difficult to secure funding for the needs of the Air Force and SAC. He would learn more about the budget wars in the years to come. Indeed, in the months to come.

The first, perhaps indirect, result of this Air Force budget triumph was that, on April 23, 1949, Secretary of Defense Louis A. Johnson canceled a $188-million Navy project, the planned construction of a supercarrier to be named the *United States*. So—there wasn't enough money in the budget for the Navy to have its carrier, but there seemed to be plenty of money for the Air Force's six-engine B-36 bomber, a whole wingful of which had already been delivered to SAC, with many more to come. By the end of 1948, SAC had 120 of the huge Consolidated Vultee bombers either on hand or on order. In early 1949, the Air Force had placed orders for seventy-five more of them. And all of this was in disregard of a rumor circulating throughout Washington that the B-36 was a lemon.

Hap Arnold had begun the B-36 development process in 1941 on the recommendation of advisers who had studied the preliminary designs. George Kenney was one of the men who had said, "Buy the B-36." Original studies indicated it would be more efficient, less costly to operate, with longer range and higher payload than any other plane then under consideration. But in 1945, when it reached the production line, problems arose. An Air Force inspection team found evidence of inferior workmanship and inferior materials in use at the Fort Worth Consolidated Vultee plant. By August 1946, when the first XB-36 made its maiden flight, Kenney, then in command of the newly organized SAC, was so disenchanted with the plane he recommended that the original order for one hundred be cut back to a few test models. Kenney cited a long list of "bugs" that, in his opinion, made the B-36 too risky to support a heavy investment. The as yet unproven defense theories on which SAC was based could hardly be proven by an impotent airplane. Others in the Air Force, however, pointed out that all new planes have bugs. Two classic examples, the B-17 and the B-29, both proved eventually to be great airplanes. This argument prevailed and the B-36 production continued.

After its shaky start, the plane gradually began to improve as modifications were introduced. In April 1948, a B-36 flew 6,922 miles in thirty-two and a half hours. In May, 8,062 miles in thirty-six hours. In December, a B-36 dropped forty-two tons of mock bombs from more than thirty-five thousand feet. And by that time the plane's speed had improved to 319 miles per hour. But there were people who either didn't know this, or didn't believe it, or didn't want to believe it. And quite a few of these people were in the Navy, where the growth of SAC was perceived as a dire threat, not only to the naval budget, but to the traditional naval function.

Since the end of World War II, such famous admirals as Chester Nimitz and William "Bull" Halsey had been crisscrossing the country, assuring the public that the atomic bomb wouldn't hurt the Navy. And here was the Air Force, buying planes which, potentially, could drop atomic bombs on any naval vessel, except a submarine, in any part of the world. If the U.S. Air Force could develop such a capability, then so, eventually, could the Russian air force. When the American people finally caught on to that obvious fact, how long would they continue to invest their tax money in a surface navy?

By the spring of 1949, rumors about the deficiencies of the B-36 were so widespread they could hardly be ignored. Since many of the plane's performance figures were classified, the Air Force could not publicly refute the charges against it. But LeMay could, at least, assure some of his fellow Air Force officers that the plane was more than satisfactory. He did so in his March 4 lecture at the Air War College.

"There has been a lot of skepticism about the B-36," he acknowledged.

I want to point out to you some proven superior features of this airplane about which you may not know. . . . The B-36 is the longest-range bomber in the world. Its present radius is 4,000 nautical miles. Based on what we know, the range . . . will steadily improve. . . . The B-36 has excellent flying qualities. It has been tested in detail by the Strategic Air Command, the Air Matériel Command, and the Air Proving Ground. [It] can operate off any airdrome from which a B-29 or B-50 [modified B-29] can operate. The B-36, already much improved in speed, will soon be faster than any other bomber except the much smaller, purely jet bomber. . . . By attaching a two-engine jet pod to each outer wing panel, the speed of the B-36 over the target can be increased to 20 percent faster than that of the B-29. . . . The B-36 has the best altitude performance of any bomber now in service. The addition of jets will increase this by 5,000 feet. . . . The B-36, without modification, can carry every type and size of bomb now developed including special bombs such as the ''A'' bomb, 12,000 pound bomb, 25,000 pound bomb, 42,000 pound bomb [and] radio controlled bomb.

While LeMay's lecture may have served to reassure the Air Force officers at the Air War College, it did nothing to stem the public rumors. And to feed these rumors, an anonymous document began circulating that contained fifty-five charges against the Air Force, the B-36 and its manufacturer. The document said, in effect, that the plane was inferior; it was chosen for development because of corruption among the highest officers in the Air Force, and, indeed, because of corruption within President Truman's cabinet, inasmuch as Secretary of Defense Louis Johnson had once worked for Convair, the new name for Consolidated Vultee.

The issue did not become public, however, until late May 1949, when Republican Congressman James E. Van Zandt of Altoona, Pennsylvania, a captain in the Naval Reserve, demanded a full investigation of the B-36 affair. He implied not only that the plane was inferior, but that the Air Force was buying it because ''the right people'' were making money on it.

Congress, being a deliberative body, which in its case often means deliberately slow, took no action until August 6, 1949, when the House Armed Services Committee opened an extensive probe of the B-36 contracts.[5] Representative Vinson, the committee chairman, announced that thirty-one military, political, and industrial leaders would testify. These included Secretaries Johnson and Symington, former Secretary of War Robert Patterson, former Air Force Secretary Robert Lovett, Undersecretary of the Navy Daniel Kimball, several aircraft manufacturers including Floyd Odlum of Convair, Donald Douglas, J. K. Northrop, W. M. Allen, J. H. ''Dutch'' Kindelberger, and R. E. Gross; plus Air Force generals Hap Arnold (now retired), Kenney, Frederic Smith, Jr., Vandenberg, Muir Fairchild, Joseph McNarney, Twining, Norstad, and LeMay.

These men were so united in their praise of the B-36 program that the whole probe began to look like a whitewash. *New York Times* military analyst Hanson Baldwin wrote on August 14 that the probe, so far, looked one-sided. Kenney acknowledged that he had been for the plane originally, then against it, but was now on record as being for it again because of its emerging improvements. Arnold, in poor health (he was destined to live only five more months), cheerfully accepted the chief responsibility for the B-36 program and declared that "the B-36 is the outstanding bomber in the world today." Then, after answering a lengthy list of questions, he turned his thoughts to his little retirement "ranch" near Sonoma, California and said, rather plaintively, "May I go back to the Valley of the Moon now?"

During his testimony, Arnold also said, about the new commander of SAC, "You can't move that cigar out of LeMay's mouth by political influence or favoritism or anything else."

When it was LeMay's turn to testify, on August 11, he told the committee that shortly after his arrival at SAC, he had decided he liked the B-36 well enough to ask that four rather than two groups be equipped with it, and that the size of these groups be increased from eighteen to thirty planes each. He said, "I believe it would be very difficult" to shoot down a B-36 in daylight, and, "I know of no night fighter . . . that would be at all effective. . . . There will come a time when a fighter can shoot down 80 percent of the B-36s—but by that time the B-36 will be obsolete."

And when he was asked if carrier-based planes could carry atomic bombs, he said simply, "No sir."

Norstad, when he took the witness stand, called LeMay "the ablest big-airplane and strategic-bomb operator in the world." He was willing at any time, he said, to accept LeMay's assessment of the B-36.

But was the American public equally willing? What did the testimony so far mean? All these fellows were in this together, all involved, one way or another, in the selection of the B-36. Maybe they were simply covering up each other's malfeasance. Congressman Van Zandt demanded that the author of the anonymous document be called to the witness stand.

From Van Zandt's point of view, this turned out to be a mistake. As the committee, and the public, soon learned, the author of the document was not so anonymous after all. He was identified as a man named Cedric R. Worth, a one-time Hollywood script writer who was now a special assistant to Undersecretary of the Navy Kimball.

On August 24, Worth took the stand to be questioned by a succession of committee members. His answers indicated he had done some reassessing since he wrote his anonymous essay, and he would have been happier, at the moment, to be somewhere else.

"Where did you get this document?"

"I wrote it."

"You wrote it, yourself?"

"Yes, sir."

"Then you claim the authorship of this document?"

"I wrote it. I am not claiming anything."

"Where did you get your information from?"

"A great many places."

"Did the Assistant *[sic]* Secretary of the Navy or anyone in the Navy Department know that you were preparing this document?"

"No, sir."

"You did this all by yourself?"

"Yes, sir."

"What prompted you to make this document? What was your motive?"

"I was greatly concerned. As the document indicates, it appears to me that the defenses of the country are going in the wrong direction and are being materially weakened by propaganda which is not true."

"Did any admiral read this document after you had prepared it?"

"No, sir."

"Did any high-ranking officer read it?"

"Not to my knowledge. I have never shown it."

"You vouch for these as facts?"

"No, I don't."

"Well, you did in the document in writing."

"That is regrettable."

While Worth swore that no admiral or high-ranking naval officer, to his knowledge, had read the document, he did admit that a Navy commander gave him much of the data he used in writing it. The grilling continued:

"You have had a little change of heart after putting that down on a paper and giving it to Congressmen, have you not?"

"Yes."

"You regret that?"

"Quite." . . .

"In any event, you realize that in this anonymous document a lot of loose, false statements have been spread around?"

"I will say that."

"Do you realize, Mr. Worth, the heartaches you have brought about by this anonymous document?"

"Yes."

"And the great disservice that you have done to the American people in the manner in which you have carried this out?"

"Yes." . . .

"Is it not true that . . . you have brought regrettable consequences to the United States Navy by your activities . . . ?"

"I will state to anybody that I believe I have done the Navy no good."

Worth's testimony virtually ended the probe, and it also ended Worth's position as special assistant to Undersecretary Kimball, who was quick to deny any knowledge of the matter. But the case of the anonymous document didn't seem to embarrass the Navy even a little bit. Six weeks later, on October 3, three high-ranking admirals, Arthur W. Radford, Louis E. Denfeld, and Gerald F. Bogan wrote joint letters to Secretary of the Navy Francis P. Matthews charging that Army and Air Force officers were trying to gain complete control of the national military establishment by obliterating naval aviation.

Five days later, on the 8th, Radford, who was commander-in-chief of the Pacific Fleet, told the House Armed Services Committee that the nation was taking a "bad risk" in depending on the Air Force and its B-36 in the event of a war. And on the 10th, several other naval officers told the same committee that the B-36 was both obsolescent and highly vulnerable to attacks by fighter planes. They agreed that the development of jet fighter strength (which was well within the Navy's capability) was much more vital to the nation's defense.

This testimony, however, came too soon after the B-36 probe, which meant that it came to naught. Congress in 1949 was not convinced that naval fighter planes, flying from woefully vulnerable carriers, could repel an armada of huge Russian bombers carrying atomic bombs to American cities. The massive deterrence promised by an armada of U.S. bombers which could reach Russian cities seemed to offer much more protection. The B-36 and SAC were now ready to fly high. As soon as they could get their act together.

CHAPTER NINETEEN

The development of SAC into the kind of organization LeMay demanded would take more time than the year that had elapsed since his arrival. This worried him to some degree because the very concept of the organization offered such extravagant promises, and there were so many people, not only in the Navy, who considered those promises outlandish. He had to be concerned also because, on September 23, 1949, President Truman disclosed that "within recent weeks" Russia had exploded an atomic device, thus ending America's atomic monopoly. It didn't mean Russia would be able immediately to launch atomic weapons against the United States. But it did mean there wasn't much time left for Americans to feel smug about their atomic superiority and safety. It also meant that, in LeMay's opinion, there wasn't much time left to get SAC ready for its ultimate capability.

By now there were about sixty-five thousand people in SAC and a thousand airplanes. Its three heavy bomb wings, eleven medium bomb wings, two fighter escort wings, three reconnaissance wings, and six air refueling squadrons were stationed at twenty-two bases throughout the United States and at several others abroad. Most of these wings had now been retrained in accordance with LeMay's requirements, and most of them had been assigned specific missions in the SAC war plan that J. B. Montgomery had put together. Each had several graduates of the lead crew school at Walker Air Base in New Mexico, well trained and practiced in the specific missions they might one day have to fulfill. But there were still many aspects of the SAC organization that fell short of LeMay's almost impossible demands. And one of them, surprisingly, was the progress of B-36 operations. After all the praise he and his colleagues had lavished on the big new bomber during the congressional probe, one might get the notion that it had eased its way into the SAC armada without encountering so much as a ripple of rough air. But not so. There were still some bugs in the plane, bugs in its maintenance system, and bugs in the coordination between its crews. Though everyone, including LeMay, thought it was a fine airplane, it hadn't yet begun to live up to its operational potential. It hadn't yet even been put into the SAC war plan.

One day in January 1950, LeMay called Bill Irvine, who was still in command of the 509th Bomb Wing at Roswell, New Mexico, and who had finally been promoted to brigadier general. LeMay began, to Irvine's considerable astonishment, by telling him he was doing pretty well with his B-29s. LeMay was much more likely to let a man know when he wasn't doing well. You could assume you were doing well if he didn't say anything. He also congratulated Irvine on his promotion. Then he said, "I suppose you've got both feet up on your desk"[1]

Irvine said, "No, I've got just one foot up, but since we won the [SAC] Combat Competition, I was about to lift the other one up."

"I've got news for you," LeMay said. "Tomorrow you're going to take over the B-36s at Fort Worth."

"That's interesting," Irvine said. "Somebody should take them over. Any special instructions?"

"Yes. Secretary Symington told me if I didn't get the B-36s running he was going to bust me. I'll bust you first if you don't get them running. I'll give you about six months."

When Irvine got to Forth Worth he called a meeting of all the B-36 pilots. He told them he had noticed that the officers' club was full of people drinking coffee at ten o'clock in the morning. He had also noticed that airplanes usually took off at such comfortable hours as eight in the morning or noon. So it seemed that the flying schedule was at the convenience of the pilots.

"I said that I expected to continue that program," he told an interviewer several years later, "but any hour of the twenty-four that an airplane was out of commission, the airplane commander or one of his officers was to be with that airplane. I ordered that every airplane out of commission was to be worked on on a twenty-four-hour basis. I told them that I was looking for someone to court martial, and the first time I found an airplane out of commission and the airplane commander or one of his officers was not with that airplane, that commander was going to be the one court martialed.''

The next thing Irvine did was to call a meeting of the pilots' wives. First he explained to them a new spot promotion policy which LeMay was then introducing. It provided that when an airplane crew met certain rigorous inspection and performance standards, everybody in the crew would get a one-step promotion. Did they want to help get their husbands promoted?

''I said that as far as I was concerned it was their job to produce for me every morning a husband that could do a day's work. Well, this produced results and I later saw wives dragging their husbands out of the club before they had one too many.''

Irvine's story about the wives illustrates one aspect of life in the Strategic Air Command that few of its veterans like to discuss at any length. What was it like to be one of those wives whose husbands had to work sometimes ninety-five hours a week and were almost always on call? Did this not strain the domestic tranquillity in many of the SAC households? Few will deny that married life in SAC could be difficult. The women, besides having to endure the long hours and often long days or weeks of separation and loneliness, had also to live with the realization that their men were in frequent danger. It was not easy.

LeMay, who took for granted his own endless dedication to his work, and therefore expected it of his men, has always felt he could also expect it of their wives. He seemed to believe that if the morale of the men was high, that meant the morale of their wives must also be high because a husband with an unhappy wife is not likely to be a happy man. It seemed to him his men were happy and he had convincing proof of it in the way they were willing to work for him.

''I have always believed that you can really work a man until he drops,'' he told an interviewer in 1971, ''if three factors exist: One, you have to be doing something important and everybody has to know it is important. Two, you have to be making a little headway toward getting the job done. And three, you have to show a little appreciation once in awhile, at least the man doing the job has to know that he is appreciated even if it only comes from his colleagues.''[2]

LeMay's introspective personality and his parsimony with words seldom allowed him to show his appreciation by pouring praise on his men, but he did find other ways, and his spot promotion system was one of them. His solution to the housing shortages on SAC bases was another, and so was the construction of hobby shops on all the bases. These were large, well-equipped buildings where SAC people of all grades and ranks could work side by side on their own personal projects.

Shortly after coming to SAC, LeMay learned that the Air Force still had a lot of promotion vacancies open from the days of World War II. After a bit of connivance in Washington, he managed to get enough of these vacancies assigned to SAC so that he could grant promotions to about 15 percent of the men in his crews. But he did not intend to issue these promotions on the basis of seniority. They would go only to crews which had proven themselves to be in the top 15 percent of combat readiness. And they would go to every man in these crews.

There was a catch, to be sure. If a crew fell below the top 15 percent, every man in the crew lost his promotion. This seems unfair on the face of it because it meant that if one crew member fell down on his job, the whole crew had to suffer for it. But LeMay found that the system worked because most men were willing to be their brothers' keepers when their own pocketbooks were affected. The best crews worked hard to stay among the top 15 percent and the others worked hard to get there. The rest of the Air Force was not enthusiastic about the notion of spot promotions, however, because they were offered only in SAC.

LeMay did not foster competition among his men in his approach to the SAC housing problem. Augie Kissner, his chief of staff, announced publicly in late 1949 "a staggering [housing] shortage over the command." At the Roswell, New Mexico, base, for instance, there were only 185 family units where eight hundred were needed. Nearly every base, he said, needed several hundred units, even though the towns near those bases were doing all they could to accommodate the families of the SAC men.

And for unmarried men who lived on the bases, the situation was almost as bad. "The Air Force was still using the Army methods, including even the early morning reveille," LeMay recalls. But since the Air Force, and especially SAC, operated on a twenty-four-hour basis, this meant people were sometimes aroused for reveille an hour or two after they got to bed, and at all hours of the day or night, people were coming and going in the old, open-bay barracks, waking each other out of their sleep. No one had any privacy.

LeMay felt that in an organization like SAC, the men should

be in rooms rather than open bays. Under the restrictions of his budget, he couldn't even dream of offering a private room for each man, but he did hope to provide a degree of privacy and dignity by building barracks that would house two men per room. What was the first objection when he went to Washington to present this plan?

"Suppose you get two 'homos' in the same room?"

His answer to that? "I thought we weren't supposed to have any of them."

Having laughed off such objections and obtained preliminary approval for the first few barracks with rooms instead of bays, he found that the Army Corps of Engineers presented his next problem. Though the Air Force and the Army were now separated, the Army Engineers were still responsible for much of the Air Force construction, under a contract arrangement between the two services.

"And the first thing they did," LeMay recalls, "was to tack a fifteen percent surcharge on top of the contract costs."

He looked out his office window one day at Offutt and saw a DC-3 parked on the ramp with no Air Force insignia. It had a big red castle painted on the side of the fuselage.

LeMay phoned his transportation department and said, "What the hell is that out there?"

"It belongs to the Army Engineers," he was told.

"Well, what's it doing here?"

"They park it out here and we maintain it for them."

"This was part of the fifteen percent, I guess." LeMay recalls. "Well, I finally threw that damned thing off the field. I thought I could build barracks cheaper than they could. And better. We sent some scouts out and we found some steel—looked like planks—made of hollow sheet steel. You could put one above another with a sealant. For siding. All metal. So I got a design laid out of what I wanted. Individual rooms with a bathroom between. As an experiment, I got permission to build them myself. So we built them at Offutt. And we built them for less money than the Army Engineers would charge for wooden, open-bay barracks. But after we had built the first three, the Army Engineers wouldn't let us build any more."[3]

He did, however, have those first three steel barracks that he could use as showcases. But not until they were furnished. And he didn't have the money to furnish them. By this time he had met a man named Arthur Storz who owned a large brewery in

Omaha. He also owned a huge hunting estate called Ducklore Lodge in western Nebraska near the Wyoming state line. Now an elderly man, he had been in the Air Service during World War I and both of his sons had served in the Air Force during World War II. He was not only one of the wealthiest men in Omaha, he was sometimes called "Mr. Air Force" in Nebraska. He was the logical man for LeMay to approach with his housing problem and when he did so, he soon found out what kind of man Storz was, then what kind of people they had in Omaha.

At Storz's suggestion, LeMay had interior and exterior models built of the as-yet unfurnished barracks. Then Storz held a dinner party at his brewery for the most influential people in town. The bar was open, the beer was flowing, and the food was delicious. After the plates were cleared an Omaha advertising executive named Morris Jacobs stood up as master of ceremonies and said to the assembled diners, "General LeMay has these three barracks built out at Offutt but not furnished. We're going to furnish them for him. The amount each of you is expected to give is on the envelope in front of you."

The men of Omaha paid without complaint and their wives did the decorating. After they were finished, but before the SAC men moved into the barracks, LeMay overheard someone saying, "It's too good for them." In fact, they took so much pride in their fancy new quarters they kept them in prime condition. They even hired civilian janitors, out of their own pockets, to do the heavy cleaning. And best of all, when the Army Engineers found out what had been done, they finally capitulated to LeMay's demands. Eventually, all the SAC barracks provided the same kind of accommodations.

Housing for the married men demanded a different approach. It began with the formation of the Strategic Air Command Housing Association. This organization was based on the idea that men in the command would contribute money for seed capital, and each man would get his money back, though without interest, when he either retired or left the command. With the funds thus collected, the association would buy prefabricated houses and put them up on the various bases. The mortgages on these houses would be serviced from the men's monthly rental allowances. The building costs would be low because the men themselves would do much of the work in their spare time. The Reconstruction Finance Corporation liked the idea so much it was willing to carry the mortgages, which LeMay figured could be paid off in about four and a half years. The entire scheme seemed about to get off the ground until it skidded to a stop on the desk of the comptroller general in Washington.

His reaction: "Negative. If you live on a base, we can't pay you any rental allowance." He refused to budge. Since the houses were to be built on government land, it would take an act of Congress to get such a plan approved.

LeMay, therefore, went to Sen. Kenneth S. Wherry of Nebraska, the Republican whip, who used his good offices to get an enabling law passed. The Wherry Housing Act entailed leasing the government land to contractors, who built the houses, then leased them back to the military.

The comptroller general wasted no time approving this plan. "He had said we couldn't do it," LeMay has observed, "but when private contractors were involved—Oh, yes. Surely."

At last, SAC got the houses needed for married personnel. But at considerably greater cost than necessary, after the contractors skimmed off their profits.

It was a disillusioning experience for LeMay in all but one respect. Again the people of Omaha gave him reason to be embarrassed about the surly remarks he had made the day he arrived there in 1948. Because he didn't have enough land within the boundaries of Offutt Air Base on which to build the required houses, the city of Omaha bought adjacent land and gave it to the government for that purpose.

When LeMay came up with his hobby shop idea, he wasn't thinking only of his men; he was thinking also of himself. He loved to putter with mechanical things, whether they were toys, bicycles, cars, airplanes, radios, or even television sets. It was his love of cars that inspired the creation of the first hobby shop at Offutt.

In his memoirs he wrote: "One night I got to yakking to Helen for about the hundredth time about that car which Bob Kalb and I rebuilt up there in Bradford, Pennsylvania [when they were in college], and how exciting it all was. Then I went over to the window and did a lot of thinking. I looked off up the street . . . that ancient Commanders' Row of the old Fort Crook days, where horses used to be tied to hitching posts out in front. . . . But . . . I was seeing cars . . . automobile engines, and an old chassis, and rebuilt transmissions and such."[4]

For that first hobby shop at Offutt, which he envisioned simply as a place where the men could work on their cars, he set aside an old, unused building, then began scrounging contributions, auto repair equipment, and even machine tools from any well-heeled civilian who made the mistake of visiting the base. But he did not arouse any immediate enthusiasm from the men on the base. Most enlisted men are too sophisticated to volunteer for anything but free beer, and a lot of them would be too suspicious to volunteer even for that. When LeMay announced the first meeting, only two appeared. Three, including himself. So he knocked some heads together the next day, which meant that at the next meeting, there may not have been any volunteers, but there were a lot of "volunteers." And when they found out what it was all about, they continued to come, in ever-increasing numbers. The hangar was soon crowded every evening with men repairing their old cars, or building new ones. And there in the middle of the crowd, dressed in an old baseball cap and greasy coveralls, without his general's stars, was Curt LeMay himself. During his years at SAC, he built for himself two full-sized sports cars. And often enough, the young fellows working beside him didn't even know that this old fellow in his forties was actually their commanding officer.[5]

As soon as the first hobby shop at Offutt proved successful, others began opening at other SAC bases and the activities expanded to every kind of mechanical hobby, including even small airplanes like Aeroncas and Piper Cubs. LeMay was soon so fascinated by his brainchild that his wife and natural child, Janie, began to wonder if he'd ever spend another evening with them.

Their house, built in 1894 on Commanders' Row at Fort Crook, not Offutt, was a great pile of red brick with a fountain that featured a stream of water pouring out of a child-statue's boot into a pool below. The house had three bedrooms and two baths on the second floor, plus a small, separate apartment on the third floor. The living room, dining room, and den on the first floor were large and formal. The kitchen was big and old fashioned.

While the necessity to entertain here was not as constant as it had been in Germany, it was frequent enough to make the LeMays realize they had to have a cook. During a five-day trip to Washington for a Pentagon conference, LeMay had stayed in a house at Bolling Field where a sergeant named Boyd Waterman had done the cooking. He wasn't a fancy chef. He was an Army, now Air Force, cook, but a good one. And he cooked the kind of plain food LeMay preferred—steak and potatoes.[6]

Shortly after LeMay's visit to Bolling, Sergeant Waterman got a call from Maj. Paul K. Carlton, one of the general's aides. Did he want to come to Omaha and cook for the SAC commander?

SAC didn't mean much to Waterman at the time and neither did Omaha, though he would one day, in retirement, choose it as his permanent home. And LeMay at the time didn't mean much more to him. Until that five-day visit to Bolling, Waterman had never heard of him. Waterman told Major Carlton he'd think about it. But he didn't think very hard or very quickly about it because he was happy where he was, at Bolling.

One day he was sitting in a little office off the kitchen storeroom at the Bolling Officers' Club when a man came in and said, "Sergeant Waterman?"

"Yes sir," he said. Then he looked up to see all those stars on the shoulders and the big cigar in the mouth and said, "Yes sir" again.

LeMay said to him, "You coming to work for me or aren't you?" Once again Waterman said, "Yes sir."

"Good. Be in Omaha by May tenth."

Always a sociable man, Waterman did so much serious socializing the night before he left Bolling that the Air Patrol had almost literally to carry him to the Omaha-bound airplane the next morning. When he landed at Offutt, woefully hung over, LeMay's driver took him to the barracks that would be his new home. About one o'clock, he walked unsteadily across the parade ground to the LeMay quarters and introduced himself to Helen LeMay, who was working in her flower garden. She stood up, surveyed him carefully, and said, "Sergeant Waterman, I think the best place for you is back in the barracks, in bed. I'll see you tomorrow morning."

The LeMays had scheduled a dinner party for 135 people about ten days after Waterman's arrival. Maybe that was why Curt LeMay had been so particular about his arriving by May 10. The Blackstone Hotel in Omaha had quoted a fee of four thousand dollars to cater the affair. But the annual entertainment allowance for the commanding general of SAC was only thirty-four hundred. And one thing the LeMays had never enjoyed was an independent income.

The general went to the sergeant and put it to him straight. Catering was out of the question. "Can you handle it?" he asked.

Fortunately, Waterman had attended a special Parties and Banquets School when he was in Washington. "Yes sir," he said, and he did. As he later recalled, "We put on the whole thing for twenty-one hundred, including the help, the linen, the flowers, and the booze."

About three times a year the LeMays staged large parties at Offutt, and Waterman managed them, but as he was always quick to acknowledge, it was with Helen LeMay's help as well as her supervision. Before each party, the two of them would spend three days in the kitchen. One day she might get up at 4 A.M. and make brownies until noon. The next day it might be two thousand patty shells. Or ice bowls for shrimp or lobster. Eventually the entertainment allowance went up to forty-five hundred dollars annually, but it was never enough. Without Waterman and Helen LeMay sweating in the kitchen, the commanding general wouldn't have had the slightest chance of discharging his social obligations.

Waterman remembers hearing the LeMays argue only once, and it hardly amounted to a serious domestic imbroglio. She was insisting that they lock up the house when they were going out. These were the days when people still dared to leave their doors unlocked.

Her husband said, "Locks only keep out honest people. A crook can always get in."

She disagreed. "I can lock this house so tight you'd never get in." He took her up on it, went outside, gave her enough time to secure the place, then jumped down a window well and kicked in a basement window.

They never argued about household matters, at least not in front of Waterman. One day he heard her telling him about some problem in the house, to which LeMay replied, "I'll run the Air Command. You run the house." If they ever differed about more serious matters, Waterman didn't know it because they held their discreet family discussions in the den. Waterman never saw them get angry at each other. He can recall only two occasions when he saw LeMay get angry at anybody.

One day the general had just emerged from the back door of his house, wearing flight fatigues but no insignia, when he saw a C-47 sputtering its way toward a landing on a path which indicated a certain crash. Noticing two airmen nearby, he ordered them to get out into the street and divert traffic. Seeing no insignia, and not knowing who he was, they told him, in effect, to go to hell.

Without arguing, he hurried off to the accident scene, but when he returned home, he was still furious at those two men. He got on the phone immediately to try to find out who they were, but fortunately for them, he never did track them down.

The second time Waterman saw him angry was during a flight from Offutt to Bolling. When he requested landing instructions (in bad weather), the flight controller there said, "You can't land here."

LeMay said he had a green instrument-flying card and intended to land.

"If you do," the controller warned, "you'll lose your green card."

LeMay, in a fury, finally banked the plane toward Andrews, several miles away, but before leaving the environs of Bolling, he picked up his microphone once more, identified himself to the controller, and said, "When I get back to Bolling, I want you and your commanding officer and the base commander to be there to meet me."

In due course, LeMay and Waterman arrived at Bolling from Andrews by automobile to find a roomful of officers and men waiting at attention. Some of them, Waterman recalls, were so frightened their knees were knocking.

"Where's the man who said I couldn't land here?" LeMay demanded.

A sergeant with a worried look on his face stepped forward.

LeMay walked up to him, looked him over, then, as if he had undergone a sudden change of heart, shook his hand. Turning to his commanding officer, he said, "I want this man promoted. The Air Force needs more like him."

Much of LeMay's time was now spent in travel, not only to Washington but to the various SAC bases. He has estimated that he was away from Offutt about half the time, inspecting bases. An experienced commander now, he had learned how to delegate authority, and in men like Augie Kissner, Tom Power, or J. B. Montgomery, he had subordinates he could trust, which gave him more time to inspect his units and to think about ways of improving procedures.

For his inspection trips he had put together a team, each man an expert in some aspect of the organization. And he had a KC-97 transport plane fitted out with bunks and a fully equipped galley. He and his team could fly off for a week's journey, to bases around the country or around the world, landing at one after another, spending a few hours, then flying on to the next.

In the beginning, he recalls, "I tried to look at everything."
But he soon "got it down to a system." Each member of his
team would check his particular specialty while LeMay himself
would look into whatever part of the operation interested him
most at the moment, or seemed most in need of improvement.
He insists that the purpose of his inspections was to improve his
units, not just to surprise them and catch them off guard. "Our
inspectors were supposed to help a commander. [We weren't]
there to gig him." But he did sometimes catch a unit off guard,
and when that happened, the people in the unit did not enjoy the
day.

"I remember landing one Sunday morning about seven o'clock
in Georgia [at Robins Air Base near Macon]. Everything was
locked up. I got hold of the SAC group commander and shook
things up. They got people out of church and off the golf course.
But I didn't fire anybody."[7]

Recollections differ about the severity of his reprimands. Gen.
John Paul McConnell, who would one day succeed him as the
Air Force chief of staff, and was for several years his director of
plans at SAC, recalls that he could be pretty hard on his men.
"We'd go on trips together and find some commander who had
screwed up. [LeMay] would be in his coveralls and he'd chew
the man's ass out from one end to the other."[8]

Maj. Gen. Timothy Dacey, Ret., who was on LeMay's staff at
SAC, remembers him differently. Before being assigned to SAC
headquarters, Dacey was with the 509th Wing at Roswell. He
recalls how the 509th would anticipate LeMay's visits and try to
be ready for him. "We'd be cranking up for it forever. And then
he'd go someplace we hadn't cleaned. We had some communications people in a big tent on the other side of the runway.
LeMay decided to go out there and say hello. Well, the place
was a mess. Guys in their underwear. Dirty dishes. Cots un-
made. LeMay looked around and marched out." But as Dacey
remembers it, all he said was, "You can do better than that."

The following year they made sure they did better. The staff
of the 509th was determined not to let him catch them again.
They built new barracks for their communications squadron and
"harassed hell out of them" to make sure they were presentable
when LeMay arrived. "We even built a road out to the place."
So what happened? LeMay wouldn't even go near it. He said he
wasn't interested.

Gen. David Wade, who also served on LeMay's staff at SAC,

recalls that he was a SAC deputy wing commander stationed at Castle Air Base near Merced, California, the first time he encountered LeMay. The big transport came to a stop on the ramp, the SAC commander emerged with a cigar in his mouth and said, "I want to see your aging racks"[10]

"I hadn't the slightest idea what he meant," Wade recalls. "I looked around for someone to help me out. There was no one there."

Finally, LeMay said, "We'll go down to the electronic shop."

In those days, before the invention of solid-state technology, vacuum tubes were used in electonic equipment. And those tubes would often prove defective. To make sure each tube was worthy of trust before being placed in an airplane, it was placed on an "aging rack" and tested at the same power input it would receive in the air. If it functioned well for three or four weeks, it would be certified satisfactory and reliable enough for the safety of an airplane to depend on it. Wade didn't know about any of this, but LeMay did. Wade soon realized that aging racks were important. "So that's what he wanted to see. Were you doing it right? Which indicated to me this guy understood what it was all about."

One problem that disturbed LeMay during these early inspection tours was the lack of adequate security on SAC bases. Russia was coming into nuclear capability. And in the United States, what came to be known as the McCarthy era was dawning. Everywhere, especially in Congress, there was talk of Communist subversives threatening not only our political institutions but our military installations. LeMay, who was second to no man in the passion of his anti-Communist conservatism, was deeply impressed by all the concern around him. And he was convinced that if there was "fifth column" activity against the American military, it would most likely be directed against SAC, which constituted the country's first line of deterrence against a Russian nuclear attack.

Unfortunately, however, if SAC was to be counted upon, there was another problem to be tackled, even more immediate than security.

Under a safety system developed shortly after the atomic bomb was invented, the Manhattan Engineering District (which had managed the creation of the bomb) retained responsibility not only for further research and development, but also for procurement, storage, assembly, and transportation of all atomic weapons. On the face of it, this system seemed sensible. Atomic weapons were not harmless baubles to be put in the hands of any agency that expressed an interest in them. But even as early as 1946, when LeMay was in Air Force Research and Development, he had seen what he considered an alarming flaw in the arrangement. If Russia were to attack the United States, the Air Force would presumably be responsible for immediate retaliation. Valuable time would be lost if the Air Force had first to go to the Manhattan District and put in requisitions for the needed bombs before transporting them to operational bases, assembling them, and sending them on their way. His concern was particularly acute because the MED, again with apparent good reason, had adopted rather stringent and time consuming procedures for release of such weapons.

LeMay raised this subject in a July 1, 1946, memorandum to the MED commander, but two years later, when he came to SAC, the Air Force was still trying without success to win authorization for SAC to store, assemble, and transport the weapons it would need. The Manhattan District, perhaps afraid that some supertough, anti-Communist general like LeMay, or even some bellicose aircraft commander, might take it upon himself to drop a bomb on Russia, clung desperately to its physical control of all atomic weapons. As SAC commander, LeMay renewed his previously expressed arguments against the established system, but when he found that his words were unavailing, he decided to try a demonstration.

Using the best trained group he had at the time, the 509th, he set up a mock war exercise in which it was assumed that Russia had just attacked the United States. The 509th was assigned the mock retaliation mission, which would, of course include the requisition of atomic bombs.

General Dacey, who was then on the staff of the 509th, remembers well that exercise: "If we were to go to war, we'd have to go to Camp Hood, Texas, to pick up the weapons. . . . My assignment was as an advance man when we moved into Camp Hood. I talked to the Atomic Energy Commission people. (The Manhattan District had now become the AEC.) They had elaborate procedures for turning over the weapons. I met with them, signed their documents, and so forth."[11]

But Dacey gradually realized that all the signatures in the world would not be enough to hasten their system. He simply had to wait for their procedures to ripen. "I finally negotiated a deal that would let me sign for all the bombs so I could pass them out. Then we had a big exercise in loading and down-loading. But the AEC at Camp Hood had only one teletype machine, so it took days before SAC headquarters [in Omaha] even found out whether its planes had arrived, or finished [the assignment] or departed.''

It was not long before Dacey became aware why he had been assigned to go through this entire rigamarole. ''One of the purposes, I later learned, was to show that we didn't have the communications to manage such a thing. LeMay had set up the exercise to prove this.''

The result of this and other frustrating demonstrations was that SAC soon had the responsibility of storing, guarding, assembling, and transporting its atomic weapons. And in addition, it had a brand new, worldwide communications system. It needed one because on June 25, 1950, war broke out between North and South Korea when troops from the Communist North crossed the 38th-parallel border in an all-out invasion of the South.

Because the United Nations and the United States had guaranteed the integrity of South Korea, the U.N. Security Council declared the invasion ''a breach of the peace'' and demanded withdrawal. The American military commander in Japan, Gen. Douglas MacArthur, sent ten fighter planes to the South Korean air force immediately. Two days later, President Truman confirmed America's intention of providing military support to South Korea, and America was officially involved in what was then called a ''police action,'' but what we now know as the Korean War.

The Strategic Air Command was placed in an awkward position by this development because its mission was not to become involved in civil wars within small nations, but to hold itself in readiness for the possibility of a nuclear attack against the United States by a major power. Since the major power most often mentioned in this respect was Russia, which shared the same political ideology as North Korea and its sponsor, Mainland China, there was now more reason than ever for SAC to be on the alert against the possible arrival of nuclear bombs in the United States. Nevertheless, because SAC was such an important part of the American military arsenal, it was natural that people should expect SAC to do its part in Korea. Curt LeMay was aware of all this, and he had a suggestion that was not surprising from a man who was never ready to stand still and who seemed always ready to fight.

"We slipped a little idea under the door up there in the Pentagon," he told a panel of interviewers of 1972. "Maybe if we turned SAC loose, not with atomic weapons but with some incendiaries, against four or five towns in North Korea, this will convince them we mean business and maybe it'll stop it. Well, the answer is, 'No, you can't do this. . . . You'll kill too many noncombatants.' "[12]

The popular conception of LeMay is that he might get quite a kick out of that. Isn't he the one-and-only Mr. Big Bang? A man who would never choose any other course if bombing were open to him? Wouldn't he rather bomb than play golf? Wouldn't he rather wipe out a city than eat a good dinner? Suggestions like the one above have tended to make a lot of people think so and he has seldom tried publicly to disabuse them. But LeMay's inclinations and theories about the use of force have never been as simple as they appeared to be. Having been for twenty-five years an Air Force general whose job it was to command aerial bombardment units, he would hardly qualify as a draft-card-burning pacifist. Yet his theories about military action were based on a belief that by quick, overpowering attacks, wars could be shortened and, thereby, lives saved. To him, the Korean conflict offered a perfect opportunity to prove this belief.

"So we go on and we don't do it," he reminded that 1972 panel of interviewers, "and [we] let the war go on. Over a period of three-and-a-half or four years [actually thirty-seven months] we did burn down every town in North Korea and every town in South Korea. . . . And what? Killed off 20 percent of the Korean population. . . . What I'm trying to say is if once you make a decision to use military force to solve your problem, then you ought to use it and use an overwhelming military force. Use too much and deliberately use too much so that you don't make an error on the other side and not quite have enough. And you roll over everything to start with and you close it down just like that. And you save resources, you save lives—not only your own but the enemy's, too, and the recovery is quicker and everybody's back to peaceful existence hopefully in a shorter period of time."

Some people would say he was overly hopeful in this appraisal. A massive, overwhelming air campaign against North Korea might have ended the war shortly after it started, as LeMay evidently believed. There are those, however, who believe that it would simply have brought Mainland China into the conflict immediately, before our ground forces were strong enough to resist theirs. This question, which is frequently argued, is not likely ever to be resolved. No one can say for certain whether a storm of bombs would have brought a quick North Korean surrender, or whether it would have produced a full-scale war with China. Many people are not yet convinced that air power can be decisive in any war, despite the evidence of what it did to Japan in World War II. But if a massive nonnuclear bombing response to the North Korean aggression had been launched, it might at least have provided a test of the air-power argument. It could conceivably have prevented a recurrence of the same argument during the subsequent Vietnam War.

In the early months of the Korean War, the strategic use of air power (as opposed to its tactical use) was tried with remarkable success. Five days after General MacArthur called for air support to help his meager forces, SAC had B-29s in action against North Korea. "I sent one crew out on such short notice," LeMay recalls, "they couldn't even go home and pack. We had what we called 'flyaway' kits. Spare parts and so forth, including necessities for the crews."

Two SAC units, the Twenty-second Bomb Group from March Field and the Ninety-second from Spokane, moved immediately to Okinawa and Japan, where they became the core of the newly organized Far East Bomber Command under Rosey O'Donnell, who was then a major general. The Nineteenth Bomb Wing of the Twentieth Air Force, then stationed on Guam, had already been moved in to augment the Thirty-first Photo Reconnaissance Squadron, which was the only SAC unit on hand when the fighting began.

Because MacArthur's immediate need was for support of his ground forces, the initial task of the B-29s was to attack the enemy's roads and rail-supply lines. Not until late July was the Far East Bomber Command freed to launch its first strategic strike, against Wonsan. This was followed by increasingly effective raids against industrial targets at Hungnam, Pyongyang, Chonglin, Kanggye, Sakchu, Pukchin, and Sinuiju. By mid-November, the strategic campaign had been brought to a virtual halt in the belief that all the strategic targets had now been destroyed. And indeed, there was considerable truth to this, as American ground forces discovered when they moved north on the drive to the Yalu River. MacArthur, who had never been a strong advocate of strategic air power, used the B-29s thereafter primarily for ground support, a function they had not been designed to fulfull.

Though LeMay never reconciled himself to this use of SAC units, he did not vigorously struggle against it. Long after the Korean War had run its tragic course, he said of SAC's participation, "It wasn't our real mission. It was a disruption of our main purpose, but it had to be done."

CHAPTER TWENTY

Directly after World War II, so many countries fell under Communist domination that by 1950, an estimated one-third of the world's population was controlled by Communist governments. And to most Americans, control by Communists meant control by Russia and its brutal dictator, Josef Stalin. How had this happened? Hadn't we fought the war to ensure freedom all over the world? And hadn't we won? How come the Russians were enjoying so many of the fruits of our victory? Whose fault was it? There had to be some people in this country who were to blame for letting them get away with it. Or even worse, for helping them get away with it. The thing to do was find those people, wherever they were, expose them, and punish them.

By the time Curtis LeMay took command of SAC, so many Americans were engaged in hunting "reds" it was almost an industry. On September 30, 1948, Rep. John McDowell, Republican of Pennsylvania, acting chairman of the House Un-American Activities Committee, charged that during the war, "one hundred or more" U.S. military secrets had fallen into the hands of the Russians. On December 6, the same committee announced that Whittaker Chambers, a confessed ex-Communist, had accused a high State Department official named Alger Hiss of giving him restricted departmental papers for transmission to a Soviet agent. Hiss was indicted December 15, on charges of perjury, and was eventually convicted after one of the most famous trials of the twentieth century.

In June 1949, another member of the House Un-American Activities Committee, Rep. John S. Wood, Democrat of Georgia, sent letters to seventy colleges and to boards of education in every state, asking them to report on textbooks that might contain Communist propaganda.

On May 2, 1950, FBI Director J. Edgar Hoover, in a New York City speech, said that the admittedly small (fifty-five thousand members) Communist Party in the United States, nevertheless had a half million fellow travelers "constantly gnawing away at the very foundations of American society." And on June 29, eight prominent Hollywood figures, all either writers, directors, or producers, were convicted of contempt of Congress because they refused to tell the House Un-American Activities Committee whether they were Communists.

It is not surprising that General LeMay, given his long-standing hatred of Communism, and surrounded by this nationwide atmosphere of distrust, should become acutely worried about military security within the Strategic Air Command. In a letter to General Vandenberg, December 12, 1949, he called attention to the importance of security measures in developing an air defense system:

> As the situation stands today, the information available to us indicates that the USSR has the capability of penetrating all Strategic Air Command stations to the extent required to immobilize through sabotage the combat units based thereon. . . . I am forced to the conclusion that we are henceforth faced with the constant possibility of losing a significant measure of our mobility because of an inability to maintain . . . both an offensive and a defensive capability. Specifically, we lack the one element which I am convinced is a prerequisite to the development of an adequate defense capability within the command—namely personnel trained, organized and distributed in sufficient strength to perform the security function as a primary mission.

What he wanted, in other words, was a highly efficient security organization that had no other duties. Looking back on this situation many years later, LeMay remarked that his basic thought in developing the now-famous SAC security system was that "we had to operate every day as if it were war. I knew that whenever an outfit went into combat, they always screwed up the first mission. We couldn't afford that."

Though he was aware that the United States was then losing its monopoly of nuclear weapons, he did not consider Russia was the immediate threat to SAC security. Like many Americans at the time, he anticipated danger from within. "The Russians didn't threaten us. But I was worried about fifth column activity. Sabotage. The Army had the chore of protecting our bases, but they weren't doing anything about it. And the stupidest people we had in the Air Force were put in the Military Police.''[1]

Since he was stuck with these people, he had to figure out how best to use them. He decided he might get some good out of them if he were to shore up their morale and instill some pride into them—convince them they were special, and their outfit was elite. ''I had to make them feel they were part of the team. If they didn't do their job, we couldn't do ours.''

This meant he had to fire some of the more incompetent people in his police section, and one of the first to go was the SAC provost marshal. Several airmen from Offutt got into trouble one night in a notoriously tough part of south Omaha and were badly beaten by a gang of hoodlums. The next morning, LeMay called the provost marshal into his office and asked him, disarmingly, to describe his job.

The provost marshal, apparently not very bright, began reciting the description of his duties as if he were reading from an Army manual. LeMay let him talk until he ran down, then said, simply, ''You're fired.''

The poor man didn't know what had hit him until one of the officers on LeMay's staff explained to him what he should have said: that he was in charge of the police around there and that he was so mad about what had happened the previous night he was about to go into Omaha and tear the town apart.

While LeMay was culling the misfits, he was also devising ways to upgrade the entire military police system in SAC. ''The first thing I did,'' he recalls, ''was to dress up the police there at Offutt. I gave them special uniforms. Got them some berets and white belts and revolvers, just to make them look different. I made them dress up and shine their boots. We had a guard mount every day. They'd pass the responsibility for the base from the old guard to the new.''

As soon as he got them spruced up, he had them retrained in modern police procedures, and in antisabotage measures, at the SAC Security School that he instituted at Fort Carson, Colorado. Then he began testing their skills with practical problems. At first they were relatively simple—how to detect and deal with forged passes, phony messages, suspicious packages. But gradually the games became more serious, and sometimes almost deadly.

"I got some teams together to try to penetrate the bases and do some simulated sabotage. They would play all kinds of tricks to fool the guards. And they got to be pretty good."

But by that time, so did the guards. It has been estimated that 98 percent of these penetration attempts by SAC teams against SAC bases end in failure. But anyone who has ever been a part of SAC can tell stories about "sabotage" plots that either succeeded or came close to it.

Perhaps the most embarrassing of these stories was one that didn't involve a penetration team. Or any team at all. It was about a teenaged Omaha boy who decided to go hunting one day. He simply slipped through the Offutt fence at a convenient place and was innocently wandering around the base with a shotgun over his arm when someone decided it would be a good idea to stop him and question him.

Sgt. Edwin O. Learnard, who spent ten years in SAC, was stationed at MacDill Field near Tampa, Florida, with the 305th Bomb Group (LeMay's old World War II outfit) when the base suffered a penetration that was more than embarrassing to all the SAC people stationed there.

"A blue Air Force van drove up to the main security gate to the flight line," Learnard recalls. "The security policeman nodded to the two white-clad occupants of the van and waved them through. Had [he] checked their flight line badges closely . . . he would have seen that one bore the photo of Josef Stalin, the other, Mickey Mouse. But it was 0630, exactly the time the mess hall sent a large container of fresh coffee for those who worked in the command post."[2]

Carrying what looked like a coffee container into the command post, the two men walked over to a door marked RESTRICTED and pressed a buzzer. Someone inside glanced at them through a window and unlocked the door. They entered, put down their "coffee" container, then handed the duty officer a note that said:

This is an exercise. Had this been a real circumstance everyone in this room would now be dead and the command post totally destroyed.

At the same time, a confederate of these "coffee planters," dressed in greasy coveralls and carrying a large toolbox, had reached one of the hangars and climbed up into the cockpit of a

SAC bomber, where he left one of several rolls of toilet paper he was carrying in his box. On the roll was a message that read:

This is an exercise: This is a simulated bomb that will detonate in 15 minutes. The time is now 0634.

When the grease-streaked conspirator climbed down out of the airplane, he found in front of him, to his great delight, an unattended staff car with a commanding officer's flag on its rear fender and the keys in the ignition. What could be more convenient? He jumped in the car and drove it straight down the flight line, tossing one of his message-tagged rolls of toilet paper under every bomber he passed.

Sergeant Learnard remembers that the embarrassment on the base was only one result of this simulated security breach. Even worse was the verdict from SAC headquarters in Omaha:

LeMay's first action was to fire the wing commander. Other heads rolled as well. . . . As a final touch, LeMay ordered that all personnel would attend a complete reading of Air Force Regulation 205-1, Security, and would be required to pass a test on this regulation. Readings would commence at 0500 each morning. Anyone failing the test would be required to go through this procedure again and again until he did pass.

As one who stood for two hours, 0500 to 0700 each morning for five days, and as one who was later used on a penetration team, I can vouch that security in Strategic Air Command improved to the point where it was the best in the Armed Forces.

Later in his career, Learnard became a noncommissioned intelligence officer, and on one occasion was assigned to penetrate a secret briefing of the 364th Squadron at MacDill. He did get into the meeting room, and was so nonchalant that when the commanding officer told everyone in the room to look each other over to make sure there were no unauthorized people present, several minutes passed before he was spotted. Fortunately for him, he escaped before they had time to pounce on him. Members of penetration teams were in for hard times when they got caught. "I kept a low profile on the base for some time after that," Learnard recalls.

The LeMay chef, Sergeant Waterman, found out one day how

dangerous it was to get caught up in this kind of security business. He and four other enlisted men were appointed as "volunteers" for a little project that some diabolical intelligence officer had devised. The five men were dropped off at various places on the base and told to snoop around in areas where they didn't belong until they were caught. If no one had caught them after two hours, they were to arrest the person with whom they were then talking.

The other four were soon caught, but because Waterman knew a lot of people on the base by this time, no one suspected him of being a security agent. He realized, when the two hours were almost up, that this had created a problem for him. He didn't want to arrest a friend.

"I was trying to find someone to take in who wasn't my buddy," he recalls. "Then I ran into this technical sergeant. I talked to him a while and he told me what he was doing. Finally I said, 'Sarge, I'm sorry. I'm gonna have to take you in. I'm a security volunteer.'

"Well, that man hit me so hard he knocked me on my butt. Broke my glasses and cut my eyebrow. Then he grabbed me by the scruff and dragged me down to the orderly room. They questioned me about who I was but nobody believed me. So they took me to the guardhouse."

Meanwhile, Helen LeMay was getting worried because Waterman hadn't shown up to cook lunch, a fact which she duly reported to her husband. He was apparently aware of the morning's security caper. "Don't worry," he told her, "I know where he must be."

LeMay drove to the guardhouse and there was Waterman, beaten and bedraggled, sitting in a cell. When the two of them got back home, Helen LeMay took a look at Waterman and immediately got mad at her husband for allowing the poor man to be so badly treated.

"We've got a slogan," Curt said to her. " 'Always keep your defense up.' Waterman didn't have his defense up."

LeMay was almost caught without his own defense up in another penetration plot which reached his very office. When asked about this story on one occasion, he said he couldn't remember it happening, but other people do remember it and recently, after stopping to think about it, he said he guessed it really did happen.

He was at his desk one morning when three men came in to

work on his telephone system. Nothing unusual about that. The commanding general of SAC has a somewhat more complicated telephone setup than the average person. It often needs repairs or upgrading. He got out of the way and allowed the men to get on with their work, which included a lot of sliding around under his desk, where there was a maze of wires.

The men weren't there long, however. They seemed to get their work done rather quickly. And they were ready to leave when he noticed something unusual about them. They were wearing green G.I. fatigues. If they were from the phone company, they'd be civilians.

As they walked toward the door, LeMay went to his desk, grabbed an automatic, followed them out, and held them at gunpoint in the corridor. When the Air Police arrived, they looked under his desk and found a beer can with a note inside. It said: "You will be blown up at 1030."

On another occasion, Mrs. LeMay was the victim of her husband's perilous and scary security system. Right after a group of Puerto Ricans tried to assassinate President Truman in November 1950, guards were stationed for a time outside the LeMay quarters at Offutt. One day, Helen was in the back yard whan a guard came up to her and asked her to show him her identification.

She told him who she was.

He said he didn't recognize her.

She said, "Well, I'm not in the habit of carrying identification every time I step out the back door."

"In that case," he said, "I'll have to take you to the guardhouse." From this moment forward, their dialogue became less and less congenial until he backed her against the wall and used his bayonet to reason with her. She soon saw the point of his logic and went into the house to get her identification. But she was still upset about his method of argument.

When her husband came home that afternoon, he stopped in the kitchen to have a sandwich and a beer. While he was talking to Sergeant Waterman, she came storming in to tell him, in her own style of persuasion, what she thought about the conduct of his back-yard guard.

LeMay looked at Waterman, winked, and smiled. "I think that boy was right," he said to her. "You are a suspicious-looking character."

As the incident with the telephone repairmen shows, LeMay

himself was not privy to all the penetration plots, or even to most of them. Many were directed at him, and that was the way he wanted it. If it was possible to capture or incapacitate the commander of SAC, he wanted to know it because that would mean the protective measures then in force were not good enough. They would have to be improved. One of the most ambitious schemes ever launched at SAC was an attempt to kidnap LeMay.

One of the standard operating procedures was to prevent any unknown plane, or any plane without a flight plan, from taxiing in to the flight line without permission after landing. If such a plane landed at a SAC base, its pilot was ordered to stop, off the end of the runway, until security police went out to establish its identity and its reason for landing.

One night a plane landed at Offutt, somehow got to the flight line without clearance, and stopped directly in front of the Operations building. A half dozen men got out of it, wearing the same kind of white coveralls the alert crew wore.

"Where's the can!" they shouted to the alert crew. "Where's the can!"

Since they seemed to be in dire need, someone said, "Right through that door."

Right through that door they went, but not to the toilet. They soon spread out through the base on the next phase of their mission, which was to disrupt the communications system before kidnapping LeMay.

They had made what seemed like a brilliant beginning except in one respect. They had alerted the entire security system which, by this time, was functioning smoothly. It was the middle of the night before LeMay even realized anything untoward was happening. He was awakened by a commotion outside his bedroom window.

"I looked out and saw this guard pointing his gun at a couple of men lying face-down in the street. It seemed as if he had things well in hand, so I went back to bed." The next morning, he found out that all the penetrators had been captured. He was beginning to think his Air Police weren't so stupid after all.

CHAPTER TWENTY-ONE

In October 1951, SAC received its first acceptable jet bomber—Boeing's B-47 Stratojet. An earlier jet, North American's RB-45, a reconnaissance bomber, had come to SAC in July 1950, but it had found no welcome there. After putting it through SAC's rigorous series of tests, LeMay had decided it could never be the intercontinental jet bomber SAC needed. Perhaps it was his lack of faith in the RB-45 that prompted him to go and learn to fly the B-47 while it was still in an experimental stage. In this plane he soon developed confidence and his confidence proved to be well placed.

At the end of 1951, the B-29 and its more advanced model, the B-50, still formed the bulk of SAC's striking force, and neither plane could be called a long-range, intercontinental bomber in the modern sense. The B-29 had been redesignated a "medium" bomber with the arrival of the B-36, which was the first American bomber capable of reaching Russia and returning nonstop. But even as 1952 began, only one of SAC's three air forces, the Eighth, had been equipped with the B-36.

The B-47 could not match the B-36 in range. It would be capable of a mission to Moscow only by refueling in flight. Fortunately, the arrival at SAC of the Boeing KC-97 tanker plane in the early summer of 1951 gave it that capability. And the jet speed of the B-47 was so much greater than that of the B-36 or any Russian bomber that its introduction could properly be said to have heralded a new era, the jet age, in strategic air power.

The arrival of the new B-47 jet was not the only thing for which Curtis LeMay had reason to be thankful in October 1951. His nomination to full, four-star generalship came that month. And unlike his nomination to one-star generalship eight years earlier, he didn't feel it was tardy. Only Ulysses S. Grant and

315

himself had earned four stars by the age of forty-five, as he later noted. Grant was forty-four when he achieved that rank.

After three years in command of SAC, LeMay had imbedded his stamp so deeply into the organization that to the public, he was the personification of SAC. And to the men of SAC, even those who had never seen him, he had become something like an iron-assed god. Lt. Gen. Richard M. "Dick" Montgomery, Ret., who was summoned to Offutt from El Paso to become Augie Kissner's deputy in 1951, still remembers with trepidation the day he had to brief "the boss" for the first time.

Though he was already a major general at the time, Montgomery recalled later that "I came in there in fear and trembling. I had never met General LeMay [but] I looked on him as if he were a god. The first day I was alone [in the office] something important came up. Shaking in my boots, I went in to brief him. This will give you [an idea of] the reaction of someone who comes in to brief LeMay. He fixes you with his eyes and just sits there. It looks as if he's going to bore a hole right through you. It's very upsetting to people not used to him. It took me months to learn that behind that stern look was a heart of gold. Tough, yes. He was tough on people who didn't do their jobs properly, but if you did a good job, he would reward you. He was understanding and, I found, very tender underneath. He could get angry and [he would] chew you out in a quiet voice but I don't think I ever heard him raise his voice."[1]

Dick Montgomery apparently did his job very well. In 1952, when Augie Kissner was dispatched to Spain and Portugal on a delicate diplomatic mission that resulted in the construction of essential SAC bases in the Azores, Montgomery took his place as chief of staff. As for the people who didn't "do their jobs properly," not many of them would say LeMay had a "heart of gold." He could be tough. But there is evidence that he had more than a little concern for the men under him. Montgomery recalls that while he was chief of staff, during the period of SAC's greatest expansion, between 1952 and 1956, LeMay "spent sixty or seventy percent of his time trying to improve the living conditions for the men, and trying to get family housing." It was during this period that he managed gradually to replace all the obsolete quarters at SAC bases throughout the world with newly designed barracks and houses.

General Dacey, who was assigned to the SAC headquarters staff as a major in 1950, had at least the advantage of one previous exposure to the LeMay personality. It was Dacey who led the flight of SAC planes to Fort Hood, Texas, in the exercise LeMay devised to prove that SAC, rather than the Atomic Energy Commission, would have to have physical custody of any atomic weapons SAC might be called upon to use. When Dacey arrived at Omaha in December 1950, he had been warned that LeMay could be severe and harsh, but what impressed him immediately was LeMay's grasp of everything happening around him.

"This was when we were beginning to build up the force," Dacey recalls. "SAC headquarters was still in the old bomber factory where the *Enola Gay* was built. The only paved street in Bellevue [the Omaha suburb adjacent to Offutt] was Mission Street. There were dirt roads and corn fields in all directions. But the B-47s were coming soon and they were going to produce them like doughnuts. We had many new stations. There was a lot going on. And LeMay was in charge. His grasp of it was exceptional. We young staff officers would go in to him with charts, and so forth. And on occasion he would countermand our plans. We'd leave his office saying [to each other], 'This time he's wrong.' But it never happened. He was right every time. The guy was something of a military genius. One definition of genius is simplicity of approach. Ability to put things in a way that a lot of dumb people can easily understand. And he could do that. But severe and harsh? No. It wasn't true. He had a great feeling for the troops. A genuine concern. He was not a showboat. Didn't try to prove what a great fellow he was. But he was a great fellow."[2]

Dacey entertained more varied feelings about some of the men around LeMay. His opinion of SAC's deputy commander, Tom Power, for instance, paralleled that of others who worked with Power. He was "a great implementer" of LeMay's ideas, Dacey agreed, but he was also "a mean S.O.B."

LeMay himself has made it clear that he realized Power's personality problems, but "he got the job done." There were others who, in Dacey's opinion, didn't do their jobs quite as well, and sometimes got themselves into trouble, but remained on the staff because they had done such good work for LeMay in previous assignments that he remained loyal to them, or simply because they had a certain flamboyance that intrigued him. Though LeMay himself didn't get into reckless adventures or drink excessively or chase women, Dacey felt that he was to a degree fascinated by some men who did.

One of them, who had quit the Air Force before World War II and flown all over the world, then returned to the service when the Japanese attacked, was a particular favorite of LeMay. They had shared some memorable flying experiences in India. But to Dacey, "he was a crazy man, with women and everything else." Another, who had been a great fighter pilot in World War II, was, "I won't say a bad actor, but a good old boy."

This good old boy got in trouble at the Offutt Officers' Club one night when the World War II Marine fighter ace, Joe Foss, visited the base. The good old boy said, "We don't want any Marines around here," and, as Dacey recalls, "knocked Foss on his ass."

Thereupon, one of the good old boy's subordinate officers said to him, "That's not a nice thing to do."

To which the good old boy replied, "I'll knock you on your ass, too."

But unfortunately for him, his subordinate was a weight lifter and a one-time boxer. In front of a crowd outside the officers' club, he gave the good old boy's head such a severe massaging with his fists that the base hospital had to swathe it in bandages.

LeMay was away at the time. When Augie Kissner, his chief of staff, called the two men into his office for an explanation, they had already sobered up and agreed on a story. They were practicing judo when the good old boy fell, hitting his head.

Kissner said, "You can tell that to LeMay when he gets back, but I don't think it will fly."

On LeMay's return, he called in the subordinate, who tried the same judo story. As Kissner had predicted, it didn't fly, but fortunately, the subordinate was also a man who had served LeMay well in years past.

"If you ever again lay a hand on your commanding officer," LeMay said, "I'll drive you out of the Air Force."

However, the subordinate later remarked, "He had a twinkle in his eye when he said it."

The demands LeMay and SAC made upon its men were so rigorous that it's not surprising if some of them drank too much and raised hell once in awhile. LeMay himself admits he worked his SAC crews sometimes as much as ninety hours a week. How he got away with that is something a lot of other military commanders would like to figure out. General Dacey recalls that when he was still a SAC aircrew commander stationed at Langley Field in Virginia on aerial alert, "We'd go for twenty-four hours. Over to the Mediterranean, circle the Mediterranean, meet a tanker out of Spain [to refuel], and come back to the United States the next day [without ever touching ground]. That drags you out."

Dacey, not only as an aircrew commander but later as a staff officer at SAC headquarters, had an excellent opportunity to observe LeMay's methods of handling the psychological burdens he was imposing on the crews. The improvement of their housing, the hobby shops, the spot promotions, the pride in belonging to an elite, unique, and perhaps militarily decisive organization were all factors in helping the men bear those burdens. Still, human limitations had to be taken into account.

"Tell those people they're good enough to do it," Dacey discovered, "and they can do it. Let them make a mistake once in awhile [then] let them know you know it. It's amazing how they respond. But the strain, day after day, year after year—I think what you have to do is make [the quality of] their lives as good as you can. Try to show them what they do is appreciated. As long as they could get promoted [it seemed to work]. We were promoting as high as lieutenant colonel. When they got to that and they knew they weren't going to get any farther, it [the psychological burden] got worse. Tom Power wanted to make them colonels but that wouldn't work because of the table of organization."

Dacey's conclusion was, "You can't spend a whole career in the cockpit. It [military flying] is not like an airline. When they wore out, we gave them jobs in operations and things like that."

Col. Stuart McLennan, a friend of LeMay's since their days at Kelly Field flying school, tells a story about another human limitation with which the commander of SAC had to contend. It's a story told to McLennan by the late Gen. Samuel Anderson who, for several years during his distinguished career, was commander of SAC's Eighth Air Force.

"Sam told me this before he died," McLennan recalls. "Every year there were competitions between the SAC air forces in navigation, bombing accuracy, and things like that. Anderson found out that some of the other SAC air forces were cheating. They were using civilian navigation aids and so forth. He flew up to Omaha and told Curt. And he said that as he told him, tears came to Curt's eyes. He couldn't believe that [men in] his wonderful organization could do such a thing." But apparently he was soon convinced. "He called in the other Air Force commanders and raised hell."[3]

Such problems and setbacks never seemed to diminish LeMay's pride in his unique command. He believed, and many experts agree, that SAC was now the most efficient military organization the world had ever seen. This had not, however, persuaded LeMay that he could relax. He hadn't run out of ideas that he thought would further improve SAC. Then in early March 1952, it suddenly began to look as if he wouldn't be around to implement them.

The White House unexpectedly announced that Gen. Hoyt Vandenberg was to be reappointed for one year as Air Force chief of staff, and LeMay was to be shipped to Washington as his vice chief, while the current vice chief, General Nathan Twining, would be transferred to Omaha as commander of SAC.

Aviation Week magazine, in announcing the LeMay-Twining shuffle, speculated that it "gave credence to previous reports that [LeMay] eventually is slated to replace Vandenberg as Chief of Staff. Apparent reasoning behind the move is to put LeMay in a role which will enable the Air Force and Administration to test his ability as a diplomat and arm chair strategist. Previously he had been in some disfavor with the State Department because of his bluntness."[4]

The *Washington Post* said in an editorial: "The brusque Gen. LeMay has acquired a reputation as a narrow partisan of strategic bombing policy, a natural result of his SAC command and his earlier bombing commands. Perhaps that is an asset to the kind of job he has held, but it has raised many questions about his breadth of outlook. . . . [The transfer] will permit closer scrutiny of Gen. LeMay in a job of wiser responsibility."

LeMay himself was apparently reconciled to the transfer and perhaps even enthusiastic about it. Gen. Frederic Smith, a colleague, remembers seeing LeMay with Helen in Colorado Springs at the time, and hearing Helen announce, without any noticeable displeasure, that Curt was to be the next vice chief of staff.[5]

However, it was not to be. The appointment was withdrawn as suddenly as it had been announced. And no explanation was forthcoming. LeMay himself, even in later life, has been reluctant to discuss the incident. But he may have been referring to it obliquely when he wrote about his eventual appointment as vice chief in 1957.

> There were those, especially in other commands, who had held to the opinion that I would never be called upon to serve in such a capacity, because I was considered to be strictly a bombardment man. It wasn't true, but newspaper columnists reaffirmed this belief from time to time. . . . They'd say, "LeMay's a bomber general. Just like the old battleship admirals." They blandly ignored the fact that I labored to get additional missiles during the same time that I battled for a manned system. I battled for interceptors to bolster up our air defenses in the same hours when I strove to get us the new manned strategic system. I concentrated as firmly as possible on my particular job at the time, whatever it was. That may have given the impression to some undiscerning souls that I didn't think about anything else. But I did.[6]

He obviously felt there were some influential colleagues in Washington who simply didn't want him there. Given his penchant for reverse diplomacy, and his tendency to dominate any scene he entered, it's a safe bet that he was right.

In January 1951, the Air Force had signed a contract with Consolidated Vultee to begin work on what was to become known as the Atlas Missile Project. This was the first overt indication that the Air Force was moving toward a serious consideration of intercontinental ballistic missiles, which might one day replace the bombers of SAC. LeMay believed at this time that it would be many years before the potential of such missiles could be realized. And everyone else believed the same thing at the time. But because LeMay's primary business had always been bombers, he became saddled with the reputation of being opposed to missiles. Though he insisted it had never been true, he was destined to be hounded by that reputation through the rest of his career.

As soon as the flurry of excitement over his abortive 1952 vice chief appointment abated, LeMay returned his attention, apparently with as much enthusiasm as ever, to the further improvement of SAC. Aware that his crews had constantly to face the possibility of a crash landing in a remote area, or even, if war were to come, within enemy territory, he founded a survival school near Reno, Nevada. By 1957, twenty-three thousand of his crew members had graduated from this seventeen-day course in how to subsist under wilderness conditions and how to escape from enemy territory.

The possibility, indeed the very real incidence, of crashes posed a problem against which he had been struggling since the day he arrived at SAC. In 1948, SAC aircraft and crews were being subjected to major accidents at the rate of sixty-five for every hundred thousand hours in the air.

This was happening, LeMay decided, because nobody at SAC in 1948 was using standard operating procedures. "It's difficult to believe that no one was using checklists for takeoff. But it's true."

He quickly took action to correct that, and he launched a safety campaign. Then he ordered that operating procedure manuals be written for every job in the command. And finally he instituted a new rule: "Every time a commander suffered a major accident in his wing, he came to Offutt to see me about it. We went into the matter from every angle. They didn't like the idea of coming up there and standing on that unpleasant piece of carpet in front of my desk, but it's what I made them do. We were going to find out how that accident happened and why."

Many of the commanders came in with the same story. They couldn't understand the crash because one of their best pilots was flying the airplane. LeMay soon developed a theory which he hoped would help them understand it. The stupid pilot follows procedures. But procedures are beneath the best pilot. He doesn't need checklists. They're for neophytes. All he has to do is get in the airplane and go. So he does it his way and he crashes. "It was the sort of education which was needed desperately," LeMay has recalled, "yet which wasn't come by popularly. It was a bitter, rigid process. Still, we made steady advances."

In fact, the advances were more than steady. They were dramatic. From the sixty-five major accidents per hundred thousand flying hours in 1948, SAC reduced its rate to forty-three in 1950 and thirty-one in 1951. This decline continued until in 1956, LeMay's last full year at SAC, the accident rate was only nine per hundred thousand flying hours.

In November 1952, LeMay did something he had done only once before, in 1928. He voted. Like most military officers, he had purposely avoided voting from the time he entered the service. "I had always felt national defense was a nonpartisan issue," he said later. "The military shouldn't participate in it. In some small towns [for instance], if the military voted, they'd control the election. That was the general Army feeling.''

As time passed, however, he gradually became convinced that the military should vote. ''In 1952 I changed my mind when I got up high enough in rank to know how much politics had to do with maintaining an adequate defense. I not only voted myself. I urged all my troops to vote.''[7]

Needless to say, given his deep conservative convictions, he voted for the Republican, Gen. Dwight Eisenhower, rather than the Democrat, Gov. Adlai Stevenson.

''I had a basic feeling that Ike knew more than Stevenson about national defense. Then too, I was always conservative and I thought Eisenhower was.'' When LeMay said this, he placed a slight emphasis on the word ''thought,'' indicating that, as time passed, he became less convinced of Ike's conservatism. LeMay's standards for judging a man's conservatism were as exacting as his standards for judging a man's military performance.

The Korean War ended in July 1953, but there were other developments to prevent any relaxation of international tensions. On June 17, Russian tanks rolled into Berlin to quell riots by East German workers. On November 1, 1952, the United States had exploded the world's first hydrogen bomb at Eniwetok, but by August 1953, the Russians had exploded one of their own. The new bomb increased the potential impact of SAC, but it created no new operating problems. Like the older atomic weapons, it fitted nicely into the SAC bombers.

LeMay felt this was a good time to impress upon the world SAC's increasing capabilities, so he arranged a well-publicized flight of two B-36s from Japan to Maine—ten thousand miles, in twenty-eight and a half hours. Then he arranged another well-publicized flight of a B-47 jet from Maine to England. That took four hours and forty-three minutes, a speed that amazed a world not yet accustomed to jet travel.

He was eager to make everyone, especially the Europeans, realize the kind of protection SAC provided. An excellent opportunity arose when a delegation of Norwegian defense officials visited SAC headquarters in Omaha. During their day-long stay, LeMay handed to each man a copy of an aerial photo of a city they soon recognized as Oslo. ''That picture,'' he informed them, ''was taken by a SAC bomber flying over your capital this morning.''

About this time, LeMay was becoming better and better acquainted with a new friend, radio and television personality Arthur Godfrey, who would prove valuable both to him and to SAC. Godfrey had joined the Navy when he was sixteen years old and had become a radio operator on a destroyer. Later, he spent some time with the Coast Guard. When he returned to civilian life, he took flying lessons and earned a pilot's license. After becoming famous on the radio, he got into the habit of talking about his Navy experiences during his shows. The Navy, as sensitive as the Air Force to public-relations possibilities, soon took him in hand, gave him an intensive flying course at Pensacola, and a reserve commission.

"From then on," LeMay recalls, "he was a Navy guy until I got hold of him."[8]

It was through General Vandenberg that LeMay "got hold" of Godfrey. Vandenberg knew Godfrey and once took a trip with him. While they were cruising in Godfrey's refurbished DC-3, Vandenberg said to him, "Why don't you come off all this Navy pitch you're putting out all the time. Put out a true story for a change."

"What is the true story?" Godfrey challenged.

"Go out to SAC," Vandenberg said, "and they'll show you."

In due time, Godfrey did fly out to SAC, and LeMay, who was waiting for him, took him on a thorough inspection trip.

"It sold him," LeMay recalls. "From then on, he did nothing [on his shows] but talk about SAC. It drove the Navy wild. They had an admiral trying to keep an eye on him, but he resigned his Navy commission."

The Air Force couldn't give him a straight commission because, by this time, he had been in an automobile accident and had only one workable lung. "But we made him a colonel in the Air Force Reserve one day," LeMay recalls, "then retired him the next day." In the meantime, Godfrey had become much more than an instrument of publicity to LeMay. They gradually became close friends. They spent time together, went on hunting trips together, corresponded, and exchanged gifts until Godfrey's death in 1983.

LeMay's personal family life at Offutt continued to be fairly smooth and uneventful. Helen kept herself busy managing the household and doing Air Force relief work. Janie, a young teenager now, had to suffer the usual problems of being a commanding officer's daughter. "Whenever you'd move to a new place," she recalls, "people would think you were going to be snobbish or stuck up. So until they get to know you, you were an outcast." She attended a private school in Omaha, Brownwood Hall, which she didn't enjoy. "It had once been a country club. The people there didn't want the military so I never did anything with those girls. I simply went to school, and then I left."

Except when he was traveling, LeMay and Helen almost always ate at home. Whenever a social engagement was avoidable, he avoided it. Janie would come to the table with them but she usually ate very little because "they were always having fish. Daddy would go fishing. Salmon. I couldn't stand it. So I'd tell Sergeant Waterman what I wanted, and half my body became Franco American spaghetti out of a can. That's what I liked. Or creamed tuna fish on toast. And tons of chocolate cookies. Waterman made the best toll house cookies."

Perhaps even better than fish, her father liked steak. He still preferred simple foods but he also developed a taste for Waterman's Chinese and Mexican dishes. For recreation, he stuck to the pastimes he had always loved. He built and rebuilt sports cars at the Offutt hobby shop, and he sponsored sports car races for the benefit of the enlisted men's housing fund. He broadcast frequently on his ham radio (his call name was Curt, with no further identification) and he built, with the help of the base electronics expert and a commercial kit, a workable color television set. He practiced target shooting and he went hunting, sometimes with Arthur Godfrey, sometimes with Arthur Storz at the Omaha brewer's hunting lodge. He had become very friendly with Storz and with many other Omaha people who went out of their way to help SAC. In May of 1954, he even went so far as to dress up in a Civil War general's uniform to attend one of their costume parties. Helen accompanied him in a long, flowing gown straight out of the 1860s. She was as svelte as ever, but Curt's weight had climbed to 190 pounds despite her efforts to restrict him to a salad diet. Fortunately, cigars were suitable with a Civil War costume because he usually had one in his mouth now, even though he sometimes went for long periods without actually smoking.

His organization was running so smoothly that he had gradually begun to realize he was keeping his key men too long in the same jobs. In May 1953, he sent his operations chief, J. B. Montgomery, to Fort Worth in command of the Eighth Air Force, and his director of plans, Cam Sweeney, to Westover in command of the Second. Then he realized that in his zeal to keep his organization intact, he had been making another big mistake.

"I was having trouble selling ideas to the Air Staff. Nobody there had been in SAC. They didn't understand our needs." It was his own fault, of course. He had been saying no whenever the Pentagon tried to transfer his men elsewhere. "So I had to start sending people to other parts of the Air Force so there would be people up there more sympathetic."

In April 1954, he took a big step in this direction by releasing Tom Power so he could take charge of the Air Force Systems Command, which, in effect, was the research-and-development department.

Power's promotion gave LeMay an opportunity to reunite with that old friend who had accompanied him into the Army Air Corps in 1928—Francis H. "Grizzy" Griswold. By a nice co-incidence, Grizzy, now a major general, had just returned from England where he commanded the Third Air Force. LeMay quickly arranged for him to come to Omaha and replace Power as deputy commander of SAC. Since Griswold had never before been connected with SAC, there may have been some in the organization who considered him an interloper, but he soon proved his worth, not only as a smooth administrator, but as an innovator.

When Griswold came to SAC, he found LeMay fussing and fuming because the radio communication system wasn't working properly. So the two of them cooked up a scheme. First of all, Griswold undertook to earn an amateur radio operator's license. Then together they built a Heathkit amateur transmitter and began a serious exploration of the ham radio bands. They soon discovered there were now so many ham operators that the ham bands were usually jammed. Then they got hold of a manufacturer of single-side-band amateur radio equipment and borrowed a set from him. Here they found it much easier to penetrate the chatter and static. So they put one of these single-band amateur sets in an airplane (despite regulations against it) and Griswold flew the plane to the Far East while LeMay, in Omaha, kept monitoring him. "It was so much better than the standard stuff we had," LeMay later recalled, "there was no comparison."[9]

All they had to do then was to sell the single-band idea to the Air Force communications department. But that wasn't easy. The possibility that amateur sets were better than their expensive, sophisticated equipment did not find much credence in the minds of the communications people. For a while, they simply ignored this nutty notion from Omaha. Finally, at LeMay's insistence, they sent a second lieutenant to see what he was trying to sell them, and to explain to him why it wouldn't work.

LeMay and Griswold put the lieutenant in an airplane, flew him up near the North Pole, and showed him he could communicate with a station near the South Pole. Still, the communications people were unimpressed.

"So I take operational funds and buy a dozen ham stations," LeMay recalled. "Put one at SAC headquarters, put one at Goose Bay, the Azores, Morocco, England . . . and we put twenty-four hour crews on them . . . and the fact that we could talk to our airplanes anyplace in the world, this finally convinced people. Then everybody went to side band after that."

Because Griswold was inventive, efficient, and very experienced, and perhaps because his methods of handling people were so different from those of Tom Power, he soon became accepted by the men around him at SAC. General Dacey recalls that "he had great ability, and he had lots more friends than LeMay." That was hardly surprising. LeMay was notoriously slow to make friends. His paucity of conversation was a barrier to most people. In contrast, Griswold was an open, outgoing man, always ready with a quip or a funny story.

Griswold was one man who had learned to deal with LeMay's wall of silence, and as a result, their friendship had grown through the years despite the fact that they would sometimes sit for long periods without saying a word to each other. Their silences would drive their wives crazy. Helen LeMay and Jeff Griswold were never short of subjects about which to chat. But occasionally one of them would pause and say to their men, "Haven't you two anything to say to each other?" LeMay felt no obligation to answer even such questions. He was happy in Grizzy's company and that was enough. It was obvious he had brought him to Omaha for personal as well as professional reasons.

In his autobiography, LeMay said, "Grizzy enjoyed messing around cars just as much as I did. There's nothing like having an old friend [pursuing a friendship that goes back almost to childhood] who can share an identical interest with you in later life. Jeff Griswold and Helen complained that they were hobby shop widows. I'm afraid this was true. Neither Grizzy nor I had much free time, but what little we had we spent being hobbyists.

During my years in that command, I built two full-scale sports cars."[10]

LeMay and Griswold, in their greasy fatigue uniforms, used to ride to and from the hobby shop, piggyback, on Griswold's Vespa motor scooter. On occasion, they would be stopped by the Air Patrol for being out of uniform, and they would listen to the lecture patiently without telling the patrolman who they were. But once when they were stopped, the patrolman recognized them, and not knowing what else to say, he said, "The order is that general officers don't ride motorcycles."

LeMay looked up at him and said, "Yeah? Who ordered that?" Thereafter, the Air Patrol looked the other way when they flashed past on the motor scooter.

Gen. Dick Montgomery recalls a time when LeMay had an Allard sports car shipped over from England. "He and Griswold worked out a better lubrication system for it, then installed a Cadillac engine in it. They wanted a higher-power output so they altered the engine block. One Sunday they closed a five-thousand-foot runway." LeMay challenged another officer who owned a Jaguar, and the two started side-by-side. Chomping his cigar and shifting gears, LeMay stayed with the Jag up to about ninety miles an hour, but then he leveled off and the Jag pulled away. "Something was wrong with [the Cad-Allard's] carburetion. LeMay and Griswold worked on it all Sunday afternoon but didn't get it straightened out. So, when LeMay came into the office Black Monday, I looked at him and said to myself, this is no day to see him about anything. I called the staff and said, 'Don't anyone come in here today.' Fortunately, he and Griswold had the car fixed by Tuesday."[11]

Their adventures with the Cad-Allard were mild compared to what they did with an old Indianapolis race car they had somehow acquired. They put a surplus jet aircraft engine in it, and one day, LeMay wheeled it out onto a closed runway. There was quite a crowd of fascinated viewers as he revved it up, but no one came very close.

Finally, he turned it loose and went speeding down the runway. For the first half mile he was in complete control, but the one thing he hadn't counted on was the fact that a jet engine has residual thrust. When he approached the end of the runway and was ready to stop, the engine was still ready to go. So away he went, into the grass and bushes. Fortunately, he wasn't hurt. He wasn't even deterred. A few days later, he tried it again, more successfully this time because he had attached a parachute to the rear of the car.

The atomic bomb was now almost ten years old, and its invention had been followed by the creation of the hydrogen bomb. Russia had also created a hydrogen bomb by this time, but Russia had not yet developed aircraft, or an air unit comparable to SAC, that could deliver such a bomb.

The initial shock of these bombs' existence and the destructive potential they implied had soaked into the intellectual and journalistic communities so thoroughly that the philosophical debate as to the permissible limits of the use of atomic weapons by a civilized nation had already become an immensely important issue within the American conscience. In the *Washington Post,* July 13, 1954, Marquis Childs wrote that "certain Air Force generals, conspicuously Curtis LeMay, chief of SAC, have from time to time openly advocated a preventive strike that would destroy or at least permanently cripple Russian war-making centers."

Had Childs been permitted to dig deeper, he could have quoted a higher authority than LeMay on the subject of atomic weapon use. Twice in 1953, President Eisenhower had suggested, first to the Joint Chiefs of Staff, then to the National Security Council, that the use of atomic weapons in the Korean War might be permissible.[12]

Both Eisenhower and LeMay were at a disadvantage in a philosophical discussion of atomic weapon use because neither man was a philosopher. They were soldiers, and they saw the world in much less complicated terms, through the eyes of soldiers. LeMay believed, at least until the middle fifties, that SAC "could have destroyed all of Russia (I mean by that all of Russia's capability to wage war) without losing a man to their defenses." He admits having discussed this capability with some of his associates, but he denies that he ever made such a suggestion formally to any of his superiors.

"We in SAC were not saber-rattlers. We were not yelling for war and action in order to 'flex the mighty muscles we had built.' No stupidity of that sort. We wanted peace as much as anyone else wanted it. But we knew for a fact that it would be possible to curtail enemy expansion if we challenged them in that way. Some of us thought it might be better to do so then, than to wait until later.

"I never discussed the problem with President Truman or with

President Eisenhower. I never discussed it with General Vandenberg when he was chief of staff. I stuck to my job at Offutt and in the command. I never discussed what we were going to do with the force we had, or what we should do with it. . . . All I did was to keep them abreast of the development in SAC. I told them what strength we had as fast as that strength grew.''[13]

In later years, he said, ''I don't think there was ever a discussion about a preemptive war. We were always weaker than Russia in conventional war [power]. Even after we got a NATO agreement on what other countries would provide, none of them ever provided it. So if we got an all-out attack from Russia, we'd have to use atomic weapons from the start. We didn't have anything else to stop them with.''[14]

LeMay has always insisted he never advocated a preemptive war, and his reputation for honesty, right up to the point of bluntness, is unchallenged. But the fact is that the American people still think he advocated a preemptive war, and all the denials in the world won't change that. Curtis LeMay is the man who built the awesome power of SAC. It's hard for him to convince people he never wanted to use that power, even though he has said many times that the purpose of SAC was to prevent war. In his straight-line soldier's mind, the matter was always simple. Atomic weapons were powerful deterrents to war. But he didn't think they would deter a potential enemy if you told him you would never use them.

''Always I felt a more forceful policy would have been the correct one for us to embrace with the Russians,'' he wrote in his memoirs. ''I can't get over the notion that when you stand up and act like a man, you win respect.''[15] Those don't sound like the words of a philosopher. They sound like the words of a soldier.

CHAPTER TWENTY-TWO

Since the day he arrived at Offutt, Curt LeMay had been less than enchanted by the appearance, convenience, and general condition of the SAC headquarters he had inherited. The old bomber plant in which it was located looked more like a huge garage than a military command post. Foremen's cubby holes and machine-tool storage rooms had been converted into offices. From the rooms that had windows, the most compelling view was of the Omaha stockyards, and so was the aroma.

"We started right away to fight for a headquarters building," LeMay recalls, "but it was not a very high priority in the Air Force budget."

In his memoirs, there is a long story about designing an underground headquarters that the Truman administration rejected because it was too expensive; then designing an aboveground headquarters that the Eisenhower administration rejected because, in the atomic age, the SAC headquarters should be underground.[1] It's a good story and it may very well be accurate, but it's not quite the way General Griswold remembers it.

As he tells it, when he arrived at SAC in the spring of 1954, LeMay was indeed frustrated in his efforts to procure a new headquarters. For six years, Congress and the Air Force had been throwing out plan after plan. And the outlook was bleak.

"Finally, Curt and I got together," Griswold recalls, "and one of us said, 'Let's not call it a headquarters. Let's call it a control center. No congressman's got enough guts to say SAC can't have a control center.' And sure enough, the next year we got it into the budget."[2] All they had to do then was to wait a couple of more years for it to be built.

In June 1955, the first B-52s were delivered to SAC's Ninety-third Bombardment Wing at Castle Air Force Base in California, foretelling the immediate dismissal of the old B-50s (converted B-29s), and the eventual dismissal of the B-36, which LeMay had praised in 1949, but which he now considered obsolete. (In 1956, he said, "If I had my desires, all B-36s would be in the junk pile.") Though the B-52 would eventually become, and would continue for many years to be SAC's standard bomber, it was second to the B-47 at the time of its introduction because, like any new bomber, it had a lot of bugs to be eliminated while the B-47, during its four years of operation, had been freed of its bugs and developed into a very efficient machine.

The B-52 had from the start a greater potential for speed and range than the B-47, and its introduction was timely for another reason. In May 1955, Russia had unveiled its first jet bomber, the Bison, the appearance of which had frightened a lot of people in Congress. Former Secretary of the Air Force Stuart Symington, now a senator from Missouri, said in a speech from the floor on May 17, "The United States . . . may have lost control of the air."

The arrival of the B-52 did much to quell such fears. As for its bugs, they neither surprised nor dismayed LeMay. In a 1957 speech to the Air Force Scientific Advisory Board, he explained his feelings about bugs in a new aircraft.

"Initially, [a commander] must expect that any new weapon system will have very low reliability. . . . Difficulties will be encountered which were unforeseen in the laboratories and not uncovered in the testing programs. Furthermore, the rate at which these difficulties will be encountered depends upon the pace of operational experience with the equipment. Since experience with manned bomber systems is accumulated rapidly, their reliability can be increased rapidly."[3]

Not content with speaking only about bombers, he went on that day to compare them with missiles in an analysis that may have provided more ammunition for those who were already criticizing him as a "bomber general" and antimissile man.

He said, "I am confident that missile systems will not enjoy such rapid improvement in reliability. In the first place, because of their great expense, the rate of expenditure of missiles in training and simulated combat firings will necessarily be small. This means that difficulties will be uncovered over a longer period of time and the opportunity to test fixes will be correspondingly limited. Furthermore, we have had forty years' experience in the operation of manned bombers. Their initial operational problems have developed into recognizable standard patterns. We know where to anticipate trouble and in general we can forecast probable techniques for fixes. Since we are just now entering the missile era, we do not have this background. We cannot anticipate the areas in which to expect difficulties . . .''

His conclusion was that ''eventually missile systems will reach a satisfactory state of reliability, but I am certain that this will come only after long and bitter experience in the field.'' In retrospect, few would argue against this conclusion, but at the time, many missile enthusiasts considered it a proof of LeMay's backward thinking.

By the end of March 1956, the Ninety-third Bombardment Wing had thirty B-52s. It soon became the training unit for crews from other wings which were about to be supplied with the new, eight-jet bomber. Eventually, SAC's B-52 fleet would exceed six hundred.

In April 1955, LeMay brought David Wade, then a brigadier general, into SAC headquarters as his inspector general. Wade had been commander of the Twenty-first Air Division at Forbes Air Force Base in Kansas. LeMay, on some of his inspection trips, had noticed him and had been impressed by his work. Though Wade had thus been exposed briefly to the LeMay personality, he was not prepared for the kind of welcome he received during his first day at Offutt. Dick Montgomery, chief of staff since the departure of Augie Kissner to Portugal, said to Wade a few minutes after his arrival, ''General LeMay is going [into Omaha] to Creighton University to make a speech today. Why don't you ride with him. Give you a chance to get acquainted.''

Wade agreed. But when he and LeMay got in the car, LeMay said nothing. On the whole eight-mile trip to Omaha, LeMay said nothing. Not a word.

At Creighton, LeMay delivered his speech, then the two men got back into the car. Still LeMay said nothing.

''I had to say something,'' Wade recalls. ''As it happened I had a cousin who was also in the Air Force. And he, too, was being transferred to Offutt. Finally I said to LeMay, 'General, I understand Horace Wade is coming into headquarters.'

''He took his cigar out of his mouth and looked at me. 'Yeah,' he said, with a twinkle in his eye. 'I wonder if two Wades are not too many in headquarters?' That's all he said, the whole trip.''[4]

LeMay was smoking only sporadically at this time, yet his cigar was almost always in his mouth. Did Wade think the cigar had become a prop to foster his tough-guy image?

"No, I don't think he ever acted. Curt LeMay was always Curt LeMay."

And whenever he could arrange it, he continued to be silent. For two years, Wade lived next door to him on Generals' Row at Offutt. "Helen would call on a Sunday," he recalls. "She'd say, 'Come on over. Curt's going to barbecue.'

"I'd go out in the yard with him. We'd be there for an hour and a half. Maybe he'd say two words."

In social situations, LeMay seemed either totally withdrawn into himself and his private thoughts, or so ill-at-ease he could cope only by resorting to silence. Several women who have been placed next to him at dinner parties and suffered his silence have speculated as to whether he disliked women or feared them. But he was often silent, even around Helen, and though she was a strong woman, quite capable of holding her own against him, no one ever suggested he was afraid of her.

When Wade was asked if he thought LeMay was ill-at-ease among women, he said, "I don't know. He might have been. But I doubt if he was ever ill-at-ease with anybody. He was usually thinking about something. Yet we've had him to dinner when he was as friendly as could be. Some nights he'd tell stories. Flying-school stories. One night he was there with Arthur Godfrey and he told about the first time he was invited to dinner in England during the war. The beef was so rare it was purple and he liked it well done. (We called the end piece the LeMay cut.) He soon had everyone at the table laughing at his account of his ludicrous and unsuccessful attempt to hide it under his vegetables so he wouldn't have to eat it."

By now, LeMay's silences were surprising only to those who were meeting him for the first time. Wade soon became accustomed to him and was sufficiently relaxed around him to suggest a change in the SAC inspection routine. Under the then current system, a unit usually received notice of an impending inspection.

"Why don't we do it without telling them?" Wade suggested. "We'll write an order. You'll sign it. I'll go onto a base with my team, completely unannounced, hand them the order and say, 'Execute your [war] plan in accordance with your operations orders, minus nuclear weapons.' "

Every SAC unit had a preplanned and prepracticed course of action it was to take in the event of war. To go through this course of action in an exercise took about two days. The unit would be given four hours to gather its crews and get off the ground. It was a type of inspection that probably didn't make Wade very popular among the units, but no one doubted that it increased the efficiency of SAC.

By the middle 1950s, the power, efficiency, and publicity of SAC had become so impressive that in the public mind, this relatively new organization, less than ten years old, overshadowed not only the rest of the Air Force but the Army and Navy as well. Could the Army or Navy protect us against Russian atomic bombs? Could the Army or Navy deter Russian aggression by threatening to retaliate? No one thought so. Only the atomic umbrellas of SAC had the power to frighten the Soviets and thus prevent war.

When LeMay took charge of SAC in 1948, it was an ineffectual force of forty-five thousand men and fourteen bomb groups, not one of which was at full strength. In no way did it pose a threat to Russia. By 1955, SAC had almost two hundred thousand men and twenty-eight hundred aircraft, stationed all over the world on bases within range of Moscow. Its jet bombers alone (twelve hundred B-47s had entered the force by then) had logged more than a million hours of simulated combat flight.

By the end of April 1956, forty-seven B-52s had been accepted into SAC, making it the most powerful military force, in terms of range, striking ability, and destructive potential, that the world had ever seen. Yet LeMay was still not satisfied. He had helped inspire, or at least did nothing to discourage, a December 4, 1955 article by Arthur Godfrey in the *Saturday Evening Post* that warned the American public about the "desperate need for air power—now!" After some extravagant praise of LeMay, Godfrey waxed enthusiastic about the B-52. But, he added, "the number in actual service is so small as to be pathetic, and at the rate they are being produced today it will be twenty-four years before we have the number required to provide the minimum protection this country must have. Are you shocked? I hope so. . . . We don't want war. We want a striking force so awesome that there won't be any war."

Six months later, LeMay followed this with a fearful warning to Congress. In testimony April 30 and May 2, 1956, before the Senate Air Force subcommittee of the Armed Services Committee, he stated that unless SAC appropriations were increased, Russia would gain air superiority over the United States by 1960. He answered 153 of the Senators' questions, 75 of them in open session. And what he said stirred up a new debate about national defense.

The substance of his testimony was that the United States could still win a war against Russia, but not "without this country receiving very serious damage. Five years ago we could have won the war without the country receiving comparatively serious damage."

It was true that the B-52 had arrived, but as of April 30, the first day he testified, only seventy-eight had been manufactured and thirty-one had been rejected by SAC because of a serious but correctable defect in the electrical system. Current production was only six planes a month.

The Russians were producing their Bison and Bear bombers "at a combined rate substantially higher" than U.S. B-52 production, and "if our estimate of Soviet production is accurate . . . they now have more Bisons and Bears in their inventory than we have B-52s."

What all this meant to him was that by 1960, "the Soviet Air Force will have substantially more Bisons and Bears than we will have B-52s. . . . I can only conclude then that they will have a greater striking power than we will have."

Whether LeMay was as convinced of this as he appeared to be is almost impossible to assess in retrospect. He knew very well that efficiency of operation, sophistication of supplementary equipment in addition to aircraft, plus the skill, experience, and advanced preparation of crews were factors as important as the planes themselves in determining the effectiveness of organizations like SAC and its Russian counterpart. And he knew the Russian counterpart was not as well prepared as SAC. But he knew also that fear was a powerful tool in getting money out of Congress.

His testimony was an almost open criticism of the Eisenhower administration's Air Force budget for 1957, and Ike's obvious spokesman on the subject, Defense Secretary Charles Wilson, was quick, though careful, in answering him. "Engine Charlie" held a news conference in which he admitted that, according to his best information, the Russians were, as LeMay had stated, producing more long-range bombers than the United States, but that the rate of production was not very high "either for us or for them." Referring specifically to LeMay, Wilson said, "A dedicated specialist usually gets pretty well sold on his particular part of the business. That is no criticism . . . but in my experience, if you add up the desires and all the stated needs and ambitions of all your specialists, you would have an impossible total on your hands."

Another "top-level" administration spokesman, unidentified, told *Time* magazine that to give LeMay what he wanted would cost another $55 billion. "Curt LeMay," he said, "thinks only of SAC."[5] Such remarks, whether true or false, were not likely to help relieve LeMay of his widening reputation as strictly a bomber general.

Needless to say, LeMay had never even dreamed of getting an extra $55 billion from Congress. But he had hoped to get something extra, and he did. Congress added another billion dollars (a significant amount in those days) to the 1957 and 1958 Air Force budgets.

LeMay's ability to get money out of Congress, and his success in convincing the public that SAC was the nation's most important defense force, did not sit well with the rest of the American military establishment. The Army and Navy were convinced that they could use to better advantage some of the funds SAC was getting. And so did the rest of the Air Force. The missile people didn't like to hear LeMay declare, as he did in his congressional testimony, that it would be several years before their revolutionary new weapons would be reliable. The tactical (fighter) air people didn't like his emphasis on bombers. And even the CIA was at odds with him because he wanted SAC to control the new U-2 reconnaissance plane which the CIA considered its own tool.

"There was a division," LeMay later admitted, "because we had built up a good outfit. Much better than the rest of the Air Force. We worked ninety hours a week, the rest about twenty. The results stuck out. It got around that we were getting all the money and the good people. Seventeen percent of the defense budget went to strategic air. So the whole defense establishment accused us."[6]

As for the accusation that he sloughed off fighter planes and tactical air support, he insists there never was any truth to that. "I demanded fighters to be assigned to SAC, and at one time we had them for escort and to protect our bases. But then we were out down to where we couldn't afford fighters just for SAC. We had to turn them back to TAC [Tactical Air Command]."

Gen. Frederic Smith, in a 1976 interview, agreed that LeMay never sloughed off fighter planes. "I was opposed to SAC getting any fighters," he said. "But LeMay insisted and Vandenberg finally agreed."[7] Smith, like most of his colleagues, conceded that LeMay "did a grand job at SAC." But he didn't indicate that LeMay was ever one of his favorite people. "I think Curt, as the years went by and he commanded SAC, became more and more dictatorial and more and more insistent on SAC being *it*. Anything else was purely secondary."

LeMay could not claim any immediate success in his effort to control the U-2 reconnaissance program. The first U-2 was airborne August 6, 1955, and that October, six SAC pilots began training to fly the plane. But not under SAC jurisdiction. LeMay did his best to take over this remarkable aircraft, which could fly at eighty thousand feet, far above the range of any antiaircraft gun or any surface-to-air missile at the time or any interceptor, but the CIA fought him from the start, and finally, Gen. Nathan Twining, who had succeeded Vandenberg as chief of staff, signed an agreement accepting a subordinate role for SAC in the U-2 program and ceding to the CIA the major control over it.

In June 1956, the U-2s, under CIA auspices, began flying routine reconnaissance missions over Russia which continued until the Russians finally managed, in 1960, to bring one down. The Soviet Union's airspace seems to have been surprisingly easy to penetrate at that time. On one occasion in the mid-1950s, LeMay flew the entire SAC reconnaissance force over the Siberian city of Vladivostok.[8]

"It wasn't my idea," he hastened to explain in recalling the incident. "I was ordered to do it. They [the Eisenhower administration's intelligence chiefs] were worried about something that was going on at Vladivostok. So I laid out a mission. From Guam or the Philippines. Maybe fifty planes. Maximum altitude about 40,000 feet. We picked a clear day and all of our electronic reconnaissance planes crisscrossed the area. They practically mapped the place. Two of our planes saw some Migs but there were no interceptions. And as far as I know, the Russians never said anything about it."

This startling story begs the question, why didn't the Russians say anything about it? Would the United States remain silent if the Russians were to do something as provocative as sending fifty planes to photograph Seattle? At about this same time, the Russians were remaining silent during four years of U-2 overflights, of which they had to be acutely aware. They said nothing about this continuing invasion of their airspace until May 1960, after they had brought one down. Again, one can only wonder why. Thomas Powers, in his book, *The Man Who Kept the Secrets: Richard Helms and the C.I.A.*, suggests a reason. By this time, the Soviets had "developed similar reconnaissance systems," including satellites, with which they could inspect and photograph whatever might be happening in the United States. Perhaps the U.S. government would have remained silent if the Soviets had flown fifty planes over Seattle. Even among enemies there are gentlemen's agreements, as John F. Kennedy and Nikita Khrushchev were destined to demonstrate in the early 1960s.

LeMay, in the middle and latter 1950s, was much more worried about proliferation of atomic weapons among other American services and commands than he was about Russian surveillance. "There was a time," he recalls, "when SAC had all the atomic weapons. But as we got more and more of them, other commands wanted them. I remember once a study was made and they asked all the theater commanders what their requirements were for atomic weapons. What targets they had to destroy to carry out their missions. Well, they asked CINCEUR [Commander-in-Chief Europe] and he had targets from the Arctic Circle down to the Indian Ocean and from the Rhine clear back behind the Urals. They asked CINCSOUTH and he had the same. And they asked CINCPAC [Pacific] and he had targets from the Arctic Circle clear down to Indonesia and clear over to the Urals. A lot of them overlapped. [But] if they had to destroy those targets to carry out their missions, you had to give them the force to do it. So they wanted SAC.

"Then the Navy got atomic weapons, and the tactical forces got some, which meant the theater commanders had some. My mission was to destroy the industrial capacity of Russia. But where were these guys going to put their bombs, and when? Am I going to be duplicating what they're doing, or what? There has to be something whole. I pointed this out. And finally, the Joint Chiefs agreed that under the rules, I could force consultation with the other commanders. So I did that. We had a meeting at Offutt. And the Navy officer from the Pacific wouldn't agree to anything. Finally I pinned him to the wall. I said, 'What orders did you get from your commander when you came here? Did you get orders not to agree to anything?' And he said yes.

"Now they've got a little better setup than that. There's a joint target committee of which the SAC commander is chairman. It operates out of Omaha.''⁹ Which means, in effect, that SAC has the major voice in determining the allotment of potential targets.

On May 21, 1956, LeMay was slightly embarrassed when one of SAC's B-52s, dropping a live hydrogen bomb for the first time ever from an American aircraft (the Russians had done it the previous November), missed its battleship target in the Bikini atoll. But knowledge of SAC's embarrassment was confined to insiders. The public was not told about the error at the time. The Atomic Energy Commission announced that the test drop was a success, and by many measurements it was. The bomb exploded ten thousand to fifteen thousand feet above the target, as it was designed to do, with a force of ten million tons of TNT. Since the spread of the bomb's destruction was more than twelve miles in diameter, its detonation did a thorough job on the intended target.

In the winter of 1956–57, SAC gave a much more convincing demonstration of its skill and readiness when its B-36s and B-47s made 751 radar-graded, simulated bombing runs on the snowbound town of Rhinelander, in northern Wisconsin.

LeMay later called this ''one of the most realistic evaluation missions we've ever conducted.'' Rhinelander was selected, he said, ''because of its size—approximately ten thousand people—and its location in a developmentally isolated area, surrounded by small lakes. Also because the entire area was snowcovered.''¹⁰

The primary target was a little airfield two miles west of town, but the crews had been given fifteen-year-old target information about Rhinelander, information assembled before the airfield was built. All they were told about the airfield was its location in relation to the town. Since the mission was conducted on a day when Rhinelander was totally hidden by clouds, their job was to locate the town by radar without seeing it, then locate the airfield in relation to the town and ''bomb'' it without seeing it. The accuracy of their radar-directed ''bombs'' was measured by radar receiving sets located on the airfield.

The results were spectacular. Though none of the crews had ever made a bomb run on this target, ''the average result for all the crews,'' LeMay announced, ''was the circle error probable of 2,650 feet [one-half mile]. Our select crews had a circle error probable of 2,075 feet.''

LeMay announced these results to an audience at Air University in February 1957, in a speech that sounded like an accounting for his stewardship at SAC. He assured the young officer-students that "the Strategic Air Command represents much of the offensive air power of the nation, and it's growing in size and in skill and in effectiveness every day. We, at the present time, consider it fully capable of affecting decisive damage on any aggressive nation that might be so unwise as to attack us, if we properly utilize the force. . . . No effort should be spared in showing that the SAC strike potential is preserved."

He sounded as if he realized that his own days at SAC were numbered. He had been there eight and a half years, a long time in any command, and he had undoubtedly heard new rumors of a shift in the making. Perhaps it was for that reason he made the opening of the new SAC headquarters (or "control center" as he and Griswold had dubbed it) an occasion for a big celebration at New Year 1957. It had taken him a long time to get that headquarters built, but by God, he had managed it before his departure.

Even in a mood to celebrate, he remained the same old Curt LeMay. David Wade remembers that at the Offutt Officers' Club New Year's Eve, as midnight approached, LeMay planted his cigar right in the middle of his mouth and kept it there. He wasn't going to have any of the women running up to him and giving him New Year's kisses. But he was proud of that hard-earned new headquarters, and he wanted everyone to know it.

Aboveground were two three-story buildings devoted to the administrative staff: LeMay's own office was on the top floor of one of these buildings. Underground, beneath these buildings, was another three-level structure, the control center, which was big enough to accommodate the operational staff at all times and the administrative staff at times of crisis. The underground facility, deep in the earth, was built of thick, steel-reinforced concrete so sturdy as to withstand all but a direct hit by a large nuclear weapon.

LeMay's commodious third-floor office commanded a view of the Nebraska countryside but not of the Omaha stockyards which he so thoroughly detested. It featured thick carpet, leather furniture, indirect lighting, and huge wall maps on which blue stars and red circles denoted SAC's worldwide air bases as well as its primary targets.

Gen. John Paul McConnell, who had come to Offutt as director of plans in 1953, recalls the typical LeMay remarks with which the new headquarters was dedicated. LeMay stood up before his assembled staff and said: "Remember this. We built this headquarters in accordance with staff specifications. Now then, if any of you don't like it just tell me about it and I'll fire your ass."

On March 4, 1957, LeMay left Grizzy Griswold in charge of SAC and took off with Arthur Godfrey, Richard Boutelle (president of Fairchild Corporation), and James Shepley (head of the Time-Life Washington Bureau) on an African hunting safari. LeMay had instigated the excursion and had made the basic arrangements through a French friend, Claude Hettier de Boislambert, with whom he had hunted for boar and deer when he was stationed in Germany after the war. Boislambert planned the trip, in LeMay's words, "commensurate with my salary since I was the poorest of the bunch. I think originally it was going to cost us about five hundred dollars apiece."[11]

Then Godfrey took over and by the time they reached Africa, their entourage included his DC-3 airplane and his helicopter (both sent on ahead), a *Life* photographer, a motion-picture crew, radio technicians, and a large supporting cast.

Surprisingly, in spite of all this excess baggage, they also managed to find time to hunt. Both Godfrey and LeMay killed bull elephants, each with a single shot. The *Life* magazine picture story of the LeMay-Godfrey safari spared none of the gruesome details, including even a gun aimed at an elephant's head some distance away, the falling beast, and its butchered carcass. Today, no general circulation magazine could approvingly publish pictures and details of hunters killing an elephant without raising a public outcry, but as recently as 1957, an African hunting safari was as socially acceptable as a dinner party.

When LeMay returned to Omaha at the end of March 1957, he knew he wouldn't be there long. The guard was changing at the Pentagon. On April 4, his appointment as Air Force vice chief of staff was announced. He was on his way to Washington, a place he had never liked very much. Had he campaigned for this job, which he almost had once before in 1952? Did he want it now?

"Not particularly," he said many years later. "Nobody likes to work on a staff. But I'd been in SAC almost nine years. A long time. And I thought I'd have a chance in Washington to be closer to Congress, the Department of Defense, and the budget people.''[12] The fact that he would be no longer with SAC didn't mean he intended to stop helping SAC get the top dollar out of the defense budget.

CHAPTER TWENTY-THREE

By 1957, the joint Chiefs of Staff, a committee composed of the chiefs of all the services, had so many high policy responsibilities that none of the chiefs could find enough time to supervise properly the business of his own service. President Eisenhower, realizing this perhaps because he was a military man himself, sent a directive to each of the chiefs informing him that his primary duty thenceforth was the business of the Joint Chiefs rather than the business of the service he commanded. His top assistant would have to handle "the day to day operation" of the service, though the chief would retain the ultimate responsibility.

Gen. Thomas D. White, the incoming Air Force chief of staff, had Eisenhower's directive in mind when, in the spring of 1957, he asked Curt LeMay to become his vice chief. If his top deputy was going to have to run the Air Force for him, he'd have to make sure he had a man who could handle the job.

"I picked LeMay," White later wrote in notes for a magazine article, "primarily because he was then commander of the most efficient component of the Air Force—SAC—and hence he was the best man to 'run' the Air Force under the Eisenhower edict. (LeMay was also, in my opinion, the greatest complement to me that I knew of. His experience, background and probably his personality were quite different from mine. I knew it might be tough but if it worked it would be terrific for the Air Force. I never had occasion to regret the choice though LeMay and I were never very close personal friends.)"[1]

As to their personal rapport, White may even have been indulging in a slight understatement. In those same notes, there is some evidence that he didn't really like LeMay, that LeMay wasn't the kind of person with whom he enjoyed spending time.

344

"LeMay has almost no social graces," White wrote. "He is not a good conversationalist and smokes cigars at the dinner table." (A charge LeMay might deny.) "He has many friends among men and perhaps as many enemies."

On the subject of LeMay's professional qualifications, however, White, in retrospect, offered the highest praise. "He was *the* architect of the Strategic Air Command. He never swerved from the profound conviction that the freedom of the U.S.A. (and the rest of the Western World) depended primarily and almost solely on SAC. In my opinion he was, at that time, absolutely correct. It is still true (in 1964) to a great degree."

When the LeMays arrived in Washington in July 1957, they moved into an attached house at Fort Myer across the Potomac, near the Pentagon in Virginia. On the other side of this double house lived the Whites, so the two four-star generals had an immediate opportunity to get to know each other socially. Though they had first met in 1941 in South America, they were only slightly acquainted. The LeMays eventually moved to Bolling Field on the Washington side of the river. They found there a single, detached house, larger and more satisfactory for their needs than the attached quarters at Fort Myer.

LeMay fitted smoothly into his new job as vice chief. White, who had as much work as he could handle as a member of the Joint Chiefs, delegated to him all the authority he needed to run the Air Force. And LeMay used the authority, apparently without abusing it. Gen. Frederic Smith said in later years that LeMay "ran the Air Force to some extent almost out from under General White. He seemed to have more prestige." But LeMay didn't see it that way. He realized he had the authority but not the responsibility.

"If I had any doubt about [White's] thinking," LeMay recalls, "I'd wait and talk it over with him."

LeMay admits "we weren't too close. He was a different sort of individual. He thought politics was the art of compromise. He would go into battle ready to compromise. I never believed in that. I thought if you believed in something, God damn it, you got in there and fought for it. Without any intention of compromising until you were convinced you were wrong or you didn't stand a chance of getting it through, so you took half a loaf. Tommy wouldn't get down in the mud and fight."[2]

But White agrees that LeMay did not abuse the authority delegated to him. "As Vice Chief of Staff, who had had world wide publicity as Commander in Chief of SAC, [he] almost completely effaced himself. The mark of a big man."

One of LeMay's first projects as vice chief was the already launched and continuing campaign to secure pay increases for Air Force personnel, which would mean, of course, increases for all military personnel. At that time, a newly recruited airman or private earned $78 a month; a second lieutenant, $222; a colonel, $592; and a full general (LeMay's rank), $1,221. In other words, at the very top of his profession, he was earning a yearly base salary of $14,652. And when he arrived in Washington, prospects for any military raises were not good. Congress was in no mood to increase the military personnel appropriation by the requested 6.5 percent.

There was one man in Congress at the time, however, who might have the power or influence to change a lot of minds there—Sen. Lyndon Johnson of Texas. As majority leader in the Senate, he had somehow learned to play Congress as if it were a musical instrument. By wheeling and dealing and threatening and cajoling, he seemed able to get any kind of a sound he wanted out of his colleagues.

LeMay, using some stratagem or other, managed to get invited to Johnson's Texas ranch one weekend. Gen. John Paul Mc-Connell, who had been LeMay's director of plans at SAC, was well acquainted with Johnson, and his recollection is that he arranged the trip. (He also recalls that it took place in 1967, but circumstances dictate that it had to be 1957.)[3]

In the evenings after dinner, Johnson liked to get into his carry-all truck, with a sizable supply of whiskey, and drive around, saying hello to his neighbors. Mostly farmers.

On the Saturday night when the two generals were there, Johnson put LeMay in the front seat next to him, with McConnell in the back seat refilling the whiskey glasses, and set out from farm to farm, extolling the beauties of Texas as the men and the whiskey became increasingly mellow.

"He'd drive up to some guy's shack with the lights shining," McConnell recalls. "Then he'd turn off the lights. The fellow would come out with a gun, peer at us, and say, 'Well, hello. Damned if that ain't Johnson.' "

The next morning at breakfast, Johnson said, "Well, let's go out again tonight."

But LeMay wasn't about to relive that experience. The two generals departed before nightfall.

LeMay's recollection is very much in accordance with Mc-Connell's but with significant additions. The whole purpose of the trip, as he remembers it, was to "try to convince Johnson that we needed the pay raise." LeMay also remembers the wild Saturday-night ride in the carry-all. "We had a couple of 'kits' as [Johnson] called them. Bottles of whiskey and boxes of ice. We got home around midnight. Not exactly sober."

It wasn't until Sunday morning, beside the pool, that LeMay managed to make his pitch for military pay raises.

Johnson said, "LeMay, you've got a good story. You need a pay raise. But you haven't got a Chinaman's chance. You couldn't get it through the Military Affairs Committee, or Appropriations. You couldn't get it onto the floor because you couldn't get it through the Rules Committee. You haven't got a chance."

LeMay returned to Washington brooding about all this. He felt discouraged but not defeated. Two weeks later, Arthur Godfrey had a party at his farm in Leesburg, Virginia, about thirty miles northwest of Washington, and he invited Senator Johnson.

"So I just happened to be there too," LeMay recalls. "I gave Godfrey the pitch and he talked to Johnson, who gave him the same answer he had given me."

But to Godfrey, Johnson added, "Of course, if you got some grass-roots support . . ."

"What do you mean by that?" Godfrey asked. "Letters to Congress?"

"That would help."

Godfrey said, "Stand by, Senator. You're going to get some mail."

On his coast-to-coast radio show, Godfrey frequently talked about SAC and about national defense. The next few days he talked about pay raises for the military and suggested that his vast audience write some letters to Washington on the subject. On May 20, 1958, President Eisenhower signed into law a congressional bill increasing military pay by about 6 percent.

On October 4, 1957, the Russians shocked the universe when they succeeded in putting the world's first space vehicle, *Sputnik,* into orbit around the globe. The repercussions from this remarkable accomplishment touched many aspects of American life and the American psyche. Our national pride suffered a severe blow. Whenever something new and amazing was done, Americans were supposed to do it. Oh, maybe the French or British once in awhile. We had very generously allowed Mme. Marie Curie to discover radium. And Marchese Marconi, an Italian, had invented the radio, but most Americans had forgotten that. They assumed it was either NBC or CBS. How then could the Russians have put a vehicle in space ahead of us? They were Communists, and everybody knew our system was better than theirs. Or was it? A lot of Americans began to wonder. There had to be something wrong with our school system if they were producing better scientists. There had to be something wrong with our industry if they were developing better technology. There had to be something wrong with our military, especially our Air Force, if they had missiles and we didn't.

Curt LeMay, as vice chief of staff, had to absorb his share of the national humiliation created by *Sputnik,* even though, as Air Force research-and-development chief in the late forties, he had suggested the development of a satellite. His suggestion had been rejected because of the high cost. On December 17, 1957, he and General White and secretary of the Air Force James H. Douglas were tossed into a frying pan before the Senate Preparedness Subcommittee, chaired by Lyndon Johnson.

Fortunately, America's first Atlas intercontinental ballistic missile was being launched that day, perhaps even slightly ahead of schedule due to *Sputnik,* but Douglas had to admit it wouldn't be ready for combat for another two years. The *New York Times* called this estimate "considerably more optimistic than most unofficial guesses," and noted that, if achieved, "it would give the United States such a weapon about the same time as the Soviet Union would begin to produce them in operational numbers."

General White told the subcommittee he was trying, though without success, to get the Defense Department to hurry the development of the Titan missile, which was more advanced than the Atlas. LeMay, who was on record many times with the opinion that it would be several years before any missile was operative, stuck to the argument he had used before, but one which post-*Sputnik* Americans weren't likely to want to hear.

The Air Force's greatest need, he said, was to maintain its "retaliatory superiority" with manned bombers—especially the B-52s while our missiles were being perfected. With General White's support, he asked for funds to disperse B-52 bases around the world and provide better maintenance crews.

Then, never hesitant to drop some diversionary fear onto an

audience, he mentioned casually that "a majority of SAC's aircraft" had been grounded for five weeks during May and June "due to lack of funds for gasoline."

This remark served to turn some congressional attention away from our apparent missile gap, and perhaps that was LeMay's purpose. At the time, he didn't explain to the senators how this had happened, but in later years, with a smile on his face, he admitted that the situation had never been quite as critical as he had made it sound that day. SAC did begin to run short of gas, and because of budget allocations, it would be a month or so before they could buy more. The Pentagon had wanted LeMay to slow down his training program and "string it out," but he had refused.

"I'll continue training," he insisted, "until there's just enough gas to execute our war plan. And that will be long enough for Congress to appropriate more money for us." For a person notoriously lacking in political tact, he was developing some remarkable techniques to get money out of Congress.

For the most part, LeMay's tour of duty as vice chief of staff was fairly uncomplicated. He had enough free time to think nostalgically about the life he once had led at SAC. He missed it. Especially the flying. There were airplanes available to four-star generals in Washington, but surprisingly, the Air Force headquarters didn't have a single jet plane attached to it, and he was accustomed to flying jets at SAC. He began looking for one that he could bring to Washington, not only for himself, but for other chair-bound flying officers.

He soon found that the research-and-development boys at Dayton were holding thirteen K-135s (the military tanker version of the new Boeing 707 airliner) for test purposes. It seemed to LeMay they could conduct their tests on twelve planes as effectively as they could on thirteen, so he told them to send him one. They said they couldn't. They needed all they had. One can imagine how well that argument worked with LeMay. He soon had his K-135 in Washington. But having brought it there, he decided he should do something with it to impress upon Russia the long range of American jet airplanes.

On November 11, 1957, he took off with a crew of mechanics and, more important perhaps, a crew of newspaper and magazine correspondents. The publicly announced reason for the flight was to carry a congratulatory message from President Eisenhower to the new Argentine president, Pedro E. Aramburu, on the occasion of his inauguration in Buenos Aires. But the much more significant reason was to show Russia we now had a tanker that could easily make a nonstop trip to Moscow. The K-135 could get there from as far away as Los Angeles.

Whether the Russians were impressed it is impossible to say, but LeMay collected a bunch of medals in Argentina, and he was later awarded the Harmon trophy for setting a speed record on the flight. He had so much fun that he staged another propaganda flight a year later, September 12, 1958, from Tokyo to Washington. The big feature of this flight was that he beat the clock. His plane reached Washington thirty-two minutes, by the clock, ahead of his takeoff time from Japan.

In early January 1959, LeMay spent a few days in the hospital for the correction of a prostate problem, but by January 13 he was back home preparing for a sojourn of rest and recuperation with Helen in the Florida sun. It was a welcome change, not only for him, but for Helen, and possibly even for Janie. It wasn't that their daughter was going with them. The change she needed was a bit of relief from a well-meaning project on which her mother had embarked.

By this time, Janie was a beautiful young woman, twenty years of age, and a student at the University of Maryland. If she had one care in the world that bothered her more than any other it was her mother's persistent campaign to find the right man for her to marry.

"I was dating a boy I had known for a couple of years," she recently recalled. "He was a lot of fun but my parents didn't like him, and they thought I was going to get married [even though] I had no such plans. I wanted to do other things when I got out of college. So my mother gets on this campaign. Everyone she knew had to find an eligible boy for me. I'd come home and mother would have someone waiting to take me out. I went on some of those dates but I got to a point where if I didn't like the fellow, I wasn't very nice."

"I lost some friends that way," Helen LeMay interjected, "because of mothers who thought their sons were pretty nice."

One day Gen. Oliver Neiss, the Air Force surgeon general, called Helen and told her about a handsome young Army doctor named Jim Lodge whom he had met at Walter Reed Hospital. Would it be all right for Jim to call Janie? In Helen's opinion it would be just fine. But to Janie this was just the latest move in her mother's campaign. Jim called twice and got no place, so he decided, as he later explained, that he wouldn't call again.

But what he didn't know was that Helen LeMay was more persistent than he was. Before long, she had arranged a boating excursion on the Potomac for six or seven couples, and behold, both Janie and Jim were invited. Equally but separately.

"I thought it was going to be another fiasco," Janie recalled. "Why couldn't he get his own date?" But this time, her mother had chosen well. Before long, Janie had a new boyfriend. And apparently a serious one.

Nineteen sixty was a memorable presidential election year. Vice President Richard M. Nixon, with what appeared to be somewhat reluctant support from retiring President Eisenhower, was favored to beat Senator John F. Kennedy, the Democratic candidate, until the campaign got into full swing and the public began reacting to the personalities of both men. Kennedy won and took office in January 1961, amidst exciting expectations that he would, as he had often promised, get the country going again.

The American people had, in fact, slipped into a certain complacency during the prosperous and world-powerful years of the Eisenhower administration. The Kennedy promise of greater national strength, more compassionate help for the poor and underprivileged, less racism, and better educational opportunities seemed to stir the imaginations of the populace, especially the young. People reacted to Kennedy's youthful enthusiasm as if it were both a tonic and a challenge. But Kennedy's youth was also to some degree a handicap. While his ideals were high, he was not as experienced in government, and the avoidance of pitfalls, as he might have wished to be. Almost the day he entered office, he was confronted by the question of what to do with a project the Eisenhower administration had begun, under some guidance by Nixon, and using the CIA as its instrument of execution. The project was the invasion of Fidel Castro's Communist Cuba, mostly by anti-Castro Cuban exiles, under the direction of a cadre of CIA agents. To his lifelong regret, Kennedy chose to continue that project on its original route, even though it obviously had to be a military operation, and the CIA was not a military organization.

Curtis LeMay, though he was Air Force vice chief of staff at the time, nevertheless knew nothing about the planned invasion of Cuba until about a month before it happened. One day in mid-March 1961, he attended a Joint Chiefs of Staff meeting as a substitute for Tommy White, who was out of town. LeMay recalls that he arrived at the meeting about five minutes early.[4] The chiefs of the Army, Navy, and Marine Corps, and the chairman, Gen. Lyman Lemnitzer, filed in and sat down. But when the time came to start the meeting, nothing happened. The minutes passed and still nothing happened except some whispered consultations between Lemnitzer and the other chiefs. LeMay began to feel very much excluded from this distinguished company. Then one of Lemnitzer's aides came in and whispered something to him. Finally the meeting began and LeMay eventually learned the reason for the delay. The Joint Chiefs that day were to discuss a subject so delicate and so secret that even the vice chief of the Air Force wasn't cleared to hear about it. Until a clearance was obtained for him, the meeting could not begin. The subject was the impending Cuban invasion.

There was a civilian in the room. As soon as the meeting began, he stood up, without introduction, and pulled back a wall curtain revealing a map of Cuba. Then he began to speak as if everyone in the room was already informed about the background of his subject. He offered LeMay no briefing.

"We've decided there has to be an airstrip on the beach," he said. "We've picked out three sites. We'd like a recommendation as to which is best."

Since the immediate reference was to airstrips, everyone turned to the Air Force representative, LeMay, who didn't even know what book they were on, let alone what page.

"I don't know what this is about," he said. "I assume you're going to make some landings there. Is this a landing operation? If so, how big a force?"

"Seven hundred," the man said.

By this time LeMay had figured the man must be from the CIA. He couldn't imagine a military man planning such an ambitious undertaking with so few troops. "I know Henry Morgan [a seventeenth-century Welsh pirate fighting in the service of England] took Panama with seven hundred men. [But] you're not intending to take Cuba? I assume this is a touch-off for an uprising."

The man said, "That doesn't concern you."

This ended the discussion. LeMay and the members of the JCS studied maps and rendered their judgment as to the most suitable beaches for airstrips, and that part of the JCS meeting came to an end.

A short time later, LeMay heard a rumor that the CIA had recruited a military force of exiled Cubans, and that "some of our people" (presumably detached members of the Army, Navy, and Air Force) were training them. He asked Lemnitzer if this was true and Lemnitzer confirmed it. That was the last thing LeMay heard about the operation until April 16, the day before the invasion was to take place.

Once again, Tommy White was out of town and LeMay was to substitute for him at a special JCS meeting the morning of the 17th. This time he was warned on the 16th that the agenda would be the invasion of Cuba, which would be in progress even as the meeting was held.

Though the Joint Chiefs were not to gather until 8 A.M., LeMay arrived at seven o'clock to find out what he could about the whole affair. "I learned that the invasion fórce had an air force based in Guatemala. It was supposed to take off the day before [actually two days before] and knock out Cuban air fields. Knock out the Cuban air force. To make sure we [the United States] didn't get the blame for this, a couple of these planes with Cuban markings were to land at Key West and say the Cuban air force was in revolt. Well, they screwed up the attack. They didn't get the Cuban air force."

At least three B-26 World War II bombers, with Cuban markings, had in fact raided three Cuban air bases April 15, killing several people but inflicting little or no significant damage on the Cuban air force. Two of the B-26s then did land in Florida with their story about the Cuban air force revolt, which, for a time, some people apparently believed.

"Part of the plan," LeMay discovered and other people have confirmed, "was to have air cover over the beach. To get there at daylight [as the invasion began], these planes would have to take off [from Guatemala] about midnight. I found out that Dean Rusk [the new Secretary of State] had canceled that air cover [the previous night] at 10 P.M. Pre Cabell [a former Air Force general who had become deputy director of the CIA] had gone to Rusk to get the cover back on, but Rusk said the president had made his decision and was now dressing to go to a party. If [Cabell] wanted to see him about it, he could go ahead.

"Cabell didn't go. It wouldn't have made any difference anyway," LeMay has concluded. "The administration didn't pay any attention to us [the military]."

As the time for the Joint Chiefs meeting approached on the

morning of the invasion, LeMay recalls that ''I stood at the door to get hold of McNamara [Robert McNamara, the new Secretary of Defense]. He didn't come. It was his deputy, Roswell Gilpatric.

''I said to him,'' LeMay recalls, '' 'Look, you just cut the throats of everybody on the beach down there.'

''He said, 'What do you mean?'

''I said, 'Rusk canceled the air cover over the beach. It's bound to fail.' ''

LeMay recalls that Gilpatric shrugged his shoulders. ''So we went in and got briefed. The landing had taken place on time and they were doing pretty well initially. But the [Cuban] air force hit them and sank the [landing] vessels [while] the reserve ammunition was still aboard. When [the invaders] had used what they carried ashore, that was all.''

LeMay has harbored through his later years a measure of bitterness about the whole episode because ''the military got blamed for the Cuban invasion, and we didn't have a God damned thing to do with it. Some of our people may have been detached to the CIA, but we didn't know what they were doing. And they didn't tell us when they came back.''

LeMay himself, despite his insistence on his lack of knowledge about or involvement in the disaster, became the butt of uncomplimentary suggestions about it afterward. Peter Wyden, discussing in his book *Bay of Pigs* the decision to remove air cover on the eve of the invasion, almost openly blames LeMay for it:

> . . . and the President perhaps heard rumors out of the Joint Chiefs . . . rumors that said not all the Chiefs were totally convinced that air cover was critical, that General Curtis LeMay, the Air Chief of Staff, had been reported less than fully convinced even though LeMay was a strategic bombing expert and not expert on tactical air support. J.F.K. would have listened to Rusk and LeMay.

No doubt JFK would have listened—and did listen—to Rusk. But he wasn't likely to have had an occasion to listen to LeMay because, though Wyden obviously didn't know it, LeMay was not the Air chief of staff at the time. Tommy White was. And White was therefore the Air Force representative on the Joint Chiefs. If the president had wanted the Air Force view, he could easily have summoned White back to Washington from wherever he had gone, and conferred with him. LeMay has emphatically stated that he knew nothing about the proposed air cover until the morning after it was canceled. But many people assume otherwise. Once again, LeMay's forceful personality and high visibility had gotten him into trouble. Though White was the chief of staff, there was a widespread feeling that LeMay was running the entire Air Force. When the experts began passing out blame for the Bay of Pigs disaster, it was inevitable that, since the lack of air cover was a factor, many fingers would point at the Air Force. And they weren't likely to point at the relatively obscure General White, who wasn't even in town at the time. They naturally pointed at the well-publicized, outspoken, and domineering Curtis LeMay, whom so many people believed to be in charge.

After his observation of the Bay of Pigs disaster, and the suggestions coming from administration sources that he and the Joint Chiefs were to blame for it, LeMay's confidence in Kennedy and his people, or however much confidence he ever had, was severely shaken. Strictly conservative as he was in his political views, he hadn't voted for Kennedy, nor did he ever think the young man would be a suitable president. By the time the previous administration ended, he hadn't even thought Eisenhower was sufficiently conservative, or sufficiently devoted to the needs of national defense. He was distrustful of Kennedy's attitudes even before Kennedy took office. And Kennedy's acceptance of Eisenhower's decision to allow the CIA to handle the Cuban invasion indicated that the new president was equally distrustful of the military.

One of Kennedy's closest advisers, Arthur M. Schlesinger, Jr., in his book, *Robert Kennedy and His Times,* was quite specific about John F. Kennedy's attitude toward the military.

> After the Bay of Pigs, the Kennedys began to question the Chiefs' professional competence. They also resented their public relations tactics. The new President was not one for men in uniform with pointers reading aloud sentences off flip charts he could read much faster himself. In the spring of 1961, Kennedy received the Net Evaluation, an annual doomsday briefing analyzing the chances of nuclear war. An Air Force general presented it, said Roswell Gilpatric, the deputy secretary of defense, "as though it were for a kindergarten

class. . . . Finally Kennedy got up and walked right out in the middle of it, and that was the end of it. And we never had another one.''

Gilpatric, who said that during a June 30, 1970, interview for the Kennedy Oral History Program, also had a few words about LeMay and Kennedy during that interview: ''Every time the President had to see LeMay, he ended up in a sort of a fit. I mean he would just be frantic at the end of a session with LeMay because, you know, LeMay couldn't listen or wouldn't take in, and he would make what Kennedy considered . . . outrageous proposals that bore no relation to the state of affairs in the 1960s.''

Everyone would have to agree that President Kennedy and Curtis LeMay were an odd couple. Kennedy was aware of LeMay's political views, his reputation as a blunt, unchangeable bomber man, his deficiencies in diplomacy and political tact. The arrival of the new administration did not augur well for this notoriously willful general. He couldn't expect to spend much more time in Washington. There was no tradition that said the vice chief of staff was the heir apparent to the chief's job. It was time for LeMay to think of early retirement.

One can imagine his surprise, therefore, when President Kennedy informed him he would be the new chief after General White's retirement at the end of June 1961. Almost everyone in Washington was equally surprised when Kennedy made the announcement May 22.

Schlesinger believed that ''LeMay's popularity in the ranks and on the hill gave him immunity,''[5] and thereby almost forced Kennedy to appoint him. Gilpatric apparently agreed. In his Oral History interview, he said, ''We would have had a major revolt on our hands if we hadn't promoted LeMay.''

LeMay says this is nonsense. ''Everybody [in the Air Force] would have been surprised if I hadn't been [appointed]. But everyone realized the president picks whomever he wants. There wouldn't have been a revolt.''

Eugene Zuckert, whom Kennedy had appointed secretary of the Air Force, agrees that there was no question of an Air Force revolt. To him, LeMay's selection as chief of staff was ''very simple. One of those things people love to overcomplicate. What happened was, I looked at the field of potential successors. I didn't think there was anybody who could get the Air

Force behind him the way LeMay could. . . . I felt LeMay was what the Air Force needed at that time. I went down and made that point to McNamara. He didn't comment. The next thing I knew, he told me the President had accepted his recommendation."[6]

Hugh Sidey of *Time* magazine believed LeMay was appointed "because he had the toughness Kennedy felt the country needed most." Sidey quoted Kennedy directly on the subject: "It's good to have men like Curt LeMay and Arleigh Burke [retired chief of Naval Operations] commanding troops once you decide to go in. But these men aren't the only ones you should listen to when you decide whether to go in or not. I like having LeMay at the head of the Air Force. Everybody knows how he feels. That's a good thing right now."[7]

One place where LeMay's appointment ran into no opposition was the Senate. At his confirmation hearing June 8 before the Armed Services Committee, he heard only praise for himself. But Sen. John Stennis of Mississippi did bring up two subjects that were destined to create serious troubles for LeMay during his term as chief of staff.

"With consideration to the actual operation of Atlas [missiles]," Stennis asked, "do you favor, or do you at all approve of, any program of reducing our manned bombers at this time?"

LeMay, as usual, jumped in with both feet: "We have missiles coming into the inventory now that are first-generation missiles, and their efficiency is not anywhere near what we would like to have or will expect to have later on after we have more experience with them, but they will take their place in the inventory and make a contribution.

"I think it only fair to say, however, that for some time to come, the bulk of the combat potential is in the manned system rather than in the missile system. . . . [The missiles] are not as good as we were hoping for. . . . Missiles are very expensive; they can be fired only once and it is going to be much more expensive and much more difficult to get a broad base of experience in missiles so that you know exactly what they will do if they are called upon to be fired in combat."

As he would soon find out, Robert McNamara, the secretary of defense under whom he'd be working, entertained different but equally firm ideas on the subject.

About fifteen people gathered at the White House for LeMay's swearing-in as Air Force chief of staff on the last day of June.

President Kennedy was there, of course. So were General White, Senator Symington, and Vice President Johnson. But McNamara wasn't there. Had LeMay already offended his boss before he even got started on his new job?

CHAPTER TWENTY-FOUR

Curtis LeMay's swearing-in as Air Force Chief of staff was not his family's only important ceremony that summer. On July 15, in the chapel at Andrews Air Force Base, his daughter, Patricia Jane, married Capt. James L. Lodge, Jr., the young Army doctor she had met through the combined machinations of the Air Force surgeon general and her mother. Jim Lodge had graduated from medical school in Georgia, served a tour of Army duty in France, then completed postgraduate medical studies in Vienna before returning to Washington for two years of residency at Walter Reed Hospital.

Their wedding was an impressive, full-church ceremony, followed by a big reception at Bolling Field. It was a great day, not only for Janie and Jim, but also for Helen. She had finally found the right man for Janie. The celebration was marked by just one, very minor, embarrassment. Sergeant Waterman's wife and the groom's mother, Mrs. James Lodge, Sr., were wearing dresses identical except in color.

After taking over his new job, LeMay had made the easy move down the hall into the chief's office, and had taken his chair among the Joint Chiefs of Staff, while Gen. Frederic Smith, Jr., settled into his old office as vice chief. Secretary Zuckert had nominated Smith for the job, but LeMay had no objections. "I had never served with him [but] we had gone through flying school together." Smith had once been in charge of the Air Force Statistical Control section in the Pentagon. He had become the resident expert in the use of those complicated new machines—computers—which Zuckert had been instrumental in introducing to the Air Force during an earlier tour as assistant secretary.

"The man we brought in to head that [computer control] program was Freddie Smith," Zuckert later recalled, "and I had a high respect for him. That was the basis for my urging LeMay to make him his vice chief.''

Smith himself recalls a certain reluctance to take the job because, while he knew LeMay, he didn't feel quite in tune with him. He told an interviewer in 1976 about a call he received on his red phone one night in the spring of 1961.

"It was Zuckert. He said, 'Freddie, I just nominated you as vice chief of staff.' I said, 'You have no right to do that without asking me about it.'

"He said, 'Well, I've done it.'

"I said, 'What does LeMay think about it?'

"He said, 'Well, he's satisfied.'

"I said, 'I know, I know just how satisfied. I don't want to do it. I'm going to talk to Norstad [General Lauris Norstad, Ret.] and I'll call you back tomorrow.'

"Well, Norstad said, 'Freddie, you had better do it for the good of the Air Force. I really think it will be good for the Air Force because LeMay is hard-nosed on one or two subjects and I think you will be a mellowing influence.'

"So, much against my better judgment, I came to Washington. . . . LeMay told me, 'You run the Air Force. I'll take care of the Joint Chiefs.'

"I said, 'Okay, that suits me fine' ''[1]

Eventually, Smith's misgivings about his ability to work with LeMay would prove to be well founded, but on the first big issue they faced together they saw eye to eye. They were both convinced the Air Force, due to growing Russian strength, needed a new, technologically advanced, all-weather fighter plane, and they basically agreed on the plane's specifications. But they realized they would not find it easy to get the project off the ground because their boss, Secretary McNamara, had already made it clear he disagreed.

Robert McNamara had been the president of Ford Motor Company when President-elect Kennedy chose him as secretary of defense. But he did not share the conservative business and political traditions of many automobile executives who had come before him. He didn't make decisions on the basis of judgment or instinct applied to past personal experience. His background was academic and his methods were based on firmly disciplined, logical, mathematical analysis of carefully prepared, often computerized, data. Before World War II he had taught at the Harvard School of Business Administration. During the war he was in charge of a team of operations analysts for the Air Force, stationed in England. In this capacity he is said to have written a letter to a Harvard colleague in praise of an Air Force colonel, Curtis LeMay, whose ideas about aerial bombardment tactics were then spreading through the Eighth Air Force. During the war years, McNamara, as an Air Force captain, found it difficult to convince generals that they should listen to his operations analyses. But his work was sufficiently impressive to draw a lot of admiring attention. And after the war, Ford grabbed him.

Norman Moss, author of the book *Men Who Play God*, called McNamara "an analyst by nature, who, when he looks at a situation, automatically strips it down to component parts with numerical relationships between them. When he asks questions of his subordinates, he calls for answers 'with numbers in them,' which means, to him, information couched in realistic terms that one can act upon."[2]

This makes him sound like a cold, calculating person more concerned about material than human values. When Moss asked him whether he felt the development of the hydrogen bomb had introduced a new moral issue to the world scene, his answer was what Moss called characteristically quantitative. "No," he said. "The moral issue comes when you kill one man. We want in our foreign policy to minimize the number of casualties, whether you're talking about one, ten, a thousand, or ten million." It was an answer that seemed to indicate a more statistical and practical than philosophical approach to governmental values. But it was an answer tailored to his uncompromising concept of his job, not necessarily to his personal feelings.

In his new job as secretary of defense, McNamara had quickly come to the reasonable conviction that whatever the big, diversified, difficult-to-manage military services were doing, they could do it for much less money. There were even a lot of military men, including Curtis LeMay, who might agree with him about that. McNamara also believed that some of what the military services did, or wanted to do, was not worth doing, and that in some of the other things they did, they duplicated each other. He was probably right about that, too. But he was destined to run into resistance in the determination of what exactly could be done less expensively, what didn't need to be done at all, and how much of the apparent duplication was unavoidable.

The issue of duplication was the first on which LeMay and McNamara seriously confronted each other. Not only the Air

Force, but also the Navy was convinced it needed a new, advanced fighter plane. McNamara was willing to concede the need on the part of both services. But committed as he was to greater economy and efficiency, he asked himself, very reasonably, what sense it would make to develop two quite different fighter planes, both of which would have the same mission—defense against Russian aggression. Why not develop just one fighter that would meet the requirements of both services? Right after he took over his job he began working on this concept, and in June 1961, shortly before LeMay became Air Force chief of staff, McNamara ordered Zuckert to proceed with the development of a plane provisionally called the TFX, to replace the Air Force F-105 and the Navy F-4.[3]

McNamara had first made his desires known on this issue in February 1961, almost the moment he became secretary of defense. And LeMay, as vice chief of staff, had made his contrary desires known several times since then. McNamara knew, therefore, that LeMay, as chief of staff, would fight him over this issue, and perhaps several others. He knew that LeMay was in some ways like himself. Both men had strong personalities. Neither was easy to sway once he made up his mind about something. Under those circumstances, it is difficult to imagine why McNamara ever forwarded the recommendation of LeMay as chief of staff. But he did. And in doing so, he invited some stormy years ahead, both for LeMay and for himself.

The Air Force and Navy, two services which seldom agreed about anything, were thrown into complete accord against McNamara's TFX concept. They agreed the TFX was certain to prove a disastrous mistake because it would fail to take into account the great and unavoidable differences in Air Force and Navy requirements.

A Navy fighter plane had to be able to take off from and land on a carrier deck, which was like a coffee table compared to the long, wide runways of an Air Force base. The necessity to operate in such a short space limited the size, weight, payload, range, and several flying characteristics of Navy fighters. But the Air Force, in designing fighters, didn't have to worry about such limitations because only under the rarest emergency conditions, if at all, would its planes ever have to land on a carrier. Why then would the Air Force be content to accept a plane with what it considered inferior performance, simply because the Navy was forced by circumstances to do so?

All of this became evident August 17, 1961, when Navy and Air Force representatives, after exhaustive meetings, agreed that they could not agree on common requirements for the kind of aircraft McNamara proposed. When they reached this stalemate, Adm. James S. Russell of the Navy suggested to LeMay that they go together and explain the situation to McNamara.

At the subsequent meeting, both men insisted every effort had been made to find agreement. Russell argued that the development of two planes was the only solution. And LeMay told the secretary that the Air Force had compromised its position "well below the state of the art." Further compromise, he said, was "out of the question if the Air Force was to accomplish its tactical mission." He also said that if only one plane was to be built, the Air Force would accept its "minimum position," but that if the secretary were to change his mind and allow development of two planes, the Air Force would "return to its original optimum position."[4]

The secretary did not change his mind. On August 22, the two services submitted their nonagreement report to McNamara. Obviously convinced he was dealing with nothing more than the usual Navy-Air Force intransigence, he notified them, on September 1, that he himself would set the plane's requirements.

McNamara later explained his decision to a congressional committee: "I would be less than candid . . . if I did not admit that the majority of experts in the Navy and Air Force said it couldn't be done. As late as the 22nd of August, 1961, after the Navy and the Air Force had been working together for almost eight months, it was reported to my by both services that development of a single TFX aircraft to fulfill stated requirements of both services was not technically feasible.

"While this attitude, based on years of going separate ways, was understandable, I did not consider it was a realistic approach, considering the versatility and capabilities that could be built into a modern aircraft because of advances in technology. I was also convinced that, if we could achieve a single tactical fighter, we would save at least $1 billion in development, production, maintenance, and operating costs. . . . I believed that the development of a single aircraft of genuine tactical utility to both services in the projected time frame was technically feasible and economically desirable."[5]

McNamara circulated his specifications for the TFX and by December 1, 1961, two companies—Boeing of Seattle and General Dynamics of Fort Worth, Texas—had submitted proposals for development of the plane. The Air Force Source Selection Board, which judged those proposals, and on which Rear Adm. Frederick L. Ashworth represented the Navy, voted unanimously January 19, 1962, in favor of the Boeing offer. But on January 24, after a review by higher authorities in the Defense Department, the Source Selection Board decision was rescinded. The competition between the two companies was extended another eight weeks and both were invited to submit second proposals at the end of that time. This meant there would be a two-month lull in the growing TFX controversy. It didn't mean the matter was settled.

Meanwhile, preliminary estimates and proposals for the 1963 defense budget (to be presented in early 1962) intensified another difference of opinion which had already surfaced between LeMay and McNamara. On September 23, 1961, McNamara sent LeMay a list of guidelines for the 1963 budget. These guidelines indicated McNamara's intention to reduce even further a key Air Force project he had already cut back drastically—the development of the B-70 long-range bomber (at this time designated the RS-70) which was expected eventually to replace the B-52.

In 1957, the Air Force had awarded North American Aviation a contract for development of the B-70. In 1960, when the development work was still in progress, the B-70 program was set at eleven to thirteen prototype aircraft. But in early 1961, after McNamara took charge of the Defense Department, he reduced the program to three prototypes and directed the Air Force to study the possible use of the B-70 for reconnaissance.

The Air Force instituted the reconnaissance study as ordered but at the same time tried to counter McNamara's obvious reservations about the B-70 by working out a new plan to reinstitute the thirteen-aircraft program with an additional $180 million in 1962, plus $675.8 million in 1963. The Air Force estimated that one wing of B-70s, forty-five planes, would cost $5 billion, including research and development.

The Air Force submitted this proposal to McNamara November 1, 1961, but never received a reaction from him. A month later, November 30, LeMay was briefed by the director of the budget on the final 1963 budget, which McNamara was then forwarding to President Kennedy for approval. It could be said that LeMay didn't much like what McNamara was proposing. In high dudgeon, LeMay discussed the matter with Zuckert, but, of course, to no avail. McNamara was also Zuckert's boss. Perhaps to release his frustrations, LeMay then dictated a memorandum of record to his executive officer, Colonel Richard H. Ellis:

> Here is what happened to the '63 budget. The Air Force has lost the additional B-52s; the B-70 is inadequately funded; the numbers of hardened and dispersed Minutemen [missiles] to be procured are inadequate; the mobile Minuteman has been canceled; and we are on thin ice with Skybolt [missile]. In other words, we have not done at all well with the funding of strategic forces for the future. This decision has been made by Sec Def against the advice of the Joint Chiefs of Staff and without consideration for the Air Force reclama [its complaint against the preliminary proposals]. The overall Air Force budget has reflected gains only in the nonnuclear tactical area. The Air Force has lost these decisions on strategic forces in spite of congressional and public support. In order to justify these decisions, it appears that a campaign is underway to discredit the judgment of the Air Force.[6]

LeMay was now so deeply immersed, and so emotionally aroused by this frustrating budget impasse it is difficult to imagine him getting involved in any other problem unless it were of major importance. But on December 1, the day after he wrote his impassioned budget memo, he found himself worrying about something which can only be described as trivial. At least from a standpoint of Air Force management it was trivial; not so, perhaps, to taxpayers who would have to pay the bill for it. Anyway, LeMay had to pay some attention to it because it concerned a person who could hardly be considered trivial—Vice President Lyndon Johnson.

On December 1, a complaint arrived in LeMay's office from Johnson's office.[7] It informed him that the vice president was "extremely unhappy with the airlift that is and has been provided him." His main complaints were "lack of jet transportation, inability to land on the airstrip at the Johnson ranch, and a continual changing of crews." After considerable to-do about the matter, LeMay called Johnson "to determine the exact nature of the latter's desires with regard to transportation."

Several back-and-forth conferences followed. Then on December 5, LeMay found it expedient to issue the following instructions: "A suitable jet aircraft [C-140 or T-39] was to be maintained on constant standby for use by the Vice President, [with] a Command Post for the purpose of providing the Vice President suitable transportation from Randolph or Bergstrom to the airstrip on the Johnson Ranch," which was to be surveyed "to determine necessary modifications or equipment additions required to insure safety . . ."

This done, LeMay could get back to more important matters. Several aspects of McNamara's budget disturbed him, but most of all, another apparent downgrading of the all-important B-70 bomber. Not the least bit inclined to surrender without a fight, he sought an appointment at the White House to talk to President Kennedy about his complaints, with Zuckert and McNamara also in attendance.[8] When he found himself unable to arrange that, he settled for a meeting, December 5, with McNamara. The B-70 took up a considerable portion of their outwardly friendly conversation.

McNamara, as usual, stated his position carefully. He didn't declare himself irrevocably against the B-70 project. He simply indicated that in view of the tremendous cost of the program, it was necessary to proceed slowly and be certain at every step that the objective could be achieved.

LeMay found it difficult to fathom exactly what that meant. Especially the part about proceeding slowly. This weapons system, he reminded McNamara, was "already years behind schedule because of stops and starts made by the administration." (He was including the Eisenhower as well as the Kennedy administration.) The B-52 would be approaching obsolescence, he said, by the time the B-70 could be deployed as a weapons system.

McNamara had already discussed several missile programs. It seemed evident that he favored missiles over manned aircraft. But LeMay, instead of tactfully avoiding the subject, confronted it. The country could not rely solely on missiles, he insisted. For this reason, "unless we proceed with the development of the B-70 as a weapons system as a matter of the highest national priority, we cannot guarantee the ability of the U.S. to maintain strategic superiority over the USSR."[9]

After this hour-and-a-half meeting, LeMay remarked to an aide that McNamara was "cordial," but that "there was no indication that he intended to change his views on strategic forces."

LeMay realized by this time that, in McNamara, he was facing something new. He had to contend with both a personality and a set of beliefs which presented a frustrating challenge. LeMay's own personality seemed so unmovable that, without necessarily trying to do so, he had for many years been able to intimidate or at least prevail over other men, even at the highest levels. In McNamara he was dealing with a man as stubborn, strong, opinionated, and positive as himself. Furthermore, this man was his boss and didn't intend to let him forget it.

Besides their differences over the TFX, the B-70, and the Air Force budget, some even more serious divergences had emerged between them concerning the basic nature of the nation's defense posture. While their contentions, on the surface, were usually about hardware—which and how many aircraft or missiles were needed—behind these arguments were their profound disagreements about what America had best do to protect itself and to keep peace in the world.

Shortly after McNamara took office, he and his staff made a thorough study of the nature and implications of nuclear war. Several years later he granted an interview to Norman Moss, who was at that time conducting research for *Men Who Play God*. McNamara's views, as quoted by Moss, represented what appear to be a unique attitude for an American secretary of defense since the beginning of the nuclear age in World War II.

"We came to the conclusion," McNamara said, "that thermonuclear war was unfeasible. Not impossible, in the sense that, technically, it couldn't happen. In that sense it was all too possible. But unfeasible in the sense that you couldn't fight such a war and hope to win in any meaningful sense."

One of the corollaries to this conclusion, McNamara said, was that "having superior strategic forces had a connotation different from what it had for centuries past. You couldn't achieve victory with them. They were not even a deterrent for more than a limited number of actions, because an enemy knew perfectly well that you wouldn't dare use them, and risk destruction of your own society . . . ."[10]

To support and enlarge his thinking about global strategy in a nuclear age, McNamara gathered around him in the Department of Defense a group of mostly young intellectuals from various universities, and from the Rand organization in Santa Monica, California, the "think tank" created by the Air Force to augment its research-and-development efforts after World War II. Some Air Force people now began to wonder about the brainchild it had spawned because these new thinkers from Rand, and the rest of McNamara's "Whiz Kids," soon began expressing important disagreements with the Air Force.

On the question of nuclear options, they adopted McNamara's thesis that a general atomic war was unfeasible, and, as alternatives to such a holocaust, developed such theories as "counterforce," the "no-cities doctrine," and the "no-first-use" position. "Counterforce" was a strategy designed to win a nuclear war by concentrating American atomic weapons against the enemy's strategic bases. The idea was to limit the enemy's civilian casualties in the hope that, perhaps out of gratitude, the enemy would try, in his attacks, to limit American civilian casualties. The "no-cities" doctrine was a more sophisticated development of the same idea. The "no-first-use" position, which originated shortly after World War II, long before Kennedy and McNamara arrived on the scene, was further developed by the Whiz Kids as a means of assuring Russia and the world that America would never launch the first bombs to start an atomic war. In McNamara's remarks to author Moss, he made it clear that he was against any "first-use" by America, and he didn't care who knew it.

LeMay and virtually all of his Air Force colleagues disagreed with many of the McNamara-Whiz-Kids theories or policies, and believed that some of those with which they might agree privately should not be announced publicly. They argued that it was damaging to divulge your plans to a potential enemy, whatever those plans might be. The divergence of opinion between the highly influential, peace-loving McNamara group, and the presumably war-loving military—Navy and Army as well as Air Force—soon became so wide that the Whiz Kids and the military men were openly contemptuous of each other.

"We in the military," LeMay later stated in his memoirs, "did not raise a blanket objection to being overruled. Sincerely we wanted to play on McNamara's team. What we did object to was the Secretary saying 'No' to something the military wished to do, and giving a *military reason* for his action. Palpably, thus, he and his coterie were setting themselves up as military experts."[11]

More recently, LeMay enlarged on his feelings about the impasse between the Kennedy administration and the military. "Every time a new administration comes in," he insisted, "the military wants to play on its team. There's no doubt in anybody's mind about civilian control of the military. There's never been any urge on the part of the military [to say], 'Stand aside, you civilians. We'll run the show.' I have never seen anything of that sort. I have seen plenty of military people who had absolutely no respect for their civilian bosses, and not without cause. But I've never met one who didn't have every respect for the job that [his civilian boss] held.

"The Kennedy Administration came in and right from the start we got the back of the hand. Get out of our way. We think nothing of you and your opinions. We don't like you as people. We have no respect for you. Don't bother us.

"My quarrel with McNamara was not so much our differences of opinion. I've had differences of opinion with a lot of people. My quarrel with him was—he has the same responsibility that I have, and he's not listening to me. [I'm] trying to do the same thing he is. I'm trying to help him and he doesn't want my help. And he does things I've known all my life are wrong."

LeMay likened McNamara to a hospital administrator. "He can run a good hospital. He doesn't have to be a doctor. But he won't run a good hospital if he dabbles in the brain surgery. This is what McNamara and his crew did. They dabbled in the brain surgery." Which was to say, military strategy.

With the Department of Defense thus divided against itself, McNamara and his civilian Whiz Kids held their deliberations and developed their theories about global strategy, while the military officers, in their offices a floor or two away, did likewise. In 1968, three years after LeMay's retirement, he published a book, *America Is in Danger,* setting forth the views he and his military colleagues had held when he was Air Force chief of staff.

"The so-called 'defense intellectuals' of the Kennedy-Johnson Administration," he wrote, "advocate parity as an ultimate goal, although not many admit it publicly. . . . Others, notably military men, think that deterrence is only possible in an atmosphere of strategic superiority. . . ."[12]

LeMay's belief, as of 1968, was that Russia, with its new intercontinental ballistic missiles, was then ahead of the United States in nuclear arms. He found the situation intolerable and called for America to regain the lead.

"Once the counter to a new weapon system had been invented and put into use," he wrote, "then, of course, the cycle repeats itself. And new offensive or defensive systems must be developed. You may call this an arms race, but it is the same kind of

arms race mankind has been running since the dawn of time."
And it was a race he believed the United States could win against
Russia.[13]

Though he has often been accused of advocating a first strike
in a preemptive war against Russia, LeMay has, on several occasions, denied that he ever favored a preemptive war. He made
it clear in *America Is in Danger,* however, that he has always
advocated a first-strike capability.

"Out general war policy should be designed to prevail and
defeat the enemy under a variety of circumstances, and not to
rule out a first strike."

He opposed a "second strike" policy which he accused Mc-
Namara of adopting, and he quoted defense specialist Paul Nitze
to explain why. In 1960, Nitze had said a second-strike retaliatory capability "provides us with no rational military strategy if
deterrence fails. . . . If deterrence fails, the only reaction open
to us is retaliation in support of a purpose that no longer exists—
the purpose of deterring the enemy from taking the action he has
already taken."

To this, LeMay added: "Deterrence is best achieved through
a real and convincing ability to win, not just to punish." He
argued for more advanced strategic aircraft, an anti-ballistic-mis-
sile system, a better air defense system, a shelter program and
"new strategic options . . . through research and development."[14]

These views, expressed publicly in 1968, were the same as
those LeMay had tried, as Air Force chief of staff, to impress
privately on Secretary McNamara. But he had little or no influence on McNamara, or on President Kennedy, both of whom
were so alarmed at the horrendous prospects of a nuclear war
that their thinking was directed toward ways of avoiding rather
than waging one. LeMay has always maintained that he was as
devoted as any man to the aim of avoiding war, but as a military
man, he had also the duty of determining how to wage and win
a war, if one should erupt. Rightly or wrongly, he argued for
strategic superiority because he believed it offered a better deterrence than did parity.

One reason LeMay published his views after his retirement
was that he believed neither McNamara nor either of the presidents under whom the two men served—Kennedy and Johnson—
had paid the slightest bit of attention to his opinions on global
defense. Speaking of McNamara in an interview at the time of

his retirement, LeMay said, ". . . we have a boss who makes a decision but he doesn't take our advice. In many cases I think he has his mind made up prior to getting our advice."[15]

In a 1972 interview, LeMay said, "President Kennedy always said that he wanted political advice as well as military advice from the Joint Chiefs, but what I think he really meant was he didn't want any advice at all. At least, I always had the feeling that I was spinning my wheels and anything that I said was not really falling on receptive ears. I think the other Chiefs felt more or less like that, too."[16]

Recently, he has elaborated on this viewpoint. Speaking again about McNamara, he said there had not been much discussion with him. "We [the Joint Chiefs] started off trying to talk to him. It was like talking into a brick wall. We got nowhere. Finally it was just a waste of time and effort. We would state opinions when we had a chance. That was all. . . . We in the military [with the exception of JCS Chairman Maxwell Taylor] felt we were not in the decision-making process. . . . [McNamara] would tell the Congress that he always consulted the JCS on important matters, and that could be construed as a true statement. But we'd get papers from the secretary's office to give an opinion on, and we knew he had already made the decision and issued the orders three days before."[17]

Given the differences between McNamara and LeMay on the subject of global strategy, it is easy to understand their differences about the kind of hardware needed to augment strategy. They weren't talking about the same strategy. While LeMay understood this perfectly, he could never overcome the frustration it caused him, nor could he give up the struggle for the more aggressive strategy he considered necessary. In his view, McNamara was simply too soft and naïve to deal with the threat of international communism.

On the same recent occasion, LeMay said, "My opinion is, [McNamara] believed if we had a deterrence, if we had forces of equal size, reasonable men could discuss things and solve [their] problems without going to war. This is, to me, too idealistic. First you've got to have two reasonable men. Are you going to have two reasonable men? Or are you going to have an idiot on one side and a smart guy on the other? Or a vindictive individual who won't agree to anything? I couldn't see any guarantee of success in this happening. And who's going to decide whether you have equal forces? I just didn't agree with that. To me it was [necessary] to have strength. If you had that strength and if you didn't push your adversary into an impossible situation, you were going to have peace. He wouldn't attack you."

These LeMay remarks, and the McNamara remarks quoted above, were made after their association at the Pentagon had ended. But it is fair to say they represented the views of the two men even as early as 1961 when they were just beginning to try to cope with each other. Each of them must have realized he had a tiger by the tail. Whether or not LeMay's problems with McNamara had anything to do with it is impossible to say, but it must be noted that LeMay, a notoriously healthy man up to that time, remained at home, sick in bed, on December 19 and most of the 20th. And on December 29 he entered the hospital at Andrews Air Force Base with what proved to be a coronary occlusion.

LeMay's heart attack kept him in the hospital until February 12, 1962. During his latter days there he relieved his boredom by firing an air pistol at a target on the wall. After his release, he and Helen flew to Hawaii for a protracted period of rest and recuperation. He sat in the sun and worked on some transistor radio kits J. B. Montgomery sent him. It wasn't where he wanted to be, with a battle in progress, but his doctors decided Washington was not the place for him until he recovered. This relieved him, at least, of having to listen to McNamara's January 24 testimony on the 1963 defense budget before the House Armed Services Committee. In this testimony McNamara stated more openly than ever his convictions about the B-70, and about manned bombers in general as opposed to missiles.

"As you well know," he reminded the congressmen, "we have had under development for some years a Mach-3 high altitude manned bomber, the B-70, for which the Congress last year provided $180 million more than President Kennedy requested. We have again restudied the role of the B-70 in our future strategic retaliatory forces and again have reached the conclusion that the B-70 will not provide enough of an increase in our offensive capabilities to justify its very high cost. . . .

"The principal advantage of the B-70 is its ability, in common with other manned bombers, to operate under positive control and to deliver a large number of nuclear weapons in a single sortie. Considering the increasing capabilities of ground-to-air missiles, the speed and altitude of the B-70, in itself, would no longer be a very significant advantage. Furthermore, it has not been designed for the use of air-to-surface missiles such as HOUND DOG or SKYBOLT, and in low-altitude attack, it must fly at subsonic speeds. In addition, the B-70 is not well suited to an era when both sides have large numbers of ICBMs [intercontinental ballistic missiles]: it would be more vulnerable on the ground than hardened missiles and it does not lend itself to airborne alert measures.''

McNamara's mention of the ''$180 million more than President Kennedy had requested'' for the B-70 referred to a partial victory, though perhaps a Pyrrhic one, that LeMay had achieved in Congress the year before, when he was still vice chief of staff. McNamara had sought, in the fiscal 1962 budget, an appropriation of $220 million for B-70 development. LeMay, because he had become surprisingly popular and prestigious with both Democrats and Republicans in Congress, had been able, without openly challenging McNamara, to get that appropriation boosted to $400 million. But McNamara had turned his defeat into victory by refusing to spend the extra $180 million. And now, in his proposed budget for fiscal 1963, he was announcing his intention to use last year's surplus in fiscal 1962, and he was asking for only $171 million to continue development of a prototype B-70, mostly for research purposes, in fiscal 1963. At the same time, he was demonstrating that the B-70 wasn't the only manned bomber he held in limited favor. He continued to refuse to use $515 million Congress had appropriated the previous year to buy more B-52s and B-58s.

When committee members questioned him about this in the budget hearings for fiscal 1963, McNamara said, ''Manned bombers present soft and concentrated targets and they depend upon warning and quick response for their survival under nuclear attack. This is a less reliable means of protection than hardening, dispersal, and mobility. (Which advantages missiles would enjoy.) Moreover, reliance on warning and quick response means that the bombers must be committed to the attack very early in the war and cannot be held in reserve to be used in a controlled and deliberate way.

''Finally, bombers are expensive. It costs well over a billion dollars to buy a wing of B-52s, together with its tankers and Skybolt missiles, and to operate it for five years. For the same cost, we can buy and operate for the same period of time 250 hardened and dispersed Minuteman missiles or six Polaris submarines.''

In these remarks, McNamara made very clear his belief that the age of missiles had come, and that manned bombers were then, in 1962, on the verge of obsolescence. Since he was the secretary of defense, his words were accepted by the public like an official announcement that had been anticipated for some time. The emergence of missiles to replace aircraft as vehicles for atomic weapons was an eventuality which had been hanging over the defense establishment since the Germans launched their V-1 and V-2 rockets against England in World War II. The fact that McNamara now indicated the missile system was ready to go confirmed in many minds the belief that LeMay, and other men of his persuasion in the Air Force, were simply fuddy-duddies who spent so much time flying around in the wild blue yonder they couldn't face the fact that their precious airplanes were becoming militarily obsolete. They were like admirals who still believed in battleships. You could sympathize with these aging flyboys for sentimental reasons, but you wouldn't want to accept their extravagant demands for larger and larger forces or the countryside would soon look like a dumpyard for useless airplanes.

It was into this atmosphere that LeMay stepped when he returned from Hawaii in mid-February, still recuperating from his heart attack. Convinced that he couldn't sway McNamara, he secured an appointment with President Kennedy and, on the 16th, repaired to the White House, charts and statistics in hand, to make his case for the B-70 and for the necessity to maintain a strong strategic force of manned aircraft, at least for several years to come. LeMay felt it was imperative to convince the president of the coming need for the B-70 and the immediate need for more B-52s and B-58s. But the president didn't seem to have his mind on the Air Force budget that day. He preferred to discuss worldwide military problem areas. When their discussion ended, Kennedy had not committed himself to supporting "any aspect" of LeMay's argument. It seemed to LeMay it had been "only with a great deal of difficulty" that he had been able to make his points. He felt that "the president was not fully informed on the adequacy of the strategic force as outlined in the '63 budget but was accepting the secretary of defense's proposed funding without question."[18]

LeMay's next stop was Capitol Hill where, on February 26, he testified before the House Armed Services Committee, the same group of congressmen to whom McNamara had stated his case a month earlier. Here, LeMay had better luck. A manned bomber force, he told the committee, was not only desirable during the years just ahead. It could make the difference between victory and defeat in a war.

After listening to his arguments, the committee showed its support by suggesting that instead of the $171 million McNamara had requested, they would ask their congressional colleagues to appropriate $491 million for the B-70 in fiscal 1963.

The next day, LeMay and his Air Force coterie visited the Defense Subcommittee of the Senate Appropriations Committee, where he presented the same arguments and expressed the hope that the senators would also recommend $491 million for the B-70. His impression afterward was that "this committee also appeared to support the Air Force position."

But he still had to contend with one important man who didn't. On March 1, LeMay went downstairs for what was described as "an informal discussion" with his angry boss, Robert McNamara. He didn't like what LeMay had said to those congressional committees. And he especially didn't like LeMay's remark that a manned bomber force could be the difference between victory and defeat in a war. It seemed to him that the Air Force had become an "all or nothing force," by which he apparently meant the Air Force would be satisfied only if it got all of what it wanted.[19]

When LeMay returned to his own office, he told his aides they had better expect the secretary of defense to "start playing rough" on the B-70 issue. And he directed his staff to "document our case" for the plane. He was especially anxious to "shoot down the secretary of defense's statement that the Air Force is an all-or-nothing force." He said he didn't think McNamara was "familiar with the technical side" of the aircraft. "We must make every effort to convince him and his staff," LeMay concluded, "that the Air Force [can], in fact, accomplish the program as presently conceived."

The next day, March 2, word sifted into the Pentagon from Capitol Hill that the House Armed Services Committee, in addition to supporting LeMay on the B-70, intended, if necessary, to "direct" the Executive Department to spend the additional money Congress would be appropriating for the B-70. And shortly thereafter, word sifted upstairs to LeMay's office that McNamara's staff had suddenly gone to work on crash studies that he intended to use before Congress in refuting the Air Force

B-70 position. One of LeMay's staff officers came up with an idea that must have seemed clever at the time, and LeMay tried it out on McNamara the next day.

After securing an appointment with the secretary of defense, LeMay suggested to him that the Air Force could be "of great assistance" in preparing the crash studies on the B-70, which he understood were in progress. But if he thought McNamara would fall for that, he didn't know McNamara. The secretary not only declined any such "assistance." He also informed LeMay that his technical staff had told him the Air Force, in the matter of the B-70, was talking beyond the state of the art. Certain subsystems on which the Air Force was counting would not be available. And there was some doubt that the aircraft industry was capable of carrying out the B-70 requirements for which the Air Force was asking.

McNamara further informed LeMay that he intended to discuss the B-70 at a meeting of the Joint Chiefs two days later. It seemed apparent to LeMay that he intended "to line up the other chiefs against the Air Force to support his position before Congress."[20]

At the JCS meeting on March 5, McNamara did exactly that, with notable success. He asked each of the other chiefs what they thought of the B-70 program. Inasmuch as it would probably, in the years to come, subtract considerable funds from their own services, they could not be expected to bubble over with enthusiasm for it. Gen. George Decker, representing the Army, was, however, surprisingly supportive of it in light of the fact that McNamara's budget indicated an intention of strengthening ground forces. Decker agreed with the Air Force that it should develop the B-70 and its components.

To this, McNamara answered that some of the components or subsystems were not technically feasible. Especially the radar system.

LeMay broke in to say that the Goodyear Company had agreed to develop the radar system on a fixed-fee basis.

McNamara said he would like to see the details of the Goodyear proposal. Then he continued polling the other two members of the JCS. The chairman, Gen. Lyman Lemnitzer of the Army, said the current strategic program seemed adequate. And Adm. George Anderson of the Navy agreed with him. It was not a good day for LeMay.[21]

Congress, however, was still to be heard from, and perhaps

because it had always been a deliberative, slow-moving body, unwilling to abandon the old until it was comfortable with the new, it was preparing to come down on the side of the airplane as opposed to the not quite proven missiles. But not only because the majority of congressmen believed that the airplane was still, at that time, more reliable than the missile. They were increasingly angry at McNamara because he was ignoring their collective will by refusing to use the B-70 funds they had allocated the previous year. Most of the members of the House Armed Services Committee were veterans who had served on it for several years. Its chairman, Carl Vinson of Georgia, had been a member for years. These men considered themselves as well qualified in matters of national defense as McNamara, who had, at that time, only one year of governmental experience.

On March 7, the Vinson committee disclosed publicly that its authorization bill recommended $491 million for the B-70 in fiscal 1963. And in a deliberate jab at McNamara, whose expertise in technical matters had long since been established, the committee report said, "Expertise is not infallibility."

Buttressing their own claim to competence and responsibility, the congressman pointed out "we are abandoning to the enemy the development and production of the flexible weapon system which has kept the peace for many years. Although there is a clear need for a manned strategic reconnaissance-strike aircraft, no manned strategic aircraft system is planned for development or production in the entire free world."

The B-70, the congressmen declared, "is ideally suited for operation in the missile era. Unlike ballistic missiles, the RS-70 [B-70] will not have to rely primarily on high speed, high altitude and low radar cross-section for penetration. It will have other important advantages—it is maneuverable, it can carry large quantities of counter-measures, it can employ tactics, it does not have to fly over or into the target, it has its own defense suppression weapons and finally, it has men aboard to exercise judgment to adjust to a changing environment."

To make sure that this time their will concerning the B-70 would be done, the Vinson committee's authorization bill used some startling and provocative language. It "directed, ordered, mandated, and required" the secretary of the Air Force to utilize the entire $491 million, or whatever amount the full Congress allocated to the bomber program.

The question as to which side was right about the potential

usefulness of the B-70 was now so complicated it was almost impossible to judge. It involved issues even the best-informed citizens could not assess concerning the state of both the aircraft and missile arts in both the United States and Russia. And it also involved the issue of who knew more about these arts— McNamara and his experts or LeMay and his. These issues were bewildering to the average person. And in the meantime, the controversy had raised two other issues of major importance.

If Congress were to pass a bill which "directed, ordered, mandated, and required" the secretary of the Air Force to carry out a program, it would be launching a horrendous constitutional challenge and confrontation between the legislative and executive branches of the government. And in this case it would not be a thoughtless, inadvertent challenge. The Vinson committee, by its wording, made that clear: "If this language constitutes a test as to whether Congress has the power to so mandate, let the test be made and let this important weapon system be the field of trial."

Here was a challenge President Kennedy could not ignore. It was probable but by no means certain that the executive branch would win in the courts. But meanwhile, the administration's relations with Congress would be badly damaged and much of its legislative program would be threatened. Kennedy decided, at this critical moment, to use one of his most powerful weapons—his charm. On March 20, he invited the elderly Carl Vinson to the White House, fed him well, and took him for a walk in the garden. By the time Vinson said good-bye, he had agreed to drop the provocative words from the bill. It would not "direct" the secretary of the Air Force. It would simply "authorize" him. And in return, the Defense Department would "restudy" the whole B-70 situation.

The second question of major importance raised by the controversy was whether a military officer was disobeying the president, his commander-in-chief, when his testimony before Congress failed to agree with that of his immediate superior, the secretary of defense. McNamara raised this question, perhaps inadvertently, during a rare press conference on March 15. The purpose of the conference was to make sure the nation's newsmen understood his position on the B-70 as opposed to the Air Force position. At one point he referred to LeMay by name as the only member of the Joint Chiefs of Staff who disagreed with his position. And he left the impression, whether purposely or accidentally, that LeMay was thereby disregarding the wishes and decisions of the president. A grave charge against a military man, punishable by courts-martial.

LeMay, who was on a short trip to Portugal that day, discussing American bases there as well as Portuguese air defense needs, returned to Washington on the 17th and heard with dismay that his loyalty to the president had been questioned. After discussing the matter with Secretary Zuckert, he decided he would "challenge Mr. McNamara's statement that he did not follow orders."

Late that afternoon he arranged a meeting with McNamara which began in a routine, friendly way. They discussed LeMay's trip to Portugal as if there were nothing else on either of their minds. But then LeMay, in his usual blunt, outspoken way, referred to the press conference McNamara had held in his absence. He said he took "a dim view" of the secretary's remarks about his failure to support presidential decisions. Not once had he ever failed to do what his commanders had ordered. As for his differences of opinion with McNamara, he had never made a public statement about them. But when he was called to testify before Congress, he was placed under oath. It was his obligation, under those circumstances, to state his honest convictions.

McNamara, who may never have intended to impugn LeMay's loyalty, was apparently astonished at this outburst. He had intended no such suggestions, he insisted, and he was sure that none of the people at the press conference had interpreted his remarks in that light.[22] Though LeMay was by no means so sure of this, he accepted McNamara's statement and the matter was closed.

As for the B-70 program, Congress appropriated $363 million to continue it in fiscal 1963. And McNamara appointed Dr. Joseph V. Charyk, undersecretary of the Air Force, to restudy the program. But there was still the question of whether McNamara would spend the allocated money on it. That matter remained open.

CHAPTER TWENTY-FIVE

While the B-70 controversy continued to draw public attention another situation was developing in Southeast Asia, to which most people paid very little heed at the time. On February 26, 1962, two "dissident" pilots in the Air Force of South Vietnam bombed the palace of their own President Ngo Dinh Diem in Saigon. Despite extensive damage to the building, President Diem was unhurt. And the whole matter would hardly have been noticed by the rest of the world were it not for the fact that the two pilots were trained by American "advisers" in Vietnam, and they were flying American-built planes.

No one suggested that this attempt to assassinate President Diem was inspired by the U.S. government, but to the American public, the incident was a reminder that we were gradually becoming involved in a war between South Vietnam and Communist-controlled North Vietnam.

A few people expressed concern about this at the time, but not many. News stories about the war in Vietnam were simply confusing to those who were bothering to read them in 1962. The French, who once held colonial sway over the country, had fought Communist guerrilla forces there since the end of World War II, and had finally given up after a humiliating defeat at Dienbienphu in May 1954. In the intervening years, Communist power had increased so alarmingly that the American government, first under Eisenhower and now under Kennedy, had gradually come to believe that it was in the national interest to intervene. As a result, we now seemed to be taking the place of the French in the tragically entangled affairs of the war-ravaged country. But the government we were supporting didn't seem much more beneficial to the Vietnamese people than the Communist government of North Vietnam which threatened it, and which, of course, we opposed.

Very little of this impressed the average American at the time. Vietnam was "a far away country of which we knew little." Its culture and its people were strange; its problems didn't seem real to most of us. To President Kennedy and the men around him, however, they did. In the fall of 1961, he sent his most trusted military adviser, retired Army Gen. Maxwell D. Taylor, to Saigon for an assessment of the situation. At that time, the United States had six hundred military "advisers" there. Taylor decided, and told Kennedy, it was not enough. In October, Kennedy decided there should be sixteen thousand. Then on December 11, thirty-three American helicopters arrived with four hundred men to fly and maintain them. This was the first direct U.S. military support for South Vietnam. But it was only the beginning. On February 8, 1962, the Defense Department announced the formation of the Military Assistance Command in Vietnam (MACV) under Army Gen. Paul D. Harkins, who was elevated to four-star rank to indicate our seriousness of purpose.

The bombing of the presidential palace February 26 apparently had little or nothing to do with the war against the Communist north. It was largely a manifestation of the widespread unpopularity of President Diem and his wealthy, Roman Catholic family, a powerful, high-handed, and arrogant clan which controlled South Vietnam. American newsmen in Saigon were well aware of the nature of the Diem government. President Kennedy should also have been aware of it, but there is some doubt as to whether he was. The one thing he knew was that Diem was anti-Communist, and in American foreign-policy decisions, that is frequently enough. Kennedy's aim was to stop the Communists and he wanted to do it quickly.

On March 1, three days after the palace in Saigon was bombed, Kennedy summoned the Joint Chiefs to a meeting, but not because of any sudden alarm about Vietnam. It wasn't even the first topic raised. The meeting began with a discussion of Okinawa and whether it could be returned to Japanese control without endangering our bases there.

When the subject of Vietnam came up, the president wanted to know if our military assistance had yet begun to show results.[1] Viewed in retrospect, the question seems shockingly naïve. Was it possible that Kennedy, even in 1962, knew so little about the true situation in Vietnam? The failure of our intelligence there must have begun early. We now know that ten more years of ever-increasing military assistance in Vietnam showed no results. At least no good results. But in 1962, the president of "the most powerful nation the world had ever seen" could hardly conceive of a spot on earth where his armies would not prevail. General Lemnitzer, answering for the assembled chiefs, told the president it was difficult to determine the success or failure of our mission at that time since we were still building up our effort. Successive chiefs of staff, successive cabinet officers, and successive civilian experts during the next ten years would continue to tell successive presidents virtually the same thing.

On April 16, 1962, LeMay and several subordinates flew to Vietnam for a five-day inspection tour. It was LeMay's first visit since the American military involvement began and he wasn't very happy with what he saw. He didn't question the fitness of the U.S. role there. His attitude was not different from that of most civilians at the time. Very few Americans were raising such questions in 1962. The public outcry against the Vietnam War did not rise to full voice until three years later, in 1965. What angered LeMay about the war was, quite characteristically, the ways in which the Americans and South Vietnamese were misusing the limited air resources at their disposal.[2]

Among the people to whom he talked were President Diem and General Harkins. The thrust of Diem's conversation was hardly surprising. It consisted largely of a list of things he wanted: improved airports, better communications and maps, more aircraft including jets, and the beginning of a "chemical crop-destruction program" in Vietcong areas. LeMay's overall impression was that Diem was "a man supremely confident, who felt he knew all the facets of the problems confronting Vietnam and knew all the solutions. The enormity of the problem did not appear to disturb him. His key solution was the prompt building up of a chain of strategic, fortified villages, inexorably increasing in number and spreading through the areas infested by Vietcong forces. Implementation of this plan would choke off the Vietcong resources and capability to live off plunder. The key to success was adequate local defense, timely intelligence, good radio communication, and prompt air support."

This need for air support was one thing about which LeMay and Diem completely agreed. LeMay was horrified by indications of what he considered inefficient use of air power. His diary summation, after his return to Washington, couched his dissatisfaction in polite words: "... the South Vietnamese Air Force and the USAF could contribute substantially greater efforts to the war." He was "particularly disturbed at the lack of knowledge on the part of U.S. Army advisers and ARVN [Vietnamese] commanders on the role of air power in counterinsurgency operations." He expressed the opinion that "while a Joint Operations Center had been established for the control of all aircraft in South Vietnam, it was not being used effectively. . . . Ground commanders were not receiving appropriate air cover with a result that ambushes were too frequent and casualties much too high." And he believed very strongly that General Harkins needed "an Air Force Deputy Commander of Lieutenant General rank."

It was for Harkins that he reserved his harshest criticism. His remarks to his colleagues on the JCS about the U.S. commander in Vietnam were so blunt and unrestrained that Harkins, ten years later, told an interviewer LeMay had preferred charges against him.[3]

"The only thing [LeMay] asked me was for five hundred thousand dollars to build a barracks for the Vietnamese up in Pleiku," Harkins recalled. "I said I'd see what I could do. Then he preferred charges against me. He preferred charges, first, that everything in Vietnam was 'business as usual,' that neither I nor my chief of staff knew anything about air support, that the air support was not being handled properly, and that nobody could get in to see me—unless they came through my chief of staff, which was untrue. My door was always open. The two charges came. And I mean they came in a 'flash' message that I was to answer within twenty-four hours. . . . When [the answer] went to Lemnitzer, he said, 'Paul, I couldn't show this to anybody,' and I said, 'You can show it to anybody you want to. I was charged and there are my answers to the charges.' About two or three days later I got a wire from Secretary McNamara, 'The charges are dropped.' "

If such charges were ever preferred, LeMay's diary and the summary report of his Vietnam visit offer no hint of them. He himself has no recollection of preferring charges against Harkins, and the assistant vice chief of staff at the time, Lt. Gen. Richard Montgomery, also has no memory of it, though he does recall LeMay's criticism of Harkins's use of air power.[4] (General Frederic Smith, the vice chief at the time, has since died.) It should be noted that LeMay, as soon as he returned to Washington, ordered that a C-123 transport be modified as a command aircraft and be made available to Harkins. It would seem an extraordinary gesture for LeMay to make toward someone he was charging with dereliction of duty.

Just before his trip to Vietnam, LeMay had been presented with a small but delicate and potentially embarrassing problem to which he had to attend as soon as he returned. On April 13, Brig. Gen. Godfrey T. McHugh, the Air Force aide to President Kennedy, informed him that the president would like to take a spin in a supersonic airplane. Which was to say, a fighter plane.

LeMay was quick to tell his staff he didn't think much of that idea. It didn't take a lot of thought for him to imagine himself on television, in front of a bereaved American public, trying to explain how the president of the United States got killed during a pointless joyride in one of his damned fighter planes.

If the president insisted on such a ride, LeMay told his staff, the flight should be in a relatively safe plane like the F-106, the pilot should be carefully selected, and the planning should be so detailed as to "provide for every possible safety precaution." But the greatest of all safety precautions, in his view, was to keep the president on the ground. It wouldn't be easy for him to say this, however, to his commander-in-chief.

Fortunately, at the right moment, help came from an unexpected source—Secretary McNamara. In this matter, he and LeMay were of one mind. On the advice of both of them, relayed through General McHugh, Kennedy canceled the flight.[5]

Within a month after LeMay's return from Vietnam, Freddie Smith's misgivings about how well they would work together proved to be well founded. LeMay decided he needed a new vice chief, not because of any explosion between the two men; simply because they didn't think alike. But LeMay, on this occasion, must have been uncommonly smooth and subtle in arranging the dismissal because Smith did not blame him for it. Smith could recall only one issue, concerning a reduction of SAC personnel, on which they disagreed. He blamed McNamara for his dismissal.

As Smith remembered the circumstances fourteen years later, McNamara wanted a major general in Logistics fired because he considered him "stupid." But Smith refused to fire the man because he would not, in his words, "ruin, at its apex, an officer's career out of sheer pique." About a month later, in early May, when faced with a repeat order that he fire the man, Smith wrote a letter of resignation that was ultimately accepted.[6]

The above incidents may have taken place as Smith recalled them, but according to LeMay, they do not explain why he was relieved. "I don't know that there was any one incident that brought things to a head," LeMay said many years later. "I wasn't completely satisfied. I didn't think I had his complete loyalty. We disagreed on things. Once I made a decision I expected wholehearted cooperation. He was happy to leave."[7]

Air Force Secretary Eugene Zuckert had chosen LeMay's first vice chief. LeMay decided he would choose the second one and he had a pretty good idea who it would be. Out in Dayton, running the Logistics Command, was a fellow named William F. "Bozo" McKee who had the distinction of being the only man in the history of the Air Corps or Air Force to achieve four-star, full-general rank without being a pilot.[8] He had begun his career in the Army but was transferred to the Air Corps as a major just before World War II when Gen. George Marshall decided Hap Arnold needed better staff officers than he had. McKee had proven to be such an excellent administrator that even the Air Force's propilot promotion system hadn't been able to hold him down. Though LeMay had never worked with him, he knew about him and decided he wanted him.

"The fact that he wasn't a pilot would be a disadvantage in the eyes of some people," LeMay said later. "I knew that. But I didn't think it would be. I thought it over a long time."

McKee's first inkling of it came when he was on his way back from an inspection trip to Europe. After landing in Bermuda, he found a message from LeMay awaiting him. He was to stop in Washington and come to LeMay's office the next day on his way back to Wright Patterson in Dayton.

McKee, despite his "Bozo" nickname, was a slender, gentle-looking man, but not one to be intimidated. LeMay's cold stare would not frighten him. He walked into the chief's office, one four-star general to another, and sat down.

LeMay, as usual, was chewing on a cigar. He glowered at Bozo for a moment or two, then said, without bothering about formalities, "You want to be vice chief of staff?"

Bozo said, "No sir. I don't have any desire to be."

"Why not?"

"Why the hell do I want to be vice chief? As logistics commander, I have my own airplane, my own staff. I can go wherever I want to go. I don't have to ask permission. If I come here and work on the Air Staff that I already worked on for years and years, I won't have any freedom. I'll work my ass off. And what'll I get out of it? I'm not rated [not a pilot]. I can't become chief of staff. So no, I'm not interested in the vice chief's job."

LeMay, after listening to him quietly and patiently, said, "All right. I've heard your bullshit. Report for duty July first. Now let's go in and see the secretary."

McKee recalls that "working with LeMay couldn't have been better. He gave me my job and he never interfered. He had this speech he made to every new group [on the Air Staff]. He'd get them in my office and say, 'I just want you people to know, General McKee is vice chief. I spend seventy-five percent of my time on the Joint Chiefs of Staff, testifying before Congress, making speeches and what not. When I'm gone, General McKee is running the Air Force. Whatever he says goes. If you don't like the way he's running it, come and see me.' I never had any problems.

"He would be going overseas [for instance]. He'd say to me, 'I'll be gone for two weeks. Don't bother me unless a war starts.' And he meant it."

The seventeen-nation conference to work out a nuclear test-ban treaty, which was in effect a two-nation conference between the U.S. and the USSR, began on June 15, 1962, mostly at the instigation of President Kennedy, and dragged on through that summer. It began with qualified hopes for success, but Curt LeMay was not among those who shared such hopes. Even before the negotiations began, he considered them unpromising and even dangerous to our national interests.

"This came up," he recalled in a 1984 conversation, "at a time when we hadn't had a test for some while. The Russians had just completed a big series, including a one-hundred-megaton H-bomb test. We never approached that. They were well ahead. I just couldn't see any military advantages."[9]

President Kennedy, who was horrified at the prospect of a nuclear war, had spent many months rounding up support for a test-ban and a disarmament agreement, provided the Russians were willing to cooperate. He had corralled the Joint Chiefs in the spring and had secured from them an "agreement in principle." But their agreement, in the opinion of Kennedy aide Theodore Sorensen, "had assumed that a test ban, like all other disarmament proposals, was only a diplomatic pose unlikely to achieve reality.''[10]

The Air Force in general, and LeMay in particular, would fit nicely into Sorensen's analysis. Almost nobody in the Air Force considered the test-ban idea practical. Concerning the Joint Chiefs' agreement in principle, LeMay said later, ''[We] got all kinds of pressure to agree to a treaty. Everybody else caved in. All the other chiefs agreed. I wondered how I could disagree without getting fired. My answer was, I couldn't see any military advantages accruing to us from the treaty. They would all be disadvantages. [But] where the administration said there would be great diplomatic gains, I couldn't pretend to be an expert in this field. These [gains] might outweigh military disadvantages. I would only agree if we would maintain our laboratories on standby, ready to go.''

In a typically hard-bitten LeMay postscript during that 1984 conversation, he added, ''I have yet to see the big diplomatic advantages.'' At any rate, none were forthcoming in the summer of 1962. On August 28 of that year, the test-ban talks at Geneva were declared to be deadlocked. And on September 7, they were recessed. But the treaty was finally signed in July and ratified in September 1963.

In late September 1962, LeMay began planning a trip to Spain and other European countries, but before his October 2 takeoff, he warned his staff about some serious troubles that might be brewing in Cuba, and he ordered that certain measures be taken in preparation for such a possibility.[11] For some time, Cuban refugees had been telling American newsmen and congressmen that there were Soviet missiles installed in Cuba. Several senators, including Barry Goldwater of Arizona and Kenneth Keating of New York, were so convinced of this they were calling for action against Fidel Castro's Communist government, and the public rhetoric had reached such a pitch that Jack Kennedy was getting worried about it. Unless he did something, people might think he was getting soft on Cuban Communism, especially after the Bay of Pigs humiliation.

Despite the rumors, however, the American intelligence community had not been able, until the end of August, to establish any hard evidence of Russian missiles in Cuba. Then on August 29, aerial photographs taken by a CIA-operated U-2 showed Russian SAM antiaircraft missile emplacements and missile-equipped torpedo boats. And more aerial photos taken September 5 showed Russian MIG-21 fighter planes. But all of these were defensive weapons and there was no way Kennedy could justify an offensive move against a country that was arming itself only for defensive purposes. CIA Director John McCone later speculated that the SAM installations could easily have been built for the primary purpose of protecting offensive ICBMs, but in early September McCone's analysis was not available because he had been married recently and was out of town on a honeymoon.

In the highest reaches of the Air Force command structure there was some knowledge of all this. Bozo McKee remembers a phone call he received from Tom Power who had succeeded LeMay as commander of SAC. "We've got a number of U-2s," McKee recalls power saying to him. "I recommend I send six of them over at low altitude and photograph every inch of Cuba."[12]

McKee's recollection is that Dr. Joseph Charyk approved the project for Zuckert, and Roswell Gilpatric for McNamara. "I went up to see the secretary of the Air Force. It happened that day to be Joe Charyk [because Zuckert was out of town]. He said, 'It makes sense to me. I'll go down and see the secretary of defense.' McNamara was also out of town so that was [Roswell] Gilpatric. It made sense to him.

"I got permission to call the CIA and tell them what we proposed. A good friend of mine, Marshall 'Pat' Carter, was the deputy director. [Carter was in charge of the CIA during McCone's honeymoon absence.] He fought it. He wanted the CIA to do it [conduct the mission] though they only had one U-2. So it went to the White House and the White House backed us up."

The Air Force, McKee recalls, used six U-2s for the mission. "They made that one pass, the first pass, and that blew the whole thing. That was the first time Kennedy really saw the extent of it."

There is disagreement among close observers at the time as to when the president first received positive evidence that there were offensive Soviet missiles in Cuba. Sorensen says it was October 14, some time after the first SAC mission. But there is no doubt that SAC's first pass over Cuba added significantly to the growing evidence that the Russians were doing something on the island that they couldn't be allowed to continue.

Because LeMay was in Europe, McKee was representing the Air Force at Joint Chiefs of Staff meetings, where the burning question under debate now was what must be done if there actually were offensive Russian missile installations in Cuba. Should the United States blockade or invade? Gen. Maxwell Taylor was the new chairman of JCS, having been brought out of retirement by Kennedy to take the job. There was agreement between him and the other chiefs that military action should be taken. "I recommended that we invade," McKee recalls, "on the simple basis that even if the Russians withdrew, they'd still have made their point and they'd end up just where they are today—controlling Cuba."

Though McKee had to represent LeMay in those early JCS deliberations about the explosive Cuban missile situation, he was uncomfortable doing so. On October 8, one day after another U-2 mission provided more missile evidence, he went to Taylor and said, "It looks to me as if we're about to get involved in a fight.

"Taylor said, 'Yes, that's right.'

"I said, 'I think LeMay ought to be here.'

"He said, 'I agree with you. But this is so supersensitive, how're you going to get hold of him without it leaking out?'

"I said, 'I know how to do that. I'll get him on the phone and tell him a final decision [presumably a decision to kill] is about to be made on the B-70. He'll be back here tomorrow morning.'

"Taylor laughed and said, 'Okay.'

"So that's what I did. LeMay (when I reached him) said, 'Who in hell is trying to stop the B-70?'

"I said, 'I'm not going to tell you anything over the telephone. You'd better get back here as soon as you can.'

"He said, 'I'll be there tomorrow morning. Don't let anything happen.'

"Next morning, he came storming into the office. Again he said, 'Who in hell is it that's trying to stop the B-70?'

"I said, 'Listen, LeMay, nobody's mentioned the B-70 since you've been gone. We're about to get in a war.'

" 'What?!'

"It was all Cuba after that."

Though LeMay hadn't expected any such news as this, he had, as previously indicated, been aware for some time of the delicate nature of the Cuban situation. On September 27, five days before his departure for Europe, he had directed Cam Sweeney, now in charge of the Tactical Air Command, "to examine the status of TAC's Cuban planning and to determine its adequacy in view of known Cuban Air Force capabilities." He had also ordered

Sweeney to work out a coordinated air plan with the Navy to be used in case of Cuban trouble.

"As I remember it," LeMay said later, "before I went to Europe I issued orders to fill up the bomb dumps in the Southeast, and the gas storage dumps, and to notify the units there to get ready for other units coming in. As I remember it, we loaded up the bases down there before I went to Europe."

On October 14, a cloudless Sunday, U-2s, flying back and forth over the western end of Cuba, where SAMs had first been spotted, were able to photograph clearly, near the town of San Cristobal, what Sorensen described as "the first rude beginnings of a Soviet medium-range missile base."

By the evening of the 15th, the photo analysts were "fairly certain of their findings" and President Kennedy, alarmed at the implications, began gathering his closest advisers for grave, secret conferences at the White House. The San Cristobal base was not designed for defensive purposes. It was designed for intercontinental ballistic missiles capable of destroying almost any city along the Atlantic coast of the United States.

On October 18, the Joint Chiefs of Staff met with the president, who had already listened to a great variety of advice from civilians, including his brother, Attorney General Robert Kennedy, Robert McNamara, Secretary of State Dean Rusk, and members of his own White House staff. Robert Kennedy, who attended the conference with the JCS, recalled that the members

were unanimous in calling for immediate military action. They forcefully presented their view that the blockade would not be effective. General Curtis LeMay argued strongly with the president that a military attack was essential. When the president questioned what the response of the Russians might be, General LeMay assured him there would be no reaction.

President Kennedy was skeptical. "They, no more than we, can't let these things go by without doing something. They can't, after all their statements, permit us to take out their missiles, kill a lot of Russians, and then do nothing. If they don't take action in Cuba, they certainly will in Berlin."[13]

There is no doubt that LeMay strongly favored an invasion of Cuba, though he himself has some doubts that the other chiefs were so unanimous about it. "We had a chance to throw the Communists out of Cuba," he later recalled in his most belligerent style. "Even though the Army and Navy weren't ready, the Air Force could have begun the attack. But the administration was scared to death they [the Russians] might shoot a missile at us. We couldn't guarantee they wouldn't. We didn't know whether we had found them all. [But] we were on alert everyplace and we made sure the Russians understood this."

At that meeting with the Joint Chiefs of Staff on Thursday, October 18, Kennedy seemed positively against LeMay's recommendation to invade. But the following Monday, October 22, he indicated to a group of congressmen that he, himself, had originally favored invasion. On Monday afternoon, after listening to four more days of advice from various quarters, and agonizing over the most difficult decision any American president had ever been called upon to make—a decision which might plunge the world into nuclear war—Kennedy called in a select group of powerful congressmen to tell them what he intended to do.

He had decided not to invade but to blockade Cuba, as a first step, unless the Soviets pulled their missiles out of there. That evening he would go on television and announce this to an American public that knew something critical was taking place but didn't know what it was. Even the members of Congress weren't sure what was happening, though there was no shortage of rumors. It was politic for Kennedy to inform the pertinent congressmen before he made any announcement to the public.

When he gathered these senators and representatives, leaders of both parties, he was surprised to learn that several of them, even Democrats, favored stronger action than he intended. Richard Russell of Georgia, chairman of the Senate Armed Services Committee, told him emphatically that a blockade would be too soft a reaction to such an aggressive Russian move. He favored an immediate invasion. And Sen. J. William Fulbright of Arkansas, chairman of the Senate Foreign Relations Committee, agreed with him. Fulbright was a peaceful man. The president was astonished to find him demanding more than a blockade. "You're for an invasion of Cuba, Bill? Is that right?" he asked. And Fulbright said, "That's right."

"Last Tuesday," Kennedy said, "I was for an air strike or an invasion myself, but after four more days of deliberations, we decided that was not the wisest first move, and you would too if you had more time to think about."[14]

On television that evening, the president revealed to the American people the presence of Soviet offensive missiles in Cuba, demanded that Russia remove them, and announced an immediate naval "quarantine" to prevent the arrival of any more Russian missile weaponry. "It shall be the policy of this nation," he warned, "to regard any nuclear missile launched from Cuba against any nation in the Western Hemisphere as an attack by the Soviet Union on the United States, requiring a full retaliatory response on the Soviet Union." And any Russian move against any American ally, anywhere in the world, especially West Germany which was particularly vulnerable, would be regarded the same way.

LeMay did not think this speech was strong enough. "According to my lights it wasn't a very tough speech." By October 22, when Kennedy made the speech, there were SAC B-52s in the air every minute of every day, loaded with atomic weapons. The Navy had 180 ships cruising around the Cuban shores. And the Army's First Armored Division, plus other combat units, were in Florida, prepared to sail. But as LeMay admitted, whatever he might have thought of the speech, "Khrushchev thought it was a tough speech." By an accident in the routing of communications, LeMay happened to see the Khrushchev message to Kennedy which arrived in Washington shortly after the speech, and its conciliatory tone convinced him that "we could have got the missiles and the Communists out of Cuba."

LeMay believes, however, that Khrushchev, despite his conciliatory tone, proved subsequently to be a tough negotiator, and that the Cuban missile crisis was finally settled, not by Kennedy's ultimatum but by a quid pro quo which the two men worked out together.

"What Kennedy actually did," LeMay is convinced, "was to make a trade with Khrushchev. If he'd take his missiles out of Cuba, we would take our missiles out of Turkey and Italy. We had two medium-range missiles, one in Italy, one in Turkey. We had just finished pouring concrete and got them set up in there when we were told to take them out. This happened about a month or two months after the missile crisis was over. When we objected, [Kennedy] said the Minuteman [missile] is coming along now. These are obsolete. We don't need them any more. I'm sure that's what happened."[15]

CHAPTER TWENTY-SIX

The controversy over the TFX, or F-111, fighter plane, which had appeared to be simply a difference of opinion between the military and the civilians in the Pentagon during 1961 and much of 1962, eventually boiled over into Congress and took on an altogether different appearance in the latter days of 1962. When Defense Secretary McNamara ignored the recommendations of the Source Selection Board in January 1962, inviting Boeing and General Dynamics each to submit a second contract proposal for the TFX, he astonished both Air Force and Navy representatives on the board. The evaluation of proposed military weapon systems was a highly sophisticated procedure involving hundreds of thousands of work hours by both civilian and military experts. It entailed the compilation and assessment of vast amounts of scientific, technical, and operational data. It was almost unheard of for a civilian secretary, whose office could not possibly match the facilities of the Source Selection Board, to have the temerity to override the judgment of such a group. But no one ever said Robert McNamara lacked courage.

On April 1, the two companies had submitted their second bids, with voluminous documentation, and the Source Selection Board had gone to work reassessing the contract competition. In May, the board again weighed its evaluations, took into account the changes and improvements enumerated, and again selected Boeing, whereupon McNamara told each of the two companies they would have to submit a third proposal if they wanted the multibillion-dollar contract. In June, the companies did so, and on the 21st of that month, the board again voted for Boeing.

General LeMay, recalling this chapter of his stormy relations with McNamara, says, "We had actually three evaluations— matériel, research and development, and performance. The pri-

mary using command evaluated how well it would carry out its
mission. We added up the evaluations. Boeing won by a country
mile. I recommended we go ahead with Boeing."[1]

McNamara, however, was not yet convinced. On July 1, he
ordered a fourth and final runoff between the two companies.
Robert J. Art, whose book, *The TFX Decision,* explains Mc-
Namara's side of the controversy, wrote that "Because the Air
Force Source Selection process diluted civilian control over a
development decision, McNamara was determined to alter it."

In September, Boeing and General Dynamics each submitted
a fourth bid for the TFX contract and again, for the fourth time,
the Source Selection Board chose Boeing. Since this had been
designated the final runoff, it appeared certain now that Boeing
would win the contract. Both the Air Force and the Navy were
unenthusiastic about the airplane because the operational needs
of both services had been compromised to create it, but since
McNamara, in the name of economy, had forced them to settle
on one plane between them instead of one for each of them, the
generals and the admirals agreed for the fourth time that both
services would be better off with the Boeing version. It appeared
now that within a matter of days, McNamara would announce
Boeing was the winner.

The days stretched into weeks, however, and there was no
announcement. Then on the afternoon of November 23, a Friday, Air Force Secretary Eugene Zuckert called Bozo McKee,
the vice chief of staff, and said he wanted to speak to the Air
Staff about the TFX.

"I'd appreciate it if you'd talk to me first," McKee said to
him. "I'd at least like to know what it is."

Zuckert agreed to get together with McKee before the meeting. They were good friends and worked well together. But in
the event, he was held up and didn't arrive until a few minutes
after five. Zuckert was in some ways a troubled man by this time.
In a 1965 interview with Col. John L. Frisbee, an Air Force
historian, he spoke about McNamara's increasingly tight control
over the secretaries of the Army, Navy, and Air Force, all of
whom were under his jurisdiction.

"If I were going to be completely frank as I want to be,"
Zuckert told Frisbee, "I was troubled considerably by this ero-
sion of the role of the service secretary. Principally, I think,
because I couldn't see where it might stop. . . . What did we
have, ninety-three studies the first spring [1961], seventy-five of

which seemed aimed at cutting back the authority of the services, the role of the services. It was pretty clear that we were going to lose our influence over policy. . . . We were always free to present our views but we were no longer policy makers. And this was troublesome."[2]

Gen. Glen W. Martin, Ret., at that time an assistant to Zuckert, later said of him, "Had McNamara not been secretary of defense at the same time Zuckert was secretary of the Air Force, I think Zuckert would have been categorized and recognized widely as being the best, or at least one of the best, secretaries of the Air Force. In fact, I think he was, but I don't think the recognition is all that wide. I think that he was overshadowed by McNamara."[3]

In the matter of the TFX, almost anyone in the Air Force at the time would agree with Martin, but Zuckert himself does not agree. In a 1983 interview, he pointed out that "I'm the only person who ever read the whole damned file on the [TFX]," and he insisted that his contract recommendation for it was entirely independent of any influence from above.[4] Nevertheless, he could hardly have been a very comfortable man when he faced McKee and the Air Staff that afternoon of November 23, 1962.

"I suspected what he was going to tell us," McKee recalls. "'With regard to the TFX,' he said, 'I find it necessary to overrule the Air Staff and your recommendtion.'[5]

"He had decided, he said, that the contract should go to General Dynamics.

"Nobody said a word. He briefly explained Why. We didn't pay any attention. I've forgotten what his explanation was. It didn't make sense to me.

"About that time, LeMay walked in [for a Joint Chiefs' meeting] and found out what the [TFX] decision was. He said, 'It doesn't make any God damned sense.' "

LeMay's personal impression of the moment is that "Zuckert lost the Air Force right then because we thought he was lying to us. He hadn't made a decision [as big as] $27,000 in the budget, let alone the two-point-seven billion we were talking about on this program. And they [the members of the Air Staff] knew he didn't do it."[6]

LeMay was and is convinced that Zuckert had nothing to do with the decision. "McNamara was not only not using the military," he insists. "I don't think he was using the secretaries of the services much either. No one will ever convince me McNamara let Zuckert make the decision on this [but] he may have convinced Zuckert he should take the rap.''

After the meeting, Zuckert got up and walked out. ''LeMay and I followed,'' McKee recalls. ''Through LeMay's office. Zuckert said he had to get in touch with McNamara right away. He'd talk to us later. We said we'd wait right here. We waited and waited. [After] about an hour, we called and asked him where he was. He came down and we gave him a hard time. . . . McNamara made the decision. He then put his whole technical staff to work to prove he was right to overrule us.''

Though LeMay and McKee may not have known it, the TFX story, at this time, had already taken another turn. About three months earlier, Sen. Henry M. ''Scoop'' Jackson of Washington had gotten wind that there was something suspiciously peculiar in the air about the TFX contract bidding. It is not clear who put this idea into his head, but Boeing is in Seattle and Seattle is in Washington. Jackson, in fact, was sometimes referred to as the Senator from Boeing. It would not have been difficult for the Boeing people to let him know that, even after winning four times in the Source Selection Board competition with General Dynamics, they still weren't confident they would win the contract. They must have been more than puzzled by these circumstances. It was not customary for the Source Selection Board to be overruled even once. It was extraordinary that it should be overruled three times on the same contract.

Jackson wondered if any political pressure could be involved in the apparent reluctance to grant Boeing a contract it seemed to have earned. Vice President Johnson, a powerful and skillful politician, was a Texan. General Dynamics was a Texas firm and it intended to build the plane at its Fort Worth factory. Furthermore, the principal subcontractor in the General Dynamics bid was Grumman Aircraft Company, a New York firm. Scoop Jackson didn't need a computer to figure out that the combined electoral votes of New York and Texas totaled sixty-nine, and both states had voted for Kennedy in 1960. Though Boeing was a Washington firm, it planned to build the TFX at its Wichita, Kansas, plant. The combined electoral votes of Washington and Kansas came to seventeen, and both states voted for Richard Nixon in 1960. General Dynamics was, in addition, suffering financial difficulties at the time, having lost $425 million in efforts to crack the commercial jet market. A lot of Texans would be out of work unless General Dynamics managed soon to scare up some business.

Scoop Jackson was curious enough about all this to put in a call for McNamara. Instead, he got Roswell Gilpatric, McNamara's deputy. Was it true, Jackson wanted to know, that General Dynamics was about to get the TFX contract? That was nothing but a rumor, Gilpatric assured him. The contract would be granted "strictly on the merits."

Jackson had so much respect for McNamara he apparently put the matter from his mind. The TFX was expected to become a vital element in the nation's defense. McNamara would surely not buy an inferior version of it for political reasons. But shortly before the November 24 announcement by the Defense Department that General Dynamics had won the contract, Jackson seems to have changed his mind. He called on Sen. John McClellan of Arkansas, chairman of the Senate Subcommittee on Investigations, to conduct hearings on the entire history of the TFX contract competition. Jackson was, himself, a member of this subcommittee.

McClellan, acting quickly, asked the Defense Department to delay its contract approval until his group had time to look into the matter. The department declined. General Dynamics received an immediate $439-million commitment for the construction of twenty-two prototype TFXs as the first step in a program expected eventually to cost about $7 billion.

McClellan, obviously unhappy, sent out his subcommittee's investigators, pads and pens in hand, to begin interviewing people who might be involved in the matter.

McNamara, no doubt displeased at this, arranged a meeting with McClellan at which he explained his reasons for choosing General Dynamics. They sounded persuasive and McClellan seemed to be mollified. But he did not withdraw his investigators from the field.

While Senator McClellan was looking into the TFX flap, LeMay was inadvertently getting into a new spot of trouble with Defense Secretary McNamara and the Kennedy administration. This time the source of trouble was a missile—the Skybolt—which seemed determined to fly the wrong way, if at all. The Skybolt was, in the words of Gene Zuckert, an attempt "to mate a ballistic missile with the B-52. [In other words, it was to be fired from a B-52 in flight.] It was to be star guided. It was to go 2,500 miles and hit within a mile or so [of its target]. This was a very difficult technical accomplishment.''

The Skybolt program had begun under the Eisenhower administration but it was not progressing very well when Kennedy moved into the White House. ''In six months, we got the program reorganized,'' Zuckert recalled during a 1965 interview. ''We got it on a good project basis.''[7]

Nevertheless, the first five test flights of Skybolt were failures, and Zuckert realized his boss, the secretary of defense, had little faith in it. ''McNamara felt that the Skybolt had all the weaknesses of both missiles and aircraft.''

Zuckert, LeMay, and the Air Force people under him, however, were not discouraged. They believed, after studying the first five failures, that Skybolt was on the verge of success. So Zuckert called a meeting December 6, 1962, to decide when they should send it up on another trip.

The technical people said they would be ready December 12. But, as Zuckert observed, ''December is when budgets are made up, and if we had six horse collars in a row, we were likely to lose the program on that basis alone. So we had a lively discussion. I said, 'All right, what's the chance of success?' They said the chances of success were sixty percent if you shoot on the twelfth, ninety percent if you shoot on the twenty-first. I think it was the twenty-first.'' Actually, the sixth Skybolt test took place December 22.

''I wrote to the secretary of defense and I said we were going to go on the twenty-first and the chances of success looked very good, so everybody was on notice. We didn't get any turn down from anybody, so we just decided to go ahead.''

LeMay also, in a January 3 letter to McNamara, was careful to point out that the secretary of defense had been notified well in advance of the sixth test:

. . . officials of the Department of Defense, the Air Force and the contractors met here on 6 December, 1962, reviewed the progress of the program and agreed that the next test would be scheduled on 19 December. They agreed also that the actual date of the test might be a few days later because of some subsidiary tests which were being made. This information was transmitted to you by the Secretary of the Air Force on 6 December. . . .

On 21 December, Undersecretary Charyk of the Air Force

discussed the matter with Deputy Secretary of Defense Gilpatric, reminding him the test was scheduled the following day and reviewing the alternative courses and asking him for a decision as to what course of action should be taken. Mr. Gilpatric told Dr. Charyk to go ahead with the program as planned . . .

The fact that McNamara's office knew about the planned sixth test of Skybolt and didn't stop it would eventually prove embarrassing because President Kennedy and McNamara, at that time, had already decided either to curtail or cancel the Skybolt program. Deeply committed to government economy, they believed they could save $2.5 billion if they were to cancel it. This may have been their primary consideration about Skybolt, but they seemed also to be convinced it would never work. The matter called for delicate handling, however, not only because the Air Force still considered Skybolt promising, but, more important, several of America's European allies were counting on it. England, in particular, expected to mate it with its Vulcan II bomber as one of the most important components of its nuclear defense. Kennedy would need some good reasons when he revealed to British Prime Minister Harold Macmillan that the Skybolt was to be grounded. But Kennedy must have felt he had five good reasons in the failures of the missile's first five tests. A sixth failure might add more strength to the Kennedy-McNamara position but they hardly needed it. From their viewpoint, there could be no sensible justification for a sixth Skybolt test. Yet no one in McNamara's office made any move to forbid it. The result was an international embarrassment for President Kennedy, as well as a few uncomfortable days for Curtis LeMay.

On December 7, the day after the Air Force scheduled the sixth Skybolt test, there were reports, which reached England, that the Skybolt program was in trouble. The British were shocked and they said so. They had spent a lot of money improving their Vulcan II bomber and outfitting it to carry Skybolt. President Kennedy, when asked if the report and the rumors about Skybolt were true, said he might curtail the program, but no final decision would be made until after he talked to Macmillan during a meeting they had scheduled for December 18 in the Bahamas.

During three days of talks in Nassau, Kennedy informed Macmillan that he did indeed intend to cancel Skybolt because, as a subsequent press release explained, "it was no longer expected that this very complex weapon system would be completed within the cost estimate or the time scale which was projected when the program was begun." In other words, the damned thing just wasn't going to work. Those were Kennedy's sentiments, of course. Not Macmillan's. He raised so much hell about the loss of Skybolt that Kennedy offered to continue the program if the British would pay for half of it. That didn't appeal to Macmillan. He preferred the previous arrangement whereby the United States paid for all of it. Then Kennedy offered him a different missile, Hound Dog, which didn't offer anything like the potential of Skybolt. Macmillan refused both offers. Finally, to make it look as if the talks had accomplished something, they announced jointly the formation of a new "multilateral NATO nuclear force in the closest consultation with other NATO allies." And Kennedy promised to implement this with some Polaris missiles, though minus warheads, for British submarines.

The Nassau conference was not the most congenial imaginable. Kennedy must have been relieved on the afternoon of December 21 when the talks ended. Now he could relax and fly back to Palm Beach for Christmas with his family. Little did he suspect the embarrassment to which he would be subjected the next day.

The Air Force had been ready for the sixth Skybolt shot on December 19, but decided to delay it because while the Nassau conference was on, it would be difficult to get much attention from the news media for a missile test. On December 22, the day after the conference ended, Skybolt took its sixth trip into space. Launched from a B-52, it flew eight hundred miles down the south Atlantic missile range.

The objectives of the test were, in the words of General LeMay, "to verify the functional operation of the missile guidance and flight control systems and evaluate the performance of all missile subsystems except the reentry vehicle and thrust reversal. The test also successfully demonstrated the ability of the aircraft from which the Skybolt was launched to determine its position in flight precisely by daylight star tracking and to transfer this data to the missile."

LeMay pronounced the flight 100 percent successful. And so did the Air Force press agents. But unfortunately, they went farther. Their press release announced that the missile had "impacted in the target area" after a perfect flight.

Actually, the missile could not have impacted in any area because it wasn't equipped with a nose cone. As expected, it burned into nothingness during its reentry to the earth's atmosphere. But the computers tracking and calculating its flight indicated to Air Force technicians that it would have come down on target if it had been equipped with a nose cone. So the Air Force public-relations people simply gave it an imaginary nose cone and announced a handsome result.

Needless to say, Kennedy and McNamara didn't like the sound of it at all. One day after the president finished convincing the British that Skybolt was a failure, his own Air Force had announced it was a great success. And the announcement made it look like an even greater success than it was. The Air Force seemed to have forgotten that the White House, and McNamara's office, also had press agents.

On December 27, "the Pentagon" let the newsmen know that the Air Force had created a false impression. The Skybolt had not returned to earth because it had not carried a nose cone, and according to Department of Defense calculations, the missile would have dropped eighty-seven miles off target if it had carried one.

For several days thereafter, the Air Force didn't get very good publicity, and neither did its chief, Curtis LeMay. There was general agreement in the press that the Air Force had exaggerated its claim. One report said LeMay had threatened to punch whoever let out that information. And another report accused LeMay of undermining his commander-in-chief, the president. For almost a week the barrage continued until LeMay and Zuckert decided they had to do something about it. Zuckert's office prepared a draft of a letter of explanation to McNamara. This draft was handed to Bozo McKee, who handed it on to five staff officers, each of whom took a shot at revising and improving it. Finally, on January 3, 1963, LeMay signed it and sent it down to McNamara's third-floor office. It began aggressively, as one might expect of a letter from LeMay:

I am sure you believe, as I do, that public trust of our military departments and their leaders is vital to the security of this country.

Accordingly, I am writing to call your attention to the recent widespread dissemination by undisclosed sources who created in the minds of press media unwarranted conclusions and implications regarding the successful Skybolt missile test of 22 December. . . . In one instance the implication is that I was disloyal to the President.

The suggestion seemed to be that LeMay was blaming Mc-Namara's office for the dissemination of false implications. From there on, the letter became a carefully honed exposition of how the sixth Skybolt test came about, the lack of forbiddance by McNamara's office, and the exact limits of the flight's success.

Two days later, McNamara sent LeMay a "Dear Curt" letter which was gracious but at the same time quite pointed. "I have complete confidence in the Military Departments and their leaders," he wrote, "and have never questioned their loyalty, devotion or motivation."

But he then went on to make it clear he wasn't letting the Air Force off the hook: "The confusing accounts in the press of the sixth Skybolt missile launch were a source of concern not only to Ros [Gilpatric] and me but to other government officials as well." (He didn't have to mention the president's name to make clear whom he meant.)

In particular we were disturbed by the implication left by the reference in the Air Force press release, issued on December 22, 1962, to the Skybolt as "an operational weapon system." Also of concern to us was the statement that the sixth Skybolt test shot "impacted in the target area."

With regard to the first point, I consider the Skybolt in its present development status far removed from operational status. The Air Force release of November 28, 1962, correctly characterized the Skybolt missile as "experimental" and the program as being "still in the test phase." As to impacting in the target area, the fact that Skybolt was not equipped with a nose cone and therefore could not have penetrated the atmosphere to land in the target area made the term "impact" misleading in the minds of those who read reports based on the press release.

In closing, McNamara was friendly but not effusive:

I regret both the confusion caused by the conflicting accounts of the sixth Skybolt test flight and any personal embarrassment suffered by you as a result of incorrect statements in the press. I trust that for both our sakes there will be no recurrence of such incidents. Sincerely, Bob.

At long last, the thunder and lightning created by Skybolt died out. But much to the chagrin of the Air Force, so did the missile itself.

CHAPTER TWENTY-SEVEN

In the continuing match between LeMay and McNamara, the score seemed to be just about even as 1963 began. McNamara had won the Skybolt contest hands down, with considerable embarrassment for LeMay, but the secretary of defense was in deep trouble with Congress over the TFX contract. As for the B-70, LeMay had won the appropriations battle in 1962 when McNamara, eager to kill the program, had sought only $171 million for continuation of the plane's development during fiscal 1963, and Congress, after listening to LeMay, gave him $363 million. But McNamara had neutralized that defeat by refusing to spend the extra money. By January 1963, the budget battle for fiscal 1964 was already under way, and again the B-70 was one of the main items of contention between the two men.

The skirmishing had begun five months earlier, on August 13, 1962, when Gene Zuckert sent LeMay a memo about the fiscal 1964 budget. "The Air Force," he reminded the chief of staff,

is currently forwarding to the Secretary of Defense numerous program change proposals and still has a number to submit which, if approved as submitted, would bring the FY 1964 program to approximately $25 billion. While I recognize that these proposals can all be defended as meeting valid requirements, I do not feel that as a practical matter we can anticipate budget approval at the $25 billion level.

Consequently I feel that it is vitally necessary that we review our currently proposed program for FY 1964 and establish a priority of missions which can be accommodated within a total budget of $22 billion—a figure almost $1 billion above the currently approved FY 1964 budget.

And just to make sure LeMay understood where this suggestion had originated, Zuckert informed him of a meeting scheduled for September 1, at which McNamara "expects us to be able to defend, page by page and item by item, the Air Force FY 1964 program and budget."

Though McNamara still lacked belief in either the quality or the need of the B-70, he seemed resigned to building three prototypes for research and mollification purposes. The Air Force, limited to three while wanting perhaps three hundred, decided at least to fight for five in the hope that the more extensive testing this would allow might convince McNamara that they had something good. But at the September 1 meeting, they couldn't get him to spring even for the two extras. The gulf between LeMay and his boss seemed to be widening.

By the middle of October, when LeMay hurried home from Europe—called back by McKee supposedly to argue for the B-70 but actually to take part in Cuban crisis deliberations—he found that while the Cuban trouble came first, there were also some newly developing B-70 troubles. Gen. Earle G. Wheeler, the Army chief of staff, and Adm. George Anderson, chief of naval operations, were supporting McNamara's position within the Joint Chiefs, and Gen. Maxwell Taylor, the new chairman, could be expected to do likewise. At the first JCS meeting on his return from Europe, LeMay had been able to talk Wheeler and Anderson into supporting the Air Force position, but he hadn't been able to budge Taylor.

On December 27, McNamara and the Joint Chiefs traveled to Palm Beach for a discussion of the fiscal 1964 budget with vacationing President Kennedy. LeMay's diary for that date notes that he "limited his comments to calling the President's attention to the progressive weakening of the strategic retaliatory force." Aware that the president was already familiar with his views about the B-70 and Skybolt, he "could only point to them as an additional weakening of the strategic force. The President acknowledged this statement but had no comment."

There could be no doubt that Kennedy stood with McNamara on both issues. But everyone was aware that Congress, including many Democrats, was likely to stand with LeMay, at least in the matter of the B-70. The deadlock between LeMay and McNamara, on a number of matters, was so well known now, despite their own public denials of any rift, that responsible people in Washington were beginning to worry about it. Philip Graham, publisher of the *Washington Post* and *Newsweek* magazine, became so concerned he called Bozo McKee and talked to him about it. Graham told McKee he considered LeMay "the key military leader in government today." He was convinced that "a McNamara/LeMay combination would be unbeatable if a common ground of understanding could be reached." It seemed to him the two men were "not as far apart in their strategic thinking as most people think." What he wanted to do was to invite both of them to his house for a frank discussion the evening of January 17.[1]

As it happened, some "personal obligations" forced Graham to cancel the meeting. At the same time, LeMay was letting it be known that he was scheduled to leave the 17th for a worldwide Air Force commanders' conference. Whether LeMay's departure schedule had anything to do with his feelings about a frank discussion with McNamara can only be left to conjecture. But after a January 14 meeting between the secretary of defense and the Joint Chiefs, McNamara asked LeMay to accompany him back to his third-floor office.

During a short conversation there, McNamara expressed disappointment that the meeting at Graham's house would not take place.

LeMay said he had always felt free to come down and talk to the secretary and he wasn't quite sure why such a meeting had to be arranged by a third party. He mentioned his scheduled departure on the 17th for the commanders' meeting but he wondered if the secretary would be free to accept a dinner invitation any time during the week following his return.

McNamara said he would prefer inviting LeMay to his house. As to the date, he would be in touch.

In the event, McNamara did not find an occasion to follow up this conversation and the projected meeting between them, to discuss and overcome their differences, never did take place. But McNamara was sufficiently concerned about their rift to have a meeting with McKee about it.

This meeting was apparently a genuine attempt to improve communications and understanding between McNamara and the uniformed Air Force. McNamara seemed to imply that "there were many pressures on him from across the river to account for many of his decisions." McKee gathered from this "the distinct impression that McNamara was taking the responsibility for many decisions which were, in effect, the president's."[2]

McNamara then voiced a complaint directed at all the service chiefs but probably aimed mostly at LeMay and at George Anderson of the Navy, with whom McNamara and Kennedy also had frequent differences. The chiefs should, McNamara declared, accept decisions without question and implement [them] without criticism.

The conversation then turned for a few minutes to an Air Force problem with the Army, which seemed determined to build its own air force. McNamara told McKee not to worry about it. There could be only one Air Force and anything approaching duplication would be cut out.

Inevitably, the subject of a mixed force—missiles and bombers—arose, and McNamara said, rather surprisingly, that he agreed on a need for one. In the Air Force there was a widespread belief that he had put all his faith in missiles instead of bombers, but he denied that. His argument with the Air Force, he said, was that he could not agree about the proposed hardware—the B-70 and the Skybolt missile. He thought the Air Force should consider a low-level penetrating aircraft and an expanded Hound Dog missile force.

McKee then returned to the problem of communication between McNamara and the services. McNamara's habit of talking to the service secretaries without the chiefs or vice chiefs present resulted, he said, "in misunderstandings and lots of lost motion."

McNamara pointed out that he was "required by law" to deal through the service secretaries.

McKee disagreed with that. He insisted that the service chiefs were "the secretary's military advisers," and he could discuss defense problems with them in their capacity either as commanders of a service or as members of JCS.

When LeMay received a report of this conversation, his first reaction was to the issue of whether service chiefs should accept administration decisions without question or criticism. He pointed out that in their relations with Congress, for example, there was a difference between a service chief and an administration appointee. He had often declared that he had no right to go to Congress, or to the public, to complain about the administration, but when a congressional committee asked him a question under oath, he was bound by law to answer it honestly. He thought, however, that some of McNamara's comments might be helpful. Especially on the subject of a mixed force of bombers and missiles. He hoped he could get the secretary to move ahead on this concept, "regardless of hardware."

The fact that the two men now seemed to agree on the need for a mixed force might be expected to downgrade the importance of the B-70 as an issue between them. If McNamara thought simply that the B-70 was the wrong airplane, perhaps he would propose a different one to develop in its place. But when he testified about the fiscal 1964 budget before the House Armed Services Committee on January 30, 1963, he made no such suggestion.

"The issue here," he said,

> was not the future of manned strategic aircraft in general. Rather it was whether this particular aircraft [the B-70 or, as it was still called, the RS-70], in either of its configurations [bombing or reconnaissance] could add enough to our already programed capabilities to make it worth its very high cost.
>
> . . . The RS-70 is said to have two distinct capabilities: (1) trans-attack reconnaissance; that is, reconnaissance during our missile attack, and (2) the ability to examine targets and attack them on the spot with strike missiles, if required. Quite apart from the technical feasibility of developing, producing, and deploying such a system within the time frame proposed by the Air Force (which we do not think possible), there are better ways, when one considers both cost and effectiveness, to obtain both of these capabilities. . . .
>
> The RS-70, by carrying air-to-surface missiles, would provide only a very small increase in overall effectiveness. In my judgment, this increase is not worth the large additional outlay of funds, estimated at more than $10 billion above the $1.35 billion already approved.
>
> Accordingly, we propose to complete the presently approved $1.3 billion B-70 development program of three aircraft and, in addition, continue the development of selected sensor components using, in the current fiscal year, $50 million of the extra $192 million provided by the Congress last year for the RS-70 program.

Earlier in his testimony, McNamara had said,

> We have made a most detailed and exhaustive review of the entire problem of the future role of [manned strategic air-

craft]. . . . Manned bombers on the ground are quite vulnerable to surprise ballistic missile attack. Minuteman, however, because it is installed in hard and dispersed sites, is far less vulnerable. An attacker would have to use several of his missiles in order to be reasonably confident that he had knocked out one Minuteman. And Polaris missiles in submarines at sea cannot be targeted for ballistic missile attack at all. Therefore we decided to concentrate our procurement dollars on the accelerated production of Minuteman and Polaris. This decision did not mean that we did not want manned bombers. We already had many bombers but few ballistic missiles. What we needed to do was to build a more balanced force. . . .

What McNamara seemed to imply was that the Air Force didn't need the B-70 or any other new bomber plane because it already had a full complement of B-52s. But LeMay was worried because the B-52 was now ten years old and far from being the best bomber available in the 1960s. The B-70, though costly, represented the very latest state of the art in aircraft, weapon, and telemetry technology. If, as McNamara said, it wasn't good enough to be worth building then what good was the older, less sophisticated B-52? While he was declaring for a mixed force, he seemed actually to be arguing against it. It was as if he knew the manned bomber was dead but didn't want to announce it publicly. He simply paid his respects to it in passing and reserved all his praise for missiles. But since LeMay, the Air Force, and a large bloc of congressmen still believed there was life in the manned bomber, the B-70 controversy was as far as ever from being resolved. In the question-and-answer period following McNamara's testimony, the congressmen grilled him sharply but they did not shake his convictions. Indeed, it seemed to one Air Force observer that the persuasive secretary of defense had managed to swing committee chairman Carl Vinson at least slightly away from the vigorous Air Force support he had shown the previous year. The best the pro-Air Force congressmen could get out of McNamara was a mention of a possible future reconnaissance plane.

In preparation for his own testimony before the committee, LeMay felt it necessary to visit McNamara February 4.[3] He referred to the many questions the congressmen had asked McNamara, especially about the B-70, and said he expected they would ask him similar questions. He wanted McNamara to know that while he would not intentionally raise the issues, he would "have to respond in accordance with previous positions taken."

McNamara said he understood. He suggested only that LeMay let the congressmen know he had been given "ample opportunity to state his views" to the secretary of defense and the president.

This was, of course, true. LeMay had also stated his views about the B-70 and the manned bomber controversy to Congress the previous year, as he reminded McNamara. On February 21 and 22, 1963, he went up to the hill and repeated those views to the members of the House Armed Services Committee. He said once more that he was not against missiles. He agreed with the need for an up-to-date missile force. But placing full reliance on missiles would destroy the capability of flexible response which not only the Air Force but Secretary McNamara himself wanted. Only manned bombers offered this flexibility. Just in case the congressmen had forgotten, he reminded them of what might be the most appealing advantage of manned bombers. When a missile was fired there was no way to recall it if you had reason to change your mind. But bombers had human crews who could exercise judgment. And they could be called back home up to the last minute before they released their bombs.

This latter argument was especially potent with the congressmen. They voted 31 to 5 in favor of the Air Force position on the B-70. And in the committee report to the full House of Representatives, they argued strongly in LeMay's favor:

> The concern of the committee stems from the growing tendency on the part of the Department of Defense to place more and more emphasis on the missiles and less and less on manned strategic systems. The committee considers this to be a most dangerous course of action. . . .
>
> The current strategic bomber force provides . . . that essential element of flexibility which spans the gap between limited war capabilities and the push-button war of long-range missiles.
>
> It embraces that highly essential element—the judgment of man.

The B-70 situation was still in contention when another controversy between LeMay and McNamara was resumed. Agents for the Senate's Permanent Subcommittee on Investigations had been in the field since November, gathering information about the award of the TFX contract to General Dynamics instead of Boeing. On February 26, 1963, Sen. John McClellan, chairman of the subcommittee, opened hearings on the subject.

The whole affair was painful to everyone in the Pentagon because it pitted the military there against their bosses, the civilian secretaries, concerning what was publicly considered a political issue—whether or not political favors had been granted. One thing military men liked to avoid in public was politics, especially in this matter since they were not involved in its political implications. All they wanted was the best airplane.

Within the Air Force, the cleavage between LeMay and his boss next door, Gene Zuckert, made everyone uncomfortable. And once the hearings had begun, the tension increased. On March 2, for instance, Zuckert suggested that LeMay discuss the whole matter of appearances before the committee with the general counsel of the Department of Defense. LeMay said he had no such intention since he was not sure the general counsel was working for the uniformed Air Force. Nor was he sure that his own testimony should coincide with that of Zuckert, who had arrived at a decision (on the TFX contract) "contrary to that of the blue suit Air Force." LeMay told his aides he wanted "to ensure that the complete history of the source selection system action, Air Council action, and his decision went into the Committee's records exactly as it had, in fact, taken place."

Despite their estrangement, a surprising kind of cooperation continued between LeMay and Zuckert. Many years later, Zuckert declared, "One great thing about the Air Force, when I had to defend [the TFX] decision, they cooperated a thousand percent with me. LeMay never spoke to me about [this] but I heard about it. He said [to his aides], "I don't agree with him but I want to see that he has everything he needs.""[4]

Lt. Gen. Maurice F. Casey, Ret., who was at that time information deputy in Zuckert's office, commented later that "Zuckert was really in a hard place because he is a very kind guy and he is a guy that really likes to be appreciated and liked and respected. He was stuck between two really overpowering men, General LeMay and Secretary McNamara. I used to tell Secretary Zuckert, 'Come on, let's get in an airplane and go somewhere. You could move your bed in here and stay here all night and you're not going to make this guy McNamara happy.'"[5]

When McClellan opened the proceedings February 26, there was little on the surface to indicate they would produce much excitement. "We anticipate the committee will be occupied with this investigation," he said, "for some five or six hearing days." But after five days, so much testimony had accumulated in favor of the Boeing over the General Dynamics plane that even the censored accounts coming out of the closed hearing room indicated some kind of scandal was being uncovered. Instead of five or six days, the extremely complicated hearings continued for eight months. Zuckert himself, for instance, testified for thirty hours during eighteen separate sessions. McNamara and LeMay both testified at length, as did a long list of civilians, Navy, Army, and Air Force officers, and representatives of the companies involved. No scandal was proven but some embarrassing questions were raised.

Within the administration, and no doubt within McNamara's office, the hearings were deeply resented as an attempt by the military to usurp civilian authority over procurement processes. Theodore Sorensen, in his book *Kennedy,* quoted an "internal government memorandum" which said the investigation was "the spectacle of a large corporation [Boeing], backed by Air Force generals, using the investigatory powers of Congress to intimidate civilian officials just because it lost out on a contract. If . . . successful, it will be impossible for any civilian official ever again to exercise judgment . . . [without] measuring the influence of large corporations with Congress or . . . to control the military men who are theoretically under his direction."[6]

The Air Force, at the same time, saw the whole matter as the result of an administration decision to buy an inferior plane. If the administration's contention was true, then McNamara and his supporters had a clear duty to fight Boeing and the Air Force generals since civilian control of the military is one of the cornerstones of American democracy. On the other hand, if an administration chooses to buy a fighter plane which military experts almost unanimously consider inferior to another equally available plane, the military men also have a clear duty to protest the decision because their pilots may have to risk their lives doing battle in that inferior plane, and the nation's security might be put at risk in such action.

When the subcommittee's investigators were through presenting the case as they saw it, the story of the TFX contract award looked, in outline, like this:

1. There was no doubt that in all four evaluations, the Source Selection Board, representing both the Air Force and the Navy,

voted for the Boeing proposal. The board found that the Boeing plane promised to be both better and cheaper than the General Dynamics plane.

2. The Boeing cost projection was at least $100 million lower, and perhaps as much as $415 million lower.

3. The Department of Defense could produce only one document favoring General Dynamics. It was a five-page memorandum signed by McNamara, Zuckert, and Navy Secretary Fred Korth. It was dated November 21, 1962, three days before the award to General Dynamics was announced, and according to Thomas Nunnally, a subcommittee accountant, it contained arithmetic errors of at least $54 million. The clear implication was that McNamara's office had put this document together hurriedly in an attempt to justify a bad decision.

When the military men began testifying, they supported this implication. Adm. Frederick L. Ashworth, the Navy's chief representative on the Source Selection Board, gave four reasons why the Navy voted for the Boeing plane:

1. Lower gross weight. A special consideration for the Navy because the plane would have to operate from carriers.

2. Better characteristics in subsonic flight. Another important factor in carrier operations because it meant better control during takeoffs and landings, especially in choppy seas.

3. Better performance in combat.

4. Lower price.

Ashworth also said McNamara had compromised the efficiency of both the Air Force and Navy by insisting they share the same plane despite differences in their requirements. "It would be an economic catastrophe," he declared, "if we end up producing an aircraft for either the Navy or the Air Force that would not do the job."

General McKee, testifying for the Air Force, said he thought the technical innovations Boeing offered, such as a thrust reverser to facilitate slower landings and greater maneuverability, gave its plane an operational advantage. "It is my view," he said, "that the operational factors should be the overriding consideration."

Gen. Walter Sweeney, commander of the Air Force pursuit arm, the Tactical Air Command, agreed with McKee about the importance of operational factors. "The Boeing plane is a much better aircraft," he insisted.

The civilian offices in the Defense Department, however, saw the entire case quite differently from the military men and the subcommittee investigators. McNamara himself, in his testimony, told the congressmen why the General Dynamics plane had been chosen. After first stating that he expected to save the taxpayers "at least one billion dollars" by making the Air Force and Navy share the same plane, he explained why he was persuaded that General Dynamics should build it:

> My examination of the facts, in consultation with my advisers, convinced me that, as compared with the Boeing proposal, the General Dynamics proposal was substantially closer to a single design, requiring only relatively minor modifications to adapt it to the different requirements of the Navy and the Air Force, and that it embodied a more realistic approach to the cost problem.
>
> . . . The Source Selection Board, using factors weighted by judgment, made a recommendation which appeared to place greater emphasis on potential bonus factors in certain operational areas, rather than on dependability of development and predictability of costs. This recommendation, understandably, was seconded by the Navy and Air Staffs, since these officers are most vitally interested in obtaining the ultimate in performance in individual weapon systems. On occasion, this desire leads to the establishment of characteristics for weapon systems which cannot be met within the time or funds available, and it has frequently resulted in lowering operational effectiveness.
>
> There is only one way I know to minimize the compounding of error that can occur through this pyramiding of judgment, and that way is to apply the judgment of the decision-maker not only to the final recommendation, but also to the underlying recommendations and facts. This I did to the best of my ability. In doing so, I found it necessary to balance the promises held out by competing contractors against the hopes and aspirations of military officers, and the limiting realities of economics and technology.
>
> . . . That I attach great importance to the recognition of economic and technological limiting conditions is, I believe, demonstrated by my selection of General Dynamics as the

contractor that most clearly recognized the effects of these limitations on the task to be achieved.

. . . In the final analysis, judgments differed. In reaching my decision, I considered the recommendations of my various military and civilian advisers as well as other available evidence, but I had the final responsibility.

McNamara concluded, in his March 13 testimony, that the General Dynamics proposal would offer "the least expensive, time-consuming research and development effort before production; the least reliance upon unknown process and materials; the earliest delivery to our fighting forces; the highest level of experience in building fighter-type aircraft."

His testimony about the economics, or cost, aspect of the contract seemed to be clouded by the contention of investigators that the Boeing cost projection was at least $100 million, and perhaps $415 million lower than that of General Dynamics. Boeing estimated that the entire program would cost $5.364 billion: General Dynamics estimated $5.455 billion. Both estimates were considered too optimistic. McNamara said he had chosen the higher one because he considered it more realistic than Boeing's.

Senator McClellan, apparently unconvinced by this assertion, asked the comptroller general to send him "an independent review of the cost standards" used in arriving at McNamara's decision.

The comptroller general replied that he could find no cost estimates other than those used by the Source Selection Board. "Both Secretary McNamara and Secretary Zuckert," he wrote, "have stated to us that the conclusions reached by them were on the basis of their judgment rather than on independent studies."

The General Accounting Office's director of defense accounting, William A. Newman, testified in regard to a meeting with McNamara, "When it came time to examine the records . . . he stated that he had the figures in his head, indicating that he did not have them on paper."

Regarding the question of evaluation, the need for four competitions between the two companies never became clear. This was especially true of the fourth evaluation because Zuckert testified August 22 that before its results were tabulated, McNamara had told President Kennedy "it looked as if General Dynamics would be chosen." This would make it difficult to escape the conclusion that McNamara had already made up his mind after three evaluations, despite the fact that all three had gone against General Dynamics. And it begged the question of whether Mc-Namara had already made up his mind before any of the four evaluations were even begun.

Adm. George Anderson, chief of naval operations, addressed himself, in his testimony, to the question of whether McNamara's rejection of the four evaluations would result in the development of the lesser of two possible airplanes. "In the military profession as in every other," he said, "an edge of advantage is of greatest importance. . . . If a potential enemy either believes or knows his prospective adversary possesses such an edge, he thinks twice before committing himself to armed conflict. If other considerations compel him to act, this edge can make the all-important difference between being able to defeat the aggressor . . . to lacking the edge, losing quickly."

But aircraft quality was not the only basis of Anderson's dissatisfaction with the proposal McNamara had accepted. From a naval viewpoint, he was also worried about the weight of the plane as specified. He suggested the worrisome possibility that it might be too heavy for use on some carriers.

"Now we will have," he said, "an aircraft 13,500 pounds heavier than our original specification and 8,500 over the revised Navy requirement." He did concede, however, that both companies were capable of building the airplane, and he couldn't go so far as to say that the General Dynamics plane would be unacceptable.

In late March, as the time approached for General LeMay's appearance before the subcommittee, Chairman McClellan invited him to his office for an informal chat. And on the 25th, LeMay went there. McClellan spoke at some length in his Arkansas twang about the hearings. His only desire, he said, was to ensure that the record had all the facts. Once the facts were determined, the record would speak for itself.

LeMay was surprisingly politic in his remarks to McClellan that day. He said he hoped the hearings would not result in "a split between the civilian portion of the Department of Defense and the uniformed services." Such a split "could only have a long-range harmful impact on the operations of the department."

On the other hand, he also hoped the hearings would not discredit the Air Force source selection system. He had considerable experience with this system and he had confidence in it. He believed the Source Selection Board's recommendation, as affirmed by the air council, the chief of naval operations, and himself, was proper. But he recognized that McNamara had the authority to change the decision, and the Air Force was already in the process of carrying out his mandate. Above all, he didn't want to downgrade the General Dynamics version of the plane before it was off the drawing board because this could have serious effects upon the Air Force and Navy pilots who would eventually have to fly it.

LeMay appeared before the subcommittee on the afternoon of April 4, and like other witnesses, began with a prepared statement. He was not quite as conciliatory in his testimony, however, as he had seemed to be in his private conversation with McClellan. He pointed out that he had taken part in about twenty-five source selections during his six years as vice chief and chief. He said the system was continually under review and he had great faith in it.

As for the TFX contract, he himself thought the Boeing plane was better than the General Dynamics plane and he had fully supported the selection board that had four times recommended it. He also said he was not once consulted by McNamara before the secretary's decision to overrule the board.

"I thought we had such a clear-cut and unanimous opinion all up and down the line," he said, "that I was completely surprised at the decision."

McClellan asked him, "Did any group, any authority at any level from you on down to the evaluation group ever recommend the General Dynamics plane?"

"No sir."

"Would you have expected . . . that you would have been consulted?"

"Yes sir. I was surprised that the decision was made without consultation. . . . The Boeing team had a much better knowledge of what was required in this sort of an airplane."

In his opinion, LeMay said, McNamara had made a "wrong" decision. But at the same time he acknowledged that McNamara had the authority to make the decision, and the Air Force had "no desire to contest" it. In fact, the Air Force was already implementing it.

Like Anderson, he also conceded that both companies were capable of building the plane, and that both proposals were militarily acceptable even though Boeing's was preferable.

This concession, by both LeMay and Anderson, practically

ended the game because it put the decision on the level of economic, political, and social as well as military judgment, where McNamara could claim superior all-around competence, rather than the level of aeronautical technology, where his claim would be weak. The hearings dragged on until December 14, 1963. The Department of Defense was further embarrassed by the disclosures that Roswell Gilpatric, McNamara's deputy, was still drawing twenty thousand dollars a year from his former law firm in New York, which did extensive legal work for General Dynamics; and that Navy Secretary Korth had been the head of a Fort Worth bank that loaned money to General Dynamics. But both men were declared free of any conflict of interest. And President Kennedy publicly defended Korth against the charge.

Despite all the questions raised by the testimony, Kennedy also continued steadfastly to support McNamara. In a March 21 press conference, he had said, "Mr. McNamara chose the [General Dynamics] plane . . . because he thought it would save the government hundreds of millions of dollars. . . . I think the secretary did the right thing. . . . My judgment is that the more this hearing goes on, the more convinced people are finally that Secretary McNamara is a very effective secretary of defense and that we are lucky to have him." As the hearings stretched on, Kennedy said nothing to make anyone think he had changed his mind.

When both LeMay and Anderson admitted that the General Dynamics plane would be at least militarily acceptable, McNamara was able to make it look like an admission that he had made the right choice. And there the matter stood. By sticking to his guns and refusing to retreat, McNamara had again shown the generals, the admirals, and the senators that he could be a very tough general himself.

Clark Mollenhoff, in his book *The Pentagon,* paid tribute to McNamara's apparent genius for making things happen his way.

Many of McNamara's decisions infuriated members of Congress and Pentagon officials. Over the recommendations of Air Force Chief LeMay he dealt the death blow to the RS-70 [B-70] program. He abandoned the Skybolt missile over the objections of many Pentagon officials as well as the British, who wanted it for part of their defensive armaments. McNamara then offered Polaris missiles to the British without informing his own Joint Chiefs of Staff until the deal was completed.

Nevertheless, from each controversy, McNamara emerged stronger than ever. If military officials disagreed with him, McNamara was hailed as putting the brass in its place. He rode roughshod over Congress and sallied forth as a man of lofty principle intent on minimizing the influence of politicians.[8]

LeMay's frustration in his contests with McNamara was now almost complete. On May 25, while the TFX hearings were still in progress, the flight of the first B-70 was postponed, and on June 21, the entire B-70 program was doomed when the House of Representatives failed to vote any new funds for it. The Skybolt missile was dead. The TFX had been compromised to such a drastic extent that the Navy almost totally rejected it, while Air Force pilots, referring to its fold-back wings, and to the fact that McNamara had once been president of Ford Motor Company, would one day call it "the switch-blade Edsel." There were plans for another new bomber to replace the soon-to-be-abandoned B-70, and LeMay already had congressional support for it, but realizing McNamara's commitment to missiles and low opinion of bombers, he could have no confidence that this new bomber would ever be built. LeMay seemed able always to get the better of McNamara in Congress. But in the real world, McNamara seemed always to win.

CHAPTER TWENTY-EIGHT

As the year 1963 progressed, the Vietnam War became an ever-increasing matter of concern within the halls of government in Washington, even though it was still not yet a major public issue. On January 2, five American helicopters there had been shot down by Communist guerrillas. Up to and including that incident, however, only thirty Americans had been killed in the fighting—enough to worry some well-informed people but hardly enough for the public to notice more than casually.

The one thing the American public did begin to grasp as the year went on was the repressive nature of the government of South Vietnam. Despite continuing censorship, U.S. correspondents in Saigon managed to report stories of violence against Buddhists by the Roman Catholic regime of President Diem and his brother, Ngo Dinh Nhu. America's Catholic President Kennedy was deeply disturbed by these stories, but not enough to withdraw military support from Diem's government. Kennedy was convinced (like the two presidents who came after him) that if he could stop the guerrilla war sponsored by the Communist governments of North Vietnam and China, he would thus enable the people of South Vietnam to choose a better government for themselves. This conviction, vaguely shared at the time by a vast majority of Americans, was leading Kennedy into a gradual though ever-deepening involvement in Vietnam. But hardly anyone was very worried about that fact, or even very interested in it. The burning issues of the day were the struggle by black people for civil rights, the question of how to contain Cuban Communism, the nuclear test-ban treaty negotiations, the race into space against Russia, and, to a lesser degree, the TFX hearings.

Curtis LeMay had visited Vietnam in 1962 and hadn't liked

the military situation as he saw it there. While he didn't disapprove of our involvement, he thought that both in field operations and in overall direction from Washington, we were going about it the wrong way. He deplored the piecemeal gradualism with which we were stepping into the fray.

In April 1963, he decided to go again to Vietnam and see if there was any improvement, at least in the methods of operation. On the 5th, the day after his TFX testimony, he flew east, beginning a journey that also included the Philippines, Thailand, Taiwan, Korea, and Japan, although it was primarily focused on Vietnam. He was no more pleased with what he found there than he had been the previous year. He came home April 21 with a list of forty things that needed to be done immediately.[1] The Army commanders, for instance, should be better informed about the possible uses of air power. While the air-ground coordination was improved over the previous year, still only 10 percent of ground operations had utilized air. More air officers were needed on the ground staffs. Communications needed closer integration and control. The Vietnamese air force should have more pilots and better planes than the T-28s they were flying. The Pacific Command should deploy more F-102s to Vietnam. The Air Defense system needed improvement. And unsatisfactory personnel at all levels should be weeded out.

All such complaints added together, however, didn't even begin to measure LeMay's basic discontent with what was happening, or rather what was not happening, in Vietnam. One of the circumstances that bothered him most was that neither he nor the other members of the Joint Chiefs, with the exception of Chairman Maxwell Taylor, had anything to say about the overall strategy or tactics employed in Vietnam. The entire operation, as far as he could see, was being run by the White House, the State Department, and Robert McNamara, with advice from Taylor. Except for Taylor, it was a war run entirely by civilians, and they weren't the slightest bit interested in the views of their top service advisers, the Joint Chiefs.

"We in the military felt we were not in the decision-making process at all," LeMay later recalled. "Taylor might have been, but we didn't agree with Taylor in most cases, so we felt that the president was not getting [from him] unfiltered military advice. The president hardly ever met with the Joint Chiefs. McNamara would come down at regular intervals. He knew what our feelings were. . . . Taylor would go with McNamara to see the president. What Taylor told him, I don't know because I, at least, differed with Taylor on practically all items of strategy. And I was never sure he [told] the president what I felt about anything."[2]

General Taylor's differences of opinion with many of his military colleagues were well known when Kennedy brought him out of retirement to make him, first, his senior military adviser, and then, chairman of the Joint Chiefs. Before retiring, Taylor had been Army chief of staff, and as such he had found frequent occasions to disagree with the other members of the JCS, especially Nate Twining, who was at that time Air Force chief. Taylor did not share the airmen's enthusiasm for air power.

"His general feeling," LeMay recalled, "was that air power was not much good. I had trouble with him all the time I was there. It would drive me practically crazy. He was a little insulting about it, I thought. It took a lot of will power to keep from letting him have one. I'd just get the back of his hand and, 'LeMay, your airplanes are no good. They're all going to be shot down. We've got these new missiles coming along, hand-held by infantrymen. An infantryman will shoot you down.' . . . He thought ground defense would make the airplane obsolete."

Taylor's book, *The Uncertain Trumpet,* published in 1959, confirms LeMay's impression that he believed aircraft were becoming obsolete. "With regard to the forces of the other services," Taylor wrote, "the Army considers that the Air Force is depending too much and too long on manned aircraft, both bombers and interceptors. In view of the tremendous growth in the destructive power of megaton hydrogen weapons, we have today an excessive number of delivery vehicles in the combination of aircraft and missiles now in the strategic deterrent forces. However, this force needs to be modernized through a more rapid replacement of bombers by missiles. . . ."

Taylor argued for what was called "flexible response," based non "agreed standards of sufficiency for strategic retaliatory forces, continental air defense, overseas deployments, limited- and general-war strategic reserves, antisubmarine warfare forces, and similar functional force groupings. Having determined how much is enough, [the Army] would then build the defense budget in consistence with the requirements of these functional forces. . . . In view of the growing ballistic missile threat, the emphasis in air defense should shift from a bomber to a missile defense faster than presently planned . . . In developing the need for a strategy of Flexible Response, the Army has become the principal spokesman for increasing the United States capability in limited war."[3]

This concept of flexible response promised economy, moderation, and an alternative to nuclear war. It was understandably attractive, because nobody wanted a nuclear war. Taylor's theories had caught the attention of then-Senator Kennedy at a time when he was preparing to seek the presidency, and they were undoubtedly a factor in Kennedy's choice of Taylor as his senior military adviser. This may explain, to some degree, why the president adopted a slow and gradual approach to his involvement in the Vietnam War.

To other, more traditional military men like LeMay, gradualism represented the worst possible way to enter a war. He believed that once you decided to fight, you had better decide to fight hard from the beginning. Though President Kennedy seldom gave LeMay an opportunity to argue in person against the administration's Vietnam policy, there was no doubt that he knew how LeMay felt about it. Both Taylor and McNamara kept him informed about sentiments within the JCS. During at least the first ten months of 1963, Taylor kept the other chiefs fairly well under control despite the pugnacious pressure they were getting from LeMay. Whether Taylor himself felt at all threatened by LeMay's pressure is impossible to know, but it is evident that Kennedy was neither afraid of his influence within the JCS, nor influenced by it.

LeMay's second year as Air Force chief of staff would be complete at the end of June, and chiefs were usually appointed for terms of only two years. Kennedy could have dismissed him into retirement with a handshake, a few kind words, and a few more ribbons for his chest. Instead, on May 6 he informed him that his term as chief was to be extended another year.

In Washington there was considerable surprise when this was announced. LeMay's continuing opposition to administration defense policies was well known even though it showed publicly only when he testified before Congress. Why did Kennedy retain him? Sorensen, in his book *Kennedy,* wrote of the extension as if it were a vote of warning rather than a vote of confidence. "[Kennedy] broke precedent by failing to reappoint Admiral George Anderson to a second term as Chief of Naval Operations and by extending Air Chief LeMay's term for only one year."[4] It is true that Anderson had also given Kennedy trouble, and it is possible he didn't want to fire two chiefs at once. But of the two, LeMay was the more difficult to handle.

Bozo McKee has offered another possible explanation. "[Kennedy] had no basis on which to fire him. Both Kennedy and McNamara knew LeMay was a great soldier. And he had a lot of support on the hill. They weren't about to run into that."

The summer of 1963 brought more disturbing developments in Vietnam. In May, a Buddhist demonstration against the persecution by Diem's regime resulted in the death of nine people at the hands of government troops. On June 11, a Buddhist priest protested against the government by burning himself to death in a Saigon street. On June 15, the government agreed tentatively to meet several Buddhist demands, but by the end of June, the Buddhists resumed their demonstrations because, they said, and American observers concurred, that the government was refusing to abide by the agreement.

While these civil disturbances continued, the Diem government, even with the gradually increasing American involvement, was running into serious trouble in its war against the Communists. Whether President Kennedy was fully informed about the worsening conditions is open to question. American newsmen in Vietnam were finding it difficult to break through Diem's censorship. And they were also getting sparse cooperation from Gen. Paul Harkins's MACV. If the U.S. Army was withholding as much information from Washington as it was from the war correspondents, then Kennedy probably knew much less than he should about military developments in Vietnam.

This situation became a public issue when the *New York Times,* on August 15, 1963, published a long dispatch which correspondent David Halberstam had managed to get through censorship. It began:

> South Vietnam's military situation in the vital Mekong Delta has deteriorated in the past year, and informed officials are warning of ominous signs. Essentially, these military sources say, a Communist Vietcong build-up is taking place in the Delta. They find it particularly disturbing because it has persisted since an American build-up twenty months ago. . . .

Halberstam, in his book *The Making of a Quagmire,* recalls, "No story I ever wrote drew a more violent reaction. The President of the United States was angry, his generals were angry and his civilian officials were angry. At a press conference Dean Rusk [secretary of state] specifically criticized the story.''[5]

Rusk held his press conference the day after the *Times* published Halberstam's piece. He insisted Halberstam was dead wrong. He declared that both sabotage and large-scale attacks by Communists were on the wane. And under the Strategic Hamlet program, the Vietnamese government was bringing more and more formerly Communist-held territory under its control.

In retrospect, Halberstam's assessment of the situation looks more convincing than that of the secretary of state. It's impossible to know whether Rusk, and therefore also Kennedy, were truly ill informed about the military situation. Perhaps they were, if the Army Command was withholding facts from Washington. The Army Command in Vietnam has been proven to have done so later, under Gen. William Westmoreland. But however little Kennedy and Rusk knew about the military situation, they seem to have been well informed about the civil turmoil created by President Diem's repression of the Buddhists.

During the summer, several more Buddhists had immolated themselves on the streets of Saigon. And Diem's sister-in-law, Madame Nhu, who seemed intent on portraying herself as the Wicked Witch of the East, had poked public fun at these suicidal martyrs. She called them Communist dupes. On August 21, Diem arrested several hundred Buddhist monks and declared nationwide martial law. But the antigovernment demonstrations continued.

On September 2, Kennedy, in a televised interview, spoke out publicly against Diem's persecution of Buddhists. ''I don't think the war can be won unless the people support the effort,'' he said, ''and in my opinion, in the last two months, the government has gotten out of touch with the people.''

Two months later, on November 2, President Diem and his brother, Ngo Dinh Nhu, were both assassinated in a coup that was probably arranged and certainly encouraged by American operatives and high American officials in Vietnam. American involvement in the coup was so deep that even the new ambassador, Henry Cabot Lodge, knew about it beforehand. Whether Diem and his brother were intended to die has never been established. And whether President Kennedy was fully informed about it is also unclear. But there is some evidence that the American military, even in Vietnam, had no prior knowledge of it. To LeMay, the coup came as a complete surprise. And it was a long time before he realized the United States had anything to do with it.

In a 1984 interview, LeMay said, "I'm convinced now that we overthrew the Diem government. But I had no knowledge of it at the time. You can see what was going on at the time. The United States was plotting the overthrow of an allied government in a war that we were engaged in, and the military didn't know anything about it."[5]

The death of Diem, ironically, worked to LeMay's advantage in his arguments within the privacy of the Joint Chiefs of Staff. LeMay had noticed that, aside from Taylor, the Joint Chiefs by this time were becoming almost as frustrated as he was by what they regarded as a "no-win" policy in Vietnam.

In a 1972 interview LeMay recalled, "General Taylor had this idea of a flexible response—of not going in with a full, all-out effort, but just enough strength out there to say, 'Look, boys, you can't do anything against us. Be sensible and negotiate.' I never was for that solution. . . . I never could condone spending lives, particularly the lives of our people, on such an operation over a long period of time without a policy of winning because I could never foresee a defensive action—and this is a defensive action—winning anything. . . . You have to go on the offensive if you're going to win. . . . So I never was for it. And this came in with Taylor. He controlled, of course, the chief of staff of the Army. And the Navy, to some extent, went along with them."[7]

When Diem was assassinated, LeMay found himself with a new argument to use against his colleagues on the JCS. "The argument I used that I think brought them over was one of: 'Look, in all of the political instability we've had in the country down there, the military has always remained loyal to the government in power. This may not always be the case and we may wind up with a situation where we're hard put to get our people out of the country. In other words, complete chaos. . . .' And this was seen for the first time, I think, after the overthrow of Diem. The argument was, 'Look, we can't go north until we get some stability in the south.' I never understood this argument, but that was the one that was advanced. And my point was that we're never going to have any stability in the south unless you went north. . . ."

Gen. David M. Shoup, Marine Corps chief of staff, had already been persuaded by LeMay's reasoning. But now, the Army's Earle Wheeler, and Adm. David L. McDonald, who had succeeded Anderson as chief of naval operations, began to agree with LeMay's aggressive philosophy.

"In spite of the arguments we've had," LeMay recalled during the 1972 interview, "everyone was of the opinion that once you choose military action as a solution to your problem, then you ought to get in with both feet and get the chore over with, and do the things that are necessary to be done. We never did that. As a matter of fact, every principle of war was violated down there. . . . So this was rather frustrating. And we always wanted to go back in full strength to get it over with. But I don't think anybody ever thought that nuclear weapons would be necessary."

LeMay has often been accused of advocating the use of atomic bombs in Asia. One report quoted him as saying to a high but unnamed State Department official, "We ought to nuke the Chinks." And there was a story about a JCS meeting at which he suppposedly said, "Maybe we ought to drop a nuclear bomb on Hanoi." He insists he never uttered either remark. But he knows how the latter one got into circulation. Just after a meeting about target selection, an admiral said, in a joking way, "Maybe we ought to drop a nuclear bomb on Hanoi and get the damned thing over with." LeMay recalls saying, also in jest, "Yeah, that's probably a good idea." The next day there were newspaper reports that LeMay advocated a nuclear attack on Hanoi. But he insists that he never, at any time, argued in favor of using atomic weapons in Vietnam. What he did advocate was a policy of keeping the enemy in suspense about the possibility.

"I think everybody [in the JCS] objected to the government making statements—'Oh, we won't use nuclear weapons, ever.' We all thought this was bad. Here we've taken a large segment of the resources of the country to put into the nuclear program for weapon systems. And if we tell our enemies that we have a policy of never using them, we've wasted the taxpayers' resources. Whether you intend to use them or not, you should never say what your intentions are. . . . Once you convince the enemy that [you won't use nuclear weapons], this relieves his mind and allows him to do a lot of things that he wouldn't otherwise do. . . . No one, including LeMay, ever advocated using atomic weapons."

LeMay also insists, perhaps even more surprisingly, that he did not advocate the use of American ground forces in Vietnam. "I don't remember that it ever came before the Joint Chiefs that we ought to send ground troops in there to fight. I would certainly have been dead set against it. As far as I know, every military man I've ever heard of advised against it. MacArthur said, 'Don't do it.' . . . Fight them where we were strong instead of fighting them in the paddies and the jungle.''[8]

In LeMay's opinion, where we were strong was in the air and on the sea. "They were getting their supplies from Communist China and Russia. With strategic bombing, naval and air power, if we had closed that off, the real effort would have died on the vine. We developed a target system that would do that. It was never done. The primary target we wanted to hit was Haiphong harbor, at Hanoi. They'd never let us do it. We had about ninety other targets that would have paralyzed North Vietnam.''

Among those he has mentioned are the other ports, power plants, transportation, and supply dumps. "If you stop the supplies coming in, there can't be too much of a war."

He recently quoted statistics comparing the tonnage of bombs his B-29s dropped on Japan with the tonnage of American bombs dropped in Vietnam. "In Japan we dropped 502,000 tons and we won the war. In Vietnam we dropped 6,162,000 tons of bombs and we lost the war. The difference was that McNamara chose the targets in Vietnam and I chose the targets in Japan."

But would China or Russia have entered the war against us if we had begun our involvement with an all-out air and naval attack on strategic targets in North Vietnam? LeMay thinks not. He acknowledges that it was one of the reasons the administration "wouldn't allow us to hit the proper targets." But even if the U.S. Air Force and Navy had been turned loose against the North, he doesn't think China or Russia would have moved against us.

"I never thought that this would happen down there. It could have happened, yes. But this is one of the things you have to think about when you make the basic decision to use military force in solving your problem. You can't get a little bit pregnant. Once you get into this, you're into it. And if you haven't the guts to see it through at the end, you shouldn't get into it to start with." He also points out that China did not enter the war, in the later stages, when President Johnson and then President Nixon sent the Air Force to bomb North Vietnam.

Though LeMay seems to have been comfortable with his aggressive convictions as to how the war should be conducted, his advice did not make President Kennedy, Robert McNamara, or

Gen. Maxwell Taylor comfortable. They looked upon LeMay as if he were a cannon trying to break loose from its fastening. They had settled on the principles of flexible response and gradual escalation. And in so doing, they had established a pattern that was to continue to the very end of the Vietnam War.

Friday, November 22, 1963, marked the beginning of one of the most tragically memorable and bizarre weekends in American history. President Kennedy was shot and killed that day in Dallas. Everybody old enough to remember can tell you where he was when he heard the news. Curt LeMay recalls that he was in Michigan on leave, but hurried back to Washington in time for the funeral.

When he arrived, he found "a lot of speculation as to whether it might be [part of] an uprising." On Sunday, November 24, he must have wondered, for a while at least, if there was something afoot even more far-reaching than the death of the president. He had gone to the White House to pay his respects to Mrs. Kennedy and was waiting in the West Wing's Roosevelt Room, also called the Fish Room because Franklin Roosevelt had kept an aquarium there, as well as trophies he had brought back after fishing trips. The Fish Room was used now as a waiting room, and in addition to its elegant Chippendale furniture, it had a television set which LeMay was watching because Kennedy's killer, Lee Harvey Oswald, was just then being marched through the basement corridors of the Dallas jail.

Suddenly, the scene before LeMay's eyes erupted into chaos. A moment later, the Fish Room door opened and Maxwell Taylor entered.

LeMay turned to him in astonishment, pointed at the TV screen and exclaimed, "Look! They just shot Oswald!"

Taylor remembers thinking "that there would be suspicion that the killing of Oswald by [Jack] Ruby had been done to suppress something."

Though LeMay recalls that a lot of people in the administration harbored such worries, he says the thought of a possible conspiracy or attempted revolution "never entered my mind." If not, he was almost alone among his fellow Americans that day. Fears of plots and attempted coups ran through most people's minds.

On November 29, the Joint Chiefs visited the White House for their first meeting with President Lyndon Johnson. He told the chiefs he needed their help and he wanted them to come to him with their advice. But first he gave them some advice. They had better cut the fat out of their military budget because if the entire budget surpassed $100 billion, Senator Harry Byrd of Virginia, chairman of the Senate Finance Committee, would see to it that it wouldn't pass. Then Johnson asked each chief how his service stood.

To this, LeMay said the Air Force was in the best shape possible with what it had, but that there were problems he would like to discuss with the president after he had a chance to see "how the overall budget shapes up."[10]

The main problem LeMay had in mind was his old nemesis, Robert McNamara, whom Johnson had retained as his secretary of defense after the death of President Kennedy. McNamara was an obstacle LeMay would have to get around if the Air Force was to attain its cherished goal—a "follow-on" bomber to replace the B-70, which was not to be.

On December 30, the Joint Chiefs, together with McNamara and Roswell Gilpatric, flew to the Johnson ranch in Texas for a meeting called "to permit the service chiefs to express their views" to the new president.[11]

When LeMay's turn to speak came, he said he understood the need for austerity. And he considered his tactical as well as his airlift forces "reasonably well balanced." But then, like a dog refusing to let go of a meaty bone, he renewed his insistence that the Air Force still needed a new bomber to replace the aging B-52.

His staff had contrived for him several points to illustrate the need. There were no plans afoot to replace the current strategic or air defense systems, in both of which our capabilities were diminishing. Especially in comparison to aeronautic capabilities elsewhere. The French and Germans, for instance, were developing supersonic transports. This would mean we wouldn't even be able to intercept commercial airliners, let alone enemy bombers. And as for air defense, we were spending more money to defend the Navy's fleet than we were to defend the whole continental United States. All he was asking for at the moment, LeMay told the president, was $5 million in fiscal 1964 and $50 million in fiscal 1965.

McNamara then pointed out that the eventual cost of the followon bomber LeMay wanted would be $10 billion. LeMay conceded it would be $9 billion.

Between LeMay and McNamara an argument ensued which

gradually became, as LeMay later described it, "pretty bloody." McNamara said he didn't know how the Air Force planned to use this follow-on bomber.

LeMay said he would send him down a paper, showing him how.

Finally the president stepped in and asked McNamara for his definitive thinking about the manned bomber, whereupon McNamara came out flatly against it. He said the manned bomber (as envisioned) was essentially a missile carrier, and as such was less reliable than the (ground- or submarine-based) missile. The meeting ended inconclusively with Johnson indicating he would want to talk more about it later.

By this time, even LeMay considered the B-70 "dead," and had said as much during an October 14, 1963, staff meeting. Though the first B-70 was almost ready for flight at that time, it seemed likely to be the last. Throughout the autumn and early winter of 1963, LeMay, Zuckert, and the Air Staff had held meetings about the development of the much desired follow-on bomber. Zuckert said the reason they had lost the B-70 was that they didn't have an operational plan.

Officers on the staff insisted the real reason was that "a decision had been made that could not be penetrated."

No doubt this was true, but if so, what made them think the same kind of decision would not be made concerning the follow-on bomber? McNamara was still secretary of defense, and as far as anyone could see, he hadn't changed his mind. Yet the hopeful planning and specification listing for a new bomber had continued. And even now, after McNamara's definitive December 30 statement, it was bound to continue because the Air Force was so deeply convinced of the need for a newer, better bomber it could not let go of its hopes.

In the early spring of 1964, when it was about time once more for LeMay to hear from the White House that he was soon to be either rehired or retired, he was talking one day to his old friend and classmate, Col. Stuart McLennan, who had been retired himself many years earlier after a remarkable recovery from a B-26 crash.

"Well, are you going to be appointed again?" McLennan asked him.

LeMay said, "I doubt it."

"You want to make a bet?"

"Yes, I'll bet you a box of cigars."

"The reason you're going to be reappointed," McLennan insisted, "is because Lyndon Johnson is not going to upset the apple cart in the Pentagon."[12]

LeMay was not impressed by this reasoning, especially when, a short time later, Gene Zuckert stopped him in the hall of the Pentagon.

"You don't get along very well with the third floor," Zuckert said, as if he were announcing something LeMay hadn't noticed. "So I didn't think it made any sense to recommend you for reappointment."[13]

"I didn't expect anything different," LeMay replied. "What's your problem?"

Zuckert said, "I just wanted you to know."

On the afternoon of April 3, LeMay went to the White House to represent the Joint Chiefs when President Johnson made a radio and television speech marking the eve of the fifteenth anniversary of the North Atlantic Treaty Organization. As soon as the speech was finished, Johnson served cocktails to the assembled dignitaries, many of them NATO officials.

"After everybody had a drink," LeMay recalls, "the president pulled me off to one of the dining rooms and said, 'Who have you got to replace you as chief of staff?'

"I wasn't about to recommend anybody. If I had, it would have been equivalent to the kiss of death. I said, 'We have a dozen people who would do a good job for you, Mr. President.'

"He said, 'Well now, something for you. How about an ambassadorship?' "

President Kennedy had rid himself of Adm. George Anderson by making him an ambassador, but Anderson, while he hadn't always gotten along well with the administration, was at least capable of diplomatic niceties. Even LeMay himself, often referred to ironically as "The Diplomat," must have been amused at the notion of the president making him an ambassador.

"My answer," he recalls, "was that it didn't make much sense to stop doing something I knew something about to take on something I knew nothing about.

"The president said, 'I want you to be a roving ambassador and sell some F-5s [fighter planes] to some of these countries up against the Iron Curtain.'

"I said, 'Well, that I can't do because I've been against the F-5 ever since its inception. It's definitely a second-line fighter. It might be all right for some small country, due to its simplicity.

They can maintain it easily. But for countries up against the Iron Curtain it's not suitable. It won't go up against a Russian first-line fighter. I'd be talking to airmen and they know that. And they know I haven't been favoring its use as a first-line fighter. I just can't do anything like that. If you haven't got anything to do that I know something about, I'll retire and go into industry or something else.'

"He said, 'You haven't made any commitments, have you?'

"I said, 'No, of course not. Not till after I retire.'

"He said, 'Well, give me about ten days.' That ended the conversation."

After only four days, LeMay was summoned back to the White House, where Johnson greeted him privately. "I don't know what's going on in the future," the president said, "but I've got an election coming up. Anyway, I don't think your military career ought to be interrupted. So I'm going to reappoint you."

"Thank you very much for your vote of confidence," LeMay said, "but I presume you've taken into account the fact that I don't think very much of what the secretary of defense has been trying to do?"

"Yes, I understand that," Johnson said. "You just keep doing what you think is best for the country."

LeMay said, "I certainly can do that," and went home to tell Helen the news. The next morning, a car pulled up in front of Stuart McLennan's house and the driver presented him a box of cigars.

Why did Johnson reappoint LeMay against all expectations to the contrary? There's a story about Johnson and J. Edgar Hoover that suggests a possible reason. When someone asked Johnson why he didn't fire the notorious Mr. Hoover, he is reputed to have said, in his earthy style, "I'd rather have him on the inside of the tent pissing out than on the outside pissing in." As Johnson said to LeMay, he had an election coming up. He must have been aware that LeMay's political persuasions were ultraconservative, and that LeMay did not approve of the administration's conduct of the Vietnam War. As a private citizen, he would be free to speak out. As Air Force chief of staff, he couldn't do so. But on the other hand, this may not explain Johnson's decision at all. Taking into account his mischievous, Byzantine mind, he may simply have enjoyed watching the in-fighting between his Air Force chief and his secretary of defense.

Whether Robert McNamara enjoyed the prospect of one more

year with Curt LeMay is another question. The morning after LeMay learned of his reappointment, he went in and told Gene Zuckert who his chief would be for the next year. "He didn't know a thing about it," LeMay recalls. "He left me standing there, practically tore the door off the hinges and ran down to tell McNamara the bad news."

President Johnson's reasons for reappointing LeMay are still open to speculation, but one thing is certain. He didn't do it because he had decided to accept LeMay's advice and reject McNamara's. In the budget for fiscal 1965, there would be no provision for a follow-on bomber. And as for the management of the Vietnam War, it was now in the hands of Johnson himself, Dean Rusk, Maxwell Taylor, Robert McNamara, and the band of civilian experts in the State and Defense departments. McNamara and Taylor visited Saigon together in March 1964, and again in May. After each of these visits, the White House announced increases in military and economic aid to South Vietnam. Neither of the increases was large enough to prove decisive in the war. Yet Taylor's concepts of flexible response and gradual escalation continued to hold favor in the Department of Defense and the White House.

Having little else to do, LeMay concentrated on running the Air Force. He took an eight-day inspection trip to Europe in June. He made another vain attempt, on August 25, to impress upon President Johnson the need for a follow-on bomber to replace the B-52. And he delivered speeches to various groups about the importance of strengthening America's air defense. But he had always hated speechmaking and he still hated it.

In 1985, Gen. John J. Vessey, Jr., the current chairman of the Joint Chiefs of Staff, reminisced in Washington about the best speech he had ever heard. It was delivered by, of all people, General LeMay.

As Vessey remembered it, LeMay stood up before his audience and said, "I have a speech. It's a good speech. It was written by a smart lieutenant colonel who works for me, and I read it on the way here. Now I'm going to put it in the library and you can read it, too."[14] LeMay, recalling the occasion, pointed out that he didn't then sit down. He fielded questions for an hour.

His speeches (or nonspeeches) and his inspection trips, and the everyday business of running the Air Force did not distract him from his deep dissatisfaction with the progress, or lack of progress, of the Vietnam War effort. On August 26, in response to news that the Vietcong had stepped up its action in South Vietnam, he reiterated his belief that the solution to the problem was "to attack North Vietnam with air and naval forces in order to force the North Vietnam government to withdraw their support and shut down the activity of the Vietcong." On one occasion he expressed it perhaps less elegantly but more eloquently: "We should stop swatting flies," he reportedly told a State Department official, "and go after the manure pile."

On September 19, when he was informed of a plan for an attack on three North Vietnam targets, he was still not satisfied. He warned that the weight of the effort was not sufficient. And on October 2, when he was briefed about another planned air strike against the North, he said it showed how much people didn't know about air power. "Rather than hit a large number of targets with a little bit of force," he told his staff, "we should pick out the most important ones and destroy them."[15] And he repeated his argument against gradual escalation—an argument which seemed to make better sense to him every day, inasmuch as gradual escalation didn't seem to be working.

"It's not right to start slowly and give the enemy a chance to build up his capabilities," he told his men. "We should hit the enemy hard with the first blow." But all of this was simply conversation. Or instruction for the younger officers who would remain after he was gone. None of his arguments had any influence in the important councils of war. LeMay was now a lame-duck chief of staff. He knew it. So did McNamara and Taylor. They felt no need to listen to him.

In November he took another inspection trip to Europe. In December, he went to Japan. For what purpose? Amazingly, the Japanese government wanted to give him a decoration. Not for burning down so many Japanese cities during World War II, but for helping to build up Japan's postwar defenses. There was a problem, though. A lot of Japanese people were still more impressed by the burndown than the buildup, so the presentation of his decoration was not the smoothest event of the year in Japan. Debate on the subject was quite spirited in the Japanese Diet and in the press.

On December 23, LeMay was back in the United States and flew to Johnson's Texas ranch with the Joint Chiefs and McNamara to discuss the budget for fiscal 1966. Again he argued with McNamara for inclusion of such Air Force projects as the follow-on bomber, but to no avail. Again he lost. On his return to Washington he told his staff, "It was a waste of taxpayers' money to buy the fuel to fly us down to the ranch. Everything had been decided beforehand."[16]

Much of LeMay's time in January 1965 was occupied with interviews by newsmen who were aware of his imminent retirement. He told an *Omaha World Herald* reporter he had a special feeling for Omaha because he had spent more time there than anywhere else. He told Lloyd Norman of *Newsweek,* in answer to a question about the manned bomber, "The deadline is long past. In peacetime, mistakes don't show up. Therefore a decision can be delayed on weapon systems such as the follow-on manned bomber and nobody will know that a mistake has been made until a war comes."

When a *Chicago Tribune* reporter asked him about his controversies with McNamara, he pointed out that he had talked to Congress when it was proper, when he had been asked to appear. He had not gone to the public with his controversies.

When Charles Corddry of United Press International asked him if there was any way out of the Vietnam situation, he said, "The direction of the war comes from Hanoi, supplies come down from the north, and so forth. We try to fight all our battles in South Vietnam. It doesn't appear that we can win this way. The only way to stop it is to make it too expensive for North Vietnam to conduct the war."

And when Jessie Buscher of the *Columbus Dispatch* asked him if he planned to enter politics after retirement, he said, "I don't think so. I don't rule this out but I am not thinking this way now."

On February 1, 1965, LeMay held his last staff meeting. His speech was characteristically short—one paragraph. He told his men they were the finest Air Staff ever. They should always push the chief and the vice chief. And they should never compromise their plans. "Make sure you are right before you move and then stick with your guns and keep fighting for what you want. It takes a long time here to get things done; however, water wears away the stone. Right prevails in the end in our form of government."

Later that day he officially retired. He had been a general officer for nearly twenty-two years and a four-star general for thirteen years. No one else had ever remained so long on active duty in four-star grade.

Though everyone in the Air Force looked upon LeMay with a certain amount of awe, not all of his colleagues or former colleagues were sorry to see him retire. Some of them were as unhappy as he was about the frustrations of his last four years.

Gen. Delmar Wilson said recently, "As chief of staff he was a complete failure because he was no politician. Though he was right in what he tried to do, he accomplished nothing."[17]

Gen. Theodore R. Milton said in 1974, "I don't think he was a very good chief, but this is my own view. Chief of staff is a job where you've got to accommodate yourself to the way that town [Washington] works, and you've got to do what's best for your service, and you've got to compete [for] the budget dollar, and you've got to get along with the civilians."[18]

Gen. Thomas White, LeMay's predecessor as chief, wrote of him at the time of his retirement:

> He did not relish Washington duty. He suffered tortures because, as a long-time field commander, he had acquired the simple virtue of being able to resolve the pros and cons of a problem into black or white. At the far more complicated level of the Washington top command, new elements such as political considerations, public relations, budget planning, and philosophies had an important bearing on the decision-making process. What seemed to LeMay like a black-and-white affair often ended up as a shade of gray which was unpalatable to his practical and initially uncomplicated view.[19]

There were no doubt others in the Air Force who harbored such feelings about LeMay and the frustrations over which he presided during the four years when he was chief of staff. But none of them, including those quoted above, had forgotten his unique contributions and accomplishments as an air commander.

General Wilson also said of him, "In World War II he was one of the great air commanders of all time. And he accomplished wonders in the organization of SAC."

Milton also said of him, "He reached his zenith as commander of SAC, and that was a hell of an achievement."

And White also wrote of him:

> True, [he] lost many battles in the nearly four years he was chief of staff. But many of the losses would have come about

in any case because of the McNamara upheaval in all the military services. . . .

LeMay's almost religious dedication to his world-saving strategic mission, his iron will, his personal technical competence, his relentless and, some say, ruthless insistence on utter selflessness in his subordinates resulted in the Strategic Air Command becoming, without question, the most efficient fighting organization ever devised . . . not only the most efficient but by far the most powerful military organization in all history. . . . Whatever one may think of him as a person, he deserves to be rated as one of America's "greats."

It would be difficult to argue against General White's assessment after reviewing the many accomplishments during LeMay's career. As a first lieutenant, he was the navigator on several of the most important pioneering navigational flights in history. As a group and then divisional commander in Europe during World War II, he contributed, more than any of his colleagues, to the tactics which finally enabled the daylight bombing strategy to work against Nazi Germany. As the B-29 commander in the Pacific, he inaugurated the incendiary tactics which left Japan prostrate even before the introduction of the atomic bomb. Directly after the war, he became the first director of the Air Force research-and-development organization. Then as Air Force commander in Europe, he initiated the Berlin Airlift. When he returned to the United States, he took over a virtually moribund Strategic Air Command and built it into what General White called "the most powerful military organization in all history." And during his years as Air Force chief of staff, he took part, albeit without immediate success, in the critical struggle over manned and unmanned defense systems.

Because he was so blunt, sometimes tactless, politically conservative, and uncompromisingly military in his outlook, he never became a popular hero in the mold of a Dwight Eisenhower, George Patton, or Jimmy Doolittle. But he inspired an admiration in his men which is surprising in light of the demands he placed upon them. An incident in Los Angeles several years ago illustrates this.

Judge Ralph Nutter, a politically liberal California jurist who had once been an American Civil Liberties Union attorney, was talking to several men at a cocktail party when a mention of General LeMay came into the conversation.

At this, Nutter turned and said, "I named my oldest child after Curtis LeMay."

Everyone there, aware of the huge gap between Nutter's liberal and LeMay's conservative political views, fell silent. Finally, one man said, "How could you name your child after that right-wing son-of-a-bitch?"

Nutter looked at the man and said, "I served under him in England during World War II. I was a navigator in his 305th Bomb Group. He was so tough on us, he trained us so hard and prepared us so well, I honestly don't believe I'd have survived to have a child if it weren't for Curtis LeMay."[20]

CHAPTER TWENTY-NINE

It was not easy for Curtis LeMay, private citizen, to adjust to his retirement. He had done almost nothing to prepare for it. While he was still on active duty as Air Force chief of staff, he didn't even consider it proper to make postretirement commitments, either to private industry or politics, the two options which seemed most possible. He was fifty-nine years old and had been a soldier for thirty-seven of them—his entire adult life. In the services, a man has to face risks, to be sure, but he is also sheltered in many ways from the vicissitudes and vagaries of civilian life. He doesn't have to worry about food on the table, housing, medical bills, etc. LeMay was not alone among soldiers if he felt a certain bewilderment at the prospect of life outside the Air Force, and a disinclination to prepare for it.

Shortly before his retirement, he had mentioned to his long-retired friend, Stuart McLennan, that he wanted to talk to him about it, find out what it was like. But then, he never got around to such a discussion, nor did he get around to making even tentative plans, which meant that on February 1, 1965, after his little retirement ceremony, he and Helen had nothing to do; in a very real sense, no place to go. When they gave up their commodious chief's quarters in Fort Myer, they moved into much smaller, presumably temporary quarters in Washington. He had no intention of staying there. He still disliked Washington.

The only thing LeMay had done, looking toward retirement, was to arrange for MacKinlay Kantor to write a book about his life and career. "I had decided," he recalled in later years, "that I was going to be one general who wasn't going to write a book. I had absolutely no talent for writing."

Then, as the end of his career approached, friends began reminding him he "had been at the places where big things happened.'' They pressed him to put it down on paper, for the record if for no other reason.

When he finally became persuaded of the merits of their argument, he realized he would have to get a professional to do the writing. He decided on Kantor because he had read some of his books and liked them. He had also known him for more than twenty years. During World War II, Kantor was a free-lance war correspondent and spent much of his time with LeMay's 305th Bomb Group in England. After that war, he visited LeMay at SAC headquarters in Omaha, and then flew into the Korean War as a correspondent with a B-29 group. So LeMay, on a trip to Florida in 1953, had stopped to see him at his home in Sarasota to propose a partnership.

For almost two years thereafter, Kantor had been interviewing him on tape, and had gathered vast amounts of material about him, but in spite of Kantor's diligence and LeMay's desire to be forthright, they were still up against a problem for which they hadn't figured out a solution. How could they get around the fact that many of the events of LeMay's career, as well as the documents which might verify and illuminate them, were still, in 1965, highly classified government secrets.

After his retirement, LeMay again flew to Sarasota, where he and Kantor finished the manuscript of the book, to be entitled *Mission with LeMay*, and to be presented in the first person as his autobiography. It was published to mixed reviews by Doubleday in November 1965. The mixed reviews were almost inevitable, first of all because LeMay's limitations in the field of public relations left a lot of people, including critics, with ambivalent feelings about him; second, because he and Kantor never could overcome the SECRET classifications that kept them from describing or explaining the controversial aspects of his career; and third, because the text, as finally published, put into LeMay's mouth a lot of unpopular political and military statements. Witness the unfortunate remark that he never uttered but failed to delete, that we should bomb the North Vietnamese ''back into the Stone Age.''

That statement, even though he never said it, did more damage to LeMay's public image than anything he ever did say. And it has made him shy about saying anything publicly. In 1985, a former Air Force officer who had never met him made a phone call to his California home. When Helen LeMay answered, she said, "Are you sure you're not a reporter? He won't talk to reporters."

He has found, since his retirement, that he has something in common with Samuel Goldwyn and Yogi Berra. Whenever a person thinks of a thoughtless malaprop about Hollywood, he's likely to put it in the mouth of Goldwyn. Whenever a person thinks of a thoughtless quip about baseball, he's likely to put it in the mouth of Berra. And whenever a person thinks of a thoughtless remark about war or nuclear holocaust, he's likely to put it in the mouth of LeMay. But while the Goldwyn and Berra "quotes" are meant to be funny, those attributed to LeMay are often frightening or appalling.

LeMay and Helen spent almost all of 1965 in Washington, wondering what they would do next, waiting for offers from industry. Retired officers at LeMay's level inevitably get a selection of lucrative offers from large corporations. But it was hardly surprising that few such offers came to him. Top management in any company might be inclined to think they had enough to do, managing their company, without trying to manage Curtis LeMay. His reputation, especially during the last four years of his career, did not make him seem like the kind of malleable man who would fit smoothly into a corporate structure.

Not until the autumn of 1965 did he get an offer he felt he could accept. A small company called Network Electronics, in Los Angeles' San Fernando Valley, asked him to come west as its board chairman at a salary of fifty thousand dollars a year—a handsome sum in those days, especially for a military man who had never, even as chief of staff, made more than $25,680 per year. In time for Christmas, he and Helen flew to California and took a house in Bel-Air, just through the Santa Monica Mountains from his new job.

"I took the job because I was tired," he said many years later. "I was through with sixteen- or twenty-hour-a-day jobs. I wanted something less strenuous, and I didn't want to go to work for a company with government contracts. So this little company that didn't have any government contracts finally sold me on coming out. The plan was . . . that I would give the owner [Mihal Patrichi] guidance from the standpoint that maybe he could get into the military business. Sounded like what I wanted. It wouldn't make me punch a time clock, or take the responsibility for making the outfit go. Well, that period was a complete disaster as far as I was concerned."[1]

He soon found he could work with Mr. Patrichi just about as well as he had with Mr. McNamara. But he stuck it out at Network for a little more than two and a half years. And it did have some advantages from his point of view. It gave him time to make speeches that he felt had to be made about America's defense needs and about our strategy in Vietnam.

In October 1966, he wrote an article about Vietnam for *U.S. News and World Report* in which he said, "Since even small wars are cruel, we must fight them in such a way as to win them as quickly as possible. . . . It's a losing game for the stronger side to deliberately drag out a conflict."

Again in this article he argued that we should increase the bombing of strategic North Vietnamese targets.

> The "flexible response" strategy championed by General Maxwell D. Taylor in his *Uncertain Trumpet* obliges us to fight according to some sort of Marquis of Queensberry rules which we, ourselves, made up and abide by unilaterally. The other side follows no such rules. . . . Of course, "flexible response" strategy is supposed to keep a small war limited so as not to unduly threaten the Sino-Soviets. But for the life of me, I can't see why the Communists would be less eager to engage us because we act equivocal rather than tough.

The retired soldier still wanted the world to know that his country may have gone soft but he hadn't.

On November 18, 1966, LeMay's father died in Mount Vernon, Ohio. He had been ill with cardiac problems for some time. During the next eight or nine months, LeMay kept after his mother to come and live with Helen and himself in California. Finally, in the late summer of 1967, she did come out, but she was too independent to stay. She returned home in September and about ten days later, on September 25, she, too, died of a heart attack.

At this time or shortly thereafter, a group of conservative California Republicans approached LeMay about running for the U.S. Senate in 1968, but he declined. "They wanted me to take on the raising of money. I wasn't interested in politics, anyway."[2] Except, of course, as a means of spreading his views about national defense and the Vietnam War.

He was approached next, in the summer of 1968, by representatives of Alabama's Gov. George Wallace, who was planning to run for president as the candidate of his newly formed American Independent Party. Would LeMay be interested in running for vice president on the same ticket?

He said no. He wasn't interested in any third party. They went away, but they came back again. "By that time I had talked to a few friends," he recalls. "They convinced me [Richard] Nixon was going to say the right things and do the right things [about Vietnam and defense policies]. So I was for Nixon. I firmly believed we had to have a conservative government or we might never have another chance. . . . At that time I thought Wallace, being a conservative Democrat, would take votes away from Nixon."

Once more he said no to the Wallace people. But as autumn approached and the campaign began to warm up, "Nixon didn't start saying the things I thought he was going to say." Then there were rumors that Nixon might appoint to his cabinet several men whom LeMay considered "left-wing Republicans." Men like Nelson Rockefeller and George Romney. "I thought, what in hell's going on here? Nixon's made so many deals to be nominated on the first ballot that his hands are going to be tied."

LeMay now became so sympathetic to George Wallace's cause that he sought out the Alabama governor and had a long talk with him. First he satisfied himself that Wallace was not a racist, despite a widespread public perception that he was. Then the two men talked presidential politics. "[Wallace] didn't think he had a chance of being elected," LeMay learned. "But he was damn sure going to try to keep [Hubert] Humphrey from being elected. He said if it went into the Electoral College, he thought he'd have enough strength there to defeat Humphrey. So I thought maybe I ought to help him."

In retrospect, the political thinking that led LeMay to this decision is difficult to swallow. "If you took votes from Humphrey," he was reminded recently, "you'd be helping Nixon."

"That was my aim," he said.

"Then you weren't really anti-Nixon?"

"Oh no. If he were elected, he'd be better than Humphrey."

It is not easy to understand why LeMay would choose to run against Nixon if he actually wanted to help him, but that was what he did. On October 3, 1968, at a televised press conference in Pittsburgh, he and Wallace jointly announced that he would be the vice presidential candidate on the third-party ticket.

The press conference itself turned out to be an embarrassment to Wallace because LeMay, in his inimitable, impolitic way, said what he believed, without much regard for political realities. The American press roundly ridiculed him. *Newsweek* magazine's report of the proceedings was particularly damaging to the Wallace-LeMay campaign:

> . . . LeMay didn't like wars, nuclear or otherwise, he said, and he didn't think nuclear bombs would be needed in Vietnam. But neither did he think that using nuclear weapons would be the end of the world. Bikini, after all, survived twenty A-tests and still came back to life (even if the land crabs are "a little bit hot"). LeMay lumbered on until, at the end, someone asked Wallace if he agreed on the use of nuclear weapons. LeMay was almost off the rostrum. Wallace tugged him back by the lapel and whispered, "They say you agreed to use nuclear weapons. You didn't say that."
>
> But LeMay missed his cue. He would "prefer not to use any weapons at all," he huffed, but if he thought it necessary he would "use anything we could dream up, including nuclear weapons." Wallace fidgeted and paced in the background, then briefly berated newsmen for pressing the question. Undeterred, LeMay bulled ahead. ". . . I'll be damned lucky if I don't appear as a drooling idiot whose only solution to any problem is to drop atomic bombs all over the world. I assure you I'm not . . ." Wallace moved to his elbow. "General," he prompted, "we got to go," and they did.[3]

LeMay may have been trying to say at that press conference what he had often said before—that even if you don't intend to use nuclear weapons, you don't make any such promises to your enemy—but that was not the message he conveyed to the nuclear-fearful American public. From this first day, his only foray into electoral politics was disastrous and sometimes ludicrous. He simply was not a politician, never had been, and never would be. Even his close friends and former colleagues were horrified at the news of his candidacy. Tooey Spaatz, Ira Eaker, and several others sent him letters and telegrams advising him against it. But by that time it was too late. He had committed himself and he plowed wearily through the hopeless campaign.

Recently, he himself admitted regrets about agreeing to run with Wallace. When asked if he now thought it was a mistake, he said, "Well, maybe it was. . . . It was a miserable mess. But I considered this my last chore for the public."

It was, indeed, his last public "chore." But unfortunately for him, it was a chore the public doesn't seem to forget. The American people seem more inclined to remember LeMay for episodes like the 1968 vice presidential campaign than for his enormously impressive achievements toward the nation's defense.

After the 1968 election, he did not return to Network Electronics. Eventually, he and Helen sold their home in Bel-Air and purchased another one, a modern, California-style, large-windowed house near the ocean in Newport Beach, about forty miles south of Los Angeles. Here they still live comfortably, only a few miles from their daughter Janie and her husband, Dr. Jim Lodge, who has retired from the medical profession to become a very successful art dealer. Helen, through the years, has developed her talents as a painter, but she doesn't paint the kind of pictures her son-in-law buys and sells. His taste inclines toward the abstract. Hers is more representational. Her interest is not so much in selling her art as in decorating her home with it.

Though Curtis LeMay is retired, he is not inactive. He flies to Washington every two or three months for meetings of the *National Geographic* board of directors, of which he became a member when he was still on active duty. While in Washington, he usually spends at least a morning being briefed at the Pentagon about current defense problems. And he has been helpful to Air Force historians, first by submitting to interviews, and now by reading and evaluating their papers and manuscripts. He also speaks on occasion, though reluctantly, before receptive groups, especially Air Force groups. And anyone who has witnessed his appearances before such groups might notice that he is still welcomed, not only with respect, but with a certain amount of awe and fear. Despite the passage of years, everyone in the Air Force still knows about old "Iron Ass." And when they talk to him they choose their words carefully. They are more aware than the general public of what he accomplished during his long career as an airman.

LeMay himself ranks two of his military accomplishments above all others. The first was getting Japan to surrender before a brutal and costly invasion became necessary. There are some modern historians who believe such an invasion would have been relatively easy because LeMay's B-29s had already destroyed so many Japanese cities. He disagrees because he is aware that the B-29s had not destroyed the Japanese army. It was intact, in hiding, and in readiness to fight. Though the Japanese people may have been near starvation, the army was not. And its leaders were in a fighting mood. It was the destruction of their cities that showed those leaders that their cause was ultimately hopeless. "Considering the problems we faced [in the air war against Japan], I think we did a hell of a job," LeMay said recently. "We got it done."

The second aspect of his career that he believes "caused a ripple" in the world was the development of the Strategic Air Command. "It was brought on by the horrible experience of World War II. We hoped we could prevent another such war," he said, "and I think it's SAC that has done so."[4] There may be people who wouldn't state it that flatly, but there are few who could deny the importance of SAC as a dominant factor in the world's power politics since the second great war.

When he's at home in California with Helen, he takes a regular morning walk, he receives and transmits on his ham radio, he practices his still amazingly accurate marksmanship at a nearby shooting range, and whenever possible, he spends time with an old pal who recently moved to California—Gen. Grizzy Griswold. LeMay is more slender than he used to be because Helen and his doctor watch his diet. Though he looks and acts like a perfectly healthy man, much younger than his years, he is a heart patient and he has to guard his temper as well as his weight. But he is still capable of anger, especially when he is reminded of the old days.

Recently, while reading a new book on the Vietnam War, he became so incensed he had to take a nitroglycerin pill and go for a walk to calm himself. He is still frustrated by the defeats he suffered in his campaigns against the policies of Robert McNamara and the Kennedy-Johnson administrations. He has, however, the consolation of his conviction that time has justified many of the stands he took during his four tumultuous years as Air Force chief of staff. Especially his stands against McNamara.

The TFX, or F-111, for instance, turned out to be a usable, but never very satisfactory fighter plane in either its Navy or Air Force configuration. As for manned bombers, McNamara was convinced in 1961 that missiles were ready to replace them, but almost twenty-five years later, the missiles have not yet been able to do so. The old B-52s are still flying for SAC. Though Mc-

Namara killed the B-70, he didn't manage to kill the need for aircraft and the judgment their human crews can exercise.

As for the Vietnam War, whether or not LeMay's assessment of it is correct, whether or not his approach to its prosecution would have worked, we'll never know, since it was never fully tried. All we know for sure is that the Taylor-McNamara methods of flexible response and gradual escalation did not work. In Vietnam, the United States lost a war for the first time in the nation's history.

A majority of Americans are now convinced that the country should never have gotten into the Vietnam War. But Curtis LeMay is not convinced of that, either. Pugnacious soldier to the end, he is convinced only that we should have won it.

SOURCES

Among the sources of material for this book are more than one hundred hours of interviews by the author with the principal subject, Gen. Curtis LeMay, mostly at the general's home in Newport Beach, California. But these constitute only a small portion of the author's research into the life and career of General LeMay. Also carefully studied and extensively used were the transcripts of LeMay's six Air Force Oral History interviews between 1943 and 1972, plus transcripts of Oral History interviews of twenty-four LeMay military associates and subordinates—some friendly to him, others less so.

In addition, the author interviewed at length thirty-two of LeMay's friends, relatives, and associates. To corroborate, and in some instances correct, the reminiscences gathered in these sixty-two interviews, the author collected thousands of pages of documents, correspondence, records, and reports, plus articles from newspapers and periodicals, searched through the collected papers of LeMay and many other prominent figures, both military and civilian, in various libraries and document repositories, and studied every available book that touches on LeMay's career.

Among the people who have been exceptionally helpful in gathering this material are, first of all, General LeMay himself, his wife, Helen, their daughter, Mrs. Patricia Lodge, his two sisters, Mrs. Methyll Kinnear and Mrs. Parica Hauger, and his brother, Leonard LeMay; James Hutson, Dr. Paul Chestnut, Gary Kohn, and Mrs. Jackie Gargan of the Library of Congress; Ms. Suzanne Forbes of the John F. Kennedy Library in Boston; Dr. Richard H. Kohn, chief of the Office of Air Force History in Washington, D.C., and among his staff members, William Heimdahl, Herman Wolk, Dr. Walton Moody, David Schoen, Ms. Margaret Peters, and Sgt. Roger Jernigan; Lloyd H. Cornett, director of the Simpson Historical Research Center at Maxwell Field, Alabama, and among his staff members, Cargill Hall, Luther E. Lee, Mrs. Judy Endicott, Pressley Bickerstaff, Warren Trest, and Richard Morse; Maj. Bernard Claxton, chief, Military History and Theory, Air University, Maxwell Field; Brig. Gen. Richard A. "Ish" Ingram, Commandant of the Air Force Command and Staff School, Maxwell Field; and perhaps most important, Brig. Gen. Brian S. Gunderson, Ret., Gen. Bryce Poe II, Ret., Col. Louis H. Cummings, Ret., Col. Kenneth Bixler, Ret., and James Parton of the Air Force Historical Foundation, which provided full and generous support to this project.

INTERVIEWED BY THE AUTHOR

Brown, Col. Mark
Cohen, Maj. Ralph
Dacey, Maj. Gen. Timothy J.
Eaker, Gen. Ira C.
Giles, Lt. Gen. Barney M.
Griswold, Lt. Gen. Francis H.
Hansell, Maj. Gen. Haywood S.
Harbold, Maj. Gen. Norris B.
Harvey, Col. Alva L.
Hauger, Mrs. Patarica
Hill, Gladwin
Kinnear, Mrs. Methyll
Kissner, Maj. Gen. August W.
Kuter, Gen. Laurence F.
Lay, Col. Beirne, Jr.
LeMay, Gen. Curtis E.

LeMay, Mrs. Helen
LeMay, Leonard
Lodge, Mrs. Patricia
McConnell, Gen. John Paul
McKee, Gen. William F.
McLennan, Col. Stuart
Montgomery, Lt. Gen. Richard M.
Mundy, Gen. George
Norcross, Carl H.
Old, Lt. Gen. Archie J.
Parrish, Brig. Gen. Noel F.
Saunders, Brig. Gen. Laverne G.
Wade, Gen. David
Waterman, Sgt. Boyd
Wilson, Gen. Delmar
Zuckert, Eugene

AIR FORCE ORAL HISTORY INTERVIEWS

Barcus, Lt. Gen. Glenn O.
Barnes, Gen. Earl W.
Carlton, Gen. Paul K.
Casey, Gen. Maurice F.
Crabb, Maj. Gen. Jarred V.
Eaker, Gen. Ira C.
Fairbrother, Brig. Gen. William H.
Giles, Gen. Barney M.
Griswold, Lt. Gen. Francis H.
Hansell, Maj. Gen. Haywood, Jr.
Harkins, Gen. Paul D.
Irvine, Lt. Gen. C.S.

Kenney, Gen. George C.
Kingsbury, Maj. Gen. William C.
Martin, Lt. Gen. Glen W.
McKee, Gen. William F.
Milton, Gen. Theodore R.
Schriever, Gen. Bernard A.
Smith, Gen. Frederic H., Jr.
Twining, Gen. Nathan F.
Waxham, Maj. Frank W., Jr. and
  Murphy, Maj. Gene D.
Wolfe, Lt. Gen. Kenneth B.
Zuckert, Eugene M.

COLLECTED PAPERS AND DOCUMENTS

Library of Congress

The Testimony of General LeMay and of Robert McNamara before various congressional committees between 1961 and 1965. Collected papers of

Fairchild, Gen. Muir S.
Foulois, Maj. Gen. Benjamin D.
LeMay, Gen. Curtis E.

Quesada, Lt. Gen. Elwood R.
Spaatz, Gen. Carl
White, Gen. Thomas D.

Simpson Historical Research Center and Office of Air Force History

Blanchard, Lt. Gen. William H.   LeMay, Gen. Curtis E.
Cabell, Gen. Charles Pearre   Martin, Lt. Gen. Glen W.
Harmon, Lt. Gen. Millard F.   White, Gen. Thomas D.
Hull, Brig. Gen. Harris B.   Zuckert, Eugene M.
Kissner, Maj. Gen. August

BOOKS

Anders, Curtis. *Fighting Airmen*. New York: Putnam, 1966.

Anderton, David A. *Strategic Air Command*. New York: Charles Scribner's Sons, 1976.

Arnold, Gen. Henry H. *Global Mission*. New York: Harper & Brothers, 1949.

Art, Robert J. *The TFX Decision—McNamara and the Military*. Boston: Little, Brown, 1968.

Barr, James, and Howard, William E. *Combat Missileman*. New York: Harcourt Brace & World, 1961.

Coffey, Thomas M. *Decision over Schweinfurt*. New York: McKay, 1977.

———. *Hap: The Biography of Gen. H. H. Arnold*. New York: Viking Press, 1982.

Craven, W.E., and Cate, J.L. *The Army Air Forces in World War II*. Chicago: University of Chicago Press, 1948.

Current Biography, 1944. New York: H.W. Wilson Co., 1945.

Enthoven, Alain C., and Smith, K. Wayne. *How Much Is Enough?* New York: Harper & Row, 1971.

Evans, Rowland, and Novak, Robert. *Lyndon B. Johnson: The Exercise of Power*. New York: Signet, 1968.

Fairlie, Henry. *The Kennedy Promise*. Garden City, N.Y.: Doubleday, 1972.

Ford, Daniel. *The Button*. New York: Simon and Schuster, 1985.

Giovannitti, Len, and Freed, Fred. *The Decision to Drop the Bomb*. New York: Coward-McCann, 1965.

Goralski, Robert. *World War II Almanac—1931–1945*. New York: Putnam's Sons, 1981.

Groves, Gen. Leslie R. *Now It Can Be Told*. New York: DaCapo Press, 1975.

Halberstam, David. *The Best and the Brightest*. New York: Random House, 1969.

———. *The Making of a Quagmire*. New York: Random House, 1965.

Hansell, Maj. Gen. Haywood S., Jr. "Strategic Air War Against Japan." Unpublished memoir, 1975.

Harbold, Gen. Norris B. *The Log of Air Navigation*. San Antonio: Naylor Co., 1970.

Hastings, Maj. Donald, and associates. *Psychiatric Experiences of the Eighth Air Force, First Year of Combat.* Prepared for Army Air Forces Air Surgeon. New York: Josiah Macy Jr. Foundation, 1944.

Herkin, Gregg. *Counsels of War.* New York: Knopf, 1985.

Hubler, Richard G. *SAC: The Strategic Air Command.* New York: Duell, Sloan and Pearce, 1958.

Jablonski, Edward. *Airwar.* Garden City, N.Y.: Doubleday, 1971.

Kaufmann, William F. *The McNamara Strategy.* New York: Harper & Row, 1964.

Kennedy, Robert F. *Thirteen Days: A Memoir of the Cuban Missile Crisis.* New York: Norton, 1969.

LeMay, Gen. Curtis E. *America Is in Danger.* New York: Funk & Wagnalls, 1968.

———. (with MacKinlay Kantor). *Mission with LeMay.* Garden City, N.Y.: Doubleday, 1965.

LeMay Family Genealogy. Published in Canada. Undated.

Link, Mae, and Coleman, Hubert A. *Medical Support in a Combat Air Force.* Washington: Government Printing Office, for the Office of the Surgeon General, 1955.

Love, George E. *The Age of Deterrence.* Boston: Little, Brown, 1964.

Mason, Herbert M., Jr. *The United States Air Force—A Turbulent History.* New York: Mason/Charter, 1976.

McNamara, Robert S. *The Essence of Security.* New York: Harper & Row, 1968.

Mollenhoff, Clark R. *The Pentagon—Politics, Profit and Plunder.* New York: Putnam's Sons, 1967.

Morrison, Wilbur H. *Fortress without a Roof.* New York: St. Martin's Press, 1982.

———. *The Incredible 305th.* New York: Duell, Sloan and Pearce, 1962.

———. *Point of No Return.* New York: Times Books, 1979.

Moss, Norman. *Men Who Play God.* London: Gollancz, 1968.

O'Donnell, Kenneth, and Powers, David F. *Johnny, We Hardly Knew Ye.* New York: Pocket Books edition, 1973.

Power, Thomas Sarsfield (with Arnhym, Albert A.). *Design for Survival.* New York: Coward-McCann, 1965.

Powers, Thomas. *The Man Who Kept the Secrets—Richard Helms and the CIA.* New York: Knopf, 1979.

Papoport, Roger. *The Great American Bomb Machine.* New York: Dutton, 1971.

Raymond, Jack. *Power at the Pentagon.* New York: Harper & Row, 1964.

Schell, Jonathan. *The Fate of the Earth.* New York: Knopf, 1982.

Schlesinger, Arthur M., Jr. *A Thousand Days.* Boston: Houghton Mifflin, 1965.

———. *Robert Kennedy and His Times*. Boston: Houghton Mifflin, 1978.

Sorensen, Theodore C. *Kennedy*. New York: Harper & Row, 1965.

Stavins, Ralph; Barnet, Richard J.; and Raskin, Marcus G. *Washington Plans an Aggressive War*. New York: Vintage Books, Random House, 1971.

Taylor, Gen. Maxwell. *The Uncertain Trumpet*. New York: Harper & Brothers, 1959.

Thomas, Gordon, and Witts, Max Morgan. *Enola Gay*. New York: Stein and Day, 1977.

Truman, Harry S. *Year of Decisions*. New York: Signet edition, 1955.

Trewhitt, Henry L. *McNamara—His Ordeal in the Pentagon*. New York: Harper & Row, 1971.

Wallace, George C. *Stand Up for America*. Garden City, N.Y.: Doubleday, 1976.

Wheeler, Keith, and the editors of Time-Life Books. *Bombers Over Japan*. New York: Time-Life Books, 1982.

White, Theodore H. *The Making of the President, 1968*. New York: Atheneum, 1969.

Wolk, Herman S. *Planning and Organizing the Postwar Air Force*. Washington: Office of Air Force History, 1984.

Wyden, Peter. *Bay of Pigs*. New York: Simon & Schuster, 1979.

NEWSPAPERS AND PERIODICALS

Aerospace Historian
Air Force Magazine
Air Force Times
Aviation Week
Columbus Dispatch
Daedalus Flyer
Los Angeles Times
Los Angeles *Herald Examiner*

National Geographic
Newsweek
The New Yorker
New York Times
Saturday Evening Post
Time
Washington Post

11. LeMay at an Eighth Air Force Memorial Museum Foundation Symposium, Los Angeles, Oct. 6, 1984.
12. *Fortress without a Roof,* p. 117–18.
13. The foregoing summary of missions was compiled from the Fourth Wing Operational Narrative for July 1943, and from *Decision over Schweinfurt.*
14. Compiled from author's interviews with more than 100 Eighth Air Force crew members; from his book, *Decision over Schweinfurt;* from the book, *Medical Support in a Combat Air Force,* by Mae Link and Hubert A. Coleman; and from a secret report entitled, "Psychiatric Experiences of the Eighth Air Force, First Year of Combat," by Maj. Donald Hastings and Associates.

CHAPTER SIX
1. *Mission with LeMay,* p. 289.
2. Ibid., p. 290.
3. The following account of the Regensburg-Schweinfurt mission was compiled mostly from *Decision over Schweinfurt,* which lists the sources in detail. They include the author's exhaustive interviews with General Eaker; Operational Narratives of the 305th Bomb Group, the Third Division, and the Eighth Air Force Bomber Command; and interviews with many participants including General LeMay (Dec. 7, 1975) and Col. Beirne Lay (Aug. 10, 1975).
4. Col. Edward D. Gray's essay, "LeMay on Aug. 16, 1943—An Early Impression."
5. Norcross to author, Sept. 29, 1983; *Mission with LeMay,* p. 293.
6. Eaker to author, Jan. 27, 1978.
7. "Personal Report in the Regensburg Mission" by Col. Beirne Lay.

CHAPTER SEVEN
1. Eaker to author, Apr. 24, 1975; Gen. H. H. Arnold's *Global Mission,* p. 451; *Decision over Schweinfurt,* p. 262ff.
2. LeMay-Hopper interview, Sept. 7, 1943, p. 21.
3. Ibid., p. 20.
4. LeMay does not remember this September 1943 meeting with Arnold, but Arnold describes it on p. 446 of *Global Mission.*
5. Arnold to Robert Lovett, assistant secretary of war for air, undated, but obviously written in 1943.
6. The following account of circumstances surrounding LeMay's promotion to brigadier general was compiled from the author's interviews with LeMay, Dec. 12, 1983; Cohen, Aug. 21, 1983; and Norcross, Sept. 29, 1983. Also useful were several conversations between the author and James Parton during 1984. Parton was a member of General Eaker's Eighth Air Force staff.
7. Gen. August W. Kissner to author (on tape), Nov. 4, 1983. General Kissner and Gen. Richard M. Montgomery, both of whom

served as chief of staff for LeMay at one time and another, prepared for the author a very useful tape of recollections about LeMay and his methods of operation.

8. LeMay to author, Jan. 25, 1984.
9. *Mission with LeMay*, p. 301ff.; LeMay to author, March 25, 1984.
10. Mrs. Helen LeMay to author, March 14, 1984.
11. LeMay to author, Dec. 12, 1983.
12. Norcross to author, Sept. 29, 1983.

CHAPTER EIGHT

1. LeMay to author, Dec. 12, 1983; *Mission with LeMay*, p. 323.
2. Concerning problems with the B-29: LeMay to author, Dec. 12, 1983; Gen. Laurence F. Kuter to author on tape, June 1979; Arnold to President Franklin D. Roosevelt, Oct. 11, 1943; Kuter to Arnold, July 7, 1944; Gen. C. S. "Bill" Irvine Air Force Oral History transcript 734, p. 36.
3. Hansell to Maj. James M. Boyle in a December 1964 letter.
4. LeMay letter to Mrs. Helen LeMay, Aug. 30, 1944.
5. LeMay to author, Dec. 12, 1983; *Mission with LeMay*, p. 330ff.
6. Col. Alva L. Harvey to author, Nov. 4, 1983.
7. LeMay to author, Dec. 12, 1983; *Point of No Return*, by Wilbur Morrison, pp. 92ff., 101ff.
8. This account of General Saunders's crash and rescue was compiled from the author's conversations with Saunders, Oct. 1, 1978, and LeMay, Dec. 12, 1983.
9. Harvey to author, Nov. 4, 1983.
10. LeMay to author, Dec. 14, 1983.
11. Ibid. Also, *Point of No Return*, pp. 112–15.

CHAPTER NINE

1. LeMay to author, Dec. 14, 1983.
2. Hansell to author, Nov. 21, 1978.
3. "A Reporter With the B-29s," by St. Clair McKelway, *The New Yorker*, June 9–30, 1945. *Hap: The Biography of Gen. H. H. Arnold*, by the author, p. 357.
4. Ibid., p. 358ff.
5. LeMay to author, Dec. 14, 1983; *Mission with LeMay*, p. 340.
6. *Mission with LeMay*, p. 340ff.
7. Brown to author, Aug. 28, 1983.
8. "Iwo Jima Cost Too Much," by Gen. Holland Smith, *Saturday Evening Post*, Nov. 20, 1948.
9. LeMay to author, Dec. 14, 1983.
10. Giles memo to Arnold, Feb. 16, 1945.

CHAPTER TEN

1. *Point of No Return*, p. 189.
2. LeMay to author, Dec. 14, 1983; LeMay Oral History K105.5–30, pp. 5, 7.
3. LeMay to author, Dec. 14, 1983; *Enola Gay*, by Gordon Thomas and Max Morgan Witts, p. 98; *Mission with LeMay*, p. 379ff.
4. Wilson to author, Nov. 21, 1983.
5. LeMay to author, Dec. 14, 1983; *Mission with LeMay*, p. 347.
6. LeMay to author, Dec. 14, 1983; *Point of No Return*, p. 189.
7. LeMay to author, Dec. 12, 1983.
8. Irvine Oral History 734, pp. 8ff, 42–43.
9. LeMay to author, Dec. 14, 1983.
10. The following account of the events and considerations leading to LeMay's low-level bombing strategy against Japan was compiled from the author's Dec. 14, 1983 conversation with LeMay; *Mission with LeMay*, p. 347ff.; *Global Mission*, p. 596; *Point of No Return*, p. 180ff.; McKelway's "A Reporter With the B-29s"; and Gen. Glen Martin's Air Force Oral History transcript dated 6–10 Feb., 1978, p. 116.
11. *Mission with LeMay*, p. 352.
12. LeMay to author, Dec. 14, 1983.

CHAPTER ELEVEN

1. LeMay to author, Dec. 14, 1983.
2. Ibid. Also, LeMay Air Force Oral History transcript 592, p. 3; and Oral History K105.5–30, pp. 7, 8.
3. Craven and Cate, *The Army Air Forces in World War II*, Vol. 5, p. 631; *Point of No Return*, p. 204, 238ff.; *Mission with LeMay*, p. 386ff.
4. Transcript of Norstad-LeMay telephone conversation, March 31, 1945. LeMay to author, Dec. 14, 1983.
5. LeMay to author, Dec. 14, 1983.
6. The details of Arnold's visit to the Marianas come from Arnold's narrative diary of the trip, his letters to his wife, and the author's book, *Hap*.
7. Mrs. LeMay to author, March 14, 1984.
8. LeMay to author, Dec. 14, 1983. Also, LeMay Air Force Oral History transcript 714, p. 2.
9. Gen. Leslie R. Groves, *Now It Can Be Told*, p. 283ff.
10. *Enola Gay*, pp. 156–57. LeMay to author, Dec. 14, 1983.
11. LeMay to author, Dec. 14, 1983; *Mission with LeMay*, p. 386ff.
12. War Department directive, July 24, 1945, written by order of President Harry S. Truman, authorizing use of atomic bomb. Also, LeMay to author, Dec. 14, 1983.
13. Harry S. Truman, *Year of Decision*, p. 462 in Signet ed.
14. *Mission with LeMay*, p. 279.

15. LeMay to author, Dec. 14, 1983.
16. Telegram, Spaatz to Norstad, Aug. 7, 1945.

PART II

CHAPTER TWELVE

1. *LeMay Family Genealogy.* Published in Canada. Undated. p. 68.
2. LeMay to author, Aug. 11, 1983. Much of the following account of LeMay's early years came from this long interview.
3. Mrs. Methyll Kinnear to author, Sept. 2, 1983. LeMay's two surviving sisters, Mrs. Kinnear and Mrs. Patarica Hauger, were interviewed together by the author at the Kinnear home in Mt. Vernon, Ohio.
4. LeMay to author, Aug. 11, 1983.
5. *Columbus Dispatch,* Nov. 25, 1955.
6. *Mission with LeMay,* p. 31.
7. LeMay to author, Aug. 11, 1983.
8. Leonard LeMay to author, Aug. 21, 1983.
9. LeMay to author, Aug. 11, 1983.
10. This account of how Patarica LeMay was named comes from the author's conversation with Mrs. Hauger and Mrs. Kinnear, Sept. 2, 1983; and with LeMay himself, Aug. 11, 1983.
11. Mrs. LeMay to author, March 14, 1984.
12. Gen. Francis H. Griswold to author, Aug. 27, 1983.

CHAPTER THIRTEEN

1. LeMay to author, Aug. 11, 1983.
2. Air Matériel Command Accident Report, March Field, Calif., June 19, 1929. Also, LeMay to author, Jan. 17, 1984.
3. Gen. Glenn O. Barcus Air Force Oral History transcript k239.0512–908, p. 19ff.
4. Accident Report, Selfridge Field, Michigan, dated Aug. 15, 1930.
5. LeMay to author, Jan. 17, 1984.
6. The story of the first meeting between LeMay and his wife, Helen, was compiled from *Mission with LeMay,* pp. 78, 86, 99; and from the author's conversations with LeMay, Jan. 17, 1984, and Mrs. LeMay, March 14, 1984.
7. LeMay to author, Jan. 17, 1984. *Mission with LeMay,* p. 504; LeMay Oral History K105.5–30.
8. LeMay to author, Aug. 11, 1983.
9. Mrs. Patarica Hauger to author, Sept. 2, 1983.
10. LeMay to author, Jan. 17, 1984.
11. Gen. Norris B. Harbold, *The Log of Air Navigation,* pp. 31–43.
12. LeMay to author, Jan. 17, 1984; Mrs. LeMay to author, March 4, 1984.
13. LeMay to author, Jan. 17, 1984; *Mission with LeMay,* p. 101ff.

CHAPTER FOURTEEN

1. The following account of the LeMay marriage, honeymoon, and assignment in Hawaii was compiled from conversations with LeMay, Jan. 17, 1984; Mrs. LeMay, March 14, 1984; and Gen. Francis Griswold, Aug. 27, 1983.

2. LeMay to author, Jan. 17, 1983; LeMay-Hopper interview, Sept. 7, 1943; and *Mission with LeMay,* p. 124ff.

3. Many times during his life LeMay has expressed his appreciation for what he learned from Olds. These remarks were to the author, Jan. 17, 1984.

4. This account of the water-bombing of the battleship *Utah* was compiled mostly from the author's Jan. 17, 1984, conversation with LeMay, but also from *Mission with LeMay,* p. 140ff.; *Global Mission,* p. 103; and the author's conversation with General Eaker, Oct. 11, 1983.

5. Eaker to author, Apr. 9, 1974.

6. John F. Royal to LeMay, letter dated Aug. 30, 1956.

PART III

CHAPTER FIFTEEN

1. LeMay to author, Feb. 2, 1984.

2. Herman S. Wolk, *Planning and Organizing the Postwar Air Force,* p. 121.

3. Lovett to Arnold, Oct. 5, 1945. Also, *Planning and Organizing the Postwar Air Force,* p. 140.

4. Eaker to Lovett, Nov. 7, 1945. Eaker to LeMay, Nov. 7, 1945.

5. LeMay Oral History 736, p. 3.

6. LeMay to author, Jan. 17, 1984.

7. Ibid.

8. *Planning and Organizing the Postwar Air Force,* p. 121.

9. LeMay to author, Jan. 17, 1984.

CHAPTER SIXTEEN

1. Mrs. Helen LeMay to author, Mar. 14, 1984.

2. Mrs. Patricia Lodge to author, Mar. 14, 1984.

3. *New York Times,* May 23, 1961.

4. LeMay to author, Jan. 24, 1984. LeMay Oral History 736, p. 8ff.

5. LeMay to author, Jan. 25, 1984. LeMay Oral History 736, pp. 13–14.

6. *Mission with LeMay,* p. 425.

CHAPTER SEVENTEEN

1. *Mission with LeMay,* p. 430.

2. LeMay to War Dept. Equipment Board, Jan. 3, 1946.

3. LeMay Oral History 736, p. 12.

4. Gen. Frederic H. Smith, Jr., Air Force Oral History transcript 903, p. 144ff.
5. Gen. Noel Parrish Air Force Oral History transcript 744, p. 144ff.
6. Gen. Irvine Oral History 734, p. 22.
7. Hubler, *SAC: The Strategic Air Command*, p. 79.
8. LeMay to author, Jan. 24, 1984.
9. Ibid. Also, LeMay Oral History 736, p. 37ff.

CHAPTER EIGHTEEN

1. LeMay Oral History 736, p. 24.
2. Irvine Oral History 734, p. 43.
3. LeMay lecture at Air War College, Mar. 4, 1949.
4. *Mission with LeMay*, p. 446.
5. The following account of the House Armed Services Committee hearing on the B-36 was compiled from Committee transcripts, current newspapers, *Mission with LeMay*, p. 474ff., and LeMay to author, Jan. 24, 1984.

CHAPTER NINETEEN

1. Irvine Oral History 734, p. 23.
2. LeMay Oral History 736, p. 40.
3. LeMay to author, Jan. 24, 1984. *Mission with LeMay*, p. 466ff.
4. Ibid., p. 450.
5. LeMay to author, Jan. 25, 1984.
6. Sgt. Waterman, on Aug. 25, 1983, gave the author this account of his association with the LeMays. And Mrs. Helen LeMay, on Mar. 14, 1984, filled in many of the details.
7. LeMay to author, Jan. 25, 1984.
8. Gen. John Paul McConnell to author, Nov. 3, 1983.
9. Dacey to author, Aug. 26, 1983
10. Gen. David Wade to author, Nov. 20, 1983.
11. Dacey to author, Aug. 26, 1983.
12. LeMay Oral History 592, p. 54ff.

CHAPTER TWENTY

1. LeMay to author, Jan. 25, 1984.
2. Sgt. Edwin O. Learnard in a letter to the *Los Angeles Times*, published Sept. 30, 1984.

CHAPTER TWENTY-ONE

1. Gen. Richard M. Montgomery to author, in a tape-recorded interview, Nov. 4, 1983.
2. Dacey to author, Aug. 26, 1983.
3. Col. Stuart McLennan to author, Nov. 21, 1983.
4. *Aviation Week*, Mar. 10, 1952.
5. Smith Oral History 903, p. 146.

6. *Mission with LeMay*, p. 503.
7. LeMay to author, Aug. 11, 1983 and Jan. 25, 1984.
8. Ibid.
9. Griswold to author, Aug. 27, 1983. LeMay Oral History 592, pp. 71ff.
10. *Mission with LeMay*, p. 452.
11. Montgomery tape for author, Nov. 4, 1983.
12. *Washington Post*, June 9, 1984.
13. *Mission with LeMay*, p. 481.
14. LeMay to author, Jan. 25, 1984.
15. *Mission with LeMay*, p. 482.

CHAPTER TWENTY-TWO

1. *Mission with LeMay*, p. 442.
2. Griswold to author, Aug. 27, 1983.
3. LeMay to Air Force Scientific Advisory Board, May 21, 1957.
4. Wade to author, Nov. 20, 1983.
5. *Time*, May 14, 1956.
6. LeMay to author, Jan. 25, 1984.
7. Smith Oral History 903, p. 145ff.
8. LeMay to author, Jan. 24, 1984.
9. Ibid.
10. LeMay lecture at Air University, Alabama, Feb. 4, 1957.
11. This account of the LeMay-Godfrey safari was compiled from *Mission with LeMay*, p. 488ff; *Life*, June 10, 1957; and LeMay to author, Jan. 24, 1984.
12. Ibid.

CHAPTER TWENTY-THREE

1. Gen. Thomas D. White, "Random Notes about Curtis LeMay," Dec. 22, 1964.
2. LeMay to author, Jan. 25, 1984.
3. This account of the LeMay-McConnell trip to Johnson's Texas ranch was pieced together from individual accounts by LeMay to author, Jan. 25, 1984, and McConnell to author, Nov. 3, 1983. Except for the time frame, the two accounts were remarkably similar, but McConnell's recollection that the trip took place in 1967 could not be accurate because LeMay had retired by that time.
4. The following account of LeMay's role in the Bay of Pigs deliberations was compiled from LeMay to author, Jan. 25, 1984; LeMay Oral History 592, p. 21; and Wyden, *Bay of Pigs*, p. 200ff.
5. Schlesinger, *Robert Kennedy and His Times*, p. 450.
6. Eugene Zuckert to author, Oct. 17, 1983.
7. Fairlie, *The Kennedy Promise*, p. 105.

CHAPTER TWENTY-FOUR

1. Smith Oral History 903, p. 149ff.
2. Moss, *Men Who Play God*, p. 567.
3. Memorandum, Zuckert to Dr. Joseph V. Charyk, undersecretary of the Air Force, June 2, 1961.
4. LeMay diary, Aug. 17, 1961.
5. Robert McNamara to the Senate Subcommittee on Investigations (McClellan Committee), Mar. 21, 1963.
6. LeMay diary, Nov. 30, 1961.
7. Ibid., Dec. 1, 1961.
8. Ibid., Dec. 4, 1961.
9. Ibid., Dec. 5, 1961.
10. *Men Who Play God*, p. 271.
11. *Mission with LeMay*, p. 8.
12. LeMay, *America Is in Danger*, p. 52.
13. Ibid., p. 94.
14. Ibid., pp. 117–18.
15. LeMay Oral History 714, p. 3.
16. LeMay Oral History 592, p. 36.
17. LeMay to author, Feb. 2, 1984.
18. LeMay diary, Feb. 16, 1962.
19. Ibid., in a summary of the B-70 controversy between Feb. 16 and Apr. 18, 1962. Item 5.
20. Ibid., Items 6, 7.
21. Ibid., Item 8.
22. Ibid., Item 14.

CHAPTER TWENTY-FIVE

1. LeMay diary, Mar. 1, 1962.
2. LeMay to author, Feb. 2, 1984; LeMay Oral History 592, pp. 50–54; LeMay Oral History 593, p. 6ff.; LeMay diary, Apr. 23, 1962.
3. Gen. Paul D. Harkins Air Force Oral History transcript 522, p. 26ff.
4. LeMay to author, Feb. 2, 1984; Montgomery on tape for author, Nov. 4, 1983.
5. LeMay diary, Apr. 13, 1962.
6. Smith Oral History 903, p. 150ff.
7. LeMay to author, Feb. 2, 1984.
8. This account of how McKee was chosen came from McKee to author, October 11, 1983; and LeMay to author, Feb. 2, 1984.
9. LeMay to author, Feb. 2, 1984.
10. Sorensen, *Kennedy*, p. 826ff.
11. LeMay to author, Feb. 2, 1984.
12. McKee to author, Oct. 11, 1983.
13. Robert Kennedy, *Thirteen Days*, p. 36.

14. O'Donnell and Powers, *Johnny, We Hardly Knew Ye*, p. 379.
15. LeMay to author, Feb. 2, 1984.

CHAPTER TWENTY-SIX

1. LeMay to author, Feb. 2, 1984.
2. Zuckert Air Force Oral History transcript 763, p. 11ff.
3. Gen. Glen W. Martin Oral History interview dated 6–10 Feb., 1978, p. 429ff.
4. Zuckert to author, Oct. 17, 1983.
5. McKee to author, Oct. 11, 1983.
6. LeMay to author, Feb. 2, 1984.
7. Zuckert to author, Oct. 17, 1983.

CHAPTER TWENTY-SEVEN

1. LeMay diary, Jan. 14, 1963.
2. McKee to author, Oct. 11, 1983; LeMay diary, Jan. 14, 1963.
3. LeMay diary, Feb. 4, 1963
4. Zuckert to author, Oct. 17, 1983.
5. Gen. Maurice Casey Air Force Oral History transcript 1058, p. 113.
6. Sorensen, *Kennedy*, pp. 467–68.
7. LeMay diary, Mar. 25, 1963.
8. Mollenhoff, *The Pentagon*, p. 301.

CHAPTER TWENTY-EIGHT

1. LeMay "Do List" dated Apr. 8, 1963.
2. LeMay to author, Feb. 2, 1984.
3. Taylor, *The Uncertain Trumpet*, p. 99ff.
4. Sorensen, *Kennedy*, p. 685.
5. Halberstam, *The Making of a Quagmire*, p. 191.
6. LeMay to author, Feb. 2, 1984.
7. LeMay Oral History 592, p. 18.
8. LeMay to author, Feb. 2, 1984.
9. LeMay to author, July 29, 1985.
10. LeMay diary, Nov. 29, 1963.
11. Ibid., Dec. 30, 1963
12. McLennan to author, Nov. 21, 1983.
13. LeMay to author, Feb. 2, 1984.
14. *New York Times*, Mar. 2, 1985.
15. LeMay diary, Oct. 2, 1964.
16. Ibid., Dec. 23, 1964.
17. Wilson to author, Nov. 21, 1983.
18. Gen. Theodore R. Milton Oral History 917, pp. 46–47.
19. Gen. White in *Newsweek*, Jan. 4, 1965.
20. Judge Nutter to author, Dec. 31, 1974.

CHAPTER TWENTY-NINE

1. *Time*, Oct. 18, 1968; LeMay to author, Feb. 2, 1984.
2. LeMay to author, Feb. 2, 1984.
3. *Newsweek*, Oct. 14, 1968.
4. LeMay to author, Feb. 2, 1984.

INDEX

FROM PERSONAL JOURNALS TO BLACKLY HUMOROUS ACCOUNTS

VIETNAM

DISPATCHES, Michael Herr
01976-0/$3.95 US/$5.50 Can
"I believe it may be the best personal journal about war,
any war, that any writer has ever accomplished."
—Robert Stone, *Chicago Tribune*

A WORLD OF HURT, Bo Hathaway
69567-7/$3.50 US/$4.50 Can
"War through the eyes of two young soldiers...a painful
experience, and an ultimately exhilarating one."
—*Philadelphia Inquirer*

NO BUGLES, NO DRUMS, Charles Durden
69260-0/$3.50 US/$4.50 Can
"The funniest, ghastliest military scenes put to paper
since Joseph Heller wrote *Catch-22*"
—*Newsweek*

AMERICAN BOYS, Steven Phillip Smith
67934-5/$3.95 US/$5.75 Can
"The best novel I've come across on the war in Vietnam"
—Norman Mailer

COOKS AND BAKERS, Robert A. Anderson
79590-6/$2.95
"A tough-minded unblinking report from hell"
—*Penthouse*